THE MOST OF
GEORGE BURNS

THE MOST OF
GEORGE
BURNS

Galahad Books
New York

First Galahad Books edition published in 1991.

Galahad Books
A division of Budget Book Service, Inc.
386 Park Avenue South
New York, NY 10016

Galahad Books is a registered trademark of Budget Book Service, Inc.

Published by arrangement with The Putnam Publishing Group.

Library of Congress Catalog Card Number: 91-73471

ISBN: 0-88365-782-1

Printed in the United States of America.

CONTENTS

Living It Up   7
The Third Time Around   253
Dr. Burns' Prescription for Happiness   501
Dear George   629

LIVING IT UP

or

They Still Love Me in Altoona!

Contents

A Day in the Life of a Late-Blooming Author! 11

Writing Humor Is Nothing to Laugh At! 27

Open-Heart Surgery Can Be Fun! 39

Gracie and Me 51

It's Fun to Look Back If There Isn't Something Cuter in Front of You! 65

Good Fathers Don't Grow on Trees! 73

A Newcomer at Sixty-Two 83

A Dresser Is Not a Piece of Furniture 89

Here She Is, Ladies and Gentlemen—Mrs. Charles Lowe! 97

No More Applause 117

Thank You, Mr. Toastmaster . . . 121

The Quiet Riot 135

Live, Love, and Enjoy It! 147

To Write a Book You Need a Sharp Pencil 155

It's Easy to Ad-Lib if You've Got It Written Down 161

Memoirs of a Warmed-Over Casanova 187

And There Was Lisa 199

The Sunshine Boys 213

Epilogue 231

Things I Forgot to Put in the Book 233

A Day in the Life of
a Late-Blooming Author!

Getting to be my age didn't happen overnight. I'm eighty years old, and I had a damned good time getting there. I run into a lot of people who ask me when I'm going to retire. I think the only reason you should retire is if you can find something you enjoy doing more than what you're doing now. I happen to be in love with show business, and I can't think of anything I'd enjoy more than that. So I guess I've been retired all my life.

In the first place, I don't see what age has to do with retirement. I've known some young men of eighty-five, and I've met some very old men of forty. In a sense that's what this book is all about; getting old doesn't mean that you have to stop having fun. When you're twenty-one you can enjoy yourself by going out with a twenty-one-year-old girl, and when you're eighty you can enjoy yourself by going out with an eighteen-year-old girl.

I got news for you. There isn't a thing I can't do now that I didn't do when I was twenty-one . . . which gives you an idea of how pathetic I was when I was twenty-one. (That's a lie, but I might as well tell you something right here at the beginning of the book. Anytime I can get a laugh I'm not going to let the truth interfere with it.)

Look, there's nothing wrong with going out with young girls. I enjoy meeting young girls. I figure some of their youth may rub off on me, and some of what I've got might rub off on them—that is, if it doesn't drop off before I meet them.

11

But I mean it—young girls are stimulating. They get you out of the house, and when you get older that's important. If you've got a date, it gives you an incentive. You shower . . . you shave . . . you choose your best cologne . . . you pick out your best shirt . . . your best tie . . . your best suit . . . and try to look as good as you can possibly look for your age. And it works. The other evening I had a date, and after I got dressed I stood in front of the mirror and I looked so good I said to myself, "Maybe that eighteen-year-old girl is too old for me!" (I'm sorry, there I go again.)

Now, I have a close friend, George Pallay, who's a seventy-five-year-old bachelor, and really a case. He's generous, he's charming, he's good company, fun to be with, but he's got one hangup. Whenever he's out with a young girl he gets embarrassed and introduces her as his niece. He's good for three or four nieces a week.

Actually he isn't fooling anybody. One night he walked into a restaurant with a young girl and said to the captain, "Could my niece and I have that corner table in the bar?"

The captain said, "I'm sorry, Mr. Pallay, but another one of your nieces is sitting there with George Burns."

That upset Pallay. He liked my niece better than the one he had with him.

Just the other day I tried to reason with him. We were having coffee after a leisurely lunch, and I said to him, "Pallay, everybody knows that these girls are not your nieces. Who do you think you're kidding? Why do you go to all that trouble? You take them to nice places, you enjoy each other's company, why don't you just relax and forget about this silly niece business?"

He looked at me sheepishly and said, "I'm embarrassed about what people might think."

"What do you care what people think?" I said. "You like the girl, the girl likes you, you've had a wonderful evening, and that's what life is all about."

He paused, let it sink in, and then said, "George, you're absolutely right. I'm going out with a young girl tonight and

12

I'm not going to introduce her as my niece. I'll just have her tell people I'm her uncle."

I said, "Pallay, I'm glad you got the message."

However, I don't want you to get the impression that this book is only about young girls. Oh, they're bound to crop up here and there—about every page or so—but they're not the important part of the book.

What's important when you get to be my age is to enjoy what you're doing. Now the young people today have a saying: "Do your own thing." Well, I go along with that, but I'd like to add something to it: "Do your own thing, but make sure you're happy doing it!"

Even when I'm doing nothing I find a happy reason for not doing it. That's the way I've been all my life. No matter what I did, I was happy doing it at that time. Back when I was a small-time vaudeville actor and couldn't get any jobs, I was still happy because I was out of work in a business that I loved.

I remember when I was sixteen I worked for Mersky & Co. in New York. They manufactured middy blouses, and I was a cutter. At that time Mersky was having a problem because nobody was buying his middy blouses, so I came up with a brilliant idea.

I said to him, "Mr. Mersky, I know how you can unload all these middy blouses. Send every store in town thirteen dozen with an invoice which says, 'Enclosed find twelve dozen middy blouses.' Even though they didn't order them, they'll keep them because they'll figure they're getting thirteen dozen for the price of twelve."

Mersky said, "Do you think it'll work?"

I said, "Mr. Mersky, trust me, it can't miss."

A big smile broke out over Mersky's face, and he gave me a $2 raise right on the spot—which brought my salary up to $16 a week.

Two weeks later he called me into his office. I got all excited—I could see the sign out front reading MERSKY AND BURNS. But as soon as I walked into his office and saw the

13

expression on Mersky's face, I knew our partnership just dissolved.

He said, "Burns, remember that idea you came up with a couple of weeks ago about the middy blouses?"

I said, "Yes, sir, did it work?"

"Certainly it worked—but not for me, for them it worked! Everybody I sent thirteen dozen middy blouses to kept the extra dozen and sent back twelve!"

Already showing my talent as a straight man, I said, "Really?"

Mersky said, "But, Burns, I'm a man of my word. I gave you a two-dollar raise, you still got it. But only until six o'clock tonight—then you're fired!"

Even this made me happy. Again I could go back to vaudeville and be out of work in a business that I loved.

But eighty is a beautiful age. It takes very little to turn me on. And sometimes when I think I'm turned on I find out I'm not even plugged in. What's the use of kidding—I've reached the point now where I can get by on about one half inch of happiness. A whole inch would overstimulate me! But who cares, I'm enjoying it.

This is what I'm trying to say. The secret of feeling young is to make every day count for something. To me there's no such thing as taking a day off. When I'm not working, which isn't often, my day goes something like this:

I usually get up at eight o'clock—sometimes earlier, but never later. I like getting up early, it gives me a longer day and more time to do things. Okay, now I'm up. The first thing I do is go to the bathroom, and in the bathroom I do what everybody does—brush my teeth. All right, so that's the second thing I do—the first thing I do is gargle. Look, I've got to take care of my vocal cords.

Now I'm wide awake and ready for my back exercises. They're not strenuous, and I have fun doing them. First, I lie on my back on the floor and grab my left knee with both hands and pull it up as far as I can, trying to touch my chin. I do this ten times with each leg. Then, still on my back, I rotate my legs in the air as though riding a bicycle. I do this twenty-five times. Now I sit on the edge of the bed and bend over and touch the floor with my hands, first to the left and then to the right. I do this twenty times.

And that's it! I feel that these particular exercises are good for me. I've always had a bad back, but I don't worry about it. If I outlive my back, fine—if my back outlives me, I'll stop doing my exercises.

Anyway, now it's time for breakfast. Those exercises always make me feel good, and when I feel good I sing. So on my way downstairs I usually sing a chorus of "Honeysuckle Rose." Breakfast consists of a piece of fresh fruit in season or a glass of orange juice, some coffee, and cornflakes. I love cornflakes. When I chew them they make a noise in my mouth . . . and when I hear that noise I think it's applause . . . and when I hear applause I go into the second chorus of "Honeysuckle Rose."

Naturally, while I'm having breakfast I read the morning papers. I think everybody should read newspapers because I feel that one should ebulliently endeavor to be cognizant of the necessity for amelioration of global détente! (Look, I didn't write that last line, I copied it out of *Time* magazine. I thought the book could use a little class.)

And then of course, I read the theatrical trade papers, the *Daily Variety* and the *Hollywood Reporter*. The first thing I look at is the obituary column. If my name isn't in it, I sing another chorus of "Honeysuckle Rose."

All right, now I'm ready for my walk. But walking can be awfully dull if you do nothing but just walk. So enjoy the beauty around you. Look at the birds! Look at the flowers! Look at the trees! And if a pretty girl passes, look at her legs! If you're worried about cheating on your wife, look at only one leg!

I do my walking in the garden; ten minutes every morning at a pretty fast clip. And while I'm walking, I rehearse. I run through the lyrics to my songs and go over the jokes in my monologues. My gardener loves my monologues be-

15

cause I do them out loud, but he always laughs in the wrong places. It isn't that my monologues aren't funny, it's just that he doesn't speak English. If I could learn to do my jokes in Japanese, I'd have him rolling in the rosebushes.

By now it's 9:30 and time to get upstairs and into the bathroom again—I love to gargle. After a good gargle I shave and then into the shower. While I'm in the shower I sing "In the Heart of a Cherry." I'd sing "Honeysuckle Rose," but by now I'm sick of it.

Picking out my wardrobe for the day is something I enjoy, because clothes have always been important to me. I came from a very poor family, and all my clothes were handed down to me by my older brother. When he outgrew a suit he gave it to me, and when I outgrew it I gave it to my younger brother. When my older brother had it, it was a blue suit; when I got it it was green; and by the time it reached my younger brother it was a sort of washed-out purple.

I was sixteen before I owned a suit of my own. I don't know how I managed to get the $12 to buy it, but I was really proud of that suit. I thought I had finally made the big time. It was a gray plaid suit and it had a four-button coat. I would only button the top button so that I could fold back the bottom part of the coat and put my hand in my pants pocket. I thought this gave me a jaunty look, and people would think I had money in my pocket. Believe me, the only thing I ever had in that pocket was my hand. I kept my hand in that pocket so long that when I outgrew the suit and gave it to my younger brother, my hand was still in the pocket.

But things have changed since then. Now I have a much larger wardrobe. I've got a closetful of suits, but mostly I wear sports clothes; jackets, slacks, and turtleneck sweaters. I think everybody should try to look as good as he possibly can. I knew an actor, Jack Desmond, seventy-two years old. He wore a wavy toupee, had his nose straightened, his face lifted, and his teeth capped. He looked gorgeous. He looked so good nobody knew he was dead. In fact, his wife still thinks she's cheating on him.

Now, where was I? Oh, yes, I'm dressed for the day and ready to leave for the office. If I'm staying home that night I stop off in the kitchen to tell my cook, Arlette, what I want for dinner. Arlette has been working for me for years, and when I walk into the kitchen, she says, "Mr. Burns, you look beautiful this morning!" That's why she's been with me for years.

Driving to General Service Studio where I've had my office for twenty-three years is another experience. While I'm driving along I smile at people in the other cars because I think everybody knows me. But everybody doesn't. Those who know me smile back, and those who don't know me think I'm an idiot. But I say if you're going to be an idiot, you might as well smile and let people think you're enjoying it.

At ten sharp I walk into my office, and my secretary, Jack Langdon, says, "Mr. Burns, you look beautiful this morning!" He's been with me for years, too.

I go into my inner office, and my writer, Elon Packard, says, "Hiya, George!"

He's only been with me ten years and he's a good writer, but he still doesn't know what to say in the morning.

We work in the office from ten until noon. As I said earlier, this is my schedule when I'm not actually working. It's only two hours but it's very concentrated effort. We answer correspondence, update the routines in my stage act, write speeches for testimonial dinners, plan what I'm going to say on the talk shows, write copy for various commercials I do . . . it's really a full two hours.

But at twelve o'clock on the nose, I quit. We could be in the middle of writing a comedy routine, and sometimes Packy follows me all the way out to my car, hollering, "George, wait a minute, I've got a great finish for the routine!" But I don't hear him. At twelve o'clock I turn my

17

head off. Anyway, I get in my car, check in the rearview mirror to see if my smile is working, and I'm off to Hillcrest Country Club.

Hillcrest Country Club is like a second home to me. It's a beautiful club and located very conveniently in Beverly Hills only ten minutes from my home. I've belonged to Hillcrest for over forty years.

Now, they have a large membership, and I know practically all of them—but not by name. I remember faces, but when it comes to names I've got a very bad memory. So I've got a little system that works for me—I call everybody Kid. When I come into the club and somebody says, "Hello, George," I answer, "Hello, Kid."

I remember one afternoon coming into the club with Jack Benny, and as we headed for the dining room one of the members came up to us and said, "Hello, George."

I said, "Hiya, Kid," and started to go on.

But the guy stopped me and said, "Wait a minute, George, you and I have been members of this club for years, and you always call me Kid. You don't even know my name."

I looked at him and said, "I don't, huh." Then, turning to Jack, I said, "Jack, tell him his name," and kept walking.

Jack turned to the man and quickly said, "I'll see you later, Kid," and hurried after me.

Of course, it's a little different when I run into Adolph Zukor, who's one hundred and two years old. A man that age deserves respect. When he says "Hello, George," I say, "Hello, MISTER Kid."

But Adolph Zukor is a remarkable man. I remember when he had his hundred and second birthday. After Mr. Zukor had his lunch, the waiter brought in this big cake to surprise him, and all the members sang "Happy Birthday." So I went over to him and said, "Mr. Zukor—" (This time I remembered his name because it was written on the cake.) —I said, "Mr. Zukor, how does it feel to be one hundred and two years old?"

18

He said, "George, I feel just as good now as I did two years ago."

At Hillcrest when I have my lunch I always sit at the same table. It's called the "Round Table." The reason it's called the Round Table is because it's a table that's round. (I hope I made that clear. My publisher told me to keep nothing from you.)

Anyway, this table is where the action is. There's very little listening but an awful lot of talking, because most of the people who sit there are in show business. Every day the cast changes—you might find Groucho Marx, Danny Thomas, Georgie Jessel, Milton Berle, and directors and producers like Eddie Buzzell, Pandro Berman, George Seaton, etc. With that bunch if you want to get a word in edgewise, you have to have an appointment. The conversations cover everything. You can hear opinions on politics, sports, religion, music—you name it, and we're all experts on it.

But over the years I've noticed a change at the table. Where the main topic used to be our sex lives, it's now about our bad backs. I can't speak for anybody else, but I know how I got my bad back—taking bows.

As in every group there is usually one person who takes charge. At our table it's Georgie Jessel. He knows all the jokes, he's a great storyteller, and he's very funny. But he does one thing that drives me up the wall. Whenever he's scheduled to do a eulogy at someone's funeral, he tries it out on us. Did you ever try eating lunch and listening to a eulogy at the same time? Jessel is the only one I know who can turn matzos, eggs, and onions into the Last Supper.

Since I'm on the subject, I'd like to tell you one story. Years ago in New York there were two great actors named Sam Bernard and Louie Mann. Jessel was crazy about Sam Bernard, they were very good friends, but he just didn't like Louie Mann. Well, Sam Bernard died, and Jessel did the eulogy at the funeral. He was absolutely marvelous; it affected everybody . . . he cried . . . we cried . . . Jessel was in top form.

19

Anyway, a couple of weeks later I happened to meet Jessel walking down Broadway, and he was wearing a black coat, a black tie, and striped pants. Right away I knew he was on his way to do another eulogy, so I said, "Georgie, who died?"

He said, "Louie Mann, and I'm on the way to do the eulogy."

"But you always told me you didn't like Louie Mann," I said. "How can you do a eulogy for a man you didn't like?"

He replied, "I couldn't pass it up, I've got some great stuff left over from Sam Bernard."

Back to the Round Table.

Groucho Marx has a very fast, caustic wit. He's well informed and extremely humorous—and above all he's loaded with CHUTZPAH! If the right situation comes up, he doesn't mind repeating the same joke twenty times in one day.

Let me give you an example. Years ago Sophie Tucker used to sing a song called "If You Can't See Mama Every Night, You Can't See Mama at All." Now I've been sitting at the Round Table for forty years, and every time I order sea bass, without fail Groucho will say, "If you can't sea bass every night, you can't see Mama at all." I laughed the first time I heard it, but after hearing it for forty years it sort of loses its freshness.

One day I wanted to order sea bass for lunch, but Groucho was sitting at the table and I didn't want to hear that lousy joke again. So I took the waiter aside and I quietly whispered, "I'll have some sea bass."

And the waiter quietly whispered back, "If you can't sea bass every night, you can't see Mama at all."

After hearing that line again from the waiter I decided it was time to change my diet. I went back to the table and said, "Groucho, do you have any jokes about whitefish?"

He said, "No, George."

I turned to the waiter and said, "I'll have some whitefish."

20

And Groucho said, "If you can't see whitefish every night, you can't see Mama at all."

I told you he had chutzpah!

Lunch usually takes about an hour or so, and then I'm off to the card room for my favorite recreation—playing bridge. I love the game; it's exciting, stimulating, and it makes you think. I don't say I'm the greatest bridge player in the world but the men I play with are just as bad as I am. I could say they're worse than I am, but that doesn't sound modest. . . . I'll say it anyway; they are worse than I am.

Sometimes I've watched some of the great bridge players play, and it's always so very quiet. They concentrate, they take their time, they speak softly—you can hear a pin drop. The table I play at sounds like a bowling alley on Saturday night. Nobody concentrates, everybody's in a hurry, and we're all screaming at the same time. That's the kind of bridge that relaxes me.

We argue, we fight, and the language we use didn't come out of *Rebecca of Sunnybrook Farm*. But there's a reason why we carry on like this—all the men that I play bridge with are practically my age or even older; sometimes I'm the youngest at the table. So we holler and shout to make sure the other members of the club know that we're still living. The only time we get quiet is when Georgie Jessel comes over to kibitz. It makes us very nervous because we know he's got four eulogies in his pocket.

One day a new member, a very distinguished attorney, came over and asked to join our game, and he did. He was lucky enough to draw me for a partner. The very first hand our opponents bid opened with a spade and their finishing bid was three no-trump. I doubled, which called for a spade lead, but my partner, this brilliant attorney, led the three of diamonds. I was shocked. I slowly folded my cards and laid them gently on the table, placed my cigar carefully in the ashtray, took three deep breaths to get some oxygen into my head, and then said to him, "Look, you may be one of our great attorneys . . . you're very well dressed . . . you're a

21

fine looking man . . . you're over six feet tall . . . which makes you one of the tallest idiots I've ever played with!"

He looked straight at me, then stood up and said, "I'm sorry, gentlemen, I've had enough. And, Mr. Burns, I would just as soon you would never talk to me again. I've never been called an idiot in my life."

"If I stopped talking to you, I'd have to stop talking to everybody at this table, because we're all idiots," I answered.

He thought this over for a moment, then he sat down, smiled, and said, "Mr. Burns, the tall idiot is back in the game." From then on he was a member of our group, screaming and hollering like the rest of us.

I don't recommend our way of playing bridge to everybody. There are times when it could lead to violence. But if you do play it our way, you better have a sense of humor. I remember a few years ago I was playing bridge at the Beverly Hills Bridge Club with George Raft, Harpo Marx, and Mack Gordon, who was one of our most prolific songwriters. He wrote "Time on My Hands," "Chattanooga Choo-Choo," "Did You Ever See a Dream Walking?"—I could go on and on.

Anyway, Mack Gordon was a very stubborn bridge player who wanted to play every hand. But I knew his game because I had played with him before. Well, in this particular rubber he was my partner, and he bid a spade. I had a heart bust—eight hearts to a queen—and no spades. In other words, I had nothing. So I bid four hearts. Now in bridge this meant I was telling my partner that this hand could only be played in hearts and for him to pass. But not Mack Gordon.

As I said, when he got a bid in his teeth he wouldn't let go. When it came around to him he didn't even look at me, he just laid his cards face down on the table, folded his arms, looked out the window and defiantly hollered, "Four spades!"

When it got to me, I never looked at him. I laid my cards face down on the table, folded my arms, and said, "I didn't

22

know we were playing with somebody across the street, but if we are, I'd like them to hear my bid, too." Then I hollered out the window, "Five hearts!"

Mack stared straight at me, and in a steely, low tone he said, "George, I've got more money than you have—seven spades."

I looked right back at him, and slowly and emphatically said, "No you haven't—seven no-trump!"

Mack threw his cards into the center of the table, stood up, and said, "Let's go downstairs and straighten this out!"

"You mean you want to fight me?" I said.

"That's right," Mack answered.

"All right," I said, "let's go down."

So Harpo, Georgie Raft, Mack, and myself started out. About halfway down the stairs I said to Harpo loud enough for Mack to hear, "I think the greatest song ever written was 'Did You Ever See a Dream Walking?'"

Mack said, "Let's go up and finish the game."

I often wondered what would have happened if I hadn't thought of that line. Mack weighed 300 pounds and I weighed 135. The world might have lost one of its great singers.

Anyway, back to Hillcrest. It's now about four o'clock and it's time for me to go home and take a nap. Oh, by the way, the Hillcrest Country Club also has a beautiful golf course. I quit playing golf several years ago. I found out I wasn't getting any exercise from it. All us members took carts, and the caddies carried our clubs. So the caddies got all the exercise and they looked great; we rode in the carts and looked pathetic.

The truth is I gave up golf because I knew I'd never be good at it. I tried very hard, but I just couldn't put it all together. Lloyd Mangrum, one of our great professional golfers, used to play at our club a lot, and one day in the locker room he said to me, "George, you look perfect . . . that beautiful knitted shirt, an alpaca sweater, those expensive slacks, argyle socks, bench-made golf shoes

23

. . . you've got an alligator bag, the finest matched irons, and the best woods money can buy. It's a damned shame you have to spoil it all by playing golf."

Now, where was I? Oh, yeah, I'm writing a book.

My nap takes about an hour and a half. I usually go to sleep at four thirty and get up at six. I really think everybody should take a nap in the afternoon. I know that when I get up after my nap I'm very refreshed and ready for the evening.

Did you ever notice how easy it is to fall asleep when you take a nap? You just lie down, and boom! you fall asleep in broad daylight. But going to sleep at night is a different story. We make such a big deal out of it. We take a sleeping pill, we put on our pajamas, we scrub our teeth, we set the alarm clock, check the window to see that just enough fresh air is coming in, get into bed and turn out the light, snuggle up under the blankets, close our eyes—and boom! we're wide awake. Then we try lying on our left side, our right side, on our back, on our stomach, and nothing happens. We've made such a production out of going to sleep that we think we're in the sleeping business and we ought to get paid for it.

Now I suppose you're saying to yourself, "Sure, he's told us why we can't sleep, but if he's so clever, why doesn't he tell us how we can get to sleep?"

Well, I'm not one of those writers who leaves you hanging there. All you've got to do is buy my next book, which covers that question. Thank you. I may not be remembered as one of the great writers, but I am polite . . . You'll notice I used three periods—I'm also a generous writer.

Now comes the most relaxing and comfortable time of my day. It's a quiet time and gives me a chance to reflect about life and things in general. Daniel and Arlette are busy in the kitchen preparing dinner, and while I'm making myself a double martini on the rocks my two cats, Ramona and Princess, are purring and rubbing against my legs as though they're anticipating the evening as much as I am.

24

Of course, I only have these quiet and relaxing evenings when I don't have a date—which means I'm quiet and relaxed about once a month. There I go again, I broke a beautiful mood just to get in one tired joke.

Anyway, when I do have a date, I usually take her to dinner at a nice restaurant. As I mentioned before, I like the company of young girls, and young girls seem to like to go out with me. It's because I don't rush them—there's no pressure on them. When I take them to Chasen's for dinner, in between courses they have time to do their homework.

On occasion if I'm in a romantic mood, I invite the young lady back to my place. And at the end of the evening she won't be disappointed. We have a little brandy, I turn the lights down low, and when I think the moment is just right—I send for my piano player. I sing her four or five songs and go upstairs and go to bed. My piano player takes her home. I've outlived four of my piano players.

Well, that's the end of my day, and it's also the end of the chapter. Being an old vaudevillian, I can't get out of a chapter without a finish—and being a singer, this is my finish. While you're reading it, hum along. I guarantee you'll be whistling it for the rest of your life:

> I'd love to call you Rose, dear,
> But roses fade away,
> Roses die when wintertime appears.
> I'd love to call you Daisy
> But daisies always tell
> What sweethearts love to whisper in your ear.
> I'd love to call you Honey
> But honey runs away,
> I'd much prefer a name like Clinging Vine.
> And if I called you Buttercup,
> The dandelions would eat you up—
> So I'll buy a ring and change your name to mine.

Catchy melody, isn't it?

Writing Humor Is Nothing To Laugh At!

This is the second chapter, and it has absolutely nothing to do with the book. But then again neither did the first chapter. I hope my style of writing isn't as confusing to you as it is to me. However, I remember something that Gracie used to do which might be of great help to you. When she read a book, first she'd read the beginning, and then she'd read the finish. Then she'd start in the middle and read toward whichever end she liked best.

Give that last line a little thought. It may sound like I'm making a joke, and I hope I am.

Well, now on with the chapter. All through my life in show business I've been a very fortunate man. When I first started out in vaudeville and it looked as if I were about to hit bottom, I always managed to bounce back. I didn't bounce very high, so even after I bounced I was pretty close to the bottom.

In those days the acts I did were pathetic, but I loved every minute of it. If I teamed up with a fellow and our act was so bad we couldn't get a job, we'd split up and I was back on the bottom again. But I didn't stay there long. A week later I'd team up with another fellow and come right back with another act that was just as bad. I must have done dozens of bad acts—singing, dancing, rollerskating, dramatic sketches. I even worked with a dog and then a seal. You name it and I've done it. But the important thing is I was in action; I was in show business and I was moving. When you did acts like I did you had to keep moving.

27

I'll tell you about one act I did when I was eight years old. I know you're not going to believe it, because it's hard for me to believe, but it's a true story and it did happen to me.

I was then singing with the Peewee Quartet. We were all about the same age, and I was the tenor. We used to sing in saloons and pass the hat around. Sometimes we'd make as much as fifteen cents, and to us that was big money. Anyway, we were singing in this saloon on Houston Street on the Lower East Side in New York, and we had just finished our second song, "Mary Ann, Mary Ann, Mary Sat in a Corner," when this man came over to me and said, "Kid, I like the way you sing, how would you like to be in my act?"

I looked up at him and there was this fellow wearing a black coat with a beaver collar, a derby hat, a diamond stickpin in his tie, and a gold chain across his vest with an elks's tooth hanging from it. I was very impressed.

"Yes, sir," I said.

It turned out his name was Jack Frye, and his act was called Jack Frye & Co. He offered me $10 a week.

Well, I had never heard of that kind of money. My whole family put together didn't make that much. I raced home to tell my mother that I got a job for $10 a week.

She listened to me and then said, "But what about your school?"

"But, Mama," I said, "it's ten dollars a week."

"Your education comes first," she said, shaking her head.

"Mama—ten dollars!!!"

My mother paused, giving that a little thought, and then said, "All right, so you'll get smart a week later."

Anyway, after five days of rehearsal Jack Frye & Co. opened at Huber's Museum on 14th Street. Now Huber's Museum was sort of a penny arcade with about ten side-show attractions like the Fat Lady, the Snake Charmer, the Sword Swallower, the Fire Eater, etc. And it also had a little theater where we played. You could come into Huber's Museum and see all of these side-show attractions plus the vaudeville show for fifteen cents.

28

Now, I'm not going to say that this sketch I was in was the worst sketch in the world, because it wasn't that good. The idea of the plot was that Jack Frye had an office—nobody knew what he did there because he didn't want to clutter up the plot with a lot of details. I was a shoeshine boy, and as I was shining his shoes he offered me a job as an office boy. All through the rest of the sketch he tried to test my honesty. And that's the plot.

Here's the way it worked. When the curtain went up, Jack Frye was sitting at his desk looking very dignified and reading *The Police Gazette*. And offstage you heard my voice singing this song:

> Shine, shine, five cents a shine;
> My name is Teddy,
> And I'm always ready;
> My brushes are new,
> My blacking is fine—
> Step right up, five cents a shine.

Then I'd stick my head through the door and say, "Shine, boss?"

Frye's opening line was memorable. He looked at me, put *The Police Gazette* down, and said, "Okay, boy, give me a shine."

As I was shining his shoes he offered me this job, which I took. Then he explained that there was $500 in the desk drawer and that I should protect it with my life, and he exited.

I turned to the audience and said, "I'm so happy that I got this job that I think I'll sing a song." Now wouldn't you think that Frye would have me sing a happy song? Nope—he picked out a sad ballad and told me to cry while I was doing it. There I was, supposed to be so happy about my new job, and I was standing up there crying my heart out.

This was the song:

29

Always think of Mother
No matter where you go.
Always think of Mother
Because she loves you so.
Your friends and many others
Will sometimes prove untrue,
But always think of Mother
'Cause she always thinks of you.

After that heartrending song the plot began to thicken. Frye returned three different times disguised as various characters. First he was a Jewish peddler, then he was an Italian immigrant, and the last one was a tough gangster. Each time he tried to trick me into giving him the $500 from the desk, but I wouldn't budge, I was a loyal office boy. When he finally came in as the gangster and I wouldn't give him the money, he advanced toward me shaking his fist, and angrily said, "Give me that money or I'll break every bone in your body!"

But that didn't frighten me. I knew there was a gun in the drawer, so I opened the drawer and put my hand on the gun, and then I made my big, dramatic speech. It went on for about three minutes and ended up with, "Threaten me if you will, sir, my mother always taught me that honesty is the best policy. Here under this ragged coat deep in my heart these words shall remain there until the last minute of my life!" Then I paused and continued, "Do you still want that money?"

"You better hand it over," snarled Frye.

"All right," I said, "then take that!" And I pulled the gun out of the drawer and pointed it at him.

With that he pulled off his wig and hollered, "Don't shoot, I'm your boss!" Then he put his arm around my shoulder and walked me to the center of the stage, and said, "My boy, your mother is right. Honesty has triumphed once again."

30

And the curtain came down with a thud!

Well, Jack Frye & Co. lasted one performance, and I was back on the bottom again. But as usual I bounced back. The next day I was singing tenor again with the Peewee Quartet.

My entire career has been filled with ups and downs like that. And if you think about it, I'll bet your life has been the same way. Everybody has his highs and lows. I remember a few years back when there was a quiet couple of months for me and nothing seemed to be happening. I still came to my office at General Service Studios every morning and met with my writer, Elon Packard, and my secretary, Jack Langdon, but this lull made these two kids nervous. They worried that I was nervous, too, so they manufactured things for us to do in order to make me believe we were busy. When I'd walk into the office, Packy would say, "George, I know what we can do today. Let's start out by writing a very funny letter to Jack Benny."

Then Jack Langdon would pipe up with, "Marvelous. And if we finish it in time, we'll send a funny telegram to Carol Channing."

This went on day after day with these two clowns trying to dream up two hours of nothing to make me think I was busy. I went along with it, but I never could figure out why they got so panicky. I was paying them every week; I was calm, but they were nervous wrecks.

One Tuesday morning we were hard at work writing a hilarious note to leave in the bottle for my milkman when the phone rang. Sure enough it was my agent. He told me that the Teacher's Scotch people were putting on a big, nationwide advertising campaign in all the leading magazines and newspapers. These ads featured humorous articles written by various personalities in show business such as Groucho Marx, Redd Foxx, Tommy Smothers, and others. The conversation ended with my agent saying, "George, the Teacher's Scotch people would like you to do one of these. Do you think you'll have time?"

31

I glanced at the other two and said, "Sure, as soon as I finish this note to my milkman I'll get right on it."

Well, there I was, up there bouncing again. I turned to the boys and said, "Fellows, you can now relax, and we'll start on this first thing tomorrow morning. Jack, you put a new ribbon in the typewriter, I'm going to the club, and Packy, you go to your favorite bar and do a little research on Teacher's Scotch." He's very good at researching scotch.

When we met at the office in the morning there was a note from my agent telling me the advertising agency handling Teacher's had suggested this title for the article I was supposed to write: "When Jack Benny has a party, you not only bring your own scotch, you bring your own rocks." They wanted me to let them know what I thought of that title. So I called them up and told them I loved it. Personally, I thought it was much too long, but after all I had a deal with the Teacher's people, and you don't get paid for writing notes to your milkman.

We talked it over in the room, and I decided that since they mentioned Jack in the title they must want an article about Jack Benny and Teacher's Scotch. So this is what I wrote:

WHEN JACK BENNY HAS A PARTY, YOU NOT ONLY BRING YOUR OWN SCOTCH, YOU BRING YOUR OWN ROCKS

By George Burns

That line about bringing your own scotch and rocks is true. But that doesn't mean that Jack Benny is a cheapskate. Don't forget, he furnishes the coasters, the water, the electricity, and the furniture you sit on. To me, that's the mark of a generous man.

Anyway, when they asked me to write this article for Teacher's Scotch they— Hold it!

To show you how generous Benny really is, one time three of us were in a bar having a drink. There was Edgar Bergen,

Jack Benny, and myself. We were all drinking scotch. (And being men of good taste, naturally we ordered Teacher's.) When we finished, Jack said, "I'll take the check." So the bartender gave him the check, and he paid it. On the way out, I said, "Jack, it was very nice of you to ask for that check."

Jack said, "I didn't ask for it, and that's the last time I'll have a drink with a ventriloquist."

(But don't forget, you can still sit on Jack's furniture for free.)

Now . . . when they asked me to write this article for Teacher's Scotch they— Hold it! I just thought of another Benny story.

Whenever Jack tries to get clever it always backfires on him. One night the two of us were having dinner at Chasen's restaurant, and he said to me, "George, I've got an idea that's absolutely brilliant. Let's both have the most expensive dinner on the menu, and we'll make Dave Chasen pay for it."

I said, "How are you going to do that?"

"Simple," Jack said, "when the check comes, you and I will get into an argument, I'll call Dave Chasen over, and I'll say, 'Dave, if George Burns pays this check, I'll never come into this restaurant again.' And then you say, 'Dave, if Jack Benny pays this check, I'll never come into this restaurant again.' We're both very good customers, so Dave will say, 'Boys, don't argue,' and he'll tear up the check. Brilliant?"

I said, "Jack, it's a great idea, and it can't miss."

So after dinner we started to argue, and Jack called Chasen over and said, "Dave, if George Burns pays this check, I'll never come into this restaurant again!" I just sat there looking at Jack and never said a word. So Dave gave Jack the check.

Jack said, "George, aren't you going to say something?"

I said, "Sure, Jack, thanks for dinner."

(Now he won't even let me sit on his furniture.)

Well, when they asked me to write this article for Teacher's Scotch they— Hold it.

I just thought of another one. During all the years of my friendship with Jack Benny, whenever we'd talk on the tele-

33

phone I'd always hang up in the middle of the conversation. The first time I did it fifty-five years ago he thought it was very funny. I still do it, but he doesn't laugh at it anymore. The reason I keep doing it, I wouldn't want Jack to think I'm not as funny as I used to be.

Now, on with the article. When the Teacher's people asked me— Hold it!

One night Benny Rubin was going to Jack's house for dinner, and I said to Benny Rubin, "If you want to have a little fun, make Jack a ten-dollar bet that if he calls me on the phone, I won't hang up on him."

Sure enough, that night my phone rang and it was Jack. We talked, and talked, and talked—oh, for about twenty minutes. Finally Jack couldn't stand it any longer. He said, "George, aren't you going to hang up on me?"

I said, "Why should I, I've got half of Benny Rubin's bet." That he didn't laugh at.

Well, I better stop talking about Jack Benny and start saying something nice about Teacher's Scotch. If you're dining at home or dining at a restaurant, the most sociable drink is Teacher's Scotch. Whether you're young, or whether you're old, Teacher's is the perfect scotch for any age. . . .

Age—that word keeps haunting me. People always want to know how old I am. They're always asking if I'm older than Jack Benny or if Jack Benny is older than me. I should settle it once and for all: I'm two years younger than Jack, and Jack is two years younger than Groucho Marx. I won't tell you our exact ages, but I will give you a little hint— Georgie Jessel, who is seventy-five years old, is the kid we send to run our errands.

Now back to Teacher's— Hold it! How do you like that, I'm finished. I wrote a whole article about Teacher's Scotch and never got to it!

The more I read this article the better I liked it. I really thought I had a very funny piece of material. In fact, I felt so enthused I drove over to Jack Benny's office to read it to him. Jack wasn't there, so I read it to his personal manager, Irving Fein, and when I had finished he said, "George, it's a very funny article. How much are they going to pay Jack for this?"

I said, "Irving, I wrote the article. Why should they pay Jack?"

"Because the whole thing is about him," Irving said. "If it wasn't for Jack, you wouldn't have an article." I couldn't argue with that. Irving continued, "George, I realize that you and Jack are very close, but I'm just being practical. When Jack Benny's name is used to promote a product, he gets paid an awful lot of money. It would be a minimum of twenty-five-thousand dollars."

Well, that made me stop and think. I said, "Irving, you're right. I'll write a whole new article and I won't even mention Jack's name."

As I got up to leave, Irving said, "George, I'm sorry you can't use that article you wrote. It's a shame it came out so funny."

I didn't bother to answer that line, I just left.

The next morning when I came into the office I said, "Fellows, we'll have to rewrite that whole Teacher's article."

Well, this brought moans and groans from Jack Langdon and Packy. Packy complained, "That's a very funny article. I can't see any reason to change it."

"You're right," I said. "But if we do the article the way it is, we have to give Jack Benny twenty-five-thousand dollars. So we'll have to split it three ways."

There wasn't a sound while that sank in. Then Packy said, "That's a damn good reason to change it."

Jack Langdon put a piece of paper in the typewriter and said, "Let's start the new article fast."

I said, "Good. And I've already thought of a title I think will work. There's a line I used to do in nightclubs, and if we just switch it a little, I think it'll make a great title."

That line I did was, "I love to sing. I'd rather sing than eat. And my friends who have heard me sing, would rather hear me eat." The boys and I switched the line, and here's the final title and the article that went with it:

35

I LOVE TO SING.
AND I LOVE TO DRINK SCOTCH.
MOST PEOPLE WOULD RATHER HEAR
ME DRINK SCOTCH.
By George Burns

When they asked me to write this article, they said to be sure and mention Teacher's Scotch, but not to drag it in, make it sound natural. Well, I just mentioned it, and that sounded natural. It sounded so natural I'll mention it again—Teacher's Scotch.

I'm a great writer. If I had a beard, I'd be another Hemingway.

They told me they wanted a fresh approach. Well, to write fresh you have to think fresh, and to think fresh you have to be fresh. I haven't been fresh January twentieth will be thirty-one years. I'm not going to tell you my age, but I've reached that point in life where I catch cold if I smoke a cigar without a holder on it.

But don't worry, I'll never give up singing. In fact, I started singing the day I was born. I remember the doctor kept slapping me, but I wouldn't stop until I finished two choruses of "Wait Till the Sun Shines, Nellie." And when I segued into the verse to "Honeysuckle Rose," he put me in the incubator and turned off the heat. It's a good thing I was smoking a cigar or I'd have froze to death.

I never did like that doctor. He wouldn't put Teacher's Scotch in my bottle.—See how naturally I mentioned that without dragging it in. I'm a great writer even without a beard. But I've found out that a little drink now and then helps my singing. It loosens my vocal cords. Sometimes my vocal cords get so loose that whenever I hit a low note I step on them. And when I step on them, I hit a high note. I lead a very nervous life. In the morning I get up a baritone, and when I go to bed I'm a soprano.

As you're reading this some of it may be funny, and then again some of it won't. So just read the funny stuff and skip the rest of it. But if the rest of it turns out to be the funny stuff, and the funny stuff turns out to be the rest of it, if I were you, I'd skip the funny stuff, too.

36

That last paragraph has so much rhythm you could almost dance to it. Well, I'll have another little sip of Teacher's Scotch, then back to the old typewriter. — How about that? — another natural mention. If I keep writing like this, I'll win the Pulitzer Prize.

Now that I've started it makes me mad after all these years to discover that something I've never done is what I do best. There may be hundreds of things I've never done that I'm great at. Tomorrow I'll take a crack at painting. I'll get a brush and some paint, and lie on my back and paint my bathroom ceiling. I may even make my own paint.

And if that works out, I'll paint the Mona Lisa. But in my version she'll have a reason to smile, because I'll have her holding a glass of Teacher's Scotch in her hand. — Another natural mention — and in oil, yet.

You know, there's an old saying which I just made up: "Don't do something that you can't do, and then do it." As soon as I get Mona out of the way, I'm going into a new project. I'll take up ballet dancing.

No, I better forget that. If I get up on my toes, I might step on my vocal cords again. I better stick to writing.

I find that writing is just like singing. But it's kind of hard to end an article with a yodeling finish. But you've got to have an ending, so here goes: I'm going to make this ending so subtle that you won't even notice I'm being natural.

Two men were standing at a bar. One was drinking Teacher's Scotch with his left hand, and the other was drinking Teacher's Scotch with his right hand. So I said to the one who was drinking Teacher's with his left hand, "Why do you drink Teacher's with your left hand?"

He said, "I always drink Teacher's with my left hand."

Then I said to the fellow who was drinking Teacher's with his right hand, "Why do you drink Teacher's with your right hand?"

He said, "Because if I didn't drink Teacher's with my right hand, you'd keep mistaking me for that fellow who drinks Teacher's with his left hand."

Well, that's the article, and I'm glad I wrote it. It's opened a whole new career for me. It turns out I write as good as I sing.

37

Well, the Teacher's people were ecstatic about it. The title with my picture appeared on billboards, and the article was published in all the top magazines and newspapers. At the height of the campaign I ran into Jack Benny at the Hillcrest Country Club. He said to me, "I just read that ad of yours in *Time* magazine."

"What'd you think of it?" I asked him.

"I've never been so hurt in my life," he said. "You're supposed to be my best friend, that article ran two full pages, and you didn't have the decency to mention my name!"

I said, "Sorry about that, Jack, you're too expensive to mention."

As Jack stared at me trying to figure out what I was talking about, I left for the card room.

Open-Heart Surgery Can Be Fun!

I came from a very large family. There were five brothers and seven sisters, and we were all healthy kids. My folks were so poor we couldn't afford to get sick.

When we were growing up we didn't worry about proteins, carbohydrates, vitamins, etc. We were happy with whatever my mother had in the pot. I still remember that pot. It was a big iron kettle that my mother kept cooking on the stove, and everything that came into the house went into that pot.

Now, feeding a family of fourteen with the few pennies my mother had to work with took a real genius. And that she was. Her secret was the sauce she always kept cooking in that pot. It was stove-hot and highly seasoned. She knew that anything she served under that sauce would taste good. You could put my mother's sauce on chipped wood and it would be delicious. In fact, I think one time I ate my brother Sammy's yo-yo.

I don't know if I owe it all to my mother's spicy sauce, but all my life I've enjoyed very good health. I've never allowed aches and pains to bother me. I just learned to live with them. There were times I didn't feel good, but no matter how bad I felt, show business came first. I'd go out on the stage, sing and dance and do my act, and then get ready for the next show. When you do five shows a day you forget anything was wrong with you in the first place.

When I was about twenty-one I was doing a song and dance act with a fellow named Billy Lorraine. We were on the Pantages circuit, and we were playing Minneapolis, when it became necessary for me to have my tonsils taken out. I found a doctor who would take care of me on a Sunday, which was our only day off, and it had to be done in the morning, because at two o'clock that afternoon Billy and I were catching the train to Vancouver. It was important that we catch that train, because if we didn't get to Vancouver in time for the matinee, we'd be canceled for the rest of the circuit.

That week I'd been going with a little usherette from the theater, and she offered to come up to the doctor's office with me. To show my appreciation I gave her a meal ticket I had from a local cafeteria which still had $3.20 worth of food unpunched on it. It wasn't that I was such a big sport, it was just that I knew that after I had my tonsils out I wouldn't be able to eat anyway.

Well, we got to the doctor's office at ten o'clock that morning, and by ten thirty my tonsils were out.

The doctor said to me, "You better rest here for about three hours, and then go home and stay in bed for two days."

I could barely talk, but I managed to whisper, "Doctor, I can't do that, I'm catching a train for Vancouver at two o'clock and I'm doing a matinee tomorrow at noon."

The doctor couldn't believe what he heard. He said, "That's impossible—you're liable to hemorrhage."

"Then I'll take the tonsils with me," I said, "and if I hemorrhage, I'll put them back in."

There was nothing he could do, so at one thirty I was all packed and standing in front of the hotel waiting to leave for the train. In a few minutes Billy Lorraine met me.

"Did you have your tonsils taken out?" he asked me.

I nodded yes and opened my mouth. Billy took one look and fainted right on the spot.

By the time we got to Vancouver I was so weak I could hardly stand up, and my voice was even worse. I told the theater manager that Billy Lorraine would have to work alone that day, but I'd be ready the next. Well, when Billy and I worked together we were not one of the great two-acts—we were just plain bad. And when Billy went out there alone doing half of a bad act, he was lucky he got off alive.

Anyway, the manager was furious. He ran into our dressing room and shouted, "Look, Burns, if both of you aren't out on that stage for the next show, the act is canceled!"

The next show I was out there. What could I do? I wanted to stay in show business. But as it worked out, it helped my entire career. From that performance on I stopped singing tenor and started singing the way I do today.

Now, I don't know whether you've heard me sing or not. I like the way I sing—I love the way I sing. I wouldn't go so far as to say I'm the greatest singer in show business, however. There are plenty of fellows who sing better than I do; there's Frank Sinatra, Tony Bennett, and that's it.

I'll let you in on something—it's a lot easier for me to work in a theater than it is for them. Guys like Sinatra and Bennett need special lighting effects, great musical arrangements, and they carry the top musicians. Their exits are very important because when they exit they need applause to bring them back. Not me. I don't have that problem; I don't exit. I just stay there and finish my songs. Sometimes the audience exits. But that doesn't phase me. As long as I'm there I know somebody loves me.

But as I was saying before I rudely interrupted myself, after having my tonsils taken out I didn't see a doctor again for the next twenty years. And oddly enough, when I did have to see one it was my throat again. I had developed sort of a tickle in my throat which caused me to constantly keep clearing it. It got so I couldn't even finish a sentence without doing it. By then I was married to Gracie, and with all this hacking of mine she couldn't get any sleep. Also, we were on radio at the time, so I was not only annoying Gracie, I was annoying the whole country.

Anyway, I went to all the great doctors, every throat specialist I could find. They all looked into my throat and said the same thing—"Stop smoking!" So I stopped, and it got worse.

One day Abe Lastfogel called me—he was the head of the William Morris Agency—and said, "George, I heard you on the radio last night, and you better do something about that throat. If you keep hacking that way, the sponsor's never going to renew your contract."

I said, "Abe, I don't know what to do. I've been to every doctor in the country."

"George," Abe said, "you haven't been to Dr. Ginsberg. He runs a little eye, ear, nose and throat clinic in downtown Los Angeles. He only charges three dollars a visit and he's a genius."

Well, I got down there as fast as I could. When I went into his office there were about forty people in the waiting room. I went over to the nurse and said, "Would you tell Dr. Ginsberg that George Burns is sitting outside."

She went into the other office, and a minute later she returned. She said, "I told Dr. Ginsberg that George Burns was sitting outside, and he told me to tell you that Dr. Ginsberg is sitting inside." So I sat down, hacked, coughed, cleared my throat and waited my turn.

When I finally got into the doctor's office I kept hacking, and hacking, and hacking. He examined my throat and said, "What's your problem?"

I said, "What's my problem! Can't you tell? I keep making this hacking noise."

The doctor said, "Why do you do that?"

I sat there stunned. Nobody had ever asked me that question before. I said, "I don't know why I do it."

Dr. Ginsberg said, "Then if I were you, I wouldn't do it anymore."

And you know something—I never did.

I paid my $3, and as I started to leave I turned to the doctor and said, "Doctor, aren't you going to give me something to take?"

42

He opened a drawer and took out a box of jelly beans. "I usually give these to children," he said, "but since you're such a big star, I'll give you one of the black ones."

Anyway, I stopped hacking, Gracie was able to sleep again, Abe Lastfogel was happy, the sponsor renewed our contract, and I was hooked on black jelly beans.

After that I enjoyed perfect health until 1947. So let's jump ahead ten years. It's easy for me to jump ahead in this book, but in real life I don't want to jump ahead ten seconds—what am I talking about, make that five.

By 1947 Gracie and I were established radio stars, and one day my agent called and told me our sponsor had just picked up our option for another season. In those days when you were picked up it wasn't just for thirteen weeks, it was for thirty-nine weeks with thirteen weeks of repeats. This meant fifty-two full weeks of very big money. Well, naturally I was excited, and I couldn't wait to rush home to tell Gracie.

When I got to the house it was midmorning, and Gracie's favorite pastime was listening to those soap operas on the radio—and that's what she was doing. I came in all out of breath and said, "Gracie, I've got marvelous news!"

She put her finger to her lips and said, "Shhh, not now, George—Ma Perkins is in trouble."

So I had to sit there and wait for fifteen minutes until Ma Perkins got out of trouble. Finally, when it was over, I said, "Gracie, the sponsors just picked up our option and we're signed for another fifty-two weeks!"

She smiled. "That's wonderful," she said. "Isn't it nice that Ma Perkins and I got good news on the same day!"

"Gracie," I said, "it's a fifty-two-week deal. Don't you want to know how much money we'll be making?"

"Of course, but you can tell me later, George. Right now *Our Gal Sunday* is coming on."

That evening we were going out to celebrate, and while Gracie was upstairs getting dressed I went behind the bar to make myself a martini. As I turned to reach for the vermouth, suddenly I fainted. I was only out for a few seconds, and when I came to I felt just fine. I also felt a little silly. When you've just signed a contract for fifty-two weeks, that's no time to faint. Fainting is for actors who are laying off. Anyway, I decided not to even mention it to anybody. Gracie and I went out that night to celebrate, and I forgot about it.

A couple of nights later Gracie was upstairs, and I wanted to ask her something. I went over to the stairs, looked up and called her, and just like that I fainted again. When Gracie came down there I was lying on the floor. In another few seconds I was fine again, but Gracie was all upset. When I told her about fainting before she said, "George, I don't want any arguments, you're going to see Dr. Kennamer first thing in the morning."

The next day, in Dr. Kennamer's office, I told him my story. He listened to the whole thing and then asked me, "George, when you reached for the gin to make your martini which way did you turn?"

I said, "I turned to the right."

"When you went to call Gracie which way did you turn?"

"To the right."

"Sit up on the table here, George," he said. "I want to see if I can make you faint." He pressed something behind my right ear, and I fainted. When I came to, he said, "George, what you've got is an exposed nerve. The next time you make a martini or call Gracie, turn to the left."

His advice was perfect. It never bothered me again. Dr. Kennamer reminded me a lot of Dr. Ginsberg. The only difference was he didn't give me a black jelly bean and he charged me a lot more than $3.

For the next twenty-seven years healthwise, the worst thing that happened to me was a badly chapped lower lip. Things had been going too well, and I figured that sooner or later something was bound to happen. And when I got to be seventy-eight years old it did. I noticed that every so often I'd experience pains in my chest. I don't remember how

44

long this went on, but the pains started to come more often. However, that didn't bother me because at my age I like a little pain once in a while—at least I know I'm alive.

Anyway, it turned out that I had to be operated on. Now I don't think you'd be interested in a long, dull medical description of my operation, so I've thought of a better way to tell it. You may not believe this, but three months after the operation I was feeling great and went on the Johnny Carson show and told all about it. Now this isn't exactly the way it happened, but when you're working with Johnny Carson you better get a few laughs. (But one little reminder; as you read this keep in mind that my good friend Jack Benny was still with us at the time.)

Now, I'm just telling you what I said. If Johnny wants to tell you what he said, let him write his own book. All right, on November 13, 1974, after Johnny Carson introduced me, here's how it went:

Thank you, Johnny. Well, here I am, right from the operating table at Cedars of Lebanon to *The Tonight Show*. I'm very glad to be here . . . in fact, I'm glad to be anyplace. . . .

But that operation I had, how that happened was pretty crazy. You see, Johnny, I had been getting these pains in my chest, and I couldn't figure out what was causing them. Then I got a bright idea. Maybe it was because I wasn't wearing a vest—so I started wearing a vest. But then I started getting pains in my left arm, and I thought maybe my cigars were too heavy—so I started smoking with my right hand. There I was, wearing a vest and smoking with my right hand, but the pains were still there. . . .

I didn't think anything more about it until a few days later at Hillcrest when I was playing bridge the pains started up again. Now, I was holding a very good hand—an opening two bid with 150 honors in hearts. If I could feel the pain while I was holding a hand like that, I knew I was in trouble. . . . I had another member play my hand, and I went right to my doctors, Dr. Rex Kennamer and Dr. Gary Sugarman.

45

After they examined me, Dr. Kennamer said, "George, this is serious."

I said, "Whatever you have to do, do it fast. I want to get back to the club, the guy playing my hand is a lousy bridge player."

He looked real serious and said, "George, you're going to have to go to the hospital."

"Okay," I said, "let's book it for next week."

He shook his head and said, "George, you've got to go right now."

"What about my bridge game?" I asked him.

He looked straight at me and said, "George, if you don't go now, you may never play bridge again."

I couldn't believe what I had just heard. I said, "Is it that serious?"

Dr. Sugarman put his hand on my shoulder and said, "George, I hate to be this blunt, but if you don't go now, you could die."

I'd never died before, but somehow I didn't think I would like it— Oh, come to think of it, I died in New Haven, Schenectady, and Altoona, but this kind of dying could cancel you out of show business.

Anyway, when I got to the hospital Dr. Kennamer told me they were going to do open-heart surgery; take some veins out of my leg and bypass some arteries in my heart. I didn't know what he was talking about. I said, "Look, doctor, whatever you have to do, do it, but make sure you don't touch my vocal cords, because that's how I make my living."

Well, they gave me some pills that made me very groggy and took me downstairs. The doctor said, "George, we're going to put some fluid into your system and show you exactly what we're going to do. And you can watch yourself on that television screen."

Johnny, can I tell you something—I looked lousy. I had no makeup on.

When the test was over, Dr. Kennamer said, "Well, George, that's what we're gonna do," and I said, "Well, do it fast, because that thing I just saw on the screen is not going to play Las Vegas."

That afternoon they operated on me. I was on the table for

46

about five or six hours, and then they put me in the Intensive Care Unit. When I came to, the first thing I did was sing "The Red Rose Rag." I wanted to make sure my vocal cords were still there.

Anyway, Johnny, my operation was a tremendous success. Dr. Kennamer and Dr. Sugarman handled the whole thing, and they're the greatest. Dr. Jack Matloff's cardiac team operated on me, and they were great. The operation was done at Cedars of Lebanon Hospital, which is also great. So because of those great people, Johnny, here I am feeling great.

And there isn't anything I did before the operation that I can't do again. That means I can do nothing. . . . I did nothing before the operation and I can do nothing now. . . . And if you don't believe me, ask Trixie Hart . . . or Lilly La-Mott . . . or Glenda Gibson . . . or Betty DeFore . . . I did nothing with a lot of girls. . . .

But naturally, Johnny, an operation like that has a big effect on your life. But don't get me wrong, I never felt better, but Dr. Kennamer did foul up my eating habits. Johnny, no ketchup . . . I put ketchup on everything. Me without ketchup is like Dean Martin splitting a milk shake with Phil Harris. . . .

Another thing—no salt. For breakfast I've always had scrambled eggs with a lot of ketchup and a lot of salt. Now I've gotta eat them just plain. Johnny, did you know eggs were yellow? You know, I'm seventy-eight years old and I've had eggs all my life, and I never knew they tasted like that . . . sort of a nothing taste . . . kind of bland. They taste like the chicken wasn't getting paid. . . .

But now I have to go every week to Dr. Kennamer's office for a checkup. And, Johnny, you're not going to believe what happened to me while I was waiting there last week—

There was a woman sitting there, and after looking at me for a minute or so she said, "It's exciting to be sitting in a waiting room with a celebrity."

I said, "Yes, it is exciting. Who are you?" She kind of laughed, and said, "I mean you. I watch you all the time, I'm a big fan of yours. By the way, how's your wife Mary?"

"Mary's just fine," I answered, "she was fine when I left her in bed this morning."

"That stingy character you play," the woman said. "You're not that way in real life, are you?"

I said, "Of course not."

Then she said something I couldn't believe my ears. She said, "Mr. Benny, is it true that everything George Burns says makes you laugh?"

"Oh, yes," I said, "he's one of the funniest men in show business. I wish I had his sense of humor."

She said, "I like George Burns, too, and I watch him all the time. How come he never finishes a song?"

"Well, he's reached the age now where he can't finish anything anymore," I said. Then I added, "What's your name?" And she said, "Mrs. Schwartz."

"Mrs. Schwartz," I said, "listen to this—

(sings)
Down in the garden where the red roses grow,
Oh my, I long to go
Pluck me like a flower,
Cuddle me an hour,
Lovie, let me learn that red rose rag . . .

"Whom does that sound like?"

Mrs. Schwartz said, "George Burns—but, Mr. Benny, Rich Little does a better imitation of him than you do."

Then the nurse came out and said, "The doctor will see you now, Mr. Burns."

Mrs. Schwartz's mouth fell open a bit, and she said, "Mr. Burns! Are you George Burns?"

"That's right," I said.

And very indignantly she said, "Well, what were you doing in bed with Mary this morning?!"

I said, "At our age it takes both Jack and myself to keep her warm. Good-bye Mrs. Schwartz."

Well, that's the way I told it on *The Johnny Carson Show.* Isn't that better than going into a lot of grim detail? Sure, I knew it was a serious operation, but I didn't allow myself to get uptight about it. That just happens to be the

48

kind of person I am. I had the finest doctors I could get, I was in a hospital with all the latest equipment, so what more could I do about it—it was out of my hands. I was fortunate, because ten years ago this bypass operation had never been heard of, and today it's very successful. So the point is, nobody should ever give up hope. Every day medical science is developing new cures for practically everything.

That's about all I'm going to say about my operation. And for you skeptics who doubt that my vocal cords came through unscathed, some night if you're giving a sociable at your house, invite me over. I'll bring my piano player and sing twenty or thirty songs for you. And if you haven't got a piano, I'll bring that, too.

Gracie and Me

I was married to Gracie for thirty-eight years, and it was a marvelous marriage. It worked. Now don't get me wrong, we had arguments, but not like other couples had. Our arguments were never about our marriage. When we had a disagreement, it had to do with show business. I know that it's a common belief among many psychologists and marriage counselors that you can't mix marriage with a career. Well, I've got news for them—they can mix, and Gracie and I proved it for thirty-eight years.

An average couple who has been married for thirty-eight years are with each other for about six hours a day. This means they see each other about one fourth of the time, so in thirty-eight years of marriage they've only been together a little over nine years.

But not Gracie and me. We got up together, we dressed together, we ate together, we worked together, we played together, we were together twenty-four hours a day. That meant in thirty-eight years of marriage Gracie and I were together four times longer than the average couple.

(I hope my fifth grade teacher, Miss Hollander, reads this. She flunked me once in arithmetic.)

You know, lots of times people have asked me what Gracie and I did to make our marriage work. It's simple—we didn't do anything. I think the trouble with a lot of people is that they work too hard at staying married. They make a business out of it. When you work too hard at a business you get tired; and when you get tired you get grouchy; and when you get grouchy you start fighting; and when you start fighting you're out of business.

(I'm another Dear Abby.)

Looking back, I really don't know why Gracie married me. I certainly know why I wanted to marry her. She was a living Irish doll; such a dainty little thing, only 102 pounds, with long, blue-black hair and sparkling eyes; so full of life, and with an infectious laugh that made her fun to be around. Besides all that she was a big talent; she could sing, she was a great dancer, and a fine actress with a marvelous flair for comedy.

But why did she marry me? As they say in music, I was tacit. I was nothing. I was already starting to lose my hair, I had a voice like a frog, I stuttered and stammered, I was a bad, small-time vaudeville actor and I was broke. I guess she must have felt sorry for me.

I'm glad she did.

I'm not going to tell you about meeting Gracie—our courtship—my proposal—or that $17 wedding ring I gave her that was marked down to $11. I've told those stories over and over again. But there is one incident that I'd like to repeat. I don't know if you'll enjoy it, but when this book comes out, I'd like to read it again.

When I first started working with Gracie she was going with a fellow named Benny Ryan. Now, Benny Ryan was in love with Gracie, I was in love with Gracie, and Gracie was in love with Benny Ryan. Benny never got jealous about Gracie working with me, because in his mind I was no competition. As far as he was concerned Gracie could have been working with a trained seal.

There was no way I could compete with Benny Ryan. He was not only a charming, witty Irishman, but he had a tremendous talent. He was considered one of our great dancers, he wrote comedy sketches for some of the biggest stars, and he was a very successful songwriter. To show you what a great sense of humor he had, one of the songs he wrote

52

was called "When Frances Dances with Me," and this was the closing couplet:

> She does a new step,
> It goes one, two, three, kick;
> She can't count so good,
> That's the worst of the trick.
> My shin bones look like they've
> Been hit with a brick
> When Frances dances with me.

How could I compete with a guy who could write a lyric like that? I always thought that "moon" rhymed with "January."

Anyway, here I was in love with this lovely girl and I knew I didn't stand a chance with her. But as I said, every time I would hit bottom something always happened that made me bounce back. Well, I bounced.

Gracie and I were booked to play eighteen weeks on the Orpheum Circuit. This was big-time vaudeville and involved a tour of all the major cities in the Western states. The day before we were set to leave, Benny Ryan arrived back in town. When he heard about our tour he asked Gracie to cancel the tour and marry him. But as much as Gracie was in love with Benny Ryan, she was too nice a person to walk out on me with such short notice. She knew how important it was for me to play these big-time theaters, so she told Benny he would just have to wait until we returned from the tour, and then she'd marry him. Benny was furious, but I was bouncing again. I figured if I had eighteen weeks on the road with Gracie anything could happen.

The team of Burns & Allen was making $400 a week, which meant $200 for each of us. Out of that I had to pay commission to my agent, send money home to my mother, pay my railroad fares, my hotel bills, and my food. So this left me with about $85 a week, and I was spending every nickel of it trying to make an impression on Gracie. Wherever we were on the tour I'd take her to dinner at the best restaurant in town, and when we were through working at night I'd often take her dancing at the finest hotels.

Well, after nine weeks we landed in San Francisco. I was still nowhere and I was broke. Now, you wouldn't think a case of appendicitis would play a big part in a romance, but in my case it did. We were playing the Orpheum Theater in San Francisco, and in the middle of the week Gracie was rushed to the hospital for an emergency appendectomy. Before she went into surgery she asked me to wire Benny Ryan in New York and let him know she was in the hospital. I sent the wire, but believe me, my heart wasn't in it—and besides that, it cost me my last seventy-five cents. It was not one of my bright moments.

Anyway, Gracie came through the operation fine, but while she recovered it meant that I had to stay in San Francisco for three weeks with no money coming in. Gracie knew this, and she said to me, "George, my mother lives here in San Francisco, and I've arranged for you to stay with her until I can go back to work." And as if that wasn't enough, she also knew I was broke, so she loaned me $200 to get by on.

Well, there I was—I had a place to stay, home cooking, and $200 in my pocket. You'd think I'd be happy—but I wasn't. All I could think of was that telegram she had me send to Benny Ryan.

Of course, I was at the hospital every day, and after about four or five days I noticed Gracie was very upset. Finally she came out and said, "I can't understand it. I haven't heard a word from Benny Ryan since we left New York. You'd think he'd at least send flowers when he knows I'm in the hospital." Then she looked at me and said, "George, are you sure you sent that telegram?"

I said, "Yes, Gracie, I sent it. I didn't want to, but I sent it."

54

When I left the hospital that day I still had $160—and the beginning of a brainstorm. I went to the nearest florist and sent Gracie $160 worth of flowers—all sorts of flowers, every kind of flower I had ever heard of. Now, in those days $160 worth of flowers not only filled Gracie's room but that hospital had flowers coming out all the windows.

But it worked! The next day, after fighting my way through the flowers to Gracie's bedside, she gave me a big smile and said, "George, anybody who would spend my two hundred dollars to send me flowers has to be a very nice man." And then she kissed me. In my mind's eye I could see Benny Ryan bite the dust.

Anyway, after the tour Gracie and I were married. And now that I look back, I don't think I ever paid her back that $200.

During the first year of our marriage everything worked. Our marriage was a success, careerwise we were doing well, our salaries were getting better—everything was getting better except me on the stage. I was still pathetic. I did absolutely nothing and put on makeup to do it. Fortunately, it didn't matter that I wasn't improving, because Gracie was so good she carried both of us.

I'll never forget the first time we were booked into the Palace Theater in New York. It was a very exciting break for us; playing the Palace was the goal of every vaudeville act in the country.

Just try to imagine two young performers being booked into the top vaudeville theater in the nation and knowing that when they walked out onstage for the opening matinee the theater would be packed with actors, critics, and bookers. Thinking about it made both of us nervous wrecks.

Gracie bought herself a brand-new outfit from head to toes, and I had my spats cleaned. The night before we opened I really went all out. I bought a couple of bottles of champagne because I thought all our friends would be coming up to our hotel room to celebrate our opening; people like Blossom Seeley, Benny Fields, Mary Kelly, Tom Swift, Jack and Mary Benny, Orry Kelly, and Archibald Leach. (He later went into pictures. I think he changed his name to Cary Grant.)

Well, we sat there waiting for a couple of hours, but nobody showed up. Finally I picked up the phone and called Jack Benny. I said, "Jack, where is everybody? I even bought some champagne because I thought you'd all be by to have a drink and help us celebrate."

Jack said, "George, we're all over here at my place. We were gonna come by, but then we talked it over. We decided since you and Gracie are opening at the Palace tomorrow night it would be better if you got some rest."

After I hung up, Gracie said, "George, what are we going to do with this champagne?" With that I opened a bottle. We both had a drink and Gracie went to bed. I didn't want that bottle of champagne to go flat, so I stayed up an extra hour. You know something? It's impossible to get a champagne cork back into the bottle.

The next thing we knew we were backstage in our dressing room putting on our makeup. There was no conversation between us. Gracie was so nervous it took her three different tries before she could get her lips on right. But for some strange reason I was as cool as a cucumber. I finally did figure it out. When you go on the stage and don't do anything, there's very little to get nervous about.

Well, the big moment finally arrived! There we were, standing in the wings of the Palace Theater, ready to go on! I took Gracie's hand, our music started to play, we made our entrance, and this is the act we did the very first time we played the Palace:

(Play-on music:)
(George and Gracie enter holding hands. Gracie stops, turns, looks toward the wings, and waves. She lets go of George's hand and walks toward the wing, still waving. Then she stops and beckons to whomever she is waving to

56

come out. A man comes out, puts his arms around Gracie, and kisses her, and she kisses him. They wave to each other as he backs offstage. Gracie returns to George center stage.)

GRACIE
Who was that?

GEORGE
You don't know?

GRACIE
No, my mother told me never to talk to strangers.

GEORGE
That makes sense.

GRACIE
This always happens to me. On my way in, a man stopped me at the stage door and said, "Hiya, cutie, how about a bite tonight after the show?"

GEORGE
And you said?

GRACIE
I said, "I'll be busy after the show but I'm not doing anything now," so I bit him.

GEORGE
Gracie, let me ask you something. Did the nurse ever happen to drop you on your head when you were a baby?

GRACIE
Oh, no, we couldn't afford a nurse, my mother had to do it.

GEORGE
You had a smart mother.

GRACIE
Smartness runs in my family. When I went to school I was so smart my teacher was in my class for five years.

GEORGE
Gracie, what school did you go to?

57

GRACIE

I'm not allowed to tell.

GEORGE

Why not?

GRACIE

The school pays me $25 a month not to tell.

GEORGE

Is there anybody in the family as smart as you?

GRACIE

My sister Hazel is even smarter. If it wasn't for her, our canary would never have hatched that ostrich egg.

GEORGE

A canary hatched an ostrich egg?

GRACIE

Yeah . . . but the canary was too small to cover that big egg.

GEORGE

So?

GRACIE

So . . . Hazel sat on the egg and held the canary in her lap.

GEORGE

Hazel must be the smartest in your family.

GRACIE

Oh, no. My brother Willy was no dummy either.

GEORGE

Willy?

GRACIE

Yeah, the one who slept on the floor.

GEORGE

Why would he sleep on the floor?

GRACIE

He had high blood pressure—

58

GEORGE

And he was trying to keep it down?

GRACIE

Yeah.

GEORGE

I'd like to meet Willy.

GRACIE

You can't miss him. He always wears a high collar to cover the appendicitis scar on his neck.

GEORGE

Gracie, your appendix is down around your waist.

GRACIE

I know, but Willy was so ticklish they had to operate up there.

GEORGE

What's Willy doing now?

GRACIE

He just lost his job.

GEORGE

Lost his job?

GRACIE

Yeah, he's a window washer.

GEORGE

And?

GRACIE

And . . . he was outside on the twentieth story washing a window and when he got through he stepped back to admire his work.

GEORGE

And he lost his job.

GRACIE

Yeah . . . And when he hit the pavement he was terribly embarrassed.

59

GEORGE

Embarrassed?

GRACIE

Yeah . . . his collar flew off and his appendicitis scar showed.

GEORGE

Gracie, this family of yours—

GRACIE

When Willy was a little baby my father took him riding in his carriage, and two hours later my father came back with a different baby and a different carriage.

GEORGE

Well, what did your mother say?

GRACIE

My mother didn't say anything because it was a better carriage.

GEORGE

A better carriage?

GRACIE

Yeah . . . And the little baby my father brought home was a little French baby so my mother took up French.

GEORGE

Why?

GRACIE

So she would be able to understand the baby—

GEORGE

When the baby started to talk?

GRACIE

Yeah.

GEORGE

Gracie, this family of yours, do you all live together?

GRACIE

Oh, sure. My father, my brother, my uncle, my cousin and my nephew all sleep in one bed and—

60

GEORGE

In one bed? I'm surprised your grandfather doesn't sleep with them.

GRACIE

Oh, he did, but he died, so they made him get up.

Well, those were the jokes Gracie and I told at the Palace, and looking back at them I still think they're pretty funny. But as I said before, Gracie was the act. I think you'll agree when you take another look at the hilarious lines I had. I said:

—"You don't know?"
—"So?"
—"And?"
—"Well, what did your mother say?"
—"When the baby started to talk?"

And those were the kind of lines that made me a star.

Following this comedy routine the lights would come down and a spotlight would hit Gracie while she sang a song. The audience loved her because her voice had a beautiful quality, pure and delightful. During this I stood over to one side in the dark. Many critics thought this was the high point of my performance.

And Gracie was a marvelous Irish clog dancer. So at the end of her song the music would segue into this very fast Irish jig, which Gracie danced to. Every part of her body went into that dance. Her feet were lightning quick and she never missed a tap. She created such excitement that at the end of her dance it brought down the house. Then the lights would come up, and while Gracie was bowing I stood there applauding her.

After the applause died down we continued with our act. This consisted of about ten more minutes of comedy dialogue, which was very easy for me because all I had to do was repeat those lines I did in the first part.

61

Our act ended with a typical boy-girl song, which led into the both of us dancing together. During this dance we used a gimmick which I think I originated. It's been used many times over the years—in fact, it's still being used and it still works. Gracie and I would dance together, and four times during the number I would stop the music—we would tell a joke—and then continue dancing. It went like this:

(George and Gracie go into dance)

GEORGE

Stop!
(Music stops)
Gracie, how is your cousin?

GRACIE

You mean the one who died?

GEORGE

Yeah.

GRACIE

Oh, he's fine now.

GEORGE

Music!
(Music starts, and dance continues)

GEORGE

Stop!
(Music stops)
Gracie, how's your uncle Harvey?

GRACIE

Oh, last night he fell down the stairs with a bottle of scotch and never spilled a drop.

GEORGE

Really?

GRACIE

Yeah, he kept his mouth closed.

GEORGE
Music!
(Music starts, and dance continues)

GEORGE

Stop!
(Music stops)

GRACIE

My sister Bessie had a brand new-baby.

GEORGE

Boy or girl?

GRACIE

I don't know, and I can't wait to get home to find out if I'm an aunt or an uncle.

GEORGE

Music!
(Music starts, and dance continues)

GEORGE

Stop!
(Music stops)
A funny thing happened to my mother in Cleveland.

GRACIE

I thought you were born in Buffalo.

GEORGE

Music!
(Music up—and into dancing exit)

Well, that was the routine Gracie and I did the first time at the Palace. And we were really a big hit. I know, I was there.

It's Fun To Look Back—If There Isn't Something Cuter in Front of You!

Now that I'm eighty I find that I have a lot in common with other people my age. There is still one thing we can all do—and we can do it standing up . . . lying down . . . sitting down . . . we can do it in any position. In fact, we can do it and drink a glass of water at the same time.

You know what it is? Being able to look back and reminisce! I'll bet you thought of a more exciting answer. Well, so did I, but this book is meant for family entertainment.

You know, most people when they look back they talk about what they would do if they could live their lives over again; how they wouldn't do this and they wouldn't do that, they'd change this and they'd change that, and all of the things they should have done differently. I've never had that problem. In all my years I've never made one mistake. Well, that's not true—on January 6, 1924, at two o'clock I made one mistake—no, I made two mistakes—look, I've made a lot of mistakes, but it never worried me. I'm glad I made all those mistakes. If it wasn't for them, when I go on the Johnny Carson or the Merv Griffin shows I wouldn't have anything to talk about. I even made a lot of those mistakes on purpose. I knew eventually Johnny Carson and Merv Griffin would grow up and have their own talk shows.

But there's nothing wrong with looking back. I know I do it, and I enjoy it. But I also enjoy looking to the future. The future I'm looking forward to tonight is about twenty-two years old and she's coming to my house for dinner. She's a beautiful little airline stewardess. We made a deal; I'm going to teach her how to sing and she's going to teach me how to fly. I'm not sure, but I think it's going to be easier for me to teach her to sing. But if this little girl can teach me to fly, it may mean a whole new chapter.

Look, I know I poke fun at everything, including myself, but that's been my philosophy all my life. I've always been able to laugh at my own problems. You'll find that most everyday little problems can be solved with laughter. For instance, if a man comes home and finds his wife making love to someone else, he should use my philosophy—don't get mad, just laugh. If it's a cold day, he could open the window so the other guy will catch cold.

Now, I may have exaggerated a bit that having a sense of humor helps get you through rough spots, but it does. I've observed that most people just take themselves too seriously, and if they do have a problem, once it's over they won't let go of it. I have actor friends who have been big stars for years. They still make fabulous salaries, they're happily married and have beautiful families, they live in magnificent homes with fine paintings on the walls, swimming pools, tennis courts, two or three cars, a staff of servants—anything money can buy. But even with all this luxury they're still bugged because during their careers they may have received three bad notices and those notices are still on their minds.

Even today I don't worry about reviews. If I get a bad review, I figure it's the reviewer who's bad, not me. If he doesn't like me, I don't have to like him. After all, we don't have to go dancing together.

When Gracie and I first started, we were playing in Oklahoma City one time and the morning after we opened there was a review of our act in the paper. This was what the man had to say in the last paragraph of his review:

. . . Number Four on the Orpheum bill was a man and woman act, George Burns and Gracie Allen. Miss Allen is not only a beautiful young lady, but a great talent. She cap-

66

tivated the audience with her lovely voice, her exciting dancing, and her all-around stage presence. On top of all this her comedy timing is flawless. There is no telling how far Miss Allen could go if she worked alone.

Reading this didn't help my ego, but what could I do about it? I admit I wondered what Gracie's reaction would be, so after the show that night I borrowed ten dollars from her and invited her out to dinner. I took her to the nicest place in town. We had a drink, a crabmeat cocktail, and right in the middle of her lamb chops I said, "Gracie, what did you think of that notice in the paper this morning?"

She looked up at me, smiled sweetly, and said, "George, pass the salt."

So I passed her the salt. I was good at it, too, because I passed Gracie an awful lot of salt.

Now, all through this book I've been telling you how bad I was, so I imagine you're saying to yourselves if he was that bad, how did the team of Burns & Allen ever make it? Well, it's true I was bad, but only onstage. Offstage was something else again. I knew show business, especially vaudeville. I knew all the ingredients involved in putting an act together; I knew exits, entrances, how to construct a joke, how to switch a joke, where the laughs were going to drop, how to build an act to a strong finish. And most important, I knew the zany, off-center character Gracie Allen played onstage. I discovered the most effective way for Gracie to get laughs was by having her tell jokes that had what I called "illogical logic"; they sounded like they made sense, but they only made sense to Gracie. This tickled the audience and they fell in love with her because her honest delivery made all this unbelievable nonsense sound believable. So when I said to Gracie, "How's your brother?" and she went into five minutes of telling me, there was a lot of me in what she said.

As time went on I got better onstage. I had to. For me there was no way to go but up. My timing got better, I got

67

more confidence in myself, and I learned how to keep out of Gracie's way so the audience would concentrate on her. I improved so much I finally got so good that nobody knew I was there.

By now Gracie and I were considered a big-time vaudeville act and we played nothing but the best theaters. We were in the third year of a five-year contract with the Keith-Orpheum circuit, and we played on the same bill with stars like Nora Bayes, Belle Baker, Eddie Cantor, Sophie Tucker, Blossom Seeley, you name them.

I was on cloud nine. In my wildest dreams I had never expected to get to this point in show business. And to top all that, here I was married to a wonderful girl who was not only marvelous onstage, but the perfect wife off. Well—not exactly perfect. Let me tell you a little personal secret about Gracie. She was everything a man could want in a wife, but her Irish background made her a very determined person. If she thought she was right about something, she wouldn't budge. Let me tell you a little something about what happened in New Orleans. This was before we were married, but it will give you an idea of what I'm talking about.

Gracie had bought a new dress, which cost her $400, to wear in our act. For her this was a very, very expensive dress, and she had saved for a long time to be able to afford it. Before we opened in New Orleans she sent the dress to a place called the Chiffon Cleaners, and when it came back the dress was ruined. It was a red and white dress and all the colors had run together and it was a mess. Naturally, when Gracie saw what they'd done she was heartbroken and went directly to the cleaners and demanded $400 to replace the dress. Well, she got nowhere. They claimed they weren't responsible and refused to do anything about it.

That afternoon in our dressing room before the matinee Gracie never said a word; she wouldn't even discuss the dress. But I could feel that her Irish was starting to bubble.

Anyway, we were on the stage doing our act, the theater was packed, and the audience was loving us. When we got

68

to our closing number we came to the joke where I stopped the music and said, "A funny thing happened to my mother in Cleveland," and Gracie was supposed to answer, "I thought you were born in Buffalo." Well, instead of answering me, she just walked right down to the footlights and matter-of-factly said, "Ladies and gentlemen, when I arrived in New Orleans I had a brand new dress which cost me four hundred dollars, and yesterday for the first time I sent it to be cleaned by the Chiffon Cleaners, which is located at the corner of St. Charles and Canal Street. When it came back it was absolutely ruined. I immediately went down there, and since I could never wear the dress again, I asked them to make good on it. They not only refused, but they were very rude to me. The reason I'm telling you this, I'll be leaving New Orleans at the end of the week, but you people live here. So I'm warning you, don't send your clothes to the Chiffon Cleaners, which is located at the corner of St. Charles and Canal Street." And with that she turned and walked back to me, and said, "I thought you were born in Buffalo." Needless to say, that joke did not get a laugh. Not only was Gracie's dress ruined, but so was that joke.

That night, during our performance, she made the same speech, but in a different part of our act. I don't have to tell you, I was a nervous wreck. We still had six more days in New Orleans and I knew there was no way of stopping Gracie. The next day, when we arrived at the theater, the only thing I could think of was, When will she do it today? Will it be the same place as last night or yesterday afternoon? When? But fortunately for my peace of mind, there was an envelope for Gracie at the stage door with $400 in it, compliments of the Chiffon Cleaners, which was located at the corner of St. Charles and Canal Street.

When Gracie had something to say she got right to the point. Let me tell you something else that actually happened onstage. One time I came up with a joke that I thought would be perfect in our closing routine. I thought it was a very funny joke, so before the matinee I told it to Gracie. I said, "When I stop the music I'll say, 'What are you doing tonight?' And you say, 'I can't see you tonight, I'm expecting a headache.'"

She shook her head and said, "I don't like it. I don't think it's funny."

I said, "Gracie, I think it's a funny joke!"

She shook her head again and said, "I don't."

Trying to reason with her, I said, "Gracie, we'll leave it to the audience to decide. If they laugh at the joke, it's in, and if they don't, we'll take it out."

She shook her head and said, "It's not funny."

Well, Gracie wanted the joke out and I wanted it in. I'm not Irish, but I've got something that bubbles a little, too. At the matinee, when we came to that bit, I stopped the music and said, "Gracie, what are you doing tonight?" She just stood there, looked at me, and never said a word. I waited through about fifteen seconds of dead silence, then finally said, "Music," and we started dancing again.

I knew that sooner or later one of us would have to outbubble the other. For two weeks at every performance I said to Gracie, "What are you doing tonight?" and she just stood there and looked at me until I said "Music." The audiences must have thought we were crazy. Anyway, she finally gave in, and that night when I said, "What are you doing tonight?" she answered with, "I can't see you tonight, I'm expecting a headache." And it got a big laugh.

Back in the dressing room, I couldn't help gloating a little. I said to her, "Well, Gracie, haven't you got anything to say?"

She looked at me, smiled sweetly, and said, "George, pass the salt."

Now, from these last two stories don't get the wrong idea about Gracie. While she stood up for her rights and didn't want to be pushed around, she certainly had no desire to be a liberated woman. She enjoyed all the little niceties that were normally extended to women. She expected a man to

70

take off his hat in an elevator, pull out her chair for her when she sat down, and open a car door for her. Gracie behaved like a refined, gentle lady and felt she should be treated like one. Except for one night.

We were coming out of Toots Shor's restaurant in New York after dinner, and without thinking I walked out ahead of Gracie and forgot to hold the door open for her. I stood there on the sidewalk looking for a cab, and the next thing I knew Gracie came right up behind me. She lifted her skirt, kicked me right in the area I had recently been sitting on, and said, "George, you're no gentleman!"

When the cab came up, believe me, I held the door open for Gracie. I wanted to make sure that she got in ahead of me.

You see, like I said, looking back and reminiscing can be fun. I know it's been fun for me, and I hope you enjoyed it, too. If I had to sum up this chapter in a few words, I'd say, Learn to laugh at your problems! When everything seems to be going wrong, there's only one thing to do—just pass the salt! If there isn't any salt, pass the pepper, it works just as well!

Good Fathers Don't Grow on Trees

At times being my age can be embarrassing. People are always asking me for advice. I guess they figure if I've been around this long, I must know everything. Actually, I know very little, but sometimes you get backed into a corner. Like the other day at the club, Archie Preissman, a very successful businessman, came up to me and said, "George, do you think changing over to the metric system will have an effect on our economy?"

Well, I puffed my cigar, thought for a minute, did my impression of Bernard Baruch, and said, "That's funny, Archie, but Judge Roth just asked me the same thing. What do you think?"

"I think it will have a drastic effect on the economy," Archie answered.

I said, "That's exactly what I told Judge Roth."

"Thank you, George," Archie said, and walked away.

That's the way I am. When people ask me an opinion, I give it to them. Imagine asking me a question like that. I thought the metric system was a way to beat the horses.

Another time one of the members came up to me and said, "George, I'm really worried about my two teen-age sons. They stay out half the night, they drive too fast, they let their hair grow long, they dress like bums—what do you think I should do?"

Again I puffed on my cigar, thought for a minute, then did my impression of Dr. Spock and said, "Patience—you've got to have patience. By the time those kids get to be my

73

age, believe me, you won't have to worry about them." He didn't even say thank you, he just walked away.

Now I don't claim to be an authority on parenthood, but Gracie and I did have two lovely children, Sandra (Sandy) and Ronnie. They're grown up now. Sandy has four beautiful daughters, Lori, Lissa, Grace-Anne, and Brooke (naturally, I'm teaching them harmony in case vaudeville comes back), and Ronnie has three handsome boys, Brent, Brad, and Bryan (with names like that they gotta wind up doing a dancing act). My grandchildren love to come over to visit me. They often come over on Friday and leave on Sunday. They look forward to these visits because I'm such a sweet, kind, considerate, lovable granddaddy. . . which is not true. The real reason they like to visit me is because of the two fine people working for me, Daniel and Arlette, who spend all their time entertaining the kids—that's the reason.

The kids don't even know I'm around. One day they were in swimming, and I was sitting by the pool. I overheard Brad say to Brent, "Who's the old man with the cigar?"

Brent looked over at me and said, "I'm not sure, but I think he's supposed to be our granddaddy."

When Gracie and I were raising Sandy and Ronnie, we were always in show business, so we had different problems than the average family. Our work hours were so irregular; sometimes we'd rehearse late, sometimes we had a very early call, sometimes we were on the road—so our problem was finding time to spend with the children. Most of the time we were able to have dinner with them. And, of course, we saw them on weekends. I don't know if Gracie and I were good parents or not, but we must have done something right, because Sandy and Ronnie turned out be a daughter and son I'm very proud of.

Naturally we had to discipline them from time to time. Once, when Sandy was five and Ronnie was four, we had a very expensive dictionary that we kept on a stand in the li-

74

My Grandchildren

Lori. *Photo by Jack Laxer.*

Lissa. *Photo by Jack Laxer.*

Left to right: Brad, Bryan, and Brent.

Grace-Anne.

Brooke.

brary. The dictionary was illustrated with beautiful colored pictures, and was actually a collector's item. When Gracie and I came home from the studio, we found the dictionary open and several of the pictures cut out of it. Well, Gracie was terribly upset and wanted to give the kids a good spanking. But I stopped her with, "Gracie, let me handle this. I'll use psychology and find out which one of them did it."

I called Ronnie into the room and said, "Ronnie, where did Sandy hide the scissors she used to cut out those pictures?"

Ronnie looked up at me and said, "I don't know, Daddy."

So I dismissed him and called in Sandy. "Sandy," I said, "where did Ronnie hide the scissors he used to cut out those pictures?"

"In that desk drawer, Daddy," she said, pointing.

Well, I looked in the drawer, and sure enough there were the scissors, and the case was solved. At that moment I thought to myself, I'm wasting my time in show business, I should be with the FBI. I went to Gracie and told her Ronnie was the one who cut out the pictures.

She said, "Well, we've got to teach him a lesson," and she called Ronnie into the room. She sat him down in a chair and said, "Ronnie, how do you spell chrysanthemum?"

Ronnie's eyes started to puddle up, and he said, "I don't know, Mommy."

Gracie said, "And you never will know if you go around cutting up dictionaries instead of reading them!"

After Ronnie had gone to his room, I said to Gracie, "How *do* you spell chrysanthemum?"

She gave me a look and said, "R-o-s-e, that's a flower, too!"

Anyway, solving that case sort of went to my head, so for years whenever anybody came to the house they had to listen to the story of how I solved the great dictionary caper. One night we were all gathered with friends in the living room, and I started to tell that story again. Sandy was now ten years old, and she stopped me. "Daddy," she said, "please don't tell that story anymore. You got it all wrong, anyway. It wasn't Ronnie. I knew the scissors were in that drawer because I was the one who cut out the pictures."

Well, that's when I resigned from the FBI and went back into show business.

When it came to entertaining the kids, again I had a problem. I knew that the average father was supposed to take his kids to the beach, go camping with them, take them fishing, hiking, go on picnics—but I just didn't have time for all those things. I'm sure Ronnie would have liked me to play baseball with him, but I knew nothing about baseball. I never played baseball. I played Mechanicsville, Schenectady, Scranton, Gloversville, Bristol, New Haven, Wilkes-Barre, Akron—but I was never booked in baseball.

I tried to entertain my kids in my own way, but I don't think they understood. I remember when they were still small and I was driving them home one night along Sunset Boulevard. They were repairing the street and they had put out about fifty of those warning lights that flash on and off. I stopped the car and said, "Look, kids, it's somebody's birthday! Now all together, let's sing!" and I started singing, "Happy Birthday to you . . . Happy Birthday to you . . . Happy Birthday, Sunset Boulevard, Happy Birthday to you. . . ." The kids looked at each other and joined in, but they didn't sing too loudly. All the rest of the way home neither one of them said a word. But as soon as we got to the house they rushed inside and went right to Gracie.

"Mommy," Sandy said, "I think something's wrong with Daddy. He saw a whole bunch of lights on the street and he thought it was a birthday cake."

Gracie kissed the children reassuringly and said, "Don't tell him it wasn't a birthday cake, it would spoil his fun."

Another time I really went to a lot of trouble to surprise Sandy and Ronnie. It was around Christmastime and Gracie and I were making a movie. On Christmas Eve I stayed late at the studio and had the wardrobe department fit me out with a whole Santa Claus outfit—the works; black

77

leather boots, padded stomach, tasseled hat, and a big bag of toys. Then I went to the makeup department and they fixed me up with a big red nose, white bushy eyebrows, and they even glued on the white beard. When they got through with me I didn't even recognize myself.

I had let Gracie in on what I was planning, so when the doorbell rang at home that night, Gracie said, "Children, see who's at the door."

The kids opened the door, looked at me, and Ronnie said, "Mommy, Daddy's home."

When I walked in Gracie said to me, "George, your outfit is beautiful, but you should have left your cigar outside."

Here's another brainstorm I dreamed up to amuse the children. Sometimes I'd pick them up after kindergarten, and this one day when I was driving home I thought it would be funny if I drove up the wrong driveway—so I did. The kids started to jump up and down excitedly, and hollered, "Daddy, Daddy, you're in the wrong driveway, we don't live here!" I acted surprised and said, "Oh?" Then I backed out and drove home.

The next time I did it again, and this time I pulled into another driveway. Again the kids got excited and hollered, "Daddy, you're in the wrong driveway again!" I looked surprised and said "Oh?" Then I backed out and went home again.

The third time I did it I pulled into this driveway and drove clear back to the people's garage, but the kids just sat there and never said a word. I stopped the car and said, "Aren't you going to tell me I'm in the wrong driveway?"

Sandy said, "No. Mommy said we should let you enjoy yourself."

That was the end of that hilarious bit.

The years flew by, the kids grew older, and so did my sense of humor. When Ronnie was about fifteen he came to me one day right at the beginning of summer vacation, full of enthusiasm, and asked me if he could build a boat in the backyard. I was all for it; I thought it was a great idea and even offered to pay for the lumber. I figured it would be worth it; building a boat would keep him occupied, teach him how to work with his hands, and he wouldn't be running around getting into trouble all summer. I was sure a project like that would take three months, but four days later Ronnie came to me and said, "Dad, the boat's finished."

I went out in the backyard and, sure enough, there was this little boat, about five feet long. I said, "Ronnie, you did a nice job, but that boat is barely big enough to hold you. I thought you were going to build a boat—a real boat—something that you and your friends could get on and sail to Catalina."

"But, Dad," Ronnie said, "that would take my whole summer vacation."

I said, "Supposing it does. That little thing you built wouldn't even get you across the swimming pool." I paused a moment, then continued with, "But wouldn't it be great when you go back to school if you could say to the other kids, 'I just finished building a boat that could take us all to Catalina'?"

I waited while Ronnie gave this some deep thought. Finally he said enthusiastically, "Dad, I'll do it. I'll get some of my pals to help me and we'll start real early at seven o'clock in the morning."

"Ronnie," I said, "you better make it eight thirty. Beverly Hills is not zoned for a shipyard."

That night I confided to Gracie, "We don't have to worry about Ronnie this summer. He'll be out in the backyard building another *Queen Mary*."

Well, the weeks went by and the boat got bigger and bigger, and so did Ronnie's labor crew. Every day there were about fifteen kids out there hammering and sawing and yelling. The swimming pool was full of shavings and sawdust, there was so much lumber stacked up we could hardly get out the back door, and every day at lunchtime we had to feed that bunch. And when it comes to food, a fifteen-year-old kid is like a human disposal. I won't say how much I spent on food, but that summer the little market where we bought our groceries became the Safeway chain.

Finally, at the end of summer, Ronnie came running in and said, "Dad, we finished the boat—but we got a problem." Boy, did we have a problem! The only way we could have gotten that boat out of the backyard would have been to tear down the house. Well, Ronnie went back to school with a hand covered with blisters, and I had to hire carpenters to come and dismantle the boat. And as the last load of lumber went down the driveway, Gracie said to me, "George, next summer try to think of something to keep Ronnie out of the backyard."

I didn't have to, Ronnie thought of something himself. During that school year Ronnie's grades were not the greatest, so at the end of the term I felt he should go to summer school. But by this time Ronnie had discovered surfing. Every daylight hour he and Freddie Astaire, Jr., were at the beach. I knew I had to do something, so I said to him, "Ronnie, you've been bugging me to buy you a car, so I'll make a deal with you. If you go to summer school, you've got the car."

Ronnie said, "Dad, it's a deal."

So I bought him a nice little car and figured that problem was solved—but it wasn't. Ronnie started getting up at five o'clock in the morning, then he'd drive to the beach and surf for a couple of hours, then drive to summer school, go to his first class, and promptly fall asleep. It took me a couple of weeks to find out I'd been had. But there was nothing I could do about it. The deal was that if I bought Ronnie a car, he'd go to summer school—and that he was doing. There was no clause in the deal that said he couldn't sleep through the classes.

This new problem might have defeated a lesser man, but not me. I came right back with what I thought was a stroke of psychological genius. The next morning at four o'clock I went into Ronnie's room, shook him awake, and sat on the edge of the bed. Remembering how Lewis Stone talked to

Mickey Rooney in the "Andy Hardy" series, I said, "Ronnie, since you don't seem to be much interested in school, you should start giving some serious thought to your future. Now, you and Freddie go to Malibu Beach every morning, and that beach is known all over the world; the sand there has got to be very valuable. If you and Freddie took that sand and canned it, you kids could sell it and make a fortune."

Ronnie looked at me like I had a hole in my head, took the covers, and pulled them over his face. Well, at five o'clock Ronnie got up, drove to the beach, did his surfing, drove to school, fell asleep—and at four o'clock the next morning I was shaking him awake again. "Ronnie," I said, "wake up. You and Freddie better get down to that beach and start canning that sand. Some other kids might steal the idea and there'll be no sand left. You and Freddie could lose a fortune." Ronnie never said a word, he just got up and went into the bathroom and locked the door.

Well, this went on for four days. Finally Ronnie came to me and said, "Okay, Dad, you win. Freddie and I have given up surfing."

I was glad to hear this because I was getting pretty tired of getting up at four o'clock every morning.

"We've now taken up scuba diving," Ronnie continued.

"Scuba diving!" I said.

He said, "Yeah, that idea of yours about canning the sand was so good we decided to branch out. Freddie and I are going to start bottling genuine Malibu salt water, too. So long, Dad." And he left.

Well, Andy Hardy had beaten Lewis Stone at his own game.

The value of my parenthood extended beyond Ronnie, however. There was my daughter Sandy, who was a beautiful girl. When she was sixteen she was going steady with a fellow named Red something-or-other, I forget his name. Anyway, Red was a football player and about six feet, five inches tall. He was so solid and had such bulging muscles

81

he didn't look like he was born; he looked like he was put together with an erector set.

Every day Sandy and Red would come home after school and sit on the floor in the library and watch television. I had never met Red until one day when I came into the library from the club, and there he was. Even sitting on the floor he was taller than I was. Anyway, they both got up, Sandy introduced me, and when Red shook hands with me he broke all my fingers. Well, he didn't really break them, but the next day when I played bridge somebody else had to hold my cards for me.

The next time I met Red the same thing happened again. This time he squeezed my hand so hard it blew out the crystal of my wristwatch. I knew I had to do something.

A couple of days later, when I came home, there stood Red with his hand out. I quickly put both of my hands in my pockets and said, "Hold it, Red. You're a nice young boy, but you don't know your own strength. From now on when we meet we don't have to shake hands. You just say 'Hello, Mr. Burns,' and I'll say 'Hello, Red.' "

He grinned and said, "I guess I am pretty strong, and I'll never do it again. Let's shake on it, Mr. Burns," and he reached into my pocket, grabbed my hand, and there went my fingers again. I was very happy when Sandy dumped Red and started going round with a small flute player in the school band.

To sum it up, it's a good thing I didn't have to make a living being a father. I would have ended up on welfare. But now that I'm older I'm much wiser, and when people come to me for advice I'm able to help them. If you don't believe me, read the beginning of this chapter again where I helped Archie Preissman and Judge Roth with the metric system.

A Newcomer at Sixty-two

Sometimes almost all of us reach a point in our life at which it becomes necessary to make a change. If this happens when you're young, it's easy, but when you have to make a change in your later years it may not be easy, but nevertheless you've still got to make it.

On June 4, 1958, the last episode of the Burns & Allen show was filmed, and Gracie retired. I didn't blame her. She had spent all her life worrying about wardrobe, makeup, getting her hair done, and rehearsals. And, after we got into television, learning thirty to forty pages of dialogue every week. Gracie wanted to relax and be able to spend some time with our grandchildren.

But I wasn't ready to retire. I was only sixty-two years old and fresh as a daisy. After all, I'd been retired all those years I was on the stage with Gracie.

Well, I came up with an idea that I thought was absolutely brilliant. Through the years of Burns & Allen we developed sort of a stock company of very talented people; like Bea Benadaret, Larry Keating, Harry Von Zell, and my son Ronnie. So why not surround myself with those same people and call it *The George Burns Show*? It seemed like a natural. I was so enthused that my writers and I knocked out a script and sold it to the Colgate people without even making a pilot. They bought it for twenty-six weeks. They made a mistake. So did I, and it was a beauty. It didn't take a genius to figure out what was wrong. Sure, we had the same people, but any minute you expected Gracie to come

83

through the door. It was like having dinner; we had the soup, the salad, and the dessert, but the main course was home playing with her grandchildren.

At the end of the twenty-six weeks the show went off the air, and there I was at the bottom again. I knew that sooner or later I'd bounce back, but I had to figure out how. I'd never worked alone before, so I had to find an image for myself. People like Jack Benny, Bob Hope, Milton Berle, all the established comedians, had spent years developing their characters, but here I was, a kid of sixty-two, struggling to get into show business.

Well, again I came up with an idea I thought was absolutely brilliant. As long as I needed an identity, why not be me? That took me right to the bottom again, because I said to myself, "Who's me?" Sure, I was funny at parties—I sang old patter songs that everybody laughed at—I told amusing anecdotes—and I was usually the hit of the sociable. . . . I thought that over for a while, and all of a sudden I said, "Wait a minute—that's me!" And it was.

I sat down with my writers and we put together a nightclub act in which I did exactly what I'd been doing at parties. I opened with a monologue of amusing anecdotes, I sang some of my old patter songs, and I booked myself into Bill Harrah's club at Lake Tahoe. But I wasn't taking any chances; I brought along Bobby Darin, who was sensational, the DeCastro Sisters, who sang up a storm, and one of the great dancing acts, Brascia & Tybee.

My opening night at Harrah's was practically one year to the day after Gracie retired. When I walked out on that stage for the first time in my life alone, believe me, it was a strange feeling. Anyway, I took a deep breath, lit my cigar, and said:

Ladies and gentlemen, this is the first time I ever played a nightclub, and I hate people who come out and say they're nervous. I despise myself, but I am.

All my friends had advice for me. I ran into Dean Martin,

84

and he told me to relax like he does. I tried it, but it gave me the hiccups.

And Frank Sinatra said, "George, there's nothing to be nervous about. When you get to Harrah's, just do what I do." At my age that's even harder than drinking.

Everybody wanted to help. Sammy Davis offered to lend me his uncle.

Sophie Tucker said, "George, I've played cafés all my life. I'm seventy-two years old, and now my voice is gone, it's practically shot, and I'm still a big hit. So you can't miss. You've got what it took me seventy-two years to get."

Even Zsa Zsa Gabor called me. She said, "George, you've got to be a hit at Harrah's if you do what I do." Not me. If I listened to her and Sinatra, I couldn't last half an hour. And if I took the advice of Frank Sinatra, Dean Martin and Sammy Davis, I'd be worn out . . . have a hangover . . . and an uncle who doesn't look like me.

And my close friend, Jack Benny, gave me some advice, too.

(Pointing)

He's sitting right down there. Before the show tonight he came backstage and said, "George, I've been working alone for a lot of years and I'll give you a little tip that's helped me. If you do this, you can't miss. After each joke you tell, just look at the audience, and keep looking, because if you look long enough, they must laugh."

"Jack," I said, "what happens if I look at the audience and they look back at me longer than I look at them?"

He said, "George, that's your problem—I'll be sitting out front."

(to Jack)

Jack, I love you.

(to audience)

And Jack is such a sport. Last night when we arrived he went to the dice table, and they're still talking about it. He held the dice for forty-five minutes. He finally threw them and rolled a crap. He lost five dollars and they had to hold *him* for forty-five minutes.

But the reason my friends are all trying to help me is that basically I'm not a comedian. I'm a straight man. You know

85

what a straight man is—he just repeats things. The comedian or comedienne asks a question, he repeats the question, and they get a laugh. I've been a straight man for so long I went fishing with a fellow once, he fell overboard and hollered "Help!" I repeated "Help!", and while I was waiting for him to get his laugh, he drowned. He must have thought he was funny, because he came up, took three bows, and disappeared.

But you know, it's awfully strange for me to be out here on the stage alone, because after all, I worked with Gracie for thirty-eight years. But now she's retired. And believe me, when Gracie retired she didn't fool around, she really retired. She's even thinking of getting twin beds.

I married Gracie in Cleveland a long time ago. And after the ceremony Gracie looked up at me and said, "I always knew a handsome man would marry me." She was right—that justice of the peace was the best-looking fellow you ever saw. Not to disappoint Gracie, I asked him to come along on our honeymoon.

But I love it here at Lake Tahoe. However, everybody is so nice to you, you can't get a good night's sleep. The owner of this place, Bill Harrah, is quite a host. At three o'clock this morning he sent up a complimentary cocktail. So what could I do? The waiter helped me out of bed, I poured it into my hot milk, and I drank it.

At five thirty the maid came in and gave me some fresh towels. I haven't had to use a fresh towel at five thirty in the morning, June the twentieth will be thirty-seven years.

Ten minutes later the honeymoon couple next door started arguing about their wedding—they couldn't decide where to have it.

And when I finally did get to sleep I had a horrible dream. I dreamed I was alone on a desert island with Ava Gardner and Lana Turner. I suppose you're wondering what would make a dream like that so horrible. In it I was Rita Hayworth.

Anyway, there we were, just three girls on this island.
. . . Who do you think was washed ashore? Lawrence Welk. Whom do you think he went for? Me. . . . All night long, a-one and a-two . . .

86

But don't worry, even though I didn't get a good night's sleep it hasn't affected my singing voice. I love to sing. I can't help it, there's something deep inside of me that just has to come out. If you had something like that inside of you, you'd want it out, too.

Now, I know you all came here to listen to some great singing, and I'm not going to disappoint you . . .

Ladies and gentlemen—Bobby Darin!

Well, Bobby Darin was a smash and so were the DeCastro Sisters and Brascia & Tybee. The whole show was great. After the opening everybody came backstage and congratulated me. But later that night when Gracie and I were alone, I said, "Gracie, how did you like me tonight?"

She said, "I thought it was a wonderful show."

"Gracie, what did you think of me?"

"George, you surrounded yourself with marvelous people."

Right then I knew she was holding something back. I said, "Come on, Gracie, let's have it."

"Well," she said, "your songs were just fine, but when you went into your monologues you knew them too well. You sounded like you were reciting them."

I was stunned! My first reaction was to be resentful, but before I could even say anything she added, "George, I know that what I just said upset you, but I think all you have to do is be natural. Like when you're entertaining at parties everybody loves you because you're just being yourself."

That's all that was said, but I didn't sleep that night. All night long I lay there wide awake, practicing how to be natural. It took quite a while, but I finally licked it. I got to the point where I could walk out on the stage and act like I was at a party, and I've been having parties with audiences ever since.

Onstage Gracie played the part of a kooky dame, but offstage I learned to listen to her because that girl knew what she was talking about.

87

Anyway, there I was, sixty-two years old and starting a brand-new career. It was a wonderful feeling. I found that audiences enjoyed my songs and laughed at my monologues. In fact, I got so darned good I invested in a new eyebrow pencil.

A Dresser Is not a Piece of Furniture

I don't know if this is common knowledge or not, but most performers in show business who are doing well have what is known as a dresser. In this case a dresser is not a piece of furniture, he's someone whose main function is to take care of your clothes and help you in and out of them. But it goes a lot further than that, especially if you're traveling. He's your road manager . . . your secretary . . . if you want a sandwich in your dressing room he gets it for you . . . he sees that your suits are pressed and your shoes shined . . . he picks up your airplane tickets and makes sure that your luggage is taken care of . . . in fact, he does everything possible to make you comfortable so you're free to concentrate on giving a good performance. That's a dresser, and believe me, it's a full-time job.

Now in all the years that Gracie and I traveled together we never thought of having a dresser. Gracie took care of her own clothes, I used to zip her up, and nobody had to help me. I always knew how to put my pants on: First you put in one leg, then you put in the other—I learned that when I was fourteen years old. My mother was so proud of me. I got so good at it she used to call in the neighbors to watch me do it.

But then, in 1958, when Gracie retired and I started working alone, I had to travel a lot, so I hired a dresser. Not that I needed one, but after all those years of working with Gracie I couldn't get used to being in a dressing room by myself. I needed company, somebody to kick gags around with.

I hired this dresser when I got booked into Las Vegas, and he was a beautiful-looking man who came highly recommended. But he was so perfect he drove me right up the wall. Everything was, "Yes, Mr. Burns"; "No, Mr. Burns"; "I'll get it for you, Mr. Burns"; "I've got it for you, Mr. Burns"; "I'll tie it for you, Mr. Burns"; "I'll untie it for you, Mr. Burns"—he wouldn't let me do anything for myself. Then one day, when he tried to help me put my socks on, that was the end. I learned to do that when I was fifteen.

After I let him go, there I was, lonesome again. One morning I was sitting in the coffee shop all by myself having breakfast when I heard a voice say, "Hi, George!" I looked up, and standing there was Charlie Reade. I hadn't seen Charlie since he was part of one of the most famous dancing acts in vaudeville, called The Dunhills. The act is still around, but with different people. Charlie was one of the original Dunhills. I was very glad to see him and invited him to sit down and have some breakfast. We got to talking about old times, and it turned out that Charlie had split up with his partners years ago and had wound up in Las Vegas looking for something to do, but so far nothing had turned up.

So I got an idea. I said, "Charlie, how would you like to work for me?"

He said, "Doing what?"

"Be my dresser."

Charlie stopped with a bite of egg halfway to his mouth. Then he put the fork down on the plate and slowly pushed the plate away. After a swallow of water he wiped his lips with the napkin, placed the napkin on the table, and then, deliberately folding his arms, he looked me right in the eye. There was a pause of about five seconds, and then he said, "George, would you mind repeating that?"

Well Charlie had given such a great performance, and not wanting to be outdone, I decided to give one, too. I dramatically put down my fork, slowly pushed my plate away, took a swallow of water, wiped my lips with the napkin, deliberately folded my arms, and stared right back at him. "How would you like to be my dresser?" I repeated.

Still looking right at me, Charlie said, "A dresser?! George, I'm a *dancer!*"

"All right, Charlie," I said, "before you say no, the job pays two-hundred and fifty dollars a week and all your expenses."

I sat there waiting for an answer. Finally Charlie said, "George, I'll take the job under one condition—promise that you won't tell anybody that I'm your dresser."

I said, "Charlie, you've got a deal. I'll tell everybody you're my road manager."

He said, "Great," and finished his breakfast. And since he was now on an expense account he ordered strawberry shortcake for dessert.

That was the beginning of a long and interesting relationship with Charlie Reade. He moved in with me and we were together practically twenty-four hours a day. He was marvelous company, and we had a lot of laughs because we both spoke the same language.

Charlie was really a beautiful dancer. He was considered to be one of the best. In fact, he was one of the few dancers who could do what is called a heel roll. He'd put his weight on the ball of his foot and tap so fast with his heel that it sounded like a machine gun. There wasn't any style of dancing that Charlie couldn't do, and his idol was Fred Astaire. Charlie dressed like Astaire, he moved like Astaire, he even walked like him. When I went down the street with him I felt like Ginger Rogers.

With Charlie everything was dancing, and me being an old hoofer, I went right along with it. We always had twin beds in our hotel room, and sometimes before we went to sleep we'd play a little game. Charlie would move his feet under the covers, and by watching the movement I'd try to guess which step he was doing. I'd say, "I've got it, Charlie, you're doing *Falling off a Log.*" He'd say, "Right, George, now it's your turn." Then he'd watch my feet under the

91

covers and say, "George, you're doing *Off to Buffalo,*" and I'd say, "You're wrong, I'm doing *Over the Top."* If anybody had walked in on us we would have wound up on the funny farm.

Charlie even talked tap dancing, and I understood him. I recall one night when I was playing at the Sahara Hotel and we were having dinner between shows. Charlie was explaining a dance routine he put together. He said, "It goes like this, George. You start with a time step and then go into—

> Boppa doppa, boppa doppa, boppa doppa dop
> Babop, babop, babop, babop, babop, babop
> Doodlely-doo bop bop, doodlely-doo bop bop
> Doodlely-doo, doodlely-doo, doodlely-doo bop!"

Right in the middle of Charlie's routine, while I was nodding my head in tempo, a man tapped me on the shoulder. He said, "Mr. Burns, I enjoyed your show very much, but I'd like to ask you something. I was sitting at the next table, and I speak seven foreign languages—but what language is your friend speaking?"

I said, "I haven't the faintest idea, but I understand him perfectly."

The man just shook his head and walked away.

Following Vegas I was booked into Harrah's Club at Lake Tahoe. By now I had found out that my new dresser (I mean road manager) had several peculiar little quirks. Like when he took my shoes down to the barbershop to be shined, he would always carry them in a flight bag so that nobody would know that was one of his duties. One day I was in the barbershop getting a haircut, and the barber said, "Mr. Burns, what's wrong with that road manager of yours? Every day around one o'clock he comes in with a pair of shoes in a flight bag and whispers to my shoeshine boy, 'I'll pick these up in an hour and don't take them out of the bag until I leave the shop,' and then he ducks out."

I said, "Well, I'm surprised he brings both of them in at the same time. He's very particular about his shoes. He usually brings in one first, and if he likes the shine, he brings in the other one. He must really trust that kid you got working for you."

The barber never said a word, all I could hear was the snipping of his scissors. But on my way out I couldn't resist taking a parting shot. I said to the barber, "If I were you, I'd give that shoeshine kid a raise. You got a gold mine there."

Besides smuggling my shoes in and out, another one of Charlie's duties was to help me on with my coat when I got dressed for a performance. But Charlie had so much pride that he always made sure the dressing room door was closed so nobody would see him holding my coat. One night the owner of the hotel, Bill Harrah, walked in while Charlie was holding my coat, and without missing a beat Charlie put it on and pretended it was his. Well, so as not to embarrass Charlie I put on his coat. Both of us looked pretty silly; him in checkered pants and a tuxedo coat, and me in a checkered coat and tuxedo pants. Bill Harrah stared at us and said, "I don't want to say anything, but you fellows have your coats mixed up."

Looking down, I said, "I didn't notice that," and so Charlie and I changed coats.

Charlie traveled with me for six years, and he was a delight to be with. He was cheerful and had a great sense of humor, and we spent hours talking together because both of us knew nothing but show business. It was never dull being with Charlie because you never knew what he'd come up with next. I was getting dressed one evening and I noticed that Charlie was standing in the hall outside the dressing room and leaning against the door frame. I said, "Charlie, why are you standing out there? Come on in."

He said, "No, George, this parquet floor out here has a nice feel to it."

Now, nobody else would have understood that, but right away I knew exactly what he meant. It was a dancer's floor.

93

So I went out there and stood with him, and Charlie was right, it was the nicest floor I ever stood on.

Another one of Charlie's duties was to go down with me and stand in the wings just before I went out on the stage. In one hand he carried a glass of scotch and water, and in the other a glass of sand. Just before my entrance I always took a healthy slug of scotch, and after my monologue I'd come offstage and pour some of the sand in my pocket. I used the sand to sprinkle on the floor for my sand dance. Well, one night just as my entrance music started, I said, "Charlie, give me the scotch." Charlie handed me the wrong glass, and I took a healthy slug of sand. Did you ever try to say, "Good evening, ladies and gentlemen," with a mouthful of sand? I don't know how I got through that performance, but in the middle of it I glanced into the wings and there was Charlie drinking my scotch and water. From that night on, Charlie's backstage duties were cut in half; he carried the glass of sand and I carried my own scotch.

I don't think I mentioned this, but this might be a good time to do so. From time to time Charlie would do a little nipping, and sometimes he'd overdo it. When this happened Charlie would get a little temperamental. In fact, he had a pretty good-sized temper. One night in Vegas we were in a taxicab on our way to see a lounge show and we got into some kind of silly argument. I don't even remember what it was about, but all of a sudden in an angry voice Charlie said to the cabdriver, "Pull over to the curb!" The cab stopped and Charlie opened the door. Without even glancing at me he said, "George, I've had enough of you! Get out!"

I very quietly said, "Charlie, you're a little mixed up. I'm not working for you, you're working for me."

"Oh?" he said. "Then I'll get out!" Which he did.

I went on to see the lounge show, and five minutes later in walked Charlie and sat down at my table. I said, "Charlie, how about a cup of black coffee?"

He said, "Good idea." Then he added, "Tell the waiter to put a little rum in it."

94

Then there was the time when Charlie just disappeared without a word. For two days I called every hotel in town, checked all the places he hung out, but there was no sign of him. I was really getting worried when on the third day Charlie showed up out of the blue. I waited for an explanation, but he acted like nothing had happened. When I couldn't stand it any longer, I said, "Charlie, where the hell have you been?"

He said, "George, I had to get away for a couple of days. You're a strong personality, and being around you all the time I was losing my identity."

Trying to make light of it, I said, "Well, Charlie, I'll try to stop smiling so much."

He said, "No, George, I'm serious. I had to be alone to see if I could find myself."

I knew he meant it, so I said, "Charlie, I hope it worked."

"I think it did," he nodded.

"Good," I said, and for the rest of the week I held my own coat.

I wouldn't say that Charlie was a particularly religious man, but every once in a while he'd go to mass. One Sunday morning, after he'd been to an early mass, we were having breakfast together. I was playing Reno that week, and I said, "Charlie, I rented a car, so after breakfast why don't we take a little drive?"

He had been very quiet all through breakfast, and when I suggested the drive, he said, "No, George, this is Sunday. I'm going to walk up into the hills, and when I get to the top I might run into Him."

I didn't want to discourage him, so I said, "Okay, Charlie, but if you do run into Him, I'm afraid you might be disappointed, He doesn't dance. And if He did, He'd be pretty awkward wearing those sandals."

Charlie gave me a look and, getting up from the table, said, "George, for a comedian you're not very funny." And then he left.

I sat there and watched through the windows as he

95

walked off toward the foothills. Only Charlie Reade would go looking for Jesus in Reno.

When Charlie came to work for me he was no kid. I'd say he was about fifty years old. But he was in great physical shape because he never stopped dancing. He had a trim waistline, he was very light on his feet, and he took great pride in his sense of balance. But there was one time when Charlie's balance deserted him. It was up at Lake Tahoe, and after one of our midnight shows I went to bed and Charlie went out on the town. I don't know whether it was the altitude or a few too many belts of booze, but around three o'clock in the morning I got a phone call from the manager of the Hi-Ho Bar and Grill. "Mr. Burns, does a fellow named Charlie Reade live with you?" he said.

"That's right," I answered.

"Well, he just fell off a barstool and hurt himself."

"Is it anything serious?" I asked.

The voice on the phone said, "No, he just got a cut on the back of his head. What should I do?"

I said, "Either take him to a hospital or have him wear his hat."

Well, after I hung up I got to thinking that maybe I should go down there and see if Charlie was okay. So I got dressed, jumped in a cab, and rushed down to the Hi-Ho Bar and Grill. When I walked in, the juke box was playing and there was Charlie with his hat on, doing one of his dance routines.

Charlie and I are still friends, and I hear from him all the time. Believe me, if I ever go on the road again, Charlie Reade will not only be my road manager, but I might even hire a dresser for him.

Here She Is, Ladies and Gentlemen— Mrs. Charles Lowe!

You know, when I started appearing in nightclubs it was quite a change for me. After working practically all my life with Gracie, here I found myself working with new people every season. And they were all very talented people. Then, in 1962, I was lucky enough to team up with a tall, wide-eyed, open-faced blonde with a wild, dizzy, cockeyed sense of humor. From that description I'm sure you know whom I mean—Mrs. Charles Lowe. Some of her intimate friends know her better as Carol Channing.

I knew Charlie and Carol before they were married. Charlie was working with the Burns & Allen television show as a sponsor representative. He got started in the business as a public relations man for Aimee Semple MacPherson (I'm not sure, but I think Charlie was the one who introduced her to Milton Berle). I met Carol through Charlie, and as soon as I met her there was an immediate feeling of mutual admiration. Carol and Charlie, and Gracie and I, became very close friends, and it seemed inevitable that Carol and I would wind up working together.

And we did! We put a show together with four other acts and called it the *George Burns-Carol Channing Show*. Everybody thought that was a very clever title for a show. In all modesty, I must say I thought of it myself.

Our first booking was at the Orpheum theater in Seattle during the Seattle World's Fair. It was a very good show, and we did very good business. We had sort of a vaudeville format, and at the end of the show Carol and I did a Burns &

Allen routine and then finished with a song and a sand dance.

I had never done a comedy routine like that with anybody but Gracie, but with Carol's off-beat personality I thought the routine we did would be a natural. But something was wrong. We were getting laughs, but there was something missing; there was no relationship . . . we weren't a team. After the third performance I finally figured out what the trouble was. When I worked with Gracie, she spoke directly to me; she looked at me and I looked at her. To Gracie there were no footlights—to her that was a wall and she never knew there was an audience out there. Now, Carol was the exact opposite. She played everything directly to the audience and didn't know I was out there.

Well, once I knew what the problem was I solved it. The next performance, when we came out on the stage, Carol didn't look at me—I didn't look at her—and we both worked straight to the audience. Now that I was working the same way as Carol, it felt right—we were finally a team. Do you know that Carol never even knew I changed my style! She was so in love with that audience she didn't know what I was doing out there anyway.

This is the way we played the routine. And remember— we both said everything directly to the audience:

Carol and George enter from opposite sides and meet center stage.

GEORGE
Ladies and gentlemen, Carol is now going to say hello to everybody.

CAROL
Hello, everybody.

GEORGE
Let's see, how should we start?

CAROL
I always like to start with a joke.

GEORGE
I think Carol's got a good idea there.

CAROL
All right. I took my girlfriend to the doctor's today, and while I was there somebody told this joke that had everybody dying laughing.

GEORGE
I'm sure we'd all like to hear it.

CAROL
Well, it went like this: "Don't let that upset you, he never says good-bye to anybody!" (A long pause)

GEORGE
That can't be the whole joke.

CAROL
There was some stuff ahead of it that I didn't hear, but that was the line that had everybody dying laughing.

GEORGE
I think we better find another way to start.

CAROL
This might be interesting. While I was in the doctor's office I read a newspaper that had the latest census report on this city. And you people out there don't look tired and worn out.

GEORGE
Tired and worn out? You don't look that way to me, either.

CAROL
Well, right at the top of the census report it said, "Population of Seattle—broken down by age and sex!"

GEORGE
I don't think she understands what that means.

CAROL
Ohhhhh, yes I do. I've known about the birds and the bees all my life.

GEORGE
That's a surprise to me.

CAROL

When I was a little girl my mother told me how the bees carry pollen from flower to flower on their feet. I even tried it, and it's nothing.

GEORGE

I'm sorry to hear that—I was getting ready to take off my shoes.

CAROL

And I read something else in the newspaper while I was in the doctor's office. A very rich man died, and the lawyer read his will to his sons and daughters and their husbands and wives. It said for every new child that was born they would get an extra half million dollars, but they weren't interested.

GEORGE

That's hard to believe.

CAROL

Well, they weren't. Before he even finished reading the will the room was empty.

GEORGE

The reason they ran out was they were probably double-parked.

CAROL

Anyway, this doctor has a beautiful redheaded nurse with the most gorgeous figure. But she was sick, too, poor little thing. She kept begging the doctor to take her appendix out.

GEORGE

Can you folks imagine a beautiful nurse asking a doctor to take out her appendix?

CAROL

It's true. Every time she went into his private office I could hear her hollering, "Doctor, please, cut it out!"

GEORGE

That doctor really knew how to operate.

CAROL

Let me tell you folks why my girlfriend went to see the doctor in the first place. She went to have the dents taken out of her knees.

GEORGE

Well, if you've got dents in your knees, that's the place to go.

CAROL

That's what she had. When I looked in the office, the doctor was pounding them out with a little rubber hammer.

GEORGE

He was trying to get a look at her reflexes.

CAROL

Well, no wonder she kept kicking at him. . . . And while she was in the doctor's office I cheered up all the patients in the waiting room. There was one little boy there who looked so sad, so I took him around and made everyone shake hands with him. It made him so happy he almost forgot he had the measles.

GEORGE

Carol's friendliness is really contagious.

CAROL

I helped the nurse, too. I answered the phone for her. Somebody wanted to know if a man eighty-five years old could have rickets.

GEORGE

I can't wait to hear what her answer was.

CAROL

I said let him have all he wants as long as he chews them well.

GEORGE

For a minute I thought she might give the wrong answer, but she fooled me.

CAROL

And then the doctor from the next office came in, and he was whistling.

GEORGE

He must have had something to whistle about.

101

CAROL

The nurse said that he was Dr. Brown, the famous obstetrician. She said that last year he had two hundred and sixty babies.

GEORGE

Well, that's wonderful.

CAROL

It might be wonderful for him, but I'll bet his wife isn't whistling.

GEORGE

I'd like to straighten her out, but she's so happy the way she is.

CAROL

I tried to have a talk with that doctor, but he was in a hurry to get back to his office. He said he had a little boy in there a year and a half old who couldn't hold on to his food. So I said, "Why don't you give him a live lobster? If he can't hold on to his food, give him food that can hold on to him."

GEORGE

I'll bet that doctor wasn't whistling when he left.

CAROL

Then this woman sitting next to me told me she sprained her back playing tennis. She told me that she hadn't held a racket in her hand for two years. So I said, "My goodness, where have you been holding it?"

That was our music cue. We sang "Some of These Days," did a sand dance, and that was the finish of the show. This whole bit ran about eight minutes, and not once did we look at each other.

That was Carol Channing onstage. Let me tell you about her offstage—the real Carol Channing—the zany one.

Now, most people have more than one personality. And I'm not speaking about only show business people, I'm talking about everybody. Just think about it—if you're at a dinner party and you're sitting next to your wife, your person-

102

ality is entirely different than if you were sitting next to somebody else's wife—especially if she's pretty—especially if she's got her hand on your knee—especially if she whispers her phone number into your ear. You're oozing charm and personality until you glance across the table and see your wife glaring at you, wise to the whole thing. One minute you're Rudolph Valentino, Cary Grant, and Warren Beatty all rolled into one, and in that split second you're back to What's-His-Name again.

And if you're a woman, this whole personality thing works in reverse. Say you're at the same party and you're dancing with your husband. You're bored to tears, you're looking around to see what the other women are wearing, and your husband is telling you about his day at the office, but you're not even listening. In fact, you don't even know the music is playing. But ten minutes later and you're dancing with that handsome Dr. Jarvis. Your feet don't even touch the floor as he's holding you close, and you're moving even closer as you laugh at all his witty remarks. You're happy—you're gay—you're Miss Universe! You look around for your husband, positive he'll be in a jealous rage. But where is he? He's at the bar with that broad he was on the make for at the dinner table. That'll put a kink in your personality!

You'll notice I had the man come out on top in that story. Look, I believe in Women's Lib, but I still like to see a guy get lucky once in a while. What I'm trying to say is that everybody changes his or her personality to fit any given situation; that is, everybody but Carol Channing. Her personality is bigger than life. To her, everything is show business. If she goes to the bathroom, it's an exit—when she comes out, it's an entrance. When she and Charlie go to bed at night she's so full of show business that Charlie has to keep applauding her until she falls asleep. And in the morning if he doesn't give her a standing ovation, she won't get up!

Now, here's a story Charlie told me. I don't believe it, but here it is anyway. One night they were staying at the Waldorf in New York, and two robbers broke into their room. Carol woke up, and one of the burglars turned his flashlight on her. She went right into two choruses of "Diamonds Are a Girl's Best Friend." The burglars applauded and left. That's such a good lie I'm sorry I gave Charlie credit for it.

During the fourteen weeks Carol and I worked together there was never a dull moment. Working with Carol was exciting, and I enjoyed it. But like with any relationship from time to time there were problems. Like the night we opened in Seattle—the first half of the show was supposed to run an hour and twenty-five minutes; then a ten-minute intermission; and the second half was supposed to run forty-five minutes, which would bring the curtain down exactly at ten thirty.

Well, the first half went fine, but in the second half when Carol came on to do her thirty minutes she stayed there an hour and a half. That night the final curtain didn't come down until eleven thirty. This meant we had to pay the musicians and stagehands one hour of Golden Time, which ran into a lot of money.

I explained this to Carol, but she looked up at me with those great big wide eyes and said, "Why, George, I can't believe I was on stage for ninety minutes. In fact, I thought I was running short tonight; I almost added another number." Well, that's Carol. When she's out there she falls in love with the audience, and the audience falls in love with her, and time means nothing. She felt terrible about what had happened, and apologized and promised it would never happen again.

However, I wasn't taking any chances. The next night when Carol was in the middle of singing "I'm Just a Little Girl from Litte Rock," I walked out onstage, stopped the music, and pointed to my watch. Carol batted those big eyes at me, then turned to the audience and said, "Ladies and gentlemen, my thirty minutes are up!" and we went into our double routine.

With Carol you never know what's going to happen next.

She lives in a world all her own. We were playing the Dunes Hotel in Las Vegas, and during the eight weeks we were there I wanted to change some of the jokes. So one day I knocked on her dressing room and said, "Carol, are you decent?"

She called out, "Sure, but I'm not dressed. Come in."

So I went in, and there she was sitting at the makeup table with absolutely nothing on but a little towel over her lap. I just stood there; I didn't know what to do. So I kept looking at the ceiling—after all, her husband, Charlie, was a very close friend of mine.

Very matter-of-factly Carol said, "What do you want, George?"

I stammered a bit. "I—I—I—I'd like to change some jokes in the act."

"Just a second, George," Carol said. "I'll be with you as soon as I put my eyelashes on."

Well, I left, in a hurry. With Carol, when she puts her eyelashes on she thinks she's fully dressed.

In all the time I've known Carol I've never known her to miss a performance. But one day in Las Vegas I thought this was it. Around five thirty in the evening one time I was over at the Riviera Hotel having a drink with Tony Martin when they paged me over the loudspeaker in the bar. When I answered the call a very excited operator said, "Thank heavens I've found you, Mr. Burns! I've paged you in every hotel in Las Vegas!"

It sounded serious to me, and the operator hurriedly continued. "Mr. Charles Lowe is trying to get in touch with you! He says it's an emergency!"

I said, "Well, put him on," and while I was waiting all sorts of thoughts flashed through my mind. Something terrible must have happened to Carol. When Charlie got on the line he could hardly talk. "George," he gasped, "you better get over here right away! Carol might not be able to go on tonight, her wig shrunk!" And he hung up.

I stood there stunned. I thought to myself, How can a wig

105

shrink? Mine doesn't shrink. If you wear them too long, they stretch, but they never shrink. And I ought to know, I've got trunksful of hair. In fact, I got one trunk I part in the middle—but-wigs-just-don't-shrink!

Well, I caught a cab and rushed over to The Dunes. When I got to their room, there was Charlie on the phone frantically trying to reach somebody in the hair business, and there sat Carol almost in tears, holding a pathetic little wig in her hands.

I said to her, "What happened?"

She poured out this sad story: "I noticed my wig was getting a little dirty, so I washed it with soap and water. Then I put it out in the sun to dry—and it shrunk!" Carol had stumbled on the one way in the world that would make a wig shrink.

I knew that she would never go onstage without that wig, because her own hair was too short. And that wild blond hair was Carol's trademark and an important part of her act. Somehow we had to get her into that wig. I had Charlie stand on one side of her, and I stood on the other. Then we both took hold of the wig and stretched it open as far as we could. When Carol got her head into the wig we let go! If you think Carol's eyes are big, when that wig snapped on her head her eyes practically popped out and changed sockets. Frankly, I don't know how she went on and did two shows that night—but she did. And you know something? She was never better.

I've never known anyone with more energy than Carol has. And I think part of it is due to the organic food diet she's on. Everything Carol eats has to be specially prepared, so she always carries food around in her purse. You should get a load of that purse. It's filled with makeup, hair spray, pantyhose, her contact lenses, Kleenex, organic cookies, her own bottled water, and maybe even a buffalo steak or a moose cutlet wrapped in a napkin. She has to have energy just to be able to lift that purse.

Well, one night Judy Garland gave a special late show at

the Sahara Hotel for all the show people in town. So the five of us went—Charlie Reade, Charlie Lowe, Carol, the purse, and myself. Four of us ordered drinks, and Carol sat there munching on her moose cutlet. As usual, Judy was just marvelous, and after the show, as we were getting ready to go back and say hello, Carol said, "I'm going to tell Judy I love her, but she should do something about her makeup. It looked dark and streaky to me."

Charlie said, "Not to me. I thought she looked fine."

"I didn't think she looked dark and streaky," I said.

Carol sort of giggled and said, "Oh . . . I must have some gravy on my contact lenses."

I guess nobody looks good through moose gravy.

It was only natural that Carol went into show business, because of her family background. Not that her parents were performers, but they did spend the greater part of their lives appearing before audiences. Carol's father, George Channing, was the head lecturer for the Christian Science Church, and he traveled all over the world on speaking tours. He was also editor-in-chief of all Christian Science publications. He passed away in 1956 on the way back from one of his most successful tours. Carol's mother, Peggy Channing, was also very active in the church as a reader and practitioner, and as a matter of fact, still is.

I first met Mrs. Channing when Carol and I were playing The Dunes, and she had come to Las Vegas to visit Carol. She was a tall, beautiful, dignified, and charming lady of around seventy. When she arrived, Carol brought her into my dressing room to meet me, and after the introductions Carol returned to her dressing room to put on her makeup, leaving Mrs. Channing with me. There was an awkward pause during which neither one of us knew quite what to say, so I thought I'd use a little humor to ease the situation. She was wearing a short-sleeved dress, so I took her by the arm and said, "Sit down, Mrs. Channing." Before she could sit, I squeezed her arm and said, "Say, that's nice tight skin you've got there."

107

She just looked at me in complete disbelief.

I gave her arm another little squeeze and said, "Mrs. Channing, I hope you're not letting this nice tight skin go to waste."

I could feel the goose pimples popping up on her arm, but she just stood there looking at me, absolutely speechless. Then, attempting to melt her further, I said, "I know that your husband has been gone for six years, but if you're looking around, I know a young rabbi who's very anxious to get married."

Well, that did it. She pulled her arm away and literally flew out of the room. There I was, left with a handful of goose pimples. A minute later Carol came rushing in and said, "George, what in heaven's name did you say to my mother? She thinks I'm working with a crazy man!"

I said, "Carol, I was just trying to put her at ease."

Later on, when Mrs. Channing realized I was just having a little fun with her, we became good friends. I called her Peggy and she called me Mr. Burns. But now that I look back, she always arranged that we were never alone together.

During my entire career in show business I've never used dirty material—maybe a little risqué, but never what you'd call out and out dirty. And Carol was the same way. However, in our show at The Dunes we did do an opening routine that could be taken two ways. In Las Vegas it was perfectly acceptable and the audience loved it, but when we played Harrah's Club at Lake Tahoe we had a problem. Bill Harrah is a very straitlaced man and wanted us to take the routine out of our act because for his audience he thought it was off-color.

To give you an idea of what the controversy was all about, here's the way it went. After Carol and I sang a chorus of "This Could Be the Start of Something Big," we went into this routine:

GEORGE

Carol, you're a delight to work with because you're a great
artist.

CAROL

Thank you, George. And it's a thrill to work with you because you've always been my idol. I've watched you work for
years, and you've really got it.

GEORGE

I got it?

CAROL

Oh, yes.

GEORGE

I hope that's a compliment.

CAROL

Oh, it is. You know, to be a star some people have to be great
singers, or great dancers, or great comedians, or great actors,
but you made it without any of that.

GEORGE

But I got it.

CAROL

Oh, yes.

GEORGE

Well, Carol, what is this thing that I've got? Is it sort of a hidden talent?

CAROL

Oh, George, what you've got isn't hidden. Anybody can see
it, it's right out in the open.

GEORGE

So before it catches cold—what would you say it is?

CAROL

Well, George, it's a certain something, and you've got it.
You've not only got it, but you've always had it.

GEORGE

Let me see—it's something that I've got. Has Sinatra got it?

CAROL

Yes, but you've got twice as much.

GEORGE

Well, maybe it's because I'm older.

CAROL

Sure, so yours is developed more.

GEORGE

Now I'm really confused. How about Dean Martin, has he got it?

CAROL

Of course he's got it. But alongside of you, you can't even notice it.

GEORGE

Now this thing that I've got—and I've got twice as much as Sinatra—and when I'm with Dean Martin you don't notice his—has . . . has . . . has Richard Burton got it?

CAROL

Of course he's got it. And I know because Elizabeth Taylor happens to be a very close friend of mine.

GEORGE

This something that I've got, and I'm glad I got it—and I certainly wouldn't like to lose it—but I'd like to know what it is—can you describe it? Is it square? Is it round? Is it . . . is it as big as a breadbox?

CAROL

George, there's no way to measure it. You can't buy it, you can't sell it, you're born with it. You can't put your finger on it.

GEORGE

That maybe I've got. . . . Now, when did you find out I had it?

CAROL

The first time I ever saw you. You were playing the Palace

110

Theater and I was in the audience. The moment you walked out on the stage I said to the woman next to me, "He's got it."

GEORGE

What did the woman say?

CAROL

She said, "He must be hiding it, because I can't see it."

GEORGE

She couldn't see it, but you could?

CAROL

Well, that's because I'm in show business. I recognized it right away because I've seen it before.

GEORGE

Anyway, this something that I've got—at my age have I got enough of it left to last until the show is over?

CAROL

Why not? It's lasted all these years.

GEORGE

Well, whatever it is, it must be pretty tired by now. . . . One more question and I'll quit. Is there anybody else who's got as much of it as I have?

CAROL

Shirley MacLaine.

GEORGE

That I didn't expect. Georgie Jessel maybe, but Shirley Mac-Laine, never. . . .

CAROL

Oh, George, everybody in show business has got it.

GEORGE

Well, if I've still got it, I hope I don't lose it at the blackjack table. . . . Carol, it's time to finish our song.

Anyway, that's the routine, and Bill Harrah wanted it out. But Carol refused. She said to Harrah, "When I'm on the stage all I'm talking about is George Burns' personality. If you're thinking of something else, then you're dirty, not the routine!"

Harrah came back with, "Well, if you're just talking about his personality, why is the audience laughing so hard?"

Very emphatically Carol said, "Because George Burns happens to have a very funny personality!"

Well, the routine stayed in. But we'd become so self-conscious about it that it lost all its humor, and after a few days we took it out. Bill Harrah had won.

In January of 1963, when John F. Kennedy was our President, the Democratic party gave a star-studded gala in Washington to celebrate the second anniversary of his inauguration. Carol and I were still working together, and we were both invited to Washington to entertain at the celebration. Naturally I took my road manager, Charlie Reade, with me.

Well, the affair was a tremendous success, and afterward we all went to Vice President Lyndon Johnson's house for a late supper. The place was full of Washington dignitaries and show business personalities, and all in all it was a very exciting evening. When I finally got back to my hotel, Charlie Reade was waiting for me and we packed our bags because we were due to fly out in the morning.

But it didn't happen. The next morning the Washington airport was fogged in and stayed that way all day. I finally got word that all flights had been canceled and we would have to leave early the following morning. So that night I decided that Charlie and I would just have dinner sent up to our rooms and we'd sit around and watch television. At about 6:30 I got into my pajamas, fixed a couple of drinks, and ordered our dinner. In the meantime Charlie had found a full-length mirror in the living room. And that's all Charlie needed. There he stood, in nothing but his jockey shorts and shoes, dancing his heart out and watching himself in

112

the mirror. Like I said, I love to watch Charlie dance, so I took my double martini, made myself comfortable, and sat there being entertained by one of the original Dunhills.

Right about then in rushed Carol Channing's husband, Charlie Lowe. He was all excited and out of breath. "George," he gasped, "the President's secretary just called, and the President couldn't make it back to Hyannisport because of the fog, so at the last minute he decided to hold a little dinner party at the White House!"

I said, "Good. That's where he lives—where else would he hold it?"

Charlie Lowe wasn't ready for any feeble attempts at humor. He blurted on, "George, you don't understand—*we're* invited! You and Carol and myself and our piano player! And we're supposed to be there in a half hour!"

"Not me," I said. "I'm not walking out in the middle of one of Charlie Reade's best routines."

Charlie Lowe was ready to have a fit. "George, this is no time to clown around!"

"But I'm all packed," I said to him. "I'm in my pajamas. And besides, I've already ordered my dinner."

With an icy look he said, "George, you don't turn down an invitation from the President of the United States. We'll meet you in the lobby in a half hour!" And he walked out.

During all this Charlie Reade hadn't stopped dancing. And after I got dressed and was ready to leave, he was still dancing.

Well, it turned out to be quite an evening at the White House. When we arrived we were met by Secret Service men who were to take us upstairs to the Kennedy living quarters. I can still remember that long walk down the hallway to the elevator in that big empty White House. You could hear the echo of your footsteps, and it made me think of Charlie Reade—he would have loved that floor.

As we entered their private living quarters, the President and Mrs. Kennedy were standing by the fireplace having a cocktail, so we joined them. Shortly the other guests ar-

113

rived, and after we finished our cocktail we all went into dinner. There were nine of us: the President and Mrs. Kennedy; the British Ambassador, Sir David Ormsby-Gore, and his wife; Jacqueline Kennedy's sister, Lee Radziwell; Carol and Charlie Lowe; Bob Hunter, their piano player; and myself.

I was a little nervous when I sat down at the table because I was expecting a formal silver service, with all those different knives and forks and spoons. When I see all that silver it confuses me; I never know which end to start from. But that night all they had were two forks, a knife and a spoon. The two forks almost threw me, but I figured it out—the short one was for the salad.

It was just the kind of dinner I like—very simple. There was onion soup, a little green salad, a minute steak with some French peas, and dessert and coffee. And the whole dinner was served by one man. I've been to dinner parties in Hollywood where for nine people they had ten butlers. One is a standby in case one of the regular butlers burns his thumb in the soup.

During dinner the President and Sir Ormsby-Gore got into a discussion about the problems of putting a man on the moon. Well, I wasn't going to sit there like a dummy, so I got into the conversation without even waiting for an opening. I said, "Mr. President, I'm a member of the Hillcrest Country Club, and every day at the Round Table I have lunch with people like Groucho Marx, Georgie Jessel, Jack Benny, Danny Thomas, Danny Kaye, Lou Holtz, Jimmy Durante—and we're all good Americans. Now, whenever you get a problem like this just throw it our way and we'll be glad to iron it out for you." There was a second of silence, then the President started to laugh. Then Sir Ormsby-Gore laughed, although he didn't know why. And then everybody at the table started to laugh except Lee Radziwill. She never could figure out who I was.

After dinner we all went into the living room. Bob Hunter sat down at the piano and started noodling, and all of a sudden it was show time. The President asked Carol to sing "Diamonds Are a Girl's Best Friend," and she followed that with "I'm Just a Little Girl from Little Rock." Again I didn't want to sit there like a dummy, so I got up without even being asked. I opened with "Red Rose Rag," then went into "Willie, the Weeper, Was a Chimney Sweeper" and finished with "Strut, Miss Lizzie." Everybody applauded except Lee Radziwill. She not only couldn't figure out who I was, she couldn't figure out what I was.

For an encore I did my French version of "La Vie En Rose." Well, this broke Jacqueline Kennedy up completely. She said, "George, I've been speaking French all my life, and now after listening to you I find out I've been doing it all wrong."

After that everybody got into the act, and we had sort of a little impromptu songfest. It turned out to be such a relaxed fun evening we forgot where we were—sitting in the White House singing along with the President of the United States.

Around eleven o'clock, when we were getting ready to leave, the President asked us if we'd like to see Lincoln's bedroom. Naturally we all said yes, so we followed the President down the hall. He started into a room, then stepped back and quietly closed the door. He turned to us and said, "I'm sorry, I forgot that my mother is sleeping in there."

As we started back down the hall, Mrs. Kennedy whispered to Carol and myself, "I knew Rose was sleeping in Lincoln's bed. But he's the President, so I let him make his own mistakes."

Anyway, when the four of us got back to the hotel we were all so stimulated from the evening we decided to have a nightcap at the bar. Carol was bubbling all over and couldn't stop talking. "What a night," she said. "Imagine having dinner at the White House and singing harmony with the President of the United States! Nothing in the world can ever top this evening!"

115

I stood up and said, "Well, for me the evening is just beginning. When I get upstairs there'll be Charlie Reade standing in front of the mirror in his jockey shorts, doing a triple-time step. Good night, everybody." With that I walked away and left them sitting there in dead silence.

When I got up to my room the phone was ringing. It was Carol. "George," she said, "tell Charlie Reade to put on a robe, we're all coming up." And they did. We all sat around and watched Charlie dance. It's the first time one of the Dunhills ever followed the President of the United States.

Carol Channing and Charlie Lowe are still two of my closest friends, and whenever Carol has a new piece of material that she's going to do on the stage she always tries it out on me. She knows I've been in show business all my life, so she's sure I'll laugh in the right spots. And not to disappoint her, I always do. I'd do anything for Mrs. Charles Lowe.

No More Applause

On August 27, 1964, Gracie passed away.

I was terribly shocked, I just couldn't believe it—it all happened so suddenly. It was true that three years before, Gracie had a severe heart attack, but afterward she came out of the hospital and was just fine. For a short time we had round-the-clock nurses, but she improved so rapidly that we dismissed two of them and kept one as a nurse-companion for Gracie during the day. From time to time Gracie had little heart flutters, but this created no particular problem, because when the nurse wasn't there I knew exactly what to do. I knew where the pills were and which pill to give her. So when she had flareups, I'd give her the pill, put my arms around her, and we'd hold each other until it passed. It usually lasted no longer than a few seconds.

After a few months we treated this whole thing very casually. We got used to living with it. As long as I had the pills with me, we lived a very normal life. I remember one night we went to a party at Vincente Minnelli's house. It was a large party, and we were having a marvelous time. I had just finished singing three or four of my songs and was at the bar having a drink when Gracie came up to me and very quietly said, "I think we better step into the other room, I need one of my pills."

So we went into another room, I gave her a pill, we held on to each other, and it passed. After it was over, Gracie said, "I feel fine, but I think I'd be more comfortable at home." So I took her home. When we got there she insisted that I go back to the party, but gave me strict orders to keep my eyes and ears open and watch everything that went on. "When you get home I want to hear everything that happened," she told me.

Back to the party I went, and I got home around midnight. There was Gracie sitting up in bed and waiting for me. She said, "Hurry up, get out of your clothes and come to bed. I want to hear every detail about the party."

Well, actually, all we did at the party was dance a little, have a few drinks, and sit around and talk. I had a perfectly fine time, but nothing out of the ordinary took place. But Gracie was sitting there primed for all the gossip, and I just couldn't disappoint her. From midnight to two in the morning I did nothing but make up a lot of lies about the wild and naughty things that went on at that party. I was in such good form that Gracie believed every word I said. In fact, I was so convincing I started to believe it myself. When I was all through, Gracie said, "Goodness, if I had known it was going to be that kind of a party, I certainly would have stayed."

Well, we finally turned off the lights and went to sleep. But about three in the morning Gracie nudged me awake. I turned over, still half asleep, and said, "What is it, Gracie?"

"Tell me again what Greg Bautzer said to that little starlet?" she begged.

I said, "Good night, Gracie"—I couldn't remember my lie.

This gives you an idea how casually we treated Gracie's illness. Those pills made me feel very secure. I figured we could go on this way year after year—it never entered my mind that anything would change it. Then one evening Gracie had another one of her attacks. I gave her the pill, we held on to each other—but this time it didn't work. When the pain continued, I called Dr. Kennamer, and they rushed Gracie to the hospital. . . . Two hours later Gracie was gone.

At first I couldn't accept it. I sat there stunned. I turned to Dr. Kennamer and said, "Doctor, how could this happen? I've still got pills left."

118

The doctor didn't say a word; he quietly ushered the other members of the family out of the room and left me there with Gracie. It was then that the full impact hit me. I knew I was alone.

There is a finality about death that is frightening, but there is nothing we can do about it. As difficult as it may be, we must all eventually realize that there's only one exit, and sooner or later every one of us has to make it. But life goes on in spite of everything, and now I had to build a whole new existence for myself. It wasn't easy—the period of adjustment to such a loss took time. Gracie had been such an all-important part of my life that everywhere I looked, everywhere I went, the feeling of her was still there. My family and friends did all they could to help me, but my days still seemed empty. For me, the most difficult time was at night. It was hard for me to go to sleep, and when I did doze off I'd soon wake with a start and look over, expecting Gracie to be there in her bed beside me.

This went on for about six months, then one night I did something, and to this day I can't explain why. I was all ready to get into bed, and then for some reason I pulled the covers down on Gracie's bed and got into it. I don't know whether it made me feel closer to her, or what it was, but for the first time since Gracie had gone I got a good night's sleep. I never did go back to my bed.

I didn't realize it at the time, but this proved to be the beginning of the end of my deep mourning period. Slowly I started returning to a more normal way of life; I began going out to dinner with my friends—I'd have people over to my house—I got interested in playing bridge again—I found myself buying new clothes—I even started going to the club and trading jokes with the fellows at the Round Table. At the time I was producing and appearing in a television series called "Wendy and Me" with Connie Stevens, and I was actually looking forward to going to work again. As I said, life does go on in spite of everything, and it did for me.

One thing I learned from all this is how strong the human spirit really is. Our ability to bounce back from what might

119

seem like the end of the world is absolutely amazing. And age has nothing to do with it. Whether you're eighteen or eighty, and whether you like it or not, you're going to go right on living.

I don't mean to imply that we can forget our loved ones who have passed on. I certainly never forgot Gracie, and I never will. She's in a mausoleum at Forest Lawn Memorial Park, and for the first year I used to take her flowers and visit her every week. The second year it was every two weeks, and after that and to this day I visit her once a month. When I first started these visits I'd put the flowers in front of the crypt and then sit there and cry and cry—I just couldn't stop. But there came a time when there were no more tears. I discovered that there are just so many tears one can cry and that crying is not going to change a thing.

I started talking to Gracie. Every time I'd visit her I'd tell her things; things about my work, things about our family, our friends, the plans that I had, etc. I don't know whether she heard me, but I like to think that she did. Later on it got so I'd tell her some of the funny things that happened to me. If I went to a party, I'd tell about all the amusing things that went on, but I made sure I always told her the truth. I figured she'd know if I was lying again.

When I was being considered for a part in the MGM movie *The Sunshine Boys,* I told Gracie all about it. I told her how I read for Neil Simon, who wrote the script, and Herb Ross, the director. I explained to her how I thought I gave a very good reading and that it was a great part, and how I knew if I got the chance I'd be able to do it. After I told her all this I said, "Gracie, maybe you can help, maybe you can put in a good word for me up there. But don't bother the head man, he's very busy. Talk to his son, and be sure to tell him I'm Jewish, too." This time she must have heard me—I did get the part.

120

Thank You, Mr. Toastmaster . . .

In the business I'm in I'm constantly being called on to make speeches at various functions. That not only goes for me, but applies to Milton Berle, Don Rickles, Buddy Hackett, Joey Bishop, Jan Murray, Nipsey Russell, Steve Allen, George Jessel, Jack Carter, Dean Martin, Johnny Carson, and many others. If I accepted all the after-dinner speeches I'm asked to make, I'd spend half of my life eating chicken croquettes and sitting between Milton Berle and Jack Carter.

Somebody is always calling me on the telephone and saying, "George, we're giving a testimonial dinner for so-and-so Friday night and the evening wouldn't be complete without you on the dais. All you have to do is get up and only do five or six minutes." Have you any idea how long five or six minutes can be? Tonight before dinner why don't you try it; stand up at the table and talk to your wife for six minutes—and try to get laughs while you're doing it.

I don't think people realize how much work and preparation it takes to prepare a six-minute speech. In the first place, when you write it, it has to be tailored to fit the guest of honor. You play off of his personality traits—things he's known for—his physical characteristics, etc. I remember once I was asked to speak at a dinner honoring Kirk Douglas. Now, one of his most discernible physical characteristics is a dimple in his chin, so naturally I wrote two or three minutes of dimple jokes. Then I got to thinking—everybody on the dais would be doing dimple jokes, so I figured

121

I'd outwit them. I threw out all my dimple jokes and concentrated on Kirk Douglas' multiple talents: acting, writing, producing, directing, etc. At the night of the affair what happened? Everybody had been trying to outwit everybody else; they'd all thrown out their dimple jokes and talked about Kirk's multiple talents. He was very upset. There he sat with this beautiful dimple and nobody mentioned it.

Not only does it take hours to write these five or six minutes, in my case it takes hours to memorize them. As a rule everyone on the dais has his speech written out on little cards and he reads it. I used to do that too, but I learned my lesson.

They gave Georgie Raft a dinner one night and I was sitting next to Milton Berle. While I was eating my chicken croquettes Milton stole my cards. What he forgot was that he and I don't work anything alike, so when he got up and did my speech he didn't get any laughs. Afterward he came over to me, slammed the cards down on the table, and said, "George, you better get yourself a new writer!" I didn't feel too bad. While he was doing my speech I stole his chicken croquettes. That's the last time I ever used cards—and it's also the last time I ate a chicken croquette.

I'd say that over the years I've made most of my speeches for the Friars Club, both here and in New York. I've belonged to the New York Friars for over fifty years, and the one out here since it was founded. They're theatrical clubs, and most of the proceeds from these functions go to worthy charities.

The Friars are famous for their "roasts," which are always stag affairs. A well-known personality is chosen to be the guest of honor, and then they literally tear him to pieces by insulting him with the dirtiest and filthiest language possible. I used to do these roasts quite frequently, but now I've stopped doing them; I don't think they're fun anymore. After all, everyone gets up and uses the same dirty words, and how many dirty words are there? In the entire English language there are only thirty-one dirty words—wait a minute, I just thought of another one—make that thirty-two.

Some of the people they roast aren't easy to talk about; they're just not colorful; they don't have any characteristics or traits that you can make jokes about. Can you imagine getting up and doing six funny minutes on Calvin Coolidge?

A good example of this happened to me when I was asked to speak at a dinner honoring General Omar Bradley. I didn't know where to begin. I tried several approaches, but nothing seemed to come out funny. I was about to call up and tell them I couldn't make it when out of the blue my show-business genius rescued me. (My show-business genius was one of my writers.) It was so simple I almost fired my show-business genius for not thinking of it sooner. What I did was take the very thing that was stumping me and turned it into a plus.

The dinner for General Bradley was held at a theatrical club, the Masquers, and Pat Buttram was the toastmaster. This was my speech:

Thank you, Pat, for that nice introduction. Excuse me while I light my cigar. I can't talk unless I smoke. Seeing me without a cigar would be like offering Pat Buttram a drink and having him say, "No, thank you." . . . I must smoke about twenty or thirty cigars a day. The older I get the more I smoke. When I was eighteen I only smoked one cigar a day. Of course, in those days I was able to do other things. I've reached the stage now that I can't even remember what those other things were. But you know, it's comfortable when you get to the point where you just smoke cigars and do nothing else. In the first place, you don't have to get undressed to smoke a cigar. And when you're finished with a cigar you don't have to call a cab to take it home.

And now to our distinguished guest of honor, General Omar Bradley. You know, I'm in a very funny spot tonight. I really don't know what to say. I've met the General, but we really have very little in common. He's a five-star general, and I'm a singer. I've never shot a gun, and I'm sure he doesn't know the verse to "Some of These Days." I've never been in the Army or the Navy, the Marines, the Air Corps. In fact, the Boy Scouts wouldn't even take me. But I felt I should do something for my country, so I joined the Girl Scouts. I got away with it for about two months until one night in the locker room after a basketball game. I thought they were going to throw me out, but the woman in charge of the troop took a look at me and said, "Let him stay, he's not going to hurt anybody." At that time I was a soprano. . . .

Anyway, when Harry Joe Brown, your program director, asked me to speak here tonight, I said to him, "Harry, you got the wrong fellow. It's not easy for me to talk about anybody unless I've been close to him. So you better count me out."

Harry said, "George, everybody on the dais is going to be talking about the General. You can be different. Do four minutes of show-business anecdotes, you know a million of them." I said, "Do you think it will work?" He said, "Of course, but one thing—the General is a very distinguished man, and there will be ladies in the audience, so don't get risqué, just do four warm and humorous minutes."

So I said, "Harry, do you think I can tell this one? It's about Georgie Jessel being married four times. In those days he considered himself a great lover, and he was—but not at home. And his four wives left him, and I don't blame them. It must be very uncomfortable to be married to a guy who goes to bed wearing all those medals, they couldn't get any sleep, all night long he tinkled."

Harry said, "George, that's a funny joke, but not in front of the General. Forget the four minutes, do about three minutes—three, nice, clean, warm minutes will be plenty."

I said, "Well, can I tell the one about Jack Benny before he was married and he was running around with this girl Lily DeFore who was working at Leon and Eddie's? She did this act where she painted her whole body gold. Jack and I were living together at the time, and one night when we were getting ready to go to bed I said, "Jack, is there anything going

124

on between you and Lily?" Jack said, "No, George, absolutely nothing." Then he turned out the lights, and the glow from his underwear kept me awake all night."

Harry said, "George, the General is in the Army and he's not used to risque things like that. Two minutes will be plenty. Believe me, at these affairs the shorter you keep it the better they like you."

I said, "Well, it won't be easy, Harry, but as long as I've only got two minutes I better tell one of my really good ones. I'll do the one about the girl I worked on the bill with in Altoona. She was a great performer. She could bend over backwards till her head touched the floor, and then she'd take both of her legs and wrap them around her neck. And she did some great stuff on stage, too. . . ."

Harry said, "Hold it, George, just do one minute . . . some short, cute little story, something that happened to you when you were a kid."

I said, "Oh, yeah, I've got a beauty. I was in the third grade, and my teacher, Mrs. Hollander, told me about the birds and the bees. I couldn't believe my ears. Those sweet little birds and those darling little bees, to think of them doing what my sister Goldie was doing was just shocking. . . . That was sixty-eight years ago, and all those birds and bees are dead now, but my sister Goldie is still trying. . . . That's not shocking, that's hopeless."

Harry said, "George, just do thirty seconds. Say something nice about the General for thirty seconds."

I said, "All right, I can tell about the only time I met him. It was at Hillcrest Country Club and he was there for lunch. Naturally we were all impressed. Then I got up and went into the men's room, and I was standing there when the General came in and stood next to me. I got so nervous I didn't know what to do, so I saluted him and ruined a perfectly good pair of shoes."

Harry said, "George, I've got an idea. There will be so many people on the dais that there's really no reason for you to show up. The next time you run into General Bradley, just wave to him."

I said, "Harry, I'd love to wave to him, but I'm afraid I might ruin another pair of shoes."

That's when Harry Joe left. I think I'm going to leave, too. I'm sorry, General, I did my best.

I thought the speech went very well, but later on I was standing at the bar having a drink when I noticed the General walking toward me. He wasn't smiling, so I didn't know what to expect. He put his hand on my shoulder and said, "George, I want to thank you for being here tonight, and I love the way you cleaned up that speech."

I relaxed a bit and said, "Thank you, General, and I'm glad you enjoyed it."

The General smiled a big smile and said, "I really did, George." Then, with just a twinkle in his eyes—"And if you ever think of joining the Army, I'll see that you get a new pair of shoes."

As he walked away, I couldn't help but compare him with Georgie Jessel. Jessel goes around with his chest covered with medals, and here's this great five-star general and he doesn't tinkle at all. I can say things like that about Jessel, and he can say anything he wants about me, because our friendship goes back a lot of years.

I could have saved myself a lot of time and worry about my approach to the General Bradley speech if I had just gone through my files. While preparing this chapter I discovered I used practically the same format at a testimonial dinner The Friars gave for Georgie Jessel back in 1948. I found out then that you can do a dirty speech without using one dirty word. You innocently plant a seed in the audience's mind, and when they read something dirty into it, you act as though you're shocked that this naughty audience could even think of such a thing. And the more shocked you look the funnier the speech gets.

Anyway, here's the Jessel speech:

Brother Friars, ladies and gentlemen, toastmaster and guest of honor, George Jessel. Well, another Friars' dinner, and on the dais practically the same faces. There's Jessel, Jol-

126

son, Cantor, Benny, Danny Kaye, Pat O'Brien, and Bob Hope. You'll notice I'm giving Pat O'Brien and Bob Hope bottom billing. If they were Jewish, I'd move them up front with us boys. . . .

Now to our guest of honor. I've known Georgie Jessel for years. I remember when he was starring in *The Jazz Singer* on Broadway. Jessel was a tremendous hit, but when they made the movie of *The Jazz Singer* Warner Brothers hired Al Jolson to star in it, and naturally this upset Jessel. He thought he should star in the movie because he originated that part. In fact, Jessel was so mad he took an oath that he'd break the Warner Brothers if it took his last cent. And I know exactly how much money Georgie Jessel has got left, so the Warner Brothers should be broke by this Thursday. . . .

Well, that's the end of my speech. I'm sorry, but I must tell you what happened. I didn't know there was going to be a mixed audience here tonight. I put together a lot of funny stuff about Jessel, but I can't use any of it. Don't you think that somebody would have told me that this was not going to be a stag affair? Who'd ever figure they'd throw a clean dinner for Jessel. . . .

Wait a minute, maybe I can take that speech of mine and clean it up as I go along. This isn't going to be easy, but I'll try.

I remember when Jessel went on the road with *The Jazz Singer* and he was playing Cleveland. There was this pretty girl who saw Jessel in the play and went for him in a big way. Well, one night Jessel invited her up to his suite at the Statler Hotel. I was in town playing the Keith Theater, so I thought I'd surprise Georgie. After the show I went up to his hotel room. Now when a guy's got a dame in his room doing what Jessel usually— Well, wouldn't you think he'd lock the door? But he didn't, so I walked right in, and there was Jessel with his— That I can't clean up.

A year later he went back into vaudeville and was booked on the Orpheum circuit. He opened in Minneapolis, and on the bill was this beautiful sister act. Well, Jessel invited one of the sisters out for dinner after the show. As you know, it gets very cold in Minneapolis, and after dinner when they

127

went back to the hotel there was no heat because the furnace had broken down. The girl said, "Georgie, can't you do something, I'm freezing?" Well, Jessel thought he'd warm things up for her, so he—

Then he played Winnipeg. . . . And in Winnipeg he was on the bill with a girl act called Lasky's Redheads—eight gorgeous showgirls. And one night he got all eight girls up into his suite and he—

Then he played Vancouver. . . . In Vancouver there was a little restaurant right alongside the theater, and there was this very sexy blond waitress—

From there he went to Seattle. . . . There he met this beautiful Chinese girl who was a stripper at the Primrose Pagoda— Then he played Portland. . . .

Then San Francisco . . .

Oakland . . .

Los Angeles . . .

Tijuana . . .

This is silly, there must be something clean I can say about Jessel. . . . Let's go back to his childhood. When Georgie Jessel was eight years old—

No, I didn't go back far enough. . . .

I'm sorry, I can't do this speech in front of a mixed audience. Later on I'll be glad to tell it to you ladies alone. . . .

Thank you very much.

Well, that speech turned out to be the hit of the evening. I never got such laughs. I really was elated. I sat there complimenting myself how I was able to make a speech like that without using one of those thirty-two words. But this ego trip didn't last too long. A matronly woman came up to me and, clutching my hand, said, "Mr. Burns, you're an amazing man. Only you could get away with a dirty speech like that in mixed company."

I didn't know what to think. I asked her, "What did I say tonight that was so off-color?"

The woman gave sort of a kittenish giggle and said, "Oh, Mr. Burns, I don't use words like that," and ran off.

There you are, this woman thought she heard me say

things that I never said, and all because I planted that little seed. It really works.

As we were all leaving later on, Lucille Ball grabbed me by the arm and pulled me aside. "George," she said, "my husband's ashamed to ask you this, but I'm not. What did Jessel do with that Chinese girl in Seattle?"

I said, "Lucy, they spent a very exciting evening—they sat around reading fortune cookies."

She gave me one of those looks, and said, "George Burns, you're the dirtiest man I know!"

But the most elegant affair I was ever invited to speak at was a testimonial dinner for Alfred Lunt and Lynn Fontanne at The Players Club in New York City. The Players is a very sophisticated theatrical club, and the membership consists of important actors, writers, producers, directors, etc., from the legitimate theater. To give you an idea of how distinguished the occasion was, besides myself here are the speakers who were on the dais that night: Sir John Gielgud, Sir Ralph Richardson, Peter Ustinov, Howard Lindsay, Russel Crouse, Marc Connelly and, of course, Alfred Lunt and Lynn Fontanne. Now, if you're wondering how a small-time vaudeville actor like me wound up in that kind of company, pull up a chair and I'll tell you.

Gracie and I had always been big fans of Alfred Lunt and Lynn Fontanne, but we had never met them. To us they were like the Royal Family of the theater, and we felt that they were way out of our league. Then, one night years ago in Beverly Hills, we were having a dinner party for ten people, and Carol Channing and her husband, Charlie Lowe, were two of the guests. At the last minute Carol called up Gracie and said, "I know this is an imposition, Gracie, but we're with Alfred Lunt and Lynn Fontanne, and I was wondering if we could bring them to dinner with us."

Gracie nearly dropped the phone. "Of course," she stammered, "you can bring them, we'll be delighted." Then she dropped the phone and came running breathlessly into the den, saying, "George . . . George, guess what's happened!

129

Carol just called and she's bringing Alfred Lunt and Lynn Fontanne to dinner!"

I looked at her and said, "You're kidding! Do you think we have time to have the house painted?"

"This is no time to be funny, George," Gracie snapped. "I'm going up to change my dress," and out she ran.

I don't mind telling you I was just as nervous as she was. I'd been making myself a martini, and I immediately turned it into a double. What do you say to people like them?

But as it turned out, there was nothing to be nervous about. When the Lunts arrived, the first thing Alfred did was hit Gracie with one of her lines that he remembered out of our first vaudeville act. In a perfect imitation of Gracie, he said, "I'm glad I'm dizzy boys like dizzy girls and I like boys and you must be glad I'm dizzy because you're a boy and I like boys!"

I don't know how he remembered that line, but it certainly broke the ice. Everybody relaxed, and we had a marvelous evening—until it was time for dinner. In the excitement Gracie had forgotten to tell our help that there would be two more place settings at the table. So when we all walked into the dining room there we were, twelve people with only ten chairs. It got pretty confusing—no matter how Gracie arranged the seating there were always two people left standing. Finally Gracie realized what had happened. "Oh, my goodness," she said, "I'm so embarrassed, I forgot the Lunts!"

The Lunts laughed, and Alfred said, "Don't worry about it, Gracie, we can always eat standing up."

And Lynn added, "Relax, Gracie, I've been married to Alfred long enough to know he likes dizzy girls." So we got two more chairs, and it was a very memorable evening.

Well, that's how we met the Lunts, and two years later it resulted in me being invited to speak at their testimonial dinner at The Players. It turned out to be quite a nerve-racking evening for me. I sat there on the dais as one after the other of these theater greats got up and made eloquent speeches extolling the Lunts and their place in the theater. Finally I realized that everyone on the dais had been called upon except me. I thought that Howard Lindsay, the toastmaster, had forgotten I was there. But he hadn't. He had saved me for the last speaker before he introduced the Lunts, which was very flattering. But it was also a little frightening. Remember, most of the people there that night had never even seen a vaudeville actor.

Well, this was my speech:

Members of The Players club, distinguished guests on the dais, toastmaster Howard Lindsay, and guests of honor, Alfred Lunt and Lynn Fontanne. First, I'd like to apologize for having this makeup on. I just came from taping a show for Jack Paar, and I was a smash. I sang some of the songs I made famous, like "Tiger Girl," and "The Heart of a Cherry," and "I'll Be Waiting for You, Bill, When You Come Back from San Juan Hill." . . .

I love to sing. You know, every night when Gracie and I go to bed I sing her seven or eight songs until she falls asleep. And it works. We've been happily married for thirty-seven years. At my age it's easier to sing. . . . And if our guest of honor, Alfred Lunt, is having the same problem, I'll be glad to teach him a few choruses of "Tiger Girl." . . .

Excuse me while I light my cigar. I can't talk unless I smoke. Seeing me without a cigar would be like seeing Sir John Gielgud playing on the same bill with Fink's Mules. . . .

What a pleasure it is to see Howard Lindsay as toastmaster. For the last fifteen years I've been looking at Georgie Jessel. Not that Jessel isn't a great toastmaster, he is. But after he gets through calling you every dirty name in the book, you've got to buy a bond for Israel. . . . You see, I'm a member of the Friars Club and I make a lot of speeches there, but it's always stag. So if I look a little nervous up here, it's not that I don't know what to say, but this just isn't the place to say it. In fact, I couldn't even say it in your men's room. This is such a high-class affair tonight that even the attendant in the men's room is wearing dinner clothes. He wouldn't give

131

me a towel to wipe my hands until I told him my name was Sir George Burns.

Let me tell you a little about myself. I never played a good theater until I met Gracie. Before that I was a small-time vaudeville actor until I was twenty-seven years old. You should have seen some of the broken-down theaters I played. I played one theater that was so bad "Madame Burkhardt and Her Cockatoos" were the headliners. I was just unbelievably bad, but who cared, I wanted to be in show business and I was. I had to change my name every week; I could never get a job with the same name twice. I was Jack Harris of Harris & Kelly. I was Phil Baxter of Baxter & Bates. I was Davis of Delight and Davis—my name was Sammy Davis. . . . Don't look so shocked—I was Jewish before he was, too. I used so many different names it got to the point where I didn't know who I was.

I remember one of the first acts I ever did was a singing, dancing and rollerskating act—Brown and Williams. Sid Brown and Harry Williams. . . . I don't remember whether I was Brown or Williams, but we got into a fight and split up the act. We both got different partners but did the same act. So now you had Brown and Williams and Williams and Brown. Then the four of us split up, got different partners, and again we all did the same act. Now we had Brown and Williams, Williams and Brown, Brown and Brown, and Williams and Williams. Then came another split. Now you had Brown and Williams, Williams and Brown, Brown and Brown, Williams and Williams, the Brown Brothers, and the Williams Boys. By the time we got through, every Jewish person on the East Side was either named Brown or Williams. There was one kid, Hymie Goldberg, he moved. He said he was afraid to live in a gentile neighborhood.

Then I did a ballroom dancing act called Pedro Lopez and Conchita. My name was Pedro Lopez. Conchita's real name was Lila Berkowitz, but I used to smoke those little Conchita cigars, so I named her after the cigar. . . . We were booked into the Farley Theater in Brooklyn, and to give you an idea of how bad we were, the music for our opening number was "La Czarina," which is a Russian mazurka. We thought it was a Spanish dance, so we wore Spanish outfits. I wore a little black bolero coat with a green sash around my

132

waist, and I parted my hair in the middle and plastered it down with Vaseline. I wanted to look like Ramon Navarro. . . .

Conchita had a red Spanish shawl with gold fringe around it, which she'd fasten under one arm, leaving one shoulder bare. And she also wore one of those big, heavy Spanish combs in her hair. It used to press on a nerve in her head and drove her crazy—they finally had to take her away. . . . She wore an evening dress under the shawl, and for our second number she'd pull the shawl off and put her arm in the sleeve of the dress. Then she'd pick up a fan, and she was ready. I'd pull off my sash, put on a top hat, grab my cane, and we were ready to do our next number, which was a Cakewalk.

At this one particular performance that comb was pressing on Conchita's nerve, and she didn't know what she was doing. She picked up the fan okay, but when she took off the shawl she forgot to put her arm in her sleeve. Well, when we started the Cakewalk, which is a very bouncy number, with her arm out of her sleeve, one of her things kept flapping up against her chest. I thought it was the audience applauding, so I kept taking bows.

Our closing number was the Turkey Trot with a whirlwind finish. For this Conchita had changed into a white evening gown with just two thin straps. Now, Conchita came from the lower East Side, and in those days a lot of Jewish girls never shaved under their arms, so she had all this hair hanging down. When we started to pivot, with that comb pressing on her nerve and me stepping on her hair, poor Conchita was sorry she ever got into show business. And for our finish she'd put her arms around my neck and I'd spin her around in the air. It looked like I was swinging two rabbis. Anyway, before the week was over they took Conchita away, and I changed my name again.

Well, that's enough about the glamor of small-time vaudeville.

Now to our guests of honor, Alfred Lunt and Lynn Fontanne. In case you're wondering why I've spent so much time talking about small-time vaudeville, it's because I just don't know our guests of honor well enough to lie about them. They did come to our house about a year ago for sort of a confused dinner, and the soup spoons they used . . . we haven't let anyone use them since. In fact, we had them bronzed.

Gracie and I always loved the Lunts. We've seen practically all of their shows for the last thirty years, and we've always sent them flowers. But we never went backstage to meet them. We never even thought that we belonged in their dressing room. And we certainly never played anyplace with the Lunts. They never played the Gus Sun Circuit, and we never played for the Theater Guild.

But I've thought it over, and I do have something in common with the Lunts. They've been in show business all their lives, and I've been in show business all my life. So if age counts, my billing is right up there with the Lunts.

Anyway, I'm thrilled that I was asked to speak here tonight. And before I sit down I'd like to say something to Lynn Fontanne. Lynn, if you're thinking of getting rid of that straight man you've been using, I've got a trunkful of stuff. I'd give anything to sing two choruses of *The Guardsman*. What a team we'd make—Lynn Fontanne and George Burns. You'll notice, of course, I'm even giving you top billing. Thank you very much.

Well, the members of The Players club were delighted with my speech, and a week later I got a telegram from the membership committee. It said that Alfred Lunt had suggested that they ask me to become a member of The Players. This was a very flattering gesture, and even though I don't play chess, shoot billiards, or drink my scotch and water without ice, I joined. I was a member for three years and never went near the place. Here I was, living in California and a member of two other theatrical clubs. It seemed silly to be paying dues to another club in New York, so I sent a telegram to the membership committee. I said, GENTLEMEN, I'D LIKE TO RESIGN FROM THE PLAYERS CLUB, BUT ONLY UNDER ONE CONDITION. PROMISE YOU DON'T TELL ALFRED LUNT. IF HE EVER FOUND OUT, HE'D MAKE ME REMOVE THE BRONZE FROM HIS SOUP SPOON. GEORGE BURNS.

134

The Quiet Riot

Somebody once said if you live long enough, sooner or later everything that can happen to you will happen. And it's true. However, I figure there must be sometime in life when you complete the cycle and start all over again. I wonder how old I'll be when I get the mumps again?

As you go through life, the good things and the bad things have a way of balancing themselves out. But there are times when you get the feeling that the bad things are winning. That's the way I felt the day my closest friend, Jack Benny, passed away. I was at the house with his family when word came down from upstairs that Jack was gone. I told Mary I'd like to go upstairs alone for a few moments and say good-bye to Jack. When I went into the room he was lying there with his hands clasped in that familiar manner and his head cocked to one side—he looked as though he were taking one of his long pauses.

Even though those of us close to Jack knew that his illness was terminal, when the end actually came we weren't ready for it. I've come to realize that death is forever, and there is no way one can completely accept it. I also realize that there is nothing one can do about it.

Jack was gone and part of me went with him, but a lot of Jack stayed here with me. Not only me—part of him stayed with people all over the world. Jack's image was so well established and the character he played was based on such reality that everybody thought of him as a personal friend.

Who could forget that walk, that voice, those familiar gestures, the outraged glances? Whenever one of Jack's self-provoked situations backfired we all suffered his humiliation right along with him. But we laughed while we did it.

That was Jack Benny the performer, the perennial thirty-nine-year-old tightwad. But the Jack Benny I knew was entirely different. He was really something special. He was the warmest and most considerate man I ever knew. Everybody who came in contact with Jack fell in love with him. And the feeling was mutual because Jack loved people. It didn't matter if they were rich, poor, tall, small, round, square, black, white, yellow or even burnt orange—Jack just loved people.

Many years ago in New York he did something that's a perfect example of what I'm talking about. He had a very important business meeting with some of the top NBC executives. Jack's manager, Irving Fein, was there also, and when Jack didn't show up on time, Irving started to get very nervous. Jack finally did arrive twenty minutes late. He apologized and explained that he had been downstairs talking to Charlie, the elevator starter. It seemed that Charlie's wife had just had a baby, and Jack was very excited about it. Irving and the NBC brass all listened to the story, and when Jack had finished, Irving said, "All right, Jack, now can we start the meeting?"

Jack said, "One more thing, Irving. On our way out remind me to ask Charlie what hospital his wife is in, I want to send her some flowers."

Then they started the meeting.

There were all kinds of little things Jack used to do that I wish I had done. I must admit I thought of them, but I never did them. A great deal of Jack's time was spent on the road making personal appearances and giving charity concerts for symphony orchestras. It was a hectic schedule, but he always found time to write fifty or sixty postcards every week. They were personal notes to his friends, and they al-

136

ways ended with some kind of a little joke. Jack had a secretary who traveled with him, but Jack wrote every one of those postcards in longhand. I'm sure he felt that a handwritten note made it more intimate and friendly. To him a typewritten note was something that came from a bank.

The longer I knew Jack the more he amazed me. Sometimes for no reason at all he would stop at a little bakery in Beverly Hills, buy a cake, and take it up to his doctor's office. The receptionist and the nurses would make coffee, and they'd all sit around and have a little gossip session. Jack didn't have an appointment with the doctor, he just got a kick out of talking to the girls.

Now, I'd love to do something like that, but I never would. I'd figure the girls would think I was doing it just because I wanted them to think I was trying to be nice. But that never entered Jack's mind. He was just naturally nice without trying.

I envied Jack because he enjoyed everything. In all the time I knew him there was just one little thing that always griped him. He could never get what he considered a good cup of coffee. He once said to me, "George, I've traveled all over the world, I've been everywhere at least once, and I've yet to find a good cup of coffee."

"Jack," I said, "if you've never tasted a good cup of coffee, how would you know if you got one?"

He gave me one of his scornful looks and said, "George, if that was supposed to be funny, it's lucky you don't make your living as a writer," and walked away.

But I think I figured out why the little things, even a cup of coffee, were just as important to Jack as the big things. He was a superstar for a lot of years and had achieved every goal it's possible to reach in show business. And when you've been on top for so many years, each major success loses its importance; you start thinking of each accomplishment as a daily routine.

Of course, when Jack was just getting started it was different. I remember when he first opened at The Palace theater in New York he was very nervous. The second time he played The Palace he was still nervous. But the third time he couldn't figure out why all the other actors were nervous. He got so used to being a hit at The Palace the only thing he worried about was whether the delicatessen next door would save him a piece of cheesecake after the show.

That's the way Jack was for the rest of his life. But sometimes those little things that thrilled him so got to be ludicrous. One day I ran into him coming out of the locker room at the club. Did he say "Hello" or "How are you?" No! He just blurted out, "George, did you take a shower today?"

I didn't know what to say; I thought maybe I had stepped in something. "Yeah, Jack, I took a shower at home this morning," I said.

"Well, you've got to take another one here," Jack urged. "I just took one and the towels are great! They're the softest, fluffiest towels I ever dried myself with!"

I just stood there and looked at him. How do you answer a thing like that? So I went into the card room. Later, when I was leaving, I passed Jack and Eddie Buzzell, and as I went by all I could hear was Jack saying, "Eddie, did you take a shower today?" I didn't look back, I ran out of the club.

There wasn't a day went by that Jack didn't come in on his toes bubbling with excitement over some new bit of trivia he'd discovered. With Jack the last thing that happened to him was always the greatest. One day he said, "George, I've just had the coldest glass of water I've ever had in my life!" Another time he said to me, "I just ate the most delicious bacon and tomato sandwich I ever tasted!" Once he interrupted me in the middle of a bridge game to tell me that Sammy in the locker room just gave him the greatest shoeshine he ever had in his life.

I usually ignored these earth-shaking discoveries of Jack's. I just passed them off as part of being Jack Benny's

138

best friend. But once in a while he'd come up with something you just couldn't walk away from. One Sunday morning Jack and I were going to play nine holes of golf and we were having breakfast together at the club. After we gave our order Jack said to me, "I was with the world's greatest comedian last night."

"Who were you with?" I asked him.

Jack sensed that he was heading for trouble. He hemmed and hawed, and finally said, "Well. . . *you* might not think he's the world's greatest comedian."

From Jack's attitude I knew he had put his foot in it, so from there on I started playing with him. I said, "Well, maybe this fellow isn't the world's greatest comedian—maybe he's the world's second-greatest comedian. Who is he?"

Jack said, "George, look—it was what he said last night that made him sound like the world's greatest comedian."

"Jack, what did he say?"

Fighting for his life, Jack stammered, "Well . . . it . . . it . . . it isn't *what* he said, it's how he said it."

Taking dead aim, I said, "Jack, you're one of the great comedians, and you've got a great delivery—tell me the line, and if he made you laugh, I'm sure you'll make me laugh."

Jack said, "George, the line wouldn't be funny now. It was the situation last night that made the line funny."

I said, "Jack, I still would like to know who this great comedian is."

There was this long pause. Then, without daring to look at me, Jack said, "Larry Adler."

Now it was my turn to take a long pause. Finally I said, "Larry Adler, the harmonica player, is the world's greatest comedian?"

Trying to dig his way out, Jack said, "George, let me tell you exactly what happened. Last night we went to a party, and the entrance to the house was this big, heavy, iron gate.

Well, Larry Adler went through first, and as I came through that's when he said, 'Jack, don't slam the door.' "

I looked straight at him and said, "He must have said something else."

Irritably, Jack snapped, "That's it, George—'Don't slam the door'!"

I said, "And that line made you think that this harmonica player was the world's greatest comedian—'Don't slam the door'? Jack, if I were you, I wouldn't go around telling people that Larry Adler said that line. It might not be his. Maybe he stole it from Borrah Minnevitch!" I could have worked on Jack for another few minutes, but by this time he was rolling on the floor laughing.

It's been a well-known fact in show business that I could always make Jack Benny laugh. And it was always silly little things that would do it—things that nobody else would laugh at. During all the years I knew Jack I never told him an out-and-out joke, because that would be the last thing he'd laugh at. He made his living writing comedy, so if you told him a joke, first he'd analyze it, then he'd start to rewrite it.

Now, here's something I did at a party one night and it made Jack hysterical. You're not going to believe this, and I don't blame you because I still don't believe it either. It started while we were both standing at the bar having a drink. We were wearing dinner clothes, and I noticed that there was a little piece of white thread stuck on the lapel of Jack's coat. I said, "Jack, that piece of thread you're wearing on your lapel tonight looks very smart. Do you mind if I borrow it?" Then I took the piece of thread from his lapel and put it on my lapel.

That was it—that was the whole thing. I'm not sure, but I think that during my life in show business I must have thought of a funnier bit—I certainly hope so. But that bit of business took Jack apart. He laughed, he pounded the bar, he kept pounding the bar, and finally he collapsed on the floor, laughing. I must admit I always loved every moment

140

of it. Being able to send this great comedian into spasms of hysterical laughter was good for my ego.

Anyway, the next day I got a little box, put a piece of white thread in it, and sent it over to Jack's house with a note that said, "Jack, thanks for letting me wear this last night."

An hour later I got a phone call from Mary. She said, "George, that piece of white thread got here an hour ago and Jack is still on the floor. When he stops laughing I think I'll leave him!"

You know, over the years I'm surprised that Jack never got mad at me. When I think back, I really did some awful things. One night Norman Krasna gave a party, and before dinner there were about thirty or forty of us standing around having cocktails and hors d'oeuvres. The room was buzzing with the usual small talk, and I happened to glance across the room and noticed that Jack was taking a cigarette and a match out of a box on the mantelpiece. I held up my hands, and in a loud voice called out, "Quiet, everybody!" A hush fell over the room, and every eye turned to me. "Ladies and gentlemen," I said, "Jack Benny is now going to do his famous match bit!" Every eye now turned to Jack. There he stood, with a cigarette in one hand, a match in the other, and a bewildered expression on his face. He didn't know what to do; he just stood there squirming uncomfortably. After a few seconds he put the cigarette in his mouth and lit it. I said, "Jack, that's much better—I notice you've got a new finish!" Well, that did it. The cigarette flew out of his mouth; he almost fell into the fireplace and couldn't stop laughing.

There are many other awful things I did to Jack, but he loved them. He enjoyed them so much it became one of the big routines in his nightclub act. He'd stand up there and spend ten minutes telling the people what a miserable man I was. I think if I had been nice, I would never have been his best friend.

Once I was playing the Majestic Theater in Chicago, and

141

at the same time Jack was playing the Orpheum Theater in Milwaukee. His show closed on a Saturday night, so he decided to come to Chicago and spend Sunday with me. He sent a wire which read: AM ARRIVING CHICAGO 10:30 SUNDAY MORNING. MEET ME AT THE RAILROAD STATION.

I wired back: LOOKING FORWARD TO SEEING YOU. WHAT TIME ARE YOU ARRIVING I'D LIKE TO MEET YOU.

Jack wired me: AM ARRIVING SUNDAY MORNING AT 10:30.

I sent off another wire saying: IF YOU DON'T WANT TO TELL ME WHAT TIME YOU'RE COMING IN, I'LL SEE YOU AT THE HOTEL.

When I got Jack's next wire I knew he was getting a little irritated. It read: STOP FOOLING AROUND. I'M ARRIVING 10:30 SUNDAY MORNING. MEET ME AT THE STATION.

My next wire was: HOW COULD I MEET YOU, DIDN'T GET YOUR LAST WIRE.

Well, the next thing I knew I was deluged with telegrams from all over the country. Every one of them said JACK BENNY IS ARRIVING 10:30 SUNDAY MORNING, MEET HIM AT THE STATION. Jack had obviously gotten in touch with all of our friends and told them to send me these wires. I got telegrams from Sophie Tucker, Blossom Seeley, Benny Fields, Jay C. Flippen, Harry Richman, Al Jolson, Belle Baker, Eddie Cantor, George Jessel, Jesse Block, Eve Sully—I must have received about twenty-five wires. I pinned them all over the wall in my hotel room, and when Jack arrived, naturally I didn't meet him. He walked into my room about eleven o'clock and said, "George, why didn't you meet me?"

Very innocently I said, "I didn't know what time you were coming in."

Well, Jack looked at me, he looked at the wires, and then he fell on the bed laughing.

But there was one time when I saw Jack mad—and boy, was he mad. He had just finished playing nine holes of golf, and he came into the grill room and sat down at my table. I made the mistake of being nice, and said, "How's Mary?"

142

This seemed to set him off, and he practically shouted at me, "Don't ever mention Mary's name to me again!"

I said, "What happened?"

Angrily he said, "And don't ever mention Irving Fein's name again!"

"I didn't mention Irving Fein's name."

"Well, don't!"

"I won't."

"Good!"

"Well, what happened, Jack?"

He said, "Treating me like some kid just getting started in show business!"

"Jack," I said, "what did they do, those two people whose names I'm not supposed to mention?"

He didn't even hear me. "I've got half a notion to divorce Mary and fire Irving Fein," he muttered.

I said, "Jack, you've been married to Mary for thirty-eight years, and Irving Fein has been your manager for twenty-six years. Now, what is this horrible thing they both did?"

He said, "They insisted I sign an exclusive contract with NBC for three years! Who needs it? Why should I be tied up with one network for three years?"

I got the feeling there was more to this than just signing the contract, so I took a stab in the dark and said, "Jack, how was your golf game today?"

Slapping the table for emphasis, he said, "I played the worst game of golf I ever played in my life!"

Nothing further was said, but a few days later Jack came waltzing into the grill room like a ballerina.

I said, "Jack you look very happy, you must have shot a good game of golf."

He beamed all over. "I was fabulous. I had a forty-one for nine holes. It's the best golf I've played in years."

"You must be in a good mood," I said. "How do you feel about that three-year contract that Mary and Irving made you sign?"

"It's a marvelous contract! I'm lucky to have two won-

143

derful people like Mary and Irving Fein looking out for me!" And he practically pirouetted out of the grill room. It's a good thing he didn't divorce Mary before he had that hot round of golf.

Before we were both married, Jack and I used to eat together almost every night. Now, eating with Jack was an experience I'll never forget. He never liked what he ordered, he only liked what you ordered. One night we were sitting in a restaurant, and he ordered a steak and I ordered roast beef. When our food came he looked at my roast beef and his mouth started to water. He said, "George, would you like a piece of my steak?"

I said, "No, then you'll want a piece of my roast beef."

Don't ask me why, but that struck him funny and he laughed so hard he fell off his chair twice.

The next night we were in the same restaurant and Jack said, "George, your roast beef looked so delicious last night I'm going to order it."

I said, "Good," and I ordered steak.

When our food came, he took a look at my steak and his mouth started to water. He said, "George, would you like a piece of my roast beef?"

I said, "No, because then you'll want a piece of my steak."

This time he only fell off the chair once because he'd heard that joke before.

Then the following night he ordered chicken and I had pot roast. He looked at my pot roast and his mouth started to water.

I said, "Hold it, you like pot roast?"

He said, "I love it," so I gave him my pot roast and took his chicken. He looked at my chicken and his mouth started to water. I got up and went to the men's room. It was making me nervous getting laughs with that kind of material. When I came back Jack wasn't there. I asked the waiter, "Did Mr. Benny leave?"

The waiter pointed and said, "No, he's right there under the table."

Now, you may think I'm exaggerating when I talk about Jack falling on the floor so often—but it's true. He'd collapse with laughter and literally fall on the floor. I don't know what his cleaning bill was, but it must have been tremendous.

I'm going to close this chapter with an anecdote about Jack Benny that you may have heard before, but I think it bears repeating. One day he went to his lawyer's office in Beverly Hills to sign a multi-million-dollar contract. I knew that it was a very big deal, so when Jack came into the club that afternoon I said to him, "Jack, you must be very excited."

"I certainly am," he said, "Do you know after I signed the contract I stopped at a little drugstore downstairs and, George, I finally found a place that serves a good cup of coffee!"

That was Jack Benny, my dearest and closest friend. And wherever Jack is I hope the coffee is good.

Live, Love and Enjoy It

When it comes to romance I'm at a very awkward age. If I go out with girls younger than me, I'm criticized. If I go out with girls older than me, I can't get them out of the rest home. But I look at it this way, I'd much rather be criticized than run around with some old kid that gets stoned on Lydia Pinkham cocktails.

My advice to any man my age is to go out with young girls—and my advice to any woman my age is to go out with young boys. But believe me, the important thing is that you go out. Don't just sit there watching game shows on television. However, if you enjoy watching television, at least do it with a young girl on your lap—that's for men. If you're a woman, have a young boy on your lap. Another thing, I think it's a good idea for couples like this to double-date. Then, about ten o'clock, when the old man and old woman get tired, the two kids can go out and enjoy themselves. Now, that's the creed I've lived by all my life, so you can see how mixed up I am.

But, on a more serious note, I should think that mothers would be tickled to death to have their daughters go out with me. After all, they meet interesting people, I take them to nice restaurants, we go to the theater . . . that's certainly better than riding around on the rear end of a motorcycle. Let's face it, I'm a very nice man to go out with. The only thing I expect from a girl is for her to light my cigar.

Now, it may come as a surprise to some people, but a lot

of these young girls I date would like to marry me. And why not? I've got a nice home in Beverly Hills with a swimming pool, two marvelous people working for me who keep the place looking like new, excellent food—all the comforts that any girl could wish for. Of course, I realize they don't want to marry me because I'm a sex symbol—I'm more of a security blanket.

It's a funny thing, but if I were their age, they wouldn't want to marry me at all. It's true, kids nowadays don't even think of getting married. If a boy and girl like each other, they live together. They have a couple of kids, the kids grow up, and if they like the looks of the kids, then they get married. And if it doesn't work out, they can always get a divorce, start living together, and be happy again.

I suppose you're all aware that nowadays anything goes. Everything is out in the open. Well, a perfect example is nudity. You go to the beaches and both men and women are sunbathing with nothing on. You can go to the theater and see a show where the entire cast is naked. And in the movies it's not uncommon to see men and women get into bed together naked. I guess that's all right for some people, but not for me. I even catch cold if I leave my house without wearing spats.

Wherever you go these days if it isn't complete nudity, it's the next thing to it. I flew in from New York recently and I had a script with me that I wanted to study on the flight. I figured those four and a half hours would be a perfect time to concentrate on learning my lines. However, I didn't even get the script open before I glanced up, and sitting opposite me was a young beautiful girl wearing a see-thru blouse. On me it was wasted. I've reached the point now where I forget what I'm supposed to look for.

That see-thru blouse made me very nervous. When I looked at it I sort of got the feeling it was looking back at me. In fact, over Albuquerque, I'm not sure but I think one of them winked at me. I not only didn't study my script, but when we landed I had trouble fastening my seat belt.

It's getting so that nothing shocks you anymore. But I remember a time when people were easily shocked. And the most shocking place of all was the burlesque theater. To be seen going in there was a disgrace. I used to go to the Olympic on 14th Street in New York City, and when I went in I'd hide my face and sit in the last row so nobody would see me. And it was quite a hassle, everybody was trying to sit in the last row. When the lights went up during intermission everybody always buried his head in a newspaper.

The big attraction then was a dancer who billed herself as "Gilda Goulay, the Girl with the American Beauty Rose." By today's standards her act was nothing, but we thought it was very wicked. It started with a loud drumroll, the houselights would go out, and a magenta spotlight would hit the stage. Then Gilda would make her entrance, and to the beat of the music she'd sensuously walk from one side of the stage to the other. She wore a black silk evening gown that clung to her body like it was painted on her. There was a slit up the front of the dress, and at the top of the slit she wore a big American Beauty rose. As Gilda paraded around, she did a series of little discreet bumps, and with each bump a single petal would fall off the rose. She had it timed so that when there was one lone petal left she made her exit. And that was her whole act. The audience went wild; they wanted her to drop that last petal. But Gilda wouldn't do that, she had too much class. She'd never stand in front of an audience with a naked stem. If any of you don't believe this story, you can check it with anybody—there was an Olympic theater on 14th Street. And if you want further proof, right across the street was Cornblatt's delicatessen store. Gilda used to eat there.

During that same era when Gilda was bumping her petals off, the average woman wore hobble skirts. These were long skirts that got very tight around the top of the shoe, and they had a slit on the side. When a woman would step up onto a streetcar, the slit would open and sometimes you could see five or six inches of her ankle. That was exciting. I

149

was twenty-two years old before I knew a woman's leg went higher than her ankle.

The favorite pastime for men in those days was to stand in front of the cigar store and watch women get onto street cars. And there was always some fresh, smartaleck wiseguy who'd whistle and holler, "Oh, you kid!" I hate myself for doing it now, but in looking back I realize that although I was only standing in front of a cigar store, I was trying to be a comedian even then. "Oh, you kid!" wasn't my only nifty remark. I had a snappy saying for every occasion. Like when I'd be dancing with a girl I'd say to her, "Honey, you're the bee's knees!" And if that didn't work, I'd hit her with my biggie, "Kid, you're the cat's pajamas!" That never missed.

Some of the other guys would use things like "23 Skiddoo!" "Ishkabibble!" or "Beat it!"—but not me. I left those corny ones for the amateurs. I had good stuff like "Make a noise like a hoop and roll away!"; "Lace up your shoe, your tongue is out!"; "Under the sink with the rest of the pipes!"; and "Turn over, your buckwheats are burning!" With comedy material like that, is it any wonder that I didn't have time for sex?

I know that today I have the reputation for being a sex kitten, but believe it or not, when I was seventeen or eighteen making out with girls didn't interest me. All I wanted to do was sing and dance and tell jokes. I was a great Peabody dancer (the Peabody came long before the Charleston and was tougher to do), and if I had a choice between two girls, one whom I knew I could make it with and the other I could enter a Peabody contest with and win a loving cup, the loving cup would win every time. I'd rather be on my toes than on my back. In those days I didn't bother with girls. The only thing I wanted to get into was show business.

There was one time when I got a crush on a little girl named Elsie McGrath. She was twelve years old, and I was thirteen—you see, I liked younger girls even then. Anyway, we used to go rollerskating in Hamilton Fish Park on

Sheriff Street, and I knew she was crazy about me because she used to let me hold her skate key.

Now, along about that time I read an article in the paper saying that the world's greatest tenor, Enrico Caruso, ate six cloves of garlic every day because he claimed it strengthened his vocal cords. Well, I loved to sing even then. I started when I was seven, and I always wanted to be a great singer, so I figured if six cloves of garlic was good enough for Caruso, it was good enough for me. I started eating six cloves of garlic a day, and believe me, this didn't help my popularity in the neighborhood. One day I played hooky from school and my mother got a thank-you note from my teacher.

I came from a big family, seven sisters and five brothers, and during my garlic period whenever I'd come into the house I'd get a standing ovation—they all not only got up but they left the room. But it did help my sleeping. I shared a small bed with my brother Sammy and my brother Willy. The minute I'd get into bed they'd go out the window and sleep on the fire escape and I had the whole bed to myself.

But my mother was smart. She knew how to take advantage of my pungent personality. Whenever a bill collector came to the door she'd have me answer it. I'd open the door and say, "What do you want?", and the guy would reel back, gasp, "Forget it!", and run down the hall.

However, it certainly did not help my romance with Elsie McGrath. Whenever I took her home I had to walk either in front of her or in back of her, depending on which way the wind was blowing. One afternoon when we reached her house she ran up to the top of her stoop, where I stopped her. "Elsie," I said, "this is the fourth time I've brought you home. Don't you think you should invite me in to meet your mother?"

Quickly she said, "You wait right there, George, and when I get upstairs I'll have my mother say hello to you from the window." And with that she bounded inside. In a couple of minutes the window opened and her mother

151

looked out. I hollered up, "Hello, Mrs. McGrath!" and she slammed the window—and they lived on the fifth floor.

It finally got to the point where Elsie wouldn't walk on the same street with me, so I had to make a decision. It was either her skate key or singing like Caruso—and she had a very cute skate key. Just think, if it weren't for her cute skate key I might be singing at the Met and using Caruso's dressing room.

Years later, when Elsie was just a memory, I was still plugging along trying to make it in show business. I couldn't get a job and time was passing by. There I was, seventeen years old, but I wasn't ready to quit. I had some pretty goofy ideas in those days. I figured if I looked like an actor, somehow I'd get to be an actor. And boy, did I look like an actor. I borrowed some money from my brother-in-law and bought myself an outfit. It was a powder-blue suit with a white chalk-stripe, and the coat had five buttons down the front. With this I wore a double-breasted, pearl-gray vest with spats to match, and a high, starched collar with a snap-on polka-dot bow tie. And I topped it all off with a wide-brimmed straw hat that had a black string attached to my lapel. Also, I always had one cigar sticking out of my handkerchief pocket. I couldn't afford to smoke it, but I thought it made me look prosperous. That entire outfit cost me $12 not counting the cigar, which cost 7¢. When I put it on, it changed my whole personality. I even walked differently. I sort of bounced when I walked so that people would know I was a dancer, too. And I always had a self-satisfied grin on my face. I thought I looked absolutely marvelous and it seemed everybody else thought so, too, because people kept staring at me.

And since I was looking like an actor I had to act like one. Now, at that time Hammerstein's Theater on 42nd Street and Broadway was the most outstanding vaudeville theater in the world. All the actors used to congregate in front of it. I reasoned if I mingled with this crowd, some agent or producer might notice me and give me a job. I had all kinds of classy theatrical poses which I thought would attract their attention. Sometimes I would only button the top button of my five-button coat so I could flare back the bottom and put one hand in my pants pocket with my thumb sticking out and my feet spread apart. Other times I'd flare back both sides of my coat and put both hands in my pants pocket with my thumbs sticking out. Then again I might hook both thumbs in my vest pocket, or hold on to both lapels, or I might even lean casually against the building with my legs crossed and gracefully hold my unlit cigar in my hand. I didn't do that one too often because I didn't want the cigar to unravel.

Anyway, producers passed, agents passed, and they always looked at me but they never offered me a job. But that didn't bother me; I felt that being out of work was part of show business.

Show business even influenced the type of girl I went out with. If I took a girl on a date, she had to be a great ballroom dancer, and wear rouge and lipstick and beaded eyelashes. That was my idea of what an actress should look like. And if she wore a beauty mark, I'd even let her stand with me in front of Hammerstein's.

With me being out of work, I suppose you're wondering how I could afford to take a girl out on a date. Well, you must remember that taking a girl out then was a lot different than it is today. In the first place, the girl didn't even expect you to take her to dinner. You'd just say, "Meet me at eight o'clock in front of Webster Hall." There was always a dance at Webster Hall, and the admission was 25¢ for women and 35¢ for men. Then, after dancing for about two hours, the two of you would have a root beer—that was another 10¢. After the dance you'd spend a dime taking the subway to Chinatown where you'd split a bowl of chow mein for 40¢, and leave a 10¢ tip for the waiter. Then you'd take the subway, which was another dime. The entire evening would cost you $1.40, and the girl let you kiss her goodnight because you'd been such a big sport.

A night on the town for $1.40—nowadays it costs you more than that just to park your car. The other night I had a date with a girl and we had dinner at a nice restaurant, went to see a show, had a couple of drinks after the show, and it cost me $82. And when she drove me home she wouldn't let me kiss her goodnight. She didn't want me to smear her makeup because after she left me she had a late date with somebody else.

Women today are very independent. All you hear about is Women's Liberation and the role they want to assume in modern society. They want to do the same work men do and get paid the same money for doing it. And I'm all for it. Last week I went out with a pretty young girl, and she was a plumber. It cost me another $82 and she couldn't do a damned thing for my pipes.

One of the big issues in Women's Lib is that they want to get out of the kitchen. My mother never would have gone along with this. There were twelve kids in my family, and my mother's idea of liberation was to get into the kitchen. She'd do anything to get out of that bedroom.

Now, just because there were twelve kids in my family didn't mean that my father was a great lover. It meant that we were very poor. We couldn't afford any coal or wood, and in the wintertime it was freezing in our house. When you get into bed and you're that cold, anybody can be a great lover. If we had lived in California, I might have been an only child.

Well, I don't know if this chapter has done anything to help your love life, but if it's given you a few laughs, I'm satisfied. But one last thought—no matter what age you are, live, love, and enjoy it!

To Write a Book You Need a Sharp Pencil

Since you've read this far into the book, I assume you must be very interested—or one of my relatives. Either way I'm going to tell you how this whole thing happened. One morning I was sitting in my office at General Service Studio with my writer, Elon Packard, and my secretary, Jack Langdon. We were in the middle of writing a silly letter to an old vaudeville friend of mine, Jesse Block, when the door burst open and in came Irving Fein, who by now was my personal manager. He was all excited and said, "George, I've got marvelous news! I just got a firm offer for you to write a book for Putnam's. What do you think of that?"

I said, "Not now, Irving, I'm in the middle of writing a letter to Jesse Block."

"But, George—" Irving stammered.

I said, "Please, Irving, this is important."

Well, a very deflated Irving Fein sat down on the couch while we finished that cockamamie letter. Then, very deliberately, I fixed myself a cup of tea, lit a cigar, crossed my legs and, turning to Irving, said in my most studied and casual delivery, "Now, Irving, what is it you wanted to talk about?"

"Two can play at this game, George," Irving said, and he deliberately got up and fixed himself a cup of tea.

Well, we finally got down to business, and Irving repeated what he'd said before about Putnam's wanting me to write a book.

I said, "Well, Irving, they came to the right guy. If I can

155

write a letter to Jesse Block, I can certainly knock out a book."

Irving put down his cup of tea and said, "Okay, George, we've both had our little fun this morning, now let's get serious. What do you think of the idea?"

I said, "Irving, I think it's a sensational idea and I'll definitely do it—but first let me think about it."

Well, that did it for Irving. He got up from the couch and headed for the door. I had to grab him by the arm to keep him from leaving. "Irving, I'm sorry," I said. "Of course I'll do it." He then told me the details, the next day I signed the contract, and that's how the deal was made.

I had written a book before back in 1955. It was called *I Love Her, That's Why!*, and I did it in collaboration with a writer named Cynthia Hobard Lindsay. She was a charming young lady and a top-notch writer. We used to meet at my house on weekends and I'd talk to her while she made notes. Then, during the week, she'd put it together. Cynthia did a very fine job, and it turned out to be a good book.

However, this time I wanted to be more personally involved with the actual writing, which I have been from the very first page. Now, I'm not the kind of a guy who can sit down at a typewriter or get a pad and pencil and start writing a book. In the first place, I never got any applause for my spelling. I spell "cat" with a capital *k* and two *t*'s. So I decided the only logical thing to do was to write the book the same way I put my comedy routines together. And that's the way it's being written. Every morning I come into my office and meet with Elon Packard, whom we call Packy, and Jack Langdon, whom we call Jack Langdon—we couldn't think of anything else to call him.

Now let me tell you how the three of us work together. Each one of us has his own particular function, and I think I'll start with me. Why not, it's my book. To begin with, in the true sense of the word I am not a writer. But I do have a good comedy mind; I think funny and I say things funny.

When Gracie and I first started to move up in show business we made eight two-reel shorts for Warner Bros. and Paramount. Each film ran nine or ten minutes, and I put them together all alone without any writers. The success of these films did a lot for our careers.

Later on, when we got into radio and television, we were able to hire writers, but I always worked right along with them. I seemed to have an instinct for what would make people laugh.

One of the most important things for a performer to learn is timing. The same thing applies to writing a comedy sketch, or a nightclub routine, or an after-dinner speech, or even to writing this book. The writing should have a rhythm to it so the reader feels he is actually listening to the words. Now that I've explained what I do, I'd appreciate it if one of you readers would write in and explain it to me.

Now let me get to the other two guys in the room. Packy has been with me for twelve years. When he was eighteen he started writing in radio for Milton Berle, and since then he has written for most of the top comics in the business. For the past eight years Packy has been with me exclusively, but only for two hours a day. When twelve o'clock comes he's on his own, and he frequently writes for his long-time friend George Gobel, and any other assignments that come up. Packy is a very funny writer, and I personally like him because he's able to phrase words in a way that fit my mouth. My only problem was breaking him of the habit of writing words with more than two syllables, because I have a very small mouth.

Anyway, Packy has a lot of free time, and if any of you readers have to make a speech at an Elk's Club, or a bar mitzvah, or even if you want to say something funny to your wife, get in touch with Packy. He can be found most afternoons at the bar of the Tail o' the Cock on Ventura Boulevard. He does some of his funniest writing on bar napkins.

Now to Jack Langdon. He's been with me for sixteen

157

years, and his is a full-time job. He runs my office, he makes sure all my bills are paid, he handles my correspondence, he coordinates all my activities—but his most important job, what you might consider his chief duty, is to make sure I don't make a date with two girls on the same night. He's a pretty shrewd kid. He's arranged things so it would be absolutely impossible for me to get rid of him. He's figured out a filing system of all my comedy routines, monologues, and songs, which is so damned complicated that when he puts something away he's the only one who knows where it is. I don't think even the CIA could break his code. If Jack ever leaves me, I'm back to being a straight man again.

Now, in the room when we're writing, Jack sits at the typewriter and he's sort of our balance wheel. Sometimes Packy and I will get hold of a funny idea and we'll work on it, kick it around, play with it and develop it until it becomes a funny little routine—and we always make sure the wording is just the way we want it. Then we're ready to tell it to Jack—and we do. But Jack isn't always ready to write it down. He just sits there stubbornly staring at the typewriter. Well, after a moment I lean toward Packy and say, "Packy, I get a feeling that Jack doesn't think our routine is funny."

Packy looks at me and says, "Why don't we ask him?"

"Well," I say, "do you want to ask him, or should I?"

Packy answers, "You better ask him. You're sitting closer to him."

"All right, I'll ask him." I turn to Jack and say, "Jack, why don't you think our routine is funny?"

Jack looks right at me and says, "All right, you and Packy have your fun, but all you do is sit there and write one joke after another. When you're writing a book you have to paint a word picture. Who are these people? How are they dressed? Where did they come from—where are they going? Are they happy—are they sad?"

Letting what he just said sink in, and being a reasonable man, I say, "Jack, I happen to think that little routine Packy and I just finished is terribly funny, and I don't want to clutter it up with where the people have been or where they're going."

His voice rising, Jack sputters, "But, George, it's important for the readers to know these things!"

Then in a very quiet voice I say, "Jack, you've made a good point, and I respect your opinion. And you certainly have the right to express yourself. But before you go any further, just stop and think—who is it that signs your paycheck every Friday?"

After a split-second pause, Jack says, "Fellows, I was wrong. I think it's a very, very funny routine. Now tell it to me again so I can write it down." By now Packy and I have forgotten the routine, and Jack has won again—I told you he was a shrewd kid.

If people knew some of the things that go on in this office, they'd back up a wagon and take us away. A while back I came into the office and said, "Jack, will you do me a favor? I'm running low on jockey shorts, can you pick me up a dozen pair?"

Jack said, "Sure, what kind do you wear?"

So I took down my pants and showed him. Well, Jack took a look and said, "Why don't you get the same kind that I wear?"

"What kind do you wear?" I said, and Jack took down his pants. There we stood, two full-grown men with our pants down, comparing jockey shorts. Well, just at that moment the door opened and in walked Packy. He took one look at us and said, "I suppose you fellows want to be alone," and walked out. Jack pulled up his pants, ran out, and brought Packy back, and we went to work on the book. It was kind of a hot day so I just sat there in my jockey shorts.

But I don't want you to get the idea that things like that happen every day—they don't. They happen four times a day. Naturally, we have our differences and our arguments, but when the air clears we always manage to get it down on paper. Packy and Jack don't even think of me as the boss.

That's because I'm the easiest person in the world to get along with—as long as they agree with me.

Well, now that I've explained our little group I suppose you're wondering how we ever get anything done. I don't know either, but somehow we do.

Now, right here I'd like to clear up something. Lots of people have the idea that all of these anecdotes and stories I tell are a bunch of lies. I resent that. I don't deny it, but I resent it. What I'm trying to say is that everything you'll read in this book actually happened. Oh, when we work on a story we might bend it a little, give it a new beginning, make the end a little funnier—but the middle is always—or maybe it's the beginning—or sometimes it's the end—but at least part of every story is based on truth! And I'm not sure of that, either.

It's Easy To Ad-lib If You've Got It Written Down

I guess by now you've got the idea that I'm in love with show business. I don't know what line of business you're in—whether you're a banker, a druggist, a used car dealer, or run a taco stand—but whatever you do, my advice would be to quit right now and get into show business. The reason I make this suggestion is that it worked for me, and for a very long time. Of course, maybe you're not cut out for show business; maybe you can't sing, or dance, or act, or be funny, but don't let that worry you—I made it.

What I'm trying to say is, whatever line of work you get into, or whatever you do, make sure it's something you love, something you enjoy doing. To my way of thinking, if you can accomplish this, you're bound to be successful. And I'm talking from experience. I fell in love with show business when I was seven years old, and for years and years and years things were very tough for me and I got very few jobs. But that didn't stop me, I'd much rather be a flop in show business than a success making felt hats. It's a damned good thing I didn't go into felt hats because they're not wearing them anymore.

To give you an idea of how much being in the theater meant to me, even when I was very young and laying off I never let anybody know it. I used to ride up and down in the elevator of the Putnam Building where all the agents had offices. I'd have makeup on the top of my collar, my music under one arm and my pictures under the other. If an agent

161

saw me, I wanted him to know I was ready. One day, after riding up and down six or seven times, the elevator boy said to me, "I know you're an actor, but do you play anyplace besides this elevator?"

In those days I'd do anything to further my feeble career. Here's an example: When I was about nineteen I knew an actor named Willie Delight, who had two thousand cards printed which read, *Willie Delight, Songs, Dances & Syncopated Patter.* Well, after he'd used about eighty of the cards he decided to go into some other business. I couldn't pass up an opportunity like that, so I bought 1,920 cards for $2, and changed my name to Willie Delight. After I used up all the cards I went back to my old name—Harry Pierce. That was a lucky name for me—I once got a job to play a Sunday concert in Ronkonkoma with it.

But through the years show business has been good to me, and it's given me a very exciting life. It's not just the spotlight, the music, the laughter, the applause, the fame, the— Not true! It *is* the spotlight, the music, the laughter, the applause, and the fame. But besides all that you meet some of the most interesting people in the world. Now, most of these people work behind the scenes. There are producers, agents, directors, stagehands, choreographers, theater managers—but there's one breed of characters that stands out from all the rest: comedy writers. Believe me I know, because as I said I've worked closely with comedy writers for the last forty-five years. I always tried to hire the best because I know how important the words are when you face an audience.

To be a good comedy writer you should have a basic intelligence, a good sense of humor, a flare for phrasing, a feeling for current comedy trends, and an understanding of human nature. Now, all comedy writers may not have every one of these qualities, but there is one characteristic that is an absolute must—they've got to be on the nutty side. By that I don't mean that they're candidates for the booby hatch, but they all have little peculiarities and idiosyncracies that the average person doesn't have. I can say this because I'm a little on the nutty side myself.

I couldn't possibly tell you about all the writers who worked for me over the years. My memory isn't what it used to be, there's a paper shortage, and I don't want to be late for my bridge game, so I'll just mention a few incidents to give you an idea of what I'm talking about.

As long as I've already mentioned Packy, I'll start with him. Back when he first started writing, he thought he should get himself some sort of identity, so he got a bright idea and decided to wear nothing but red socks. He figured if a producer couldn't remember his name, he'd say, "Why don't we hire that kid who wears red socks?" So that's all Packy ever wore. No matter what kind of an outfit he had on, or what color it was, he always wore his red socks. However, it backfired on him. He was up for a job one time and he was turned down. Later he found out the reason why—the producer had said, "I'd never hire that kid, he never changes his socks." Personally I'm glad he still wears red socks, because sometimes I can't remember his name.

Back in the early days of radio there was a writer named Harry Conn, who not only worked for me, but also worked for Jack Benny. He was with me about four or five months, but he did certain things that I couldn't take. He went on to work exclusively with Jack and did a great job because he was a fine writer—but he was not for me. One of the things I couldn't take was his colossal ego. He'd come in with three of four pages of jokes, then he'd tear off one joke and give it to me to read. After I read it he'd tear off another joke and give that to me. Well, the first time he did this, I said to him, "Harry, what is it with this tearing bit? Why don't you just give me the four pages and let me read them?"

He said, "George, I want my jokes to be appreciated. I write them one at a time, and I want you to read them one at a time. It's like fine wine—you don't gulp it down, you sip it." After he hit me with that last line I had the feeling that Harry Conn was soon going to be drinking alone.

163

Anyway, the way we worked there were three of us in the room. Besides Harry Conn and myself there was Carroll Carroll, a writer who was hired by the J. Walter Thompson Agency. But this setup didn't agree with Harry because he thought he could do everything by himself. One day while Carroll was out of the room, and after Harry had torn off two pages of jokes, he said, "George, I can't work with another writer in the room. Either you get rid of Carroll or you get rid of me."

Well, I just sat there with my hands full of this funny confetti he had just handed me. "Harry," I said, "I happen to think Carroll Carroll is a fine writer, but that's beside the point. Carroll Carroll is paid by J. Walter Thompson—I am paid by J. Walter Thompson—you are paid by me. So I can't fire Carroll Carroll. In fact, I think Carroll Carroll might be able to fire me. So, Harry, why don't you take a walk around the block, think about it and cool off. And if you still want me to fire Carroll Carroll, just keep walking."

Harry left, slamming the door behind him. Ten minutes later he was back, tore off another joke, and we all went back to work again.

Now let me tell you what ended our relationship. This particular morning he came in, tore off his first joke, and gave it to me.

I read it, tore it up, and said, "I don't like it."

He was indignant. "What do you mean you don't like it?"

I said, "It's not funny. Your fine wine has fermented."

"George," Harry snapped back, "if you don't like that joke, you know nothing about comedy. If you lock me in a room with George S. Kaufman and Moss Hart, I guarantee you I'll write funnier stuff than they do!"

I said, "I'm sorry to hear that, Harry. George S. Kaufman and Moss Hart are very expensive writers. Now, if your stuff is better than theirs, you might as well leave because you deserve a lot more money than I can afford to pay." With that I opened the door and said, "Good-bye, Harry!"

So Harry left. After he was gone I glued the pieces of that

164

joke together, and Gracie and I did it on the air. It didn't get a laugh. Harry was wrong, I do know something about comedy.

Another writer who worked with me during that same period was John P. Medbury. To me, Medbury never looked like a writer. Come to think of it, none of my writers ever looked like writers. In fact, I don't know what a writer is supposed to look like, but they can certainly look better than they do. I think I look more like a writer than my writers did. I wear expensive clothes, I always have a silk scarf tied around my neck, I always carry a couple of ballpoint pens along with a little notebook pad, and when I come to the office I always wear my suede jacket with the leather patches on the elbows. But there's one problem—I can't write.

Anyway, Medbury was about 5'5" or 5'6", and must have weighed 250 pounds. He was not only a writer, but he was a big eater. And he looked more like an eater than a writer. But even though he was one of the best writers I ever had, he never laughed at anything, not even his own stuff. He never changed his stone-faced expression. It wasn't that he didn't have a marvelous sense of humor, it was just that he knew practically every joke that was ever written. So if you tried to tell him a joke, before you got the first line out of your mouth he'd tell you the punch line.

Even when he wasn't working at it he always had a quick dry wit, and he was never stuck for an answer. I remember one time standing with him on the corner of Hollywood Boulevard and Vine Street, and a strange man came up to him and asked, "Can I get to Sunset Boulevard this way?"

Without batting an eye, Medbury answered, "Yes, but only this once!" That was about twenty-five years ago and I'll bet that man is still standing there trying to figure out what Medbury meant.

At that time Medbury had an office in the Hollywood Plaza Hotel and was writing two syndicated humor columns for the newspapers. One was called "Mr. & Mrs." and the other was called "Mutter and Mumble." He hired a young fellow named Frank Williams to work for him. Frank was an ambitious young fellow trying to get started as a writer.

Now, right here I think I should explain that from time to time Medbury would entertain certain young ladies in his office. Well, one day Mrs. Medbury happened to drop in, and while looking for a stamp she opened the top drawer of Medbury's desk, and there was a pair of black lace panties. Gingerly holding them up, she looked at Medbury and said coldly, "John, what are these doing here?"

Again, without batting an eye Medbury angrily called into the other office, "Frank, get in here!"

The bewildered young writer walked in, and Medbury threw the panties at him, saying, "Give these back to your girl. You're fired!"

On her way out, Mrs. Medbury stopped at Frank's desk and said, "Frank, you're not fired. And tell lover-boy it didn't work. He's not as fast as he used to be."

Now, earlier in this chapter I stated that comedy writers are a little on the nutty side. And if this next story doesn't prove my point, nothing will. When this incident took place I was in radio and Medbury was my head writer. By now he had his offices on Gower Street, right next to Columbia Pictures, and every year I had to go there to negotiate a new contract with him. And it wasn't easy.

His outer office was a comfortable room with several chairs, a couch, and a well-stocked bar. Behind the bar were a number of shelves filled with all sorts of canned exotic foods. He had things like rattlesnake meat, chocolate-coated bumblebees, and fried grasshoppers. I remember one year at contract time I walked into his office, and after he fixed me a drink he said, "George, I just made myself a kangaroo sandwich and it's really delicious. Would you like one?"

I said, "No thanks, John, it would ruin my appetite. For dinner Gracie's fixing me some sautéed antelope ears."

Well, now it was time to talk business, so we took our

166

drinks and went into the other office where Medbury did his writing. In there was a large desk with a swivel chair behind it, and on the desk were four containers full of sharpened pencils. Medbury wrote everything in longhand. Over in one corner of the room was a table with four chairs.

Now get a good grip on the book. Seated in one of the chairs was a life-sized dummy of an American Indian in full regalia. This didn't shock me because it happened every year. The Indian was part of a little game Medbury played whenever he would sign a contract. I never did figure out whether Medbury was serious or not, but I played right along with him because I had to. He was my top writer and I didn't want to lose him.

Here's the way it went: We sat down at the table with the Indian, and Medbury said, "George, you remember the Chief."

"Of course," I said. Then, turning to the Chief, "Nice seeing you again, Chief. I notice you got a new headdress."

Medbury said, "That's not new, that's the same one he had last year."

I said, "Oh, I'm sorry, Chief, it looked new to me." Then I tried to get down to business. "John, it's contract time again. How about signing for next season?"

Medbury took a sip of his drink, then said, "George, we'll do it the same way we did it last year. You know I don't make a move unless the Chief okays it. So you better explain the deal to him."

I took a swallow of my drink and said, "Chief, it's very simple. You know, John has been with me for four years now, and every year I give him a hundred-dollar raise . . . and I'd like to do the same thing this year. It's been a very good relationship, and you okayed it last year, and I'm sure you will again."

"George," Medbury said, "you're coming on a little strong. Don't put words in the Chief's mouth. Give him time to think this out himself."

So we just sat there. After I finished my drink I said,

"John, the Chief's been thinking now for about ten minutes. When is he going to come up with an answer?"

Getting up from the table, Medbury said softly, "George, the Chief's in one of his quiet moods. You better leave now before you louse up the deal."

I whispered back, "Well, when can I expect his decision?"

Medbury said, "I'll talk it over with him and call you in the morning."

With that the meeting was over and I tiptoed out. The last thing I wanted was an Apache mad at me. As soon as I left there I got into my car and drove straight home to see Gracie. I wanted to talk to somebody who made a little sense. But the next morning Medbury called up and said, "George, the Chief slept on it and he's okayed the deal," and he hung up.

At that time Gracie and I were in the Top Ten of all the shows on radio, and here we were at the mercy of a stuffed Indian!

One thing I learned in my long association with comedy writers is that they come from all walks of life. I knew one writer who started out as a taxi driver; another was a tailor; then there was a policeman and a carpenter; I even hired one who was a cutter of ladies' dresses. One night some friends brought a young priest over for dinner. He was a very funny fellow and had us screaming all night long. After dinner I said to him, "Father, you've got a terrific sense of humor. Now, I don't know if you're allowed to do it or not, but we could certainly use a writer like you on our television show. In your spare time would you like to work for us?"

He gave me a benevolent smile and said, "That's a very flattering offer, George, but I don't think I could get away with moonlighting—I've got a very sharp Boss."

But there was one writer I discovered accidentally. He started out working for his father as a jewelry salesman. Gracie and I were playing Shea's theater in Buffalo, and one day before the matinee a young man came into my dressing room. He was a tall, gangling fellow with big feet and stooped shoulders. He said his name was Al Boasberg and asked if I would like to buy some jewelry. He opened his sample case, and as I was looking at the jewelry he started telling me jokes he'd written. And they were darned funny. After I heard a few I closed the case and said to him, "Did you really write this stuff yourself?"

He said, "Yeah."

"Well, then, you're in the wrong business," I said. "You ought to be a writer."

With that we started talking, and in the course of the conversation I got an idea. I knew a very old joke that I was crazy about. I had always wanted to use it in our act, but I couldn't figure out a way to switch it to make it sound new. I thought this would be a good chance to test this kid and see if he could really write. So I said to Boasberg, "See if you can switch this joke," and I told it to him.

I had no sooner gotten it out of my mouth than another comedy team, Harris & Pilsner, came into my dressing room. Well, I wanted to make Al Boasberg feel good, so I introduced him as a bright new comedy writer. Harris' face lit up, and he said to Boasberg, "Boy, can we use you! There's a hole right in the middle of our act where we need one good joke. If you can come up with one we can use, I'll give you fifty bucks for it."

What do you think Al Boasberg did? Without even looking at me he told Harris & Pilsner that same old joke that I had just told him. Well, they loved it, bought it, gave him $50, and left the dressing room on cloud nine.

I just sat there staring at Boasberg. "Kid," I said, "you've got a big future as a writer. You've not only got a great sense of humor, but you already learned how to steal!"

Boasberg grinned at me and put the $50 in his pocket.

I continued, "Now, Boasberg, I'd like to get serious with you. I've been in this business for a long time, and, kid, that's not the way to start. If you want to really succeed, one—you have to be original; two—you have to be honest; and three—you owe me twenty-five dollars!"

Anyway, three weeks later I brought Al Boasberg to New York and he went on to become one of the top comedy writers in the business. Besides Gracie and myself he worked for Jack Benny, Buster Keaton, the Marx Brothers, and many others. Now, as far as writing went, Boasey wouldn't sit down at a typewriter and put together a script. But if somebody else wrote the script, you'd give it to Boasey and he'd punch it up for you. He was sort of a doctor of comedy, and he was great at it. His lines always made the script funnier.

Boasey looked at the funny side of everything, and he loved practical jokes. I remember right after he got married, he was living here in California, but he'd never met his wife's folks. Well, her parents planned a trip out here to meet their new son-in-law, and the day they arrived Boasey's wife asked him to meet them at the airport while she prepared a nice meal for them. This started the wheels turning in Boasey's head. At that time Boasey was driving a big, black Cadillac, and on the way to the airport he stopped off at Western Costume Company and rented a chauffeur's outfit. When he got to the airport and met his wife's parents he was a picture of the perfect high-class chauffeur. He put their luggage into the trunk, helped them into the back seat, made sure they were comfortable, etc. They were very much impressed.

While driving home the mother said to Boasey, "I really didn't expect a chauffeur-driven car. My daughter's husband must be doing very well."

Playing it straight, Boasey said, "Oh, yes, he's probably the best comedy writer in Hollywood."

"Well, I've never met him," the mother continued. "What kind of a man is he?"

Boasberg answered, "He's probably the finest man I ever met in my entire life." Then, "Maybe I shouldn't say this, but it's a shame what his wife is doing to him behind his back!"

170

In a shocked voice, the mother gasped, "What on earth is she doing to him?"

"Well, for one thing she started sleeping with me even before she got married," Boasberg stated.

The rest of the trip was in absolute silence. When Boasey pulled the car into the driveway, his wife came out the front door to greet them, and as the stunned parents looked on, he grabbed her in his arms, spun her around, patted her fanny, and gave her a great big kiss. Then he said, "Honey, your folks are here."

As soon as his wife saw the chauffeur's uniform she knew he was up to one of his practical jokes. She patiently explained to her confused parents that Boasey was her husband, and after everything was straightened out they all had a good laugh—that is, everybody except the mother. She never did really warm up to Boasberg.

Although Boasey was a master of the practical joke, there was a time when one of them backfired. One of his best friends was another writer named Andy Douglas. One day Boasey went to visit Andy and when he arrived at the house he found a bicycle on the front porch. Well, Boasey couldn't pass that up. He took off his pants, opened the front door, and rode the bicycle into the living room in his shorts. There were about twelve people sitting there, and Boasey kept circling around the room on the bicycle. When he noticed that nobody was laughing, he stopped circling and said, "What's wrong with you people? You act like somebody died."

Andy said, "Somebody did—my mother. She's in the next room." Boasey peddled out the front door, and I don't think he pulled another practical joke for about two days.

The writers I've spoken about up to this point worked for me in vaudeville and radio. Later on, when I became involved in television, I remember hiring a team of very good writers named Seaman Jacobs and F-F-F-Fred F-F-F-Fox. The reason I wrote it that way is that Freddie stuttered. I don't mind telling a few stories about Freddie's stuttering be-

171

cause he never stops making jokes about it himself. On the other hand, his partner, Seaman Jacobs, whom we always call Si, is a very articulate, well-spoken man. What didn't make any sense was when they came into a meeting Freddie did all the talking and Si just sat there.

Now, when we used to put a script together the first step was for Freddie and Si to come in with a story line and read it to me. If I liked it, then it would be developed further into a complete script. A story line could sometimes be as long as five or six pages, and who do you think read it to me—F-F-Freddie. And the way Freddie told a story line, it took a l-l-l-long time. When Freddie started reading a story line I'd never stop him, because it took him an hour to get s-s-s-started. But it was worth it; they were always good and the scripts turned out funny.

Once when I was alone with Si I asked him, "Si, you could read that story line in one-tenth the time it takes Freddie. Why do you have him do it?"

Si said, "George, the way Freddie talks he needs all the practice he can get."

Well, I couldn't argue with that, so every Monday morning Freddie would come in and read the story line. One morning he was going along as usual when he came to a scene that he got very enthused about. In his excitement he read through the entire scene without once stuttering. When he was finished I said, "Freddie, do you realize that you just read three pages without stuttering?"

Freddie's eyes widened, and he jumped up, shouting, "My God, I'm c-c-c-cured!"

During this time there was another writer working for me, and the other fellows found out he was part Polish. Well, naturally they made him the butt of all those Polish jokes that were going around. He put up with it for a while, then one day he said to Freddie, "I wish the guys would stop hitting me with those lousy Polish jokes."

Freddie said, "Well, it's your own f-f-f-fault. You shouldn't have told them you were p-p-p-part Polish. Just like I shouldn't have t-t-t-told them I st-st-st-stutter."

172

The season was going along smoothly, and then one day Freddie had to go to the doctor. So on that Monday morning Si came in and read the story line. What usually took Freddie two hours took Si ten minutes. Well, I was so used to hearing Freddie's delivery that the whole thing fell flat. I said, "Si, I don't like this story line. You guys better come up with another one."

The next morning they came back and Freddie took two hours to read me that same story line, and I loved it. Si just shook his head and said, "George, that does it. If I want to stay in this business, I better learn how to st-st-st-stutter."

Now, before I lock up this section on Si and Freddie, I must tell you one quick little line that Freddie hit me with once. As he left the office he said, "G-G-G-George, if you have a p-p-p-problem with the script, just c-c-c-call my house. If nobody answers, th-th-th-that's me."

Anyway, Seaman and Freddie are still together, and I'm sure they'll never split up, because neither of them could ever find a nicer partner to work with.

Of all the writers I've worked with I've yet to find two with the exact same temperament. Some are easy going, some are excitable, some work fast, some work slow, some work alone, some need a partner, and some work best just kicking jokes around in a room with other writers.

At one time my writers would bring in four or five pages each morning, and each writer would take his turn reading his own material. This created a problem for me to decide what was funny or not. You see, some writers had a great delivery and made everything sound funny, while others were more introverted and just mumbled their words. I found myself being sold on stuff that wasn't funny and not using stuff that was. However, I finally solved the problem; I let my secretary, Jack Langdon, read everybody's material. That way everybody got a fair shake because Jack had no delivery at all.

Let me quickly give you an idea of how bad Jack's delivery was. When I did the television series "Wendy and Me"

173

with Connie Stevens, I'd have Jack read Connie's part when I auditioned other actors. His readings were so awful that I almost got rid of Connie and hired another actress. (I hope that last anecdote gets into the book, because Jack is typing this stuff.)

You know, when you're working with four or five writers sitting in a room things do not always go smoothly. There was one time when one of my writers who was very high-strung came up with a joke that I didn't think was funny. He jumped up and started to argue with me. He said, "I know it's funny! I told it at a party last night and had the people screaming!"

I said, "After three martinis it might be funny, but in this room it isn't."

Well, the veins in the guy's neck popped out, his face turned red, and he started pounding my desk, hollering, "George, I've been a comedy writer all my life, and I know this is a very funny joke, and it's going to get a tremendous laugh!"

By now he was screaming right in my face. I smiled sweetly and said, "You're cute when you get mad."

He stormed out of the office, and that took care of the writing for that day. The next morning when he came in, before he had a chance to say anything I said, "You're right. I thought the joke over; it's a funny joke and I'm going to use it."

He jumped up again and his face turned red. "Don't! I told that joke last night in a bar and it didn't get a snicker! It only proves that you know nothing about humor!"

I told you things don't always go smoothly.

The next writer I'm going to tell you about is not easy to describe. But before I try, let me say this about him; his name is Norman Paul and he's one hell of a writer. There's not a comedy series on the air that wouldn't like to hire him. He's not only a good joke writer, but he has a marvel-ous story mind and is a fine constructionist. You know, sometimes when you're writing a script you'll be right in the middle of it and find yourself up a blind alley with nowhere to go. Well, whenever we found ourselves in that kind of a spot we'd struggle with it for a while, and finally I'd say, "Fellows, let's break it up. We'll try again in the morning."

I never gave it another thought and had a good night's sleep, because I knew that in the morning Norman would have the solution—and he never disappointed me. His mind was always on the script, whether he was sitting in a bar, driving his car, sitting in a bar, relaxing at home, sitting in a bar, eating at a pizzeria, or maybe even sitting in a bar— he never stopped thinking.

Now that I've said all these nice things about Norman, let me try to describe him. He's really a very good looking man, but he does his best to disguise it. If Norman stood up, he'd be about six feet tall, but he always walks around in sort of a half crouch. He looks like he's taking a bow and nobody's applauding.

About Norman's clothes. He never wears a necktie, and his suit looks like he just sent it out to have it wrinkled. He wears his pants a little below his stomach, so they hang down and appear to be about five inches too long for him. This is good because they cover up his socks, which never match. His shoes are so scuffed up they look like he had somebody break them in for him at a lumber camp. I don't know where Norman buys his clothes, but the guy who sells them to him must have a hell of a sense of humor.

One thing Norman is proud of is his full head of wavy hair. It's beautiful. However, when you look at the overall picture his hair looks like it should be on somebody else's head. Now, in describing Norman Paul I admit that I did exaggerate a little bit. In all fairness I'd like to say that he came in one day and his socks did match.

Norman always drives a car that looks exactly like he does. The reason is that Norman's mind is so absorbed in his work he can't be bothered with trifles. When he buys a

175

car he never has it serviced. He puts in gasoline, but he never checks the tires, changes the oil, or puts in water. He just drives it until it stops running and then he buys a new one. The back seat of his car always looks like a mobile disaster area. It's cluttered with old scripts, newspapers, magazines, discarded clothing, a half-eaten ham sandwich, anything Norman happens to throw back there.

One day he was driving down Santa Monica Boulevard and he flicked a cigarette out the window, but it blew into the back seat. Well, naturally all that debris back there caught on fire, but Norman didn't even notice it. Other drivers were honking and hollering and waving at him, but he drove for three blocks before he finally noticed his car was on fire. He was concentrating on how to finish a story line, so a fire meant nothing to him. He drove into a gas station, they put out the fire, he left the car there, and bought a new one.

When Norman worked for me I always made sure I had a full-length couch in the office. That's the only way he could write; lying on his back and looking up at the ceiling. One day I said to him, "Norman, why don't you stand up for a while, you're pressing all the wrinkles out of your suit." He never even heard me; he was figuring out how to start the next scene.

Norman was a very sensitive man, who didn't accept criticism too well. He was always quitting his job. I'd say he quit me about three times a week, sometimes three times a day. I was always able to calm him down and we'd go back to work, but on one day things got more heated than usual. I don't know what we were arguing about, but we finished up screaming at each other. Finally Norman jumped up off the couch, shouting, "I know I've quit before, but this time I mean it!" And out he walked. Well, I walked out with him. When we got to the parking lot Norman turned to me and said, "What are you doing here?"

I said, "Well, as long as you quit, I figured I'd quit, too."

Five minutes later Norman was back on the couch and we were working again.

I must have upset Norman a lot, because no matter how hard he tried he just couldn't quit me. One day after work Norman stopped off at a bar to have a drink, and while the bartender was making it Norman's foot accidentally slipped off the bar rail and he broke his ankle. That's the story that Norman told us; the bartender probably had a different version.

Anyway, the next morning Norman's wife, Kay, pushed him into the office in a wheelchair. His leg was in a cast up to his knee. We all helped get him on the couch, and then Kay left, saying she'd pick him up later in the day. Well, after we ran out of broken-leg jokes we all settled down and went to work. Within twenty minutes Norman and I were at it again; another one of our silly arguments that ended up with Norman hollering, "I can't take this anymore! I quit!"

You should have seen him try to quit. He'd forgotten he had the cast on his leg and he couldn't get off the couch. He floundered around like a beached whale. We just sat there looking at him. Finally I said, "Okay, Norman, you're not working for me anymore, so would you please lie there and be quiet. The other fellows and I have a script to get out." So we ignored him and went to work. Well, Norman couldn't stand it. In no time he was in there pitching jokes with the rest of us.

"Norman," I said, "don't you want to save those funny lines for your next job? You're not on salary anymore."

He grumbled, "Well, I can't just lie here like a dummy. When Kay comes to get me then I'll quit."

We finished out the day with no more problems. When Kay came we all helped Norman into the chair, and while she was wheeling him out I said, "Norman, you want me to write a little farewell note on your cast?"

For the first time that day Norman laughed. He said, "George, I'll see you in the morning."

Well, Norman was in that cast for six weeks, and during that time he didn't quit me once because he couldn't. The first day he walked into the office without the cast I said to him, "Norman, these past six weeks have been the most pleasant we've ever spent together. If you were any kind of a sport, you'd go back to that same bar and break your other leg."

Norman and I went on like that for years. The more we fought, the more we liked each other. He never really did quit me. When I stopped producing television shows Norman went on to other things. However, he still drops by the office every once in a while, and I'm always glad to see him. I know we haven't stopped liking each other because we still argue. And I'm sure when Norman finishes reading about himself in this book he'll throw it into the back seat of his car.

In terms of time there was one writer who was with me longer than any of the others. His name was Harvey Helm. I'd say he wrote for me about thirty-five years. He started by selling me loose jokes in vaudeville and stayed with me through radio and television right up until Gracie retired. Harvey was more than a writer, he was a personal friend. He and his wife, Ruth, and Gracie and myself used to go out socially all the time.

One time the four of us spent a week's vacation in Honolulu. Gracie and I were very big in radio then, and our sponsor was Chesterfield cigarettes. When we arrived in Honolulu naturally the press interviewed us. One of the reporters asked me what was my first impression of Honolulu. I had an answer right on the tip of my tongue. I said, "Seeing Diamond Head was very exciting. I've never seen a volcano before, but if it smokes again, I hope it smokes Chesterfields."

That line was picked up by the wire services and printed in papers all over the country. It made my sponsor very happy, and everybody thought I was a great wit for ad-libbing a

178

line like that. What I didn't tell them was that Harvey Helm gave it to me the night before.

The same thing happened in New York City when Billy Rose opened his big hit musical, *Jumbo*. For one reason or another the opening had been delayed for almost a year. When I arrived at the theater I was interviewed for radio. I said, "I'm looking forward to seeing *Jumbo*, and I only hope it stays open as long as it stayed closed."

I had scored again. I got so I could ad-lib without looking at the paper that Harvey wrote it on.

When it came to writing, Harvey had a wild, wild imagination. His jokes were perfect for Gracie's character, and the words he put in her mouth made sense, but only to Gracie. I doubt if any writer ever worked the way Harvey did. He'd sit for hours at a typewriter, a cigarette dangling from his lips, and thumb through a copy of *Popular Mechanics* magazine. The magazine was full of pictures, and that's where Harvey got his inspirations for those mad jokes he'd write. Let me give you a few samples of what Harvey came up with. Now, you may have heard some of these jokes, but when Harvey wrote them they were new:

A picture of a plastic swimming pool inspired this one:

GRACIE: My sister Hazel just put a new swimming pool in her backyard. Yesterday we had a marvelous time swimming and diving. And tomorrow we'll even have more fun when they put water in it.

When he saw a picture of a glassblower he came up with this:

GRACIE: My brother Willy got into trouble on account of his new job. He's a glassblower, and yesterday he got the hiccups and blew himself into a bottle.

Then he saw a picture of a saxophone:

GRACIE: My brother's taking a correspondence course on how to play the saxophone and he's going to be very good at it. Every night he blows his lesson into an envelope and mails it to the teacher.

179

This one came from an ad for an iron grill door:

GRACIE: My uncle Harry just got out of jail because he's a
great artist. He painted a picture of an open window on the wall of his cell, and when the guard
came in to close the window, uncle Harry
walked out the door.

Antique salt and pepper shakers:

GRACIE: The reason I put the salt in the pepper shaker,
and the pepper in the salt shaker is that people
are always getting them mixed up. Now when
they get mixed up they'll be right.

Well, that was Harvey Helm's mind at work!

But Harvey didn't get all of his inspirations out of *Popular Mechanics*. A lot of it came out of a bottle. I can honestly say that Harvey used to drink a little. Well, as long as I'm
going to be honest, Harvey didn't drink a little—he drank a
lot. Most of the time he held his liquor very well. When he
first came to work for me I didn't know whether he was
drinking or not. There's an old line that describes Harvey in
those days: "I never knew he drank until one day he
showed up sober."

Having Harvey work for you was a very nerve-racking experience. But in the long run it was worth it. He'd go along
okay for a while, and then he'd go off the deep end and dis-
appear for a couple of weeks, and then into a sanatorium to
dry out. He'd be fine for a few months, then the same thing
would happen again. One time in New York after one of his
escapades, Harvey showed up at my hotel room in bad
shape. I called Dr. Leo Schoenfeld, who was not only a well-
known society doctor, but a close personal friend of mine. I
asked him if he would come over and pick up Harvey and
check him into Bellevue Hospital in order to get him so-
bered up. Dr. Schoenfeld didn't want any part of it, but as a
favor to me he finally agreed. He called the hospital and arranged for Harvey to be admitted. A half hour later he had
Harvey in a taxi and they were on their way to Bellevue.

Well, Harvey wasn't ready to spend four days in Bellevue,

so he pulled himself together just long enough to put that tricky little mind of his to work. While Dr. Schoenfeld was paying off the cabdriver, Harvey rushed into the hospital and up to the admission desk. Assuming a very dignified manner, he said to the nurse in charge, "I'm Dr. Leo Schoenfeld."

The nurse said, "Oh, yes, Doctor, I got your call. Where's your patient, Harvey Helm?"

Just at that moment Dr. Schoenfeld was coming through the door, so Harvey pointed to him, saying, "That's him. I suggest you rush him right upstairs before he becomes violent."

Before Dr. Schoenfeld knew what hit him, two burly interns grabbed him and hustled him into an elevator, and he was gone. In the meantime Harvey got into a cab, and I didn't hear from him for two weeks. However, I did hear from Dr. Schoenfeld. He sent me a bill, and it was a very sizable one. But it was two years before I could get Leo to speak to me again.

A strange thing about Harvey was that he was always terribly concerned about any friend who had a drinking problem. One morning he came to work very upset. He said, "George, I had a horrible experience last night. You remember Joe Talbot?"

I said, "Sure, an actor. He worked for me a few times."

Worriedly, Harvey said, "Well, I ran into him in a bar last night, and he was so loaded he didn't know where he was. I had to carry him home, undress him, put him to bed, and call the doctor."

I had always liked Joe Talbot, so I asked, "I'm sorry to hear that, how was he when you left him?"

Harvey shook his head and said, "Not good, George. When the doctor got there he asked him if he saw anything like pink elephants, or blue mice, or purple alligators, but Joe said no. That's why I'm so worried, George. The room was full of them!" I knew right then that Harvey was getting ready for another trip.

181

This may all sound funny now, but it wasn't funny when it happened. But, in spite of all the troubles, I often wish I could have gotten my other writers to do a little drinking, because Harvey's stuff was the greatest.

My younger brother, Willy Burns, belongs in this chapter because he worked with all the writers I had over the years. Willy wasn't the kind of a writer who put a piece of paper in a typewriter and knocked out a scene, but he was great in a room where everybody would sit around and pitch funny lines. But besides contributing to the scripts, Willy also handled all my business activities. He checked all my contracts to see that they were drawn up right, he okayed all my bookings, he set up interviews with the press, and when I played Las Vegas he would go up there and make sure everything was right. To sum it up, Willy ran interference for me so I didn't have to worry about anything except writing and performing.

Willy did so many things for me that it often conflicted with his writing. There was one time when we were writing a scene that took place in a hospital. It was all about our neighbor, Harry Morton, going in for an operation. Well, in the middle of it Willy got a phone call and had to go see my lawyer in Beverly Hills. While he was gone we decided the scene in the hospital wouldn't work so we threw it out. Two hours later, when Willy got back, he was all excited. He said, "George, I've got a great finish for that scene in the hospital."

I said, "Well, I hope it works in a car wash."

Willy shrugged his shoulders and said, "I get it. You switched the scene. Instead of a hospital it's now a car wash. Well, that takes care of that great finish I thought of."

I said, "Don't feel bad, Willy, we'll try to get Harry Morton in a hospital before the season is over."

Poor Willy had another function that I'm sure he didn't enjoy. Whenever I would get mad at one of the writers I'd scream at Willy. I didn't dare scream at the writer, because he was liable to quit me, but I knew Willy understood me. When my temper flares up I holler and shout, but in a minute it's over. And when I'm hollering I have no idea what I'm talking about.

One day when things were going slow and we weren't getting anywhere I went into my hollering bit. I jumped up and started shouting at Willy, and I got so confused I ended up by yelling, "Damn it, Willy, just don't sit there wearing those same red socks again, come up with something!"

He leaned back in his chair, and with a little smile, said, "George, the only one in the room wearing red socks is Packy."

I sputtered and stammered, and finally said, "Well, put on Packy's red socks and come up with something!" Everybody laughed, and by then I was all sputtered out. In a calm voice I said, "I guess that was pretty funny. Now let's see if we can think of something that funny to put in the script."

Willy's favorite recreation was gambling. He loved to go to Las Vegas. He'd shoot craps, play blackjack, roulette, baccarat, and he had a real knack for it—he knew how to lose at every game. But I guess his greatest love was playing the horses, and he considered himself an expert at hand-icapping. With this he had a soulmate in the man on the couch, Norman Paul. When we were working and I had to leave the room to go to the bathroom, out would come the Racing Form and they'd call their bets into the bookmaker. I knew what was going on, so every morning at exactly ten thirty I went to the bathroom, ready or not. Sometimes I'd just stand there and wash my hands for ten minutes. I was afraid if they didn't get all their bets down, they wouldn't be able to concentrate on writing the next scene. When I came back from the bathroom I'd always hum a few bars so they'd know I was coming and have time to hang up the phone and put the Racing Form away.

When four guys are sitting in a room trying to write comedy, the toughest part is to get started. Once you get a hook on the scene everybody begins to talk at once, and the jokes come so fast there isn't time to write them down. Well, one morning we were sitting there and nothing happened. There was complete silence; we just couldn't seem to get rolling. After about an hour of looking at one another, I said, "Fellows, we've got a script to finish. Now if somebody doesn't get funny pretty soon, I'm not going to the bathroom at ten thirty." That did the trick. At ten thirty I was back in the bathroom as usual washing my hands again.

Willy was with me practically from the time I started doing well in show business. I must tell you one cute story that happened when I was working with Gracie, but before we were married. At that time I was already in love with Gracie, but she was in love with Benny Ryan. Well, we were playing in Cleveland, and Gracie had a small two-room suite in the hotel and I was living with Willy. One night after the show Gracie insisted she was going to cook dinner for us. Now, a cook Gracie wasn't, but she decided to fix a big platter of spaghetti and tomato sauce. I happen to know that when you make tomato sauce you put in two or three of those little white peppers, and you put them in whole to give the sauce a tang. Gracie didn't know that. She put in about ten peppers and sliced them open, which released all that heat.

She had made an occasion of it because this was the first time she'd ever cooked dinner for us. There were two little candles burning on the table, flowers, a bottle of red wine, soft music—she'd gone all out. Well, Willy and I had a couple of drinks, and finally Gracie announced that dinner was ready. We sat down at the table, and in she came with this big platter of spaghetti covered with tomato sauce. Can I tell you something? The sauce on that spaghetti was so strong that it could have come in by itself.

Gracie served both of us a heaping plateful and then went back to the kitchen for the salad. Willy and I both took a mouthful and then turned and looked at each other. Willy's ears had turned a bright red, and I could feel the fillings

184

melting out of my teeth. After Willy finally got his breath back, he gasped, "George, this sauce is so hot I can't eat it! I'm going to go! You make some excuse to Gracie."

I said, "Willy, you can't walk out."

Barely able to whisper, Willy said, "Oh, yes I can. You're the one who can't walk out. If you don't eat that spaghetti, she'll marry Benny Ryan."

I whispered back, "And if you don't eat that spaghetti, you'll be looking for another job."

At that point in came Gracie with the salad and sat down at the table. Willy and I started on our salads, carefully avoiding the spaghetti. Gracie took a big mouthful of spaghetti, and both Willy and I stopped and stared at her, waiting for her reaction. It wasn't long in coming. She sat there unable to speak. Finally, smiling bravely through the tears streaming down her cheeks, she managed to say, "This tastes terrible—I didn't put enough peppers in the sauce. Let's go to a Chinese restaurant and have dinner."

Willy picked up his glass of wine and said, "I'll drink to that," and off we went.

That happened a long time ago. Willy passed away in 1966, and I miss him very much. And just in case you're interested, before that television season was over we did do the scene where Harry Morton went into the hospital for an operation—and we used Willy's finish.

Memoirs of a Warmed-Over Casanova

It's amazing to me how many people seem to be interested in my love life. I've been giving a lot of interviews lately, and the first question they ask is usually, "Is it true that you only go out with young girls?" Well, I'd like to clear that point up once and for all—it is not true. Sometimes I go out with a girl who's twenty or twenty-one. But I guess Warren Beatty, Robert Redford, Jack Nicholson, Paul Newman, and Burt Reynolds all get asked the same question. It's just something us sex symbols have to learn to live with.

I promised the publisher of this book that I'd hold nothing back, so I'm going to let my hair down. I not only can let my hair down, I can walk away and leave it there. But to me a promise is a promise, so here are the facts. In my long and checkered career I've loved many women. There was Clara Bow, Nita Naldi, Vilma Banky, Dorothy Gish and her kid sister Lillian, Pola Negri, Valeska Surratt, Helen Hayes, and Garbo. I loved them all! I never met them, but I loved them! So at last it's out in the open. Now I hope the press will stop hounding me.

But in all seriousness, the only real love in my life was Gracie, and I was happily married to her for thirty-eight years. After she was gone it took a long time before I even thought about going out with anybody else. And when I did start dating it was never with a thought of serious involvement. I had a wonderful marriage, and I don't intend to get married again.

187

Going out with a girl now and then is enjoyable—someone to have dinner with, to take to the theater, to watch television with, someone to talk to and— Now, there's a reason why I prefer going out with young girls to older women. If I decide to spend an evening at home watching television with a girl my age (and there are very few girls my age left), I don't think it's very interesting for her. I love to watch old movies, and chances are she's already seen it before, so she'd be bored. On the other hand, with a young girl all the old movies are brand new, so if I happen to doze off, she can still enjoy herself.

Before any of you readers get the wrong idea about me, I'd better clear something up. I do not chase after girls, and I do not try to pick up any girls. You'll never find me cruising down Sunset Boulevard with the top down; I do not hang out in bars offering to buy drinks; and I certainly don't put ads in the *Free Press* enumerating my charms. I'm just like the grandfather of the boy next door.

What I'm trying to say is the girls I go out with are girls I've met through friends, or girls I've worked with. For instance, some time ago I did a television show in New York. It was a musical show, and one of the dancers in the show was a charming little girl named Debbie Phillips. Well, during the four days of rehearsal we got to know each other, and before I left I told her if she happened to get to California to be sure and give me a call. I didn't think any more about it until a month later my phone rang and there she was. I asked her if she'd like to go out to dinner that night and she said yes. You see, you don't have to cruise down Sunset Boulevard with your top down to get a date.

Anyway, Debbie and I went out that night and we had a marvelous time. For the next six months we saw a lot of each other. She was very attractive, she had a good sense of humor, and she always woke me up when the movie was over.

Then one day I got a phone call from her and she was all excited. She told me she was going back East to get married to the fellow she used to go with. She thanked me for all the good times we'd had together, I wished her the best of luck with her marriage, and that was the end of it. Of course, I did miss Debbie, I missed her very much. It's no fun sleeping through an old movie and having nobody to wake you up. Then I finally bought an alarm clock and I didn't miss her anymore.

Now, that should be the end of that story, right? Well, you don't know my sincere but misguided friend, George Pallay. You may remember him earlier in the book—he's the fellow who told everybody the young girls he went out with were his nieces. Well, Pallay is a perennial romanticist. I'd say that he falls madly in love at least once a month, and twice on Fridays. And every time one of these romances is over he goes to pieces. He can't eat, he can't sleep, his whole world comes to an end. He can't find a building tall enough to jump off. When he goes through one of these experiences he refers to it as "carrying a torch," which I think is a very quaint phrase for a seventy-five-year-old man.

Anyway, the same week that Debbie left I was booked to do a television show in Toronto. At that time Pallay was in Miami, but somehow he got the news that Debbie and I had split up. He assumed that my splitup would affect me the same way that his always affected him, so he caught the first plane to Toronto to save me from killing myself.

Meanwhile, during my television rehearsals I met a bouncy little French-Canadian girl, Yvonne, who was the assistant to the producer, and we were having lunch up in my suite. We finished lunch and she went into the bathroom to freshen up, and right about then Pallay came bursting into the room. He rushed over to me, put his arm around my shoulder, and said, "George, I just got the news about your breakup with Debbie. I know how you feel so I'm going to stay right here with you all week."

We hadn't even said hello yet, but he kept rambling on. "I've been through all this myself, and there's only one way

189

you're going to get over it. You've got to forget Debbie and look around for somebody else! And believe me, George, you'll meet another girl in no time!"

Just then Yvonne walked out of the bathroom. I said, "Pallay, is that fast enough?"

Pallay just stood there staring at Yvonne with his mouth open. I introduced him to her, and she went back to work. After she left, Pallay said, "I really admire you, George, pretending that you're interested in that little French girl. It takes a lot of courage to put up such a great front when I know you feel terrible on the inside!"

"You're right, Pallay," I said. "I shouldn't have had that cucumber salad for lunch."

A smile came across his face. He shook his head and said, "George, I don't know how you do it. Standing there with a broken heart and you can still make jokes."

Even though he was sincere, I was starting to get a little sick to my stomach. I said, "Look, Pallay, I've got to do a television show in an hour. Now, if everything goes well and the audience likes me, you and Yvonne and I will all go out to dinner. But if it's a bad audience and I don't get any laughs, I want you to find the tallest building in Toronto and you and I will go up to the top, we'll hold hands, and we'll jump off together."

Well, it turned out to be a good audience, and Pallay, Yvonne, and I had dinner that night. And during the week Yvonne introduced him to her sister. It's the first time Pallay ever had a French niece.

Being an eligible bachelor in Beverly Hills made me very much in demand. Whenever there was a party and one of my friends had to be out of town, it wasn't unusual for him to call me and ask if I'd mind taking his wife. Well, this was fine with me because I like parties. I'd not only take his wife, but I'd take my music with me in case there was a piano player there. Whenever I took Danny Kaye's wife,

Sylvia, to a party, I didn't have to bring my music because she knew how to play in my key.

One time the Irving Lazars took over the upstairs room at the Bistro for a private dinner dance. The day of the party Mary Lazar called me and asked if I would pick up Cyd Charisse because Tony Martin was playing Las Vegas. It turned out to be a wonderful evening because Cyd is great to dance with. Once when we were out on the floor dancing, the band went into "La Vie en Rose." Well, that's one of my big numbers, so I sang it into Cyd's ear. When I finished the first chorus, I whispered, "Cyd, you've made movies with Fred Astaire, who's a great dancer, and you're married to Tony Martin, who's a great singer—it must be very exciting for you to be on a dance floor with a combination of both." She started laughing so hard we couldn't even finish the dance! I must be a great comedian—I get laughs even when I'm serious.

One of the first times I took a friend's wife to a party was when Jean Negulesco's wife, Dusty, called me and asked me to be her escort. Jean was in Spain at that time directing a picture, so I told Dusty I'd be glad to. This was before I had much practice taking out married women, so at the end of the evening the "eligible bachelor" almost made an idiot of himself.

Anyway, we had a lot of fun at the party, and at one o'clock I drove Dusty home. I pulled my car into her driveway, and she said, "George, would you like to come in for a martini?"

I said, "Dusty, it's one o'clock in the morning!"

She looked at me with sort of a puzzled expression. "Is there some Beverly Hills law that says you can't drink a martini at one o'clock in the morning?"

"No," I answered, "but at this hour a martini seems so—so intimate."

Dusty laughed and said, "Oh, George, stop acting like Andy Hardy. I know it's wicked, but nobody will ever know

191

that you and I had a martini at one o'clock in the morning. My help is off—my husband's in Spain—and I'm sure my cocker spaniel will keep his mouth shut." So I went in, we had a martini, I said goodnight, and went home. But the next day it was all over Beverly Hills. Do you know that cocker spaniel blew the whistle on us!

Rosalind Russell is one of the first ladies of film. She has a great sense of humor, she's very witty and always a delight to be with. I'm glad her husband, Freddie Brisson, is out of town so much because I really enjoy taking Roz out. One morning after taking her to one of these parties, Freddie called me on the phone. "George," he said, "I just flew in from New York, and I want to thank you for taking Roz out last night. She's still talking about what a terrific dancer you are."

"It's easy to be a terrific dancer, Freddie," I said, "all you have to do is hold the girl very close with your right hand and she's got to follow you."

He said, "George, who are you kidding? I've seen you dance, and the reason you hold them close is you're a very sexy dancer."

"Freddie," I said, "I don't want you to tell this to Roz, but being sexy had nothing to do with it. The reason I hold them close is at my age I've got to hang on to something!"

That's what I told Freddie Brisson, but when he reads this he'll find out he was absolutely right—I *am* a very sexy dancer.

There was one dinner party I went to alone, and at dinner I found myself seated between Pamela Mason and Zsa Zsa Gabor. Everybody was telling jokes and anecdotes, and it was a very gay table. I didn't know Zsa Zsa too well then, so I directed most of my stories to her because she got to laughing so hard she started to hiccup. Well, after three or four minutes she still couldn't get rid of them.

"Vy don't von of you dahlings frighten me so I can get rid of my hiccups," she gasped in between them.

Well, I wanted to be helpful, so I took her hand and put it under the table on the napkin in my lap. She pulled her hand away and jumped up indignantly. "Mr. Burns, you're a very naughty man!" Then she thought a moment and smiled down at me. "But I forgive you, dahling, you cured my hiccups!"

That surprised me. I never thought a napkin would shock Zsa Zsa.

Relating these party incidents reminds me of something that happened while I was still married to Gracie. She had gone up to San Francisco to visit her sister Hazel, so I went by myself to a party we were invited to in Sherman Oaks. Sophie Tucker was there, and she was alone, too, so at the end of the evening she asked me to drive her home. Well, I'd known Sophie practically all my life, so on the way home I thought I'd be funny and get a little laugh. Driving along Mulholland Drive, I pulled the car over to a secluded spot and turned off the engine. "Sophie," I said, "we're out of gas—let's neck."

She just looked at me, and without cracking a smile, she said, "George, we're both out of gas, let's go."

I said, "Sophie, you're not laughing, didn't you think that was funny?"

"Of course," she answered, "what I said was very funny, and thanks for the straight line."

Well, we both laughed and I drove her home. But I never pulled that gag again. I hate to be topped twice in the same evening.

Now, aside from acting as an escort for his friends' wives, the eligible bachelor has to think of himself once in a while. For the last two years I've been sharing myself with two charming young ladies, Lita Baron and Joanna Baer. They're both very pretty, and they fit in beautifully no matter where you take them.

I met Lita Baron at a party given by Mr. and Mrs. Harry Jameson. The Jamesons are famous for their lavish formal parties, and they always serve squab for dinner. That eve-

193

ning I happened to be sitting next to Lita, but we hadn't been introduced, so I thought I'd break the ice. I looked over at her and said, "Miss Baron, I couldn't help admiring your squab."

She gave me a look, then she laughed and said, "Yours is cute, too."

Now I doubt if that's the way the Duke of Windsor introduced himself to Wally Simpson, but it worked for me, and Lita and I have been sharing our squab ever since. I always enjoy going out with Lita because she enjoys me. Everything I say makes her laugh, and it's good for my ego. When I'm around her I think I'm one of the great comedians. And when I use those same lines on somebody else I think I'm back in Altoona again.

Lita is a very social person; she knows everybody in Hollywood and remembers all their names. This is great for me because I can't remember my own name. Whenever we'd be sitting in a restaurant and somebody we knew would start over to our table, she'd whisper their name in my ear so I wouldn't be embarrassed. Her always leaning close to me like that gave people the idea that we were very lovey-dovey. One time it even landed us on the front page of a newspaper. There was a picture of us having dinner at Chasen's, and the caption underneath said, "It must be serious between Lita Baron and George Burns. As usual Lita is whispering sweet nothings into George's ear!" Actually she wasn't whispering sweet nothings at all. She was saying, "George, that man coming towards you is your brother Willy."

When I first started dating Lita I was amazed at the size of her wardrobe. Every time we went out she wore a different gown. I don't ever remember her wearing the same dress twice, and they were all beautiful. She always looked so dressed up that I felt I had to get dressed up, too. Well, if there's anything I hate it's getting dressed up. I like to look as good as I can, but I'm much more comfortable when I'm dressed casual. In fact, I prefer going to restaurants where I don't even have to wear a tie. Can you imagine us walking into a place with Lita in one of those gorgeous outfits and me in an open sport shirt? People would think she was taking her gardener out to dinner.

This went on for months. Every time we went out I wore a dark suit and tie, and it makes me nervous to wear a dark suit and a dark tie. I always get the feeling there are eight guys in back of me waiting for me to lie down.

Anyway, one night we were going out to dinner, so I went over to her house to pick her up. Naturally I was wearing my Utter-McKinley outfit. But when Lita opened the door I got a real surprise. There she stood, wearing blue jeans, a pullover sweater, loafers, and her hair tied back with a little ribbon. She looked absolutely darling, but I'd never seen her that way before. I said, "Lita, did you forget we were going out to dinner tonight?"

Hesitantly she said, "George . . . I don't know how to tell you this . . . but I'm getting tired of getting all dressed up every time you take me out. I know how you always love to get dressed up, but just once couldn't we be casual?"

I couldn't believe my ears. "Lita," I said, "as long as you feel that way, from now on we'll always dress casual. And I'm going to do something I've never done for any other girl—even though it's my favorite, I'll never wear this black suit again."

She put her arms around me and gave me a kiss. "George," she said, "you're so considerate." I was kind of sorry she didn't have the hiccups.

Anyway, we stopped by my house, I got into some comfortable clothes, and we went to a quiet little restaurant called Dominick's and had a wonderful evening.

Now let me tell you about the girl who shared the other half of me during that time. I met Joanna Baer over the telephone. She was working for Michael Viner, the man who produced my concert at the Shubert Theater in Los Angeles, and for weeks I knew her only as a voice. Well, I'm not stupid, I figured there must be a body to go with that voice, so I invited her to lunch. And I was right, there was a body—and what a body—tall, dark-haired, beautiful, voluptuous, and she had a driver's license. That's important. I won't go out with a girl unless she can drive me.

Now, Lita and Joanna had something in common; Lita was married to Rory Calhoun, and Joanna was married to Max Baer, Jr., and both husbands were very tall, handsome, virile men. It was only natural that after their divorces the girls went for me; I'm not tall, I'm not handsome, and I'm certainly not virile, but who wants to take out a girl who has no imagination?

I never met a girl who was interested in as many things as Joanna. She flies an airplane, she designs her own clothes, she's a great cook, she's a plumber, an electrician, a carpenter, and she built the house she's living in. She's the only girl I know who ever came to my house with a tool kit.

But there was never anything for Joanna to fix when she came over. Daniel, the man who works for me, can do everything, so everything in my house is always in perfect order. Well, this upset Joanna, because she wanted to fix my toilet to prove that she loved me. To show you what a nice man I am, the next time my plumbing broke down I told Daniel not to touch it. That night when Joanna came over I let her work on it. She was so happy to fix my toilet that she thought we were engaged. Well, I admit that's a slight exaggeration, but now that I'm an author I sometimes take a few literary liberties. But Joanna's still the prettiest plumber I've ever seen.

It was always a joy to go out with Joanna because I never had to move a muscle. Whenever we'd go out in the evening she'd always drive the car. I recall one evening we were going to a party at Jim and Henny Backus' house in Bel Air. About halfway up the hill all of a sudden the car sputtered and stopped. Well, I just sat there; I know nothing about cars. Sometimes even when I blow the horn I get my finger

196

caught in the crack. I turned to Joanna and said, "What's wrong?"

"I think your regulator's off," she answered.

Well, I couldn't pass that up! I said, "My regulator's been off for years, but why did the car stop?" She never even heard that comical line; she was already out of the car with her head under the hood.

Right about then a car pulled up, and two good-looking young fellows got out. Now, get this picture: There I was sitting in a dinner jacket, smoking a cigar, and a beautiful girl in a white, clinging evening gown was under the hood. In a cocky voice one of the fellows said, "Look, doll, when you're through fixing your grandfather's car, how'd you like to go out with us?"

Joanna raised her head and, looking right at this kid, she said, "I'm nobody's doll, and that's not my grandfather, that's my date. Now if you two clowns don't split, you're both asking for a karate chop!"

I forgot to mention, she does that, too. But while all this was going on I was a nervous wreck. I rolled up the window and caught my finger in it. And it hurt, because it was the same one I usually catch in the horn.

Now, don't get the idea from my pathetic literary liberties that Joanna is anything but a beautiful, feminine girl. And what's more, she looks absolutely marvelous on a dance floor. I enjoy dancing with her because again I do absolutely nothing. I stand there and sway to the music, then I push Joanna out, and she spins and twirls and circles the whole dance floor and eventually comes back to me. Sometimes I push her out and sit down, and when she finishes circling and comes back I get up and give her another push. I don't like to brag, but when it comes to pushing I'm in a class with Gene Kelly.

One of my more memorable evenings with Joanna started with dinner at The Luau, which is a very popular Polynesian restaurant in Beverly Hills. We started drinking an

197

Aku-Aku, which is a rum drink served in a hollowed-out coconut shell, and you sip it through a straw. It's full of shaved ice and tastes like a fruit punch, but it's very potent. I don't know why, but I was feeling good and having fun, so I drank three. In the middle of my third Aku-Aku without my knowing it my necktie had fallen into the coconut and froze there. So when I got up to go to the men's room, the coconut went with me.

Well, it turned into one of those silly evenings in which everything seems funny. After dinner Joanna drove me to my house, where she usually picked up her car and drove on home. But this time when we got to the front door and I took out my house key, it slipped out of my hand and fell into the grass. It was very dark, so the two of us got down on our hands and knees and started groping around the grass trying to find the key. What with the rum and this ridiculous situation, Joanna and I got to giggling. All of a sudden the beam of a flashlight hit us, and when we looked up there stood a Beverly Hills policeman. He looked at us for a moment, then shaking his head he said, "Mr. Burns, I've heard of people smoking grass, but I never saw anybody eating it before." That's what I like about living in Beverly Hills, we have very funny policemen.

I still see Joanna, and I still see Lita Baron. When I go out with Lita I dress casual, and when I take out Joanna I stay away from rum and I make sure my house key is on a chain.

And There Was Lisa

During the last several years I've taken out a lot of girls. I've enjoyed being with every one of them, and they always told me they enjoyed being with me. They had to—I told them I was very sensitive, and they didn't want to see an old man cry. But long before I started dating all these girls there was one girl in particular who played a very important role in my life for about three years. Her name was Lisa Miller, and I met her when she was eighteen years old. Now, don't ask me how Lisa and I got together in the first place, because I really don't know. It just seemed to happen.

I was playing an engagement at the Riviera Hotel in Las Vegas, and on the bill was a group called "The Kids Next Door." It was a group of seventeen young singers, and Lisa was one of them. They opened the show and then I'd follow them. I always came down a little early because they all wanted to make it big in show business and I enjoyed watching them work. To me they were a bunch of nice-looking kids who all looked alike until one night after the early show. I was on my way to change clothes when I heard somebody playing the piano in my dressing room. I couldn't imagine who it was, and besides they were playing "The Maple Leaf Rag," which goes back to the turn of the century. I thought maybe one of my old buddies like Teddy Roosevelt had come backstage to surprise me. I opened the door and walked in, and there was Lisa.

When she heard me come in she stopped playing and looked up a little apprehensively. "I'm sorry, Mr. Burns,"

199

she said, "I hope you don't mind my using your piano while you were onstage."

"No, I don't mind," I said, "but what I'd like to know is how a young girl like you would know the 'Maple Leaf Rag.'"

With a smile Lisa said, "My mother taught it to me, and my grandmother taught it to my mother."

I thought I'd have a little fun with the kid, so I said, "Well, maybe you could get your grandmother to teach it to me."

She came back with, "I'll try, but it will have to be in the afternoon when my grandfather isn't home. He's a very jealous man." And out she went.

I was sort of amused, but I didn't think any more of it. Then the next afternoon I decided to kill some time before the first show, so I went down to the casino to play a little blackjack. I played along for a while, then I remember I had a hand with a ten in the hole and a four showing, so I asked for another card. The dealer hit me with a nine, and I busted out. Just then I heard a voice behind me say, "Mr. Burns, when you've got fourteen and the dealer has a five showing, you should never ask for another card."

I looked over my shoulder and there stood Maple Leaf Rag. And she was right, so I said, "Look, kid, how do you know so much about blackjack?"

With a straight face she said, "My mother taught me, and my grandmother—"

Well, I wasn't going through the grandfather bit again, so I stopped her. "Hold it, kid. If you know so much about blackjack, I've got thirty dollars left. Sit down and play for me." And she did. I stood there and watched her, and this kid played blackjack better than she did "Maple Leaf Rag." Within fifteen minutes she'd won $200. I said, "You really know what you're doing, kid."

She smiled at me and said, "Mr. Burns, my name isn't kid, it's Lisa Miller."

I said, "Well, the way you play blackjack your name

200

should be Nick the Greek." I picked up the chips and offered her some. "You won two hundred dollars, so half of these are yours."

"No, no," she said, "Thanks, but it was your money and I wouldn't think of it."

Well, I thought the least I could do was invite her to dinner, so I asked her to join Charlie Reade, my road manager, and me for a late supper that night. After the show Charlie and I sat at a table in the dining room, and I began to wonder if Lisa would show up or not. Well, I'd no sooner taken a sip of my martini when I looked up and there was Lisa, coming into the room. And when Lisa comes into a room, you know she's there. She's very animated and vivacious, and there's something very alive about her. As she crossed to the table I got my first really good look at her. Lisa's a tall girl, about 5'8", with straight blond hair, large blue eyes, and a mischievous smile.

She sat down with Charlie and me and we had dinner. Afterward we sat there talking, and before I knew it it was three o'clock in the morning. That night I learned a lot about Lisa Miller. She was born in Long Beach, California, and her parents were divorced when she was a very little girl. Her mother, Imogene, had reared Lisa and her two older brothers, Graham and Philip.

Lisa was a very smart, well-educated girl. She had graduated from Long Beach Polytechnic High School, gone on to Long Beach City College, then to Pierce College and finished up at UCLA. When I heard that list of credits I felt a little intimidated. The only school I ever went to was PS 22, and I stayed in the fourth grade so long I wound up dating my teacher, Mrs. Hollander.

As we sat there talking it became apparent to me that Lisa had always been in love with show business, and her mother had encouraged her. At a very early age Lisa started taking piano lessons, singing lessons, dancing lessons, acting lessons, etc. She told me her whole childhood had been devoted to taking lessons. In fact, she remembered one time

201

when she was about six years old and she watched a little neighbor boy climbing a tree. He went up the tree, swinging from one branch to another like a squirrel, and when he came down Lisa went up to him and asked, "I never saw anything like that! Who do you take your climbing lessons from?"

By the time she was sixteen Lisa thought she knew everything there was to know about show business. And like most young people she had lots of ambitions and very little patience. She fully expected to be a superstar by the time she was seventeen—and by the time she was eighteen at least a living legend. Well, the moment of truth arrived when she learned that the Long Beach Civic Light Opera Association was auditioning for their production of *Funny Girl*. Lisa went right to work. She learned all of Fanny Brice's songs and all of her dialogue, and when she went to the audition they hired her—to play the part of a maid! During a party scene in the second act she came on with one line: "Would anyone care for some oyster dip?"

Lisa's mother came opening night to watch the "living legend," and Lisa told me that after the show her mother was waiting for her when she got home. She hit her with a line Lisa never forgot. As soon as Lisa walked in the door her mother said, "Thirteen years of lessons and you wind up passing the oyster dip!"

Well, that did it for Lisa. She retired from show business, switched her major at UCLA to economics, and decided to become a teacher. And you know, I think the kids would have loved her. She could do a split, kick the back of her head, and teach the multiplication tables to the tune of "Maple Leaf Rag."

Naturally I wondered how she got sidetracked from a teaching career and wound up with a singing group in Las Vegas. Well, here's what she told me, and if the story sounds familiar, I'm sure it must have happened to Ruby Keeler in one of those Warner Bros. musicals.

Auditions were being held for a new singing group called

The Kids Next Door, and Lisa's best friend, Cathy, was going down to try out. Lisa was helping Cathy out by playing the piano for her while she rehearsed. Well, the day of the auditions came, and Cathy was a nervous wreck. She was ready to give the whole thing up until Lisa agreed to go to the audition with her for moral support. When they got to the auditorium there were about thirty or forty kids who were being called up one at a time to audition. As it got closer to Cathy's turn she became more and more nervous. Finally she panicked, shoved her music into Lisa's hands, and ran out the door. Just then the man in charge pointed to Lisa and said, "You're next!" She went over to the man, but before she could explain about Cathy he took the music, the piano player started to play, and before Lisa knew it she was singing. That same afternoon she signed a contract with The Kids Next Door and retired from becoming a teacher.

But that's not the end of the story. Two weeks later Lisa was playing Las Vegas, and Cathy was teaching school. Wouldn't Ruby Keeler have loved that story? And Joan Blondell would have been perfect as Cathy.

Well, that three o'clock session with Lisa was the beginning. I had three more weeks at the Riviera, and during that time I saw Lisa practically every night. She was an absolute joy to be with, and we had a marvelous time together. Now, you may wonder how a man of seventy-two and a girl of eighteen could have anything in common. I can't really explain it, but there was something there that made it work. Part of it was she made me feel young. She treated me like I was one of The Kids Next Door. After a week with Lisa she almost had me convinced that I was twenty years old. I was ready to go out and buy a long-haired toupée and rent some pimples.

When the engagement ended at the Riviera, Lisa went on tour with The Kids and I went back home to Beverly Hills. After I'd been home for several days I just didn't feel right; I was restless and bored. Finally I figured out what it was; I

203

wanted to hear "The Maple Leaf Rag" again. About three weeks later I was sitting at home when the phone rang. I picked it up and a voice said, "If you're going to be home tonight, I'd like to bring over some oyster dip."

Lisa was back!

We picked up right where we left off in Las Vegas, and it was just as much fun here as it was there. It wasn't long before I realized that this little girl was filling a need that was missing at this particular time in my life. I always felt very comfortable when I was with Lisa, because there was never any problem about the difference in our ages. Now, when some older men take out a young girl they get very self-conscious; like my friend George Pallay who introduces his young dates as his nieces, or the type who takes his date to some out-of-the-way place and sits at a table in a dark corner so nobody should see them. It was never that way with Lisa and me. Whenever I took her out to dinner we always went to places where my friends were, and we didn't sit in some dark corner, we sat at a front table with the lights up.

One night at Chasen's I kiddingly said to Lisa, "I get a feeling that some of the people in this room might think you're a little too young for me."

Without batting an eye she said, "You're wrong, you're too young for me. As soon as I find an older man I'm leaving you." That didn't bother me; I knew there weren't any older men.

One night after we had been seeing each other for about two months, we were watching television together, and I said, "Lisa, you've told me so much about your family, I'd like to meet them. Why don't I have them all over here to dinner some night."

She didn't even answer me. She jumped up, made three phone calls, came back, and said, "They'll all be here Saturday."

That night I had a little trouble getting to sleep. I kept saying to myself, "What are you getting yourself into? Even

204

her mother is too young for you! All of them will probably hate you. You must be out of your mind!" I went on talking to myself like that all night. I said some pretty funny things, but I was too worried to enjoy them.

Well, Saturday night came, and so did the Miller family. When I met Lisa's mother, Imogene, I couldn't get over it. She looked and acted exactly like an older version of Lisa. She was a charming woman, and I felt right at home with her the moment I met her.

And I knew I was going to like Lisa's brother, Philip, because he brought along his guitar. She must have told him I was a singer. He was a schoolteacher, and his lovely wife, Andi, was planning to enter college to study law.

Lisa's other brother, Graham, was a former All-American football player; 6'2", 240 pounds, and all muscle. When he went to shake my hand I pulled it back; I didn't want to hurt the kid. He was working in a brokerage house, and Laurel, his very pretty wife, was a speech therapist.

Well, I said hello to everybody, and that's the last thing I said for the next three hours. When the Miller clan gets together they don't need anybody else. I was all prepared to make a good impression on the family; I had about twenty-five minutes of my real funny anecdotes worked out, but I never got a chance to use them. I sat there while they told stories, laughed, kidded each other, and had a marvelous time. This went on all through dinner. Then, afterward, they all trooped into the living room and Lisa's mother played the piano, Philip played his guitar, and the rest of the Millers sang and danced. I just sat there with a mouthful of anecdotes. I couldn't believe this family. Just before they left, Imogene started playing "The Maple Leaf Rag" and everybody else lined up and went into a time step. Then they did an off-to-Buffalo and finished with a brake. After they left I was in a daze—this wasn't a family, this was a Fanchon & Marco unit.

The next time I saw Lisa she told me her family had had a

marvelous time at my house. She said, "G.B., my family all loved you." (Oh, I forgot to tell you, she always called me G.B.) Then, with that pixie smile of hers, she added, "But they were sort of surprised, they wondered why a man who'd been in show business as long as you have didn't get up and do something."

Shortly after this I was booked to play three weeks at the Frontier Hotel in Las Vegas, so I got an idea. Lisa was a talented girl, so I put together a little routine in which we talked and danced and sang and worked it into my act. We did it in Las Vegas, and the routine was a hit. Lisa was not only good in the act, but she was great company to have around. At the risk of hurting Charlie Reade's feelings, a man gets tired of looking at his road manager twenty-four hours a day.

Well, after the Frontier we played the Palmer House in Chicago, we did two television shows with Bob Hope, one with Jackie Gleason, and another with Dean Martin. Then we went to London and appeared on *The Max Bygraves Show*. While we were in London, one day we decided to visit Westminster Abbey. When our cab pulled up front I got out one side and Lisa got out the other. Now, English money has always been hard for me to figure out, so it took me some time to pay the driver. After the cab pulled away I looked around, but there was no Lisa. I thought she must have gone in ahead of me, so I went into the Abbey to look for her. What I didn't know was that she had gone into a nearby shop to price something.

When I got inside the Abbey it was breathtaking. There was a reverent quietness about it that was overwhelming. There were a number of people there tiptoeing around looking at this impressive display of England's history, and if anyone so much as cleared his throat it reverberated from wall to wall. When my eyes became accustomed to the dim light I quietly moved around looking for Lisa. Suddenly the stillness was shattered with the loudest stage whisper I ever heard: "G.B., ARE YOU IN THERE?" I went into a state of shock as those words echoed all over the Abbey. I sneaked out as fast as I could, and when I found Lisa out front I grabbed her by the arm and started looking for a taxi.

"G.B.," she protested, "we came to see Westminster Abbey!"

"Some other time, Lisa," I muttered. About then a cab came up, and as we got in I said, "I only hope the people in there thought that G.B. stood for Great Britain."

A few months after we returned from London Lisa moved into my house. Now hold it, I know what you're thinking! I admit I was thinking the same thing, but it didn't happen that way. It all started with Lisa's mother, Imogene. She had been going with a very nice man named Lee White, and several times I had both of them to dinner at my house. Well, one day I got a phone call from Imogene asking me if she could come by the house and see me alone that afternoon, it was important. It turned out that Lee had asked her to marry him, but she didn't know what to do.

I said, "Well, Imogene, the first thing is, do you love Lee?".

"I love him very much," she answered, "but I'm worried about Lisa. If I marry Lee, I'll have to move up north to Ukiah because his business is there. I just can't stand the thought of leaving my baby all alone in that big house in Long Beach."

Well, this sort of amused me. I said, "Your baby? Imogene, your baby Lisa can not only take care of herself, she can take care of me, you, Lee, her two brothers, and their wives—and if Kissinger has a problem, she can straighten that out, too."

Imogene laughed and said, "G.B., you said exactly what I hoped you'd say. You've really taken a load off my shoulders."

Well, we had a martini and toasted her coming marriage,

which took place two weeks later. The newlyweds moved to Ukiah, and the "Baby" was left alone in that big house in Long Beach.

After that, when Lisa and I had a date and got in late, instead of taking that long drive to Long Beach she'd stay over at my place. I have a rather large home, and upstairs there's an extra suite that my children used to live in when they were growing up. When Lisa stayed over I'd have Arlette and Daniel make it ready for her. This arrangement worked out fine for everybody.

On one of the nights when she didn't stay over we had an early dinner, watched a little television, and Lisa drove home to Long Beach. Well, at two o'clock that morning my phone rang and it was Lisa. She was crying, and when I asked her what the trouble was she sobbed into the phone, "G.B., my ting-a-ling is missing!"

I wasn't quite awake, but *that* woke me up. I had no idea what a ting-a-ling was, but I was hoping it wasn't what I thought. Anyway, trying to calm her down, I said, "Look, Lisa, I'll have Daniel and Arlette look around, and if you left your ting-a-ling here, you can pick it up tomorrow."

"Oh, G.B.," she wailed, "this is serious. I left the window open and it got out!"

"Lisa," I said, "calm down. Now—what got out?"

She said, "Ting-a-Ling, my cat!"

Well, this was a pretty dull finish, but she was genuinely worried, so I said, "Just leave the window open, and I'm sure Ting-a-Ling will come back." And he did. When it comes to a crisis I always know how to handle it.

One night things came to a head. Lisa and I had been to a movie and we were sitting having a nightcap and watching Johnny Carson. After a few minutes Lisa got up and turned off the television. Looking very serious, she sat down beside me on the couch and said, "G.B., I think it's time we discussed something very important."

I said, "Well, it must be important, you just turned off an interview between Johnny Carson and Lyle Talbot."

208

Instead of a laugh all I got from her was a weary sigh, and then she continued. "Please, G.B., I really mean it. I hate being alone in that big house down in Long Beach—and since I spend half my time here anyway—why couldn't I just move in?"

The same thing had crossed my mind, but I did have certain reservations. "Lisa," I said, "it's all right with me, but aren't you worried about what people will think?"

She said, "No. If you're not worried, and I'm not worried, let people think what they want and let them worry."

"Then it's settled," I said. "You can move in tomorrow."

She took me by the hand and said, "Come upstairs, G.B., I want to show you something." Well, we walked into the suite she used, and there hanging in the closet was her entire wardrobe; her slippers were under the bed, her toothbrush was hanging by the washbasin, and all her luggage was there. She gave me a big innocent smile and said, "I'm so glad you said I could move in, G.B., now I won't have to move out."

Now, that's the story of how and why Lisa moved into my house. You must admit that it's a very believable story. In fact, I just read it over and I'm beginning to believe it myself.

During the time that Lisa lived at my house we had a lot of wonderful times together, but that doesn't mean each of us didn't have a life of his own. Lisa had her circle of young friends she went out with, and I still went to the club and enjoyed the company of my friends. Of course, her life was a little more exciting than mine, because my youngest friend was Georgie Jessel. It was a perfect arrangement for both of us.

Along about then Lisa decided to continue her education and retired again from show business. Maybe I should say semiretired, because she was still interested in the theater. She enrolled in Immaculate Heart College where she eventually received her Bachelor of Arts degree in Theater and English. It was while attending Immaculate Heart that she

209

came home one evening with a friend of hers whom she introduced as Albin Konopka. Albin was a promising young pianist and seemed to be a very nice young man. I didn't realize it at the time, but this was the beginning of the story of how Lisa moved out of my house.

Now, moving out didn't take as long as moving in. It was only a week or two after I had met Albin that Lisa turned off Johnny Carson again and sat down next to me on the couch. This time she said, "G.B., I'm in love with Albin, and we plan to be married."

For a minute I panicked; I thought Albin was going to move in, too. But I realized she was serious, so I said to her, "Lisa, this is a very important step in your life, have you talked it over with your mother?"

"Oh, yes," she answered, "I talked to her on the phone this morning, and she said 'If it's all right with G.B., it's all right with me.'"

I gave her a little hug and said, "Anything that makes you happy, kid, is okay with me." So she and Albin set the date for their marriage.

The wedding was a lovely affair. It took place in a very picturesque setting, high in the Palos Verdes Hills, overlooking the ocean. There were about one hundred and fifty relatives and friends there. After the ceremony, when I danced with Lisa, I said, "Lisa, I've never seen you look happier."

She said, "I am. It's because I'm in love with Albin." Then, after a pause, she smiled at me and added, "G.B., you'll always be the best friend I've ever had."

The following day the bride and groom moved to New York, where Albin had a scholarship at the Juilliard School of Music. Subsequently they moved to Paris, where they live at the time this is being written. Albin has developed into a very accomplished concert pianist, and is continuing his studies with Mademoiselle Nadia Boulanger, an internationally famous music instructor. I hear from Lisa frequently, and both she and Albin are very happy. When they

210

return to the United States I'm sure Albin will be giving concerts, and Lisa will be able to play "The Maple Leaf Rag" in French.

When Lisa got married I don't want you to get the idea that I didn't miss her. I did—a great deal. There was a very special affection between Lisa and me, and there always will be. This had been a very enjoyable interlude in my life, but as I've said before in this book, I believe you've just got to take life as it comes. In the words of one of our foremost philosophers, Doris Day—*"Que será, será!"*

The Sunshine Boys

We all know that Neil Simon wrote a hit play called *The Sunshine Boys*, and we all know that Neil Simon wrote a hit movie called *The Sunshine Boys*. And since he did so well with that title, I don't see why I shouldn't have a chapter called *The Sunshine Boys*, so that's why this chapter is called—The Sunshine Boys. I don't say it's going to be a hit, but then again I'm not Neil Simon.

Now that I started off with a little laugh—a very little one—I'd like to get serious for a moment. As I said at the beginning of this book, I don't believe anybody should retire, no matter what his or her age is. In fact, that thought is so important I'm going to repeat it again—*I don't believe anybody should retire, no matter what his or her age is!* And I'm living proof of this point. Well, not completely living; I must admit that every Tuesday at five minutes after one I cough a little.

Now, you all know that I've spent my entire life in show business, then at the age of seventy-nine I made one movie, *The Sunshine Boys*, and it's like I'm just getting started. That should be an example to everyone. I didn't quit, I stayed in there, and I finally got so old that I became new again.

Playing the part of Al Lewis in *The Sunshine Boys* was the most exciting thing that ever happened to me. Let me tell you how it all came about. Originally in 1974 Jack Benny was signed to play the part of Al Lewis, and Ray Stark,

213

the producer, was testing other well-known vaudeville comedians to play opposite Jack in the role of Willie Clark. Well, on August 7 of that year I received a script from Ray with a note asking me to look over the part of Willie. I knew I was wrong for the part, but it didn't make any difference, because on August 9 I was in Cedars of Lebanon Hospital having open-heart surgery. I was wrong for that part, too, but I figured I better not turn it down or I might be making a quick exit.

Fortunately I had a very rapid recovery period, and by the time I was back on my feet, Walter Matthau had been cast to play opposite Jack in the picture. I was very glad for both of them because I knew they'd make a marvelous team.

Then Fate took a cruel twist. Jack Benny became very ill, and in a matter of a few weeks he was gone. This was one of the low points of my life. My best friend was gone, career-wise I wasn't in great demand, and I wasn't getting any younger. To some people this might be the time to throw in the towel, but that's not the way I think. I truly do believe that if you can't do anything about a bad situation, you've got to learn to live with it. So I continued my habit of coming into the office each morning and meeting with Packy and Jack Langdon. I wasn't booked anyplace and we had nothing to do, so we just sat around writing funny routines. And it's hard to know whether a routine is funny or not when you've got no place to play it.

One day we were sitting around the office playing with our pencils when my manager, Irving Fein, came in. He seemed unusually ill at ease, and after a bit of small talk he got to the point. He said, "George, how would you feel about playing the part of Al Lewis in *The Sunshine Boys*?"

I was stunned. For a moment I didn't know what to say. "Irving, I don't think I should do it. That was Jack's part, and if I played it, I just wouldn't feel right."

"George, I think I can help you," Irving said. "I was Jack's manager for twenty-six years, and nobody knew the man any better than I did. Take my word for it, nothing would make Jack happier than to have you do that part."

I still didn't know what to say. Irving turned to Packy and Jack Langdon and said, "Boys, what do you think?" They both enthusiastically agreed it was a marvelous idea. But in spite of all this encouragement I still had reservations. I said, "Irving, give me a chance to think it over."

Irving opened his briefcase and pulled out a copy of the script of *The Sunshine Boys*. "Good. And while you're thinking it over tonight read this script and call me in the morning."

Well, that night I read the script and all of my doubts vanished. It was a beautiful script, and I fell in love with every word. It was like everything Al Lewis said came out of my mouth. I didn't even wait until morning. I called Irving that night. When he picked up the phone I said, "Irving, this is Al Lewis speaking."

He laughed and said, "George, I knew this would happen. I've arranged for you to read for Neil Simon and Herb Ross at ten o'clock Thursday morning."

Well, for the next three days I buried my head in that script, and when Thursday came around I not only knew my part, I knew everybody else's part. I wasn't a bit nervous about reading that morning, because the character of Al Lewis fit me like a glove. Al Lewis was supposed to be born in New York, he was a vaudevillian, he was old, and he was Jewish. Well, I was born in New York, I was a vaudevillian, I was old . . . but how they found out I was Jewish I'll never know. They must have seen me in the locker room at Hillcrest.

At ten o'clock I read for Neil Simon and Herb Ross, who was directing the picture. They must have liked me because when I finished and started to hand the script to Herb, he said, "You keep it, George, I think you're going to be needing it."

Well, the next few days were very nervous ones for me,

215

wondering whether I had the part or not. But I didn't hear a word. Then one day the trade papers, *Variety* and the *Hollywood Reporter* came out saying that I was set for *The Sunshine Boys*.

But nobody called me and said, "George, you've got the part!"

A couple of days later I received a beautiful leather scriptholder from Ray Stark. On the cover embossed in gold letters was THE SUNSHINE BOYS and my name.

But nobody said, "George, you've got the part!"

Next I was invited to a luncheon at MGM in the private executive dining room. There were six of us: Frank Rosenfelt, president of MGM; Dan Melnick, vice-president in charge of production; Walter Matthau; Herb Ross; Irving Fein, and myself. It was a delightful luncheon. We laughed and talked, told anecdotes, the food was delicious, and everybody was very friendly. When we broke up, Herb Ross said to Walter Matthau, "Come on, Walter, let's go downstairs and pick out your wardrobe for *The Sunshine Boys*." Then Frank Rosenfelt shook hands with me, and Dan Melnick shook hands with me.

But nobody said, "George, you've got the part!"

By now two weeks had passed. When the phone rang again, it was Irving Fein. He told me MGM wanted me to go see their doctor for an insurance examination. Well, I'd gone this far, so I figured why not. The next day I went to the doctor's office, and he turned out to be a young doctor, about forty years old. He got right down to business and put me through all the preliminary examinations. They turned out fine. Then he got very serious. "Mr. Burns," he said, "I happen to know that five months ago you had open-heart surgery, and now to complete this examination I have to give you an electrocardiogram to test your heart."

I could see he was a little tense, so I thought I'd soften up the situation. I said, "Doctor, go ahead, that's what I'm here for. And if I enjoy it, let's do it every Monday."

216

He was not amused. Very slowly he explained, "Before I give you this test you've got to walk on this treadmill. Now it's uphill, you've got to walk for two minutes, and it's very strenuous. Do you think it will be too much for you?"

"Doctor," I said, "Neil Simon is a great writer, I read the script and I love my part—start the treadmill."

Before he turned it on he cautioned me, "Now, Mr. Burns, when you're on the treadmill, if you feel the least bit of pain, or dizziness, or get short of breath—anything at all—tell me immediately and I'll stop the machine."

Well, he started the treadmill, I got on it and started to walk. He stood right next to me and never took his eyes off me. Every five seconds he'd say, "How do you feel?" . . . "How do you feel?" . . . "How do you feel?" And I'd answer, "Fine!" . . . "Fine!" . . . Fine!" This went on for two minutes, and when I got off the machine I felt great. Then I took a look at the doctor. He was white as a sheet, trembling all over, and wringing wet. I said, "Doctor, did you ever have open-heart surgery?"

He said, "No."

I said, "Well, you ought to have it, you look bad."

The following morning I got the results of my tests and everything came out perfect. But still—

Nobody said, "George, you've got the part!"

Well, for three more days we sat around the office and heard nothing. Finally, I said to Packy and Jack, "Fellows, it doesn't look good. I've done everything they asked me to do, so I guess we might as well forget about it and start playing with our pencils again." Wouldn't you know, the phone rang. I knew who it was. I picked up the phone and said, "Hello, Irving."

Irving said, "George, the picture starts Monday. They want you to be on Stage 28 at nine o'clock to start rehearsals."

Do you know, that was almost two years ago? I made the picture, it turned out to be a big hit, I traveled all over the

217

world to promote it, and I won an Academy Award for Best Supporting Actor. Would you believe that to this day nobody has ever said—

"George, you got the part!"

During my many years in show business with Gracie, whether it was vaudeville, radio, television, or movies we were always Burns and Allen, and I played George Burns. Now here I was playing the part of Al Lewis in *The Sunshine Boys*, and it was a brand-new experience for me. But, as I said, I felt the character of Al Lewis so strongly I could hardly wait to get to the studio that Monday morning. At the time I said to myself, "If I'm a hit as Al Lewis, I might never go back to being George Burns again. I'll let somebody with less talent play him."

For the first two or three days the cast sat around a table and read the script to get familiar with it. Now, one of the actors was a method actor who needed a motivation for everything he did. He wouldn't make a move unless he knew why he was making it. There was a scene in the script that called for him to go to the bathroom, and he said to the director, Herb Ross, "*Why* am I going to the bathroom?"

Herb said, "*Why?* Who knows?—for the same reason that everybody goes to the bathroom."

"I know that, but *why?*"

Herb just looked at him. "Well, maybe in the scene before that you had breakfast."

"Did I have a big breakfast, or did I have a small breakfast?"

Herb's eyes narrowed a bit. "What difference does that make?"

"I want to know how long to stay in the bathroom."

Herb thought a second, then he said, "I just decided you're not going to use the bathroom."

"*Why* am I not going to use the bathroom?"

Very calmly and quietly Herb answered, "You won't be able to get in. The actor who's taking your place will be using it."

218

That was the end of the method actor. And from then on I didn't take any chances. Whenever Herb Ross looked at me I went to the bathroom!

By the end of the first week something happened that proved to me that no matter how long you're in this business you're never really sure of yourself. By now we were on our feet walking through the scenes, and every day when we broke for lunch Neil Simon and Herb Ross would come to the commissary and eat with us. However, this one day I heard Herb say to Neil, "I've ordered lunch for us in my office. We've got a problem and we have to make a decision today."

When I heard this I got an awful sinking feeling. I'd seen what had happened to the method actor, and for some reason I figured I was next. It looked like I was going back to being George Burns again. Well, I couldn't eat a bite of my lunch. My new movie career was ending before it started. All sorts of thoughts went through my head and I was absolutely miserable. When I got back to the set I noticed Herb and Neil sitting with their heads together. I knew it would be embarrassing for them to tell me they were letting me go, so I thought I'd make it easier for them and bow out gracefully. I went over to them and said, "Gentlemen, I know what your problem is, and I'm going to solve it for you."

They both gave me a blank look, then they looked at each other, and Herb said to me, "We just decided during lunch to change the ending of the picture, how would you know that?"

Well, it was my turn to look blank. I realized I had let my imagination run away with me, but I didn't want them to know it. I said, "Fellows, I'm glad to hear that because I felt the picture needed a new ending, too!" And without waiting for their reaction I ran into my dressing room and ordered lunch.

Finally the day came when they were going to shoot my first scene. I had a very early call, and while I was driving to

219

the studio I remembered something that Edward G. Robinson once told me. He had said that in every picture he ever made, before they shot the first scene if he got nervous, he knew he was going to give a good performance. This kind of worried me, because in one hour I was going to shoot my first scene and I wasn't a bit nervous. But then I figured it would happen when I got to my dressing room. Well, I got to my dressing room and sat down and waited. I must have sat there four or five minutes. Nothing happened. I almost fell asleep. I thought maybe if I started putting on my wardrobe that would do it. While I was dressing I began talking to myself. "George, remember what Eddie said—if you want to give a good performance, you've got to get nervous." Did you ever try to make yourself get nervous? Get butterflies in your stomach? Make your palms sweat? You can't do it. In fact, I almost got nervous because I wasn't getting nervous.

When I finished dressing I stood in front of the mirror, and I forgot all about being nervous. I couldn't get over the way I looked. I had on a dark pin-striped suit, a polka-dot bow tie, and a white silk scarf. Over that I wore a blue top-coat with a black velvet collar and, to top it all, a black felt fedora hat and a heavy cane with a gold top and gloves. I stared at myself for a minute, but it wasn't what I expected. I didn't look like Spencer Tracy, or Jimmy Cagney, or Paul Muni, or Marlon Brando—I didn't even look like an actor. I looked like an honorary pallbearer.

Then I looked at myself from different angles; first from the left, then from the right, then straight ahead. Then I threw back my head and laughed; then I looked down and frowned, but something was missing. Finally I realized what it was—no cigar. Even with all those clothes on I felt naked. And there wasn't going to be any cigar, because Neil and Herb had decided I wasn't going to smoke in the picture. I couldn't imagine myself without a cigar. It would be the first time I ever worked alone.

Well, the big moment arrived for me to start my new career as an actor. They called for me, and I walked onto the set with no cigar, no butterflies, and dry palms. Now, my first scene was with Richard Benjamin. I knock on the door, and he opens it. When he sees me he says, "Hello, Mr. Lewis, come on in." Well, when he opened the door and said, "Hello, Mr. Lewis, come on in," I just looked around. I didn't know whom he was talking to. When I heard the name Lewis I thought maybe Jerry got the part.

Well, Herb stopped the scene and came over to me and said, "George, you're Mr. Lewis." I felt better right away. I knew if I couldn't remember that my name was Lewis, I was nervous enough to give a good performance. Well, after that there was no problem. Dick Benjamin and I went through the whole scene, and Herb Ross loved it.

Now, I'll let you in on a little secret. I found out that acting is easy. It's much easier to be an actor than it is to walk out on the stage by yourself and tell jokes and sing for an hour. On the stage if it's no good, that's it, you don't have a chance to do it over, but when you're acting in a movie and it's no good, you do it over and over and over until you get it right. And when you're on the stage you're all by yourself, you don't have Walter Matthau on one side and Richard Benjamin on the other to help you.

Another great thing I discovered about acting is that you don't have to stand on your feet all the time. Ninety percent of the time you're sitting down. At this stage of the game if I can sit down and get paid for doing it, I'm in the right business. Makes me wonder why I've been standing up all these years.

Now, let me tell you what I meant about acting being easy. To be a good actor all you have to do is listen. In that first scene when Dick Benjamin opened the door and said to me, "Hello, Mr. Lewis, come on in," I went in. Now, that's good acting! If I had stayed out in the hall, that's bad acting. When I got inside, Dick Benjamin said, "How do you feel, Mr. Lewis?" And I said, "Fine, thank you." Again, that's good acting! Now, when he said, "How do you feel, Mr.

Lewis," if I had said, "Look on the floor, maybe it fell down," that's bad acting. That means you're not listening. And to be a great actor you've got to listen. So when I said, "Fine, thank you," that meant I was listening. I was listening so hard that in my next picture I might even ask for more money.

I had always heard that the toughest thing about acting was to be able to laugh and to be able to cry. I say nonsense! If I'm doing a scene in which I'm supposed to cry, all I do is think of my sex life. If I'm doing a scene in which I'm supposed to laugh, all I do is think of my sex life. I must really be a hell of an actor. This morning after taking a shower I looked at myself in the mirror and laughed and cried at the same time.

There are those who say that the most difficult emotion to portray on the screen is pain. Again, I say nonsense! If a scene calls for me to register extreme pain, it's simple. All I do is wear tight jockey shorts.

That sums up my formula for being a good actor. Of course, there are other schools of thought on the subject, but everyone must decide which works best for him. As Harry Fink of "Fink's Mules" once said, "Every mule has his own personality." Personally, I don't know what that means, but Harry Fink went around saying things like that.

But I've been serious long enough. Back to *The Sunshine Boys*. I never had such kid-glove treatment in my life as I did during the shooting of that picture. The producer, the director, the assistants, the crew, the cameraman, the makeup man, they all treated me as though I were a china doll. They acted as though any minute I might break into little pieces. I suppose they were nervous because Jack Benny had passed away, and I had had open-heart surgery five months before. I don't know if they were worried about me personally; they probably just wanted to make sure I lasted until the picture was finished.

If I so much as mentioned a cup of tea, before I could

move there'd be four cups of tea in front of me. If I sneezed, before anybody could say "Gesundheit!" I was surrounded by Kleenex. And everywhere I went somebody was following me with a chair. They'd say, "Sit down, Mr. Burns. . . ." "Take it easy, Mr. Burns. . . ." "Rest, Mr. Burns. . . ." I got so tired of sitting down whenever I wanted to stand up I'd have to sneak into the men's room. One day the property man even followed me in there. I said, "Please, this is one thing I like to do by myself."

I didn't wear any makeup in the picture, but they hired Dick Smith, one of the top makeup men in the business, for Walter. Walter is only in his mid-fifties, but they had to make him look as old as I did. It took Dick two hours to put on Walter's makeup. He had to shave part of his head to make him look bald, he put wrinkles in his face and neck, and even protruding veins on the back of his hands. It was a tremendous makeup job, and Dick Smith is very expensive. I'm not sure, but I think he got more money for making up Walter than I got for making the picture.

Now, when Walter arrived in the morning, he had a lively bounce in his walk, and he used to do little dance steps while he was singing or whistling; he was full of life. To show you what a complete actor Walter Matthau is, when he got up from that makeup table he not only looked like an old man, he *was* an old man. His whole body slumped, his shoulders sagged, his clothes hung on him, and when he walked he dragged his feet. The first day I saw him shuffle onto the set I jumped up and gave him my chair. After I helped him down, he looked up and said, "Thanks, son."

I don't hesitate to say that *The Sunshine Boys* was a fine picture. Everyone involved with the picture enjoyed making it, and nobody was ever late for work in the morning. All of the pieces seemed to fit, and the man who put them together was Herb Ross, the director. He was a tremendous help to me, and he got the most out of everybody without even raising his voice.

223

Let me give you an example of how Herb worked. In this one particular scene he thought I was playing it too serious, but he didn't say a word to me. Between takes he went to Walter and quietly told him he thought I was a little tight in this scene and asked Walter to do something to loosen me up. Well, that's all he had to say to Walter. Now, this scene was a single shot of me, and Walter was standing behind the camera feeding me lines. Herb called for action so we started doing the scene. Right in the middle of it Walter dropped his pants. I'm sure it must have loosened me up a little, but I never lost my concentration. I went right on with the scene and, believe me, it's not easy to look a man in the eye when he's standing there with his pants down. I admit when the scene was over I did take a little peek. Walter's eyes are prettier.

Anyway, Herb liked the scene, so Walter pulled his pants up and we went on with the picture. By using a little psychology Herb got the job done, and he didn't even have to raise his voice. All he had to do was lower Walter's pants.

Another thing I learned is that acting in a movie is entirely different than appearing on the stage in front of an audience. On the stage I'm very conscious of the audience because I need them. If I look out there and see them laughing and enjoying what I'm doing, it's like having a love affair with them. But in a movie it's just the opposite. The only audience you have is the crew, and they can't make a sound. No matter how funny the scene might be, they don't dare let out a snicker. When Walter and I would do a funny scene we knew where the laughs should be, but there was nothing but silence. He was used to this, but for me it felt strange; no reaction, no laughs, no applause—I felt like I was playing Altoona again.

This is where concentration is important. You know there are fifty or sixty people gathered around you so close you can practically touch them, but you have to block them out completely. Your concentration has to be so strong that you don't even know there's a camera there. I worked so hard at concentrating I even took it home with me. One night when I arrived home Daniel opened the door for me. I said, "Why are you opening the door? Where's Daniel?"

Daniel said, "Mr. Burns, I'm Daniel."

"Excuse me," I said, "I thought you were Dick Benjamin."

Now, you know the above story is true. George Burns might lie a little, but not Al Lewis.

Well, after we wrapped up our scenes here at MGM, the company went on location to New York City for five weeks. We shot several scenes in the lobby of the Ansonia Hotel. Now, the Ansonia Hotel has been around as long as New York has been around. At the turn of the century it was a very elegant hotel where all the famous opera stars used to stay. On the second day of shooting the manager of the Ansonia brought out an old registration book he had in his office and proudly opened it up and showed me some of the people who had registered there. There were Enrico Caruso, John McCormack, Mary Garden, and Jenny Lind. Then he said, "Mr. Burns, wouldn't you like to sign your name in the book?" I was happy to, so I did. It was exciting having my name there on the same page with four other great singers.

But the highlight of the trip was when the Friars Club in New York gave Walter and me a testimonial dinner. It was a big affair, and practically all of Walter's speech was about me. He said I was the most natural actor he ever worked with, and every day he was learning something new from me. Then he went on to say what a joy I was to work with, and it was such a pleasure to be around me that he couldn't wait to leave home and come to work in the morning.

I was sitting on the dais next to Walter's wife, Carole. Right about then I felt a little nudge in my ribs. Carole leaned over and whispered into my ear, "George, I'm afraid I've got a problem. I think my husband is in love with his leading man."

I whispered back, "Your husband is the one who has the problem. I think I'm in love with his wife."

But everywhere we went, if there was an interview, Walter kept saying these flattering things about me. It got to be embarrassing. I mean, it would have been embarrassing if they weren't true.

(Here's a little footnote that I'm too tired to put at the bottom of the page. Packy and Jack said that line about me not being embarrassed makes me sound conceited. But I don't care, at my age I haven't got time to be humble.)

Whenever I'm in New York I always manage to spend some time with my friends Jesse Block and his wife, Eva. I've known Jesse and Eva since the old vaudeville days, when they did a great man and woman act, and they were billed as "Block and Sully." Jesse has been a member of the Friars Club as long as I have, and one day we were having lunch there. Some of the scenes for *The Sunshine Boys* were being shot there at the club, and it so happened that I wasn't in any of them. Jesse couldn't understand that. He said to me, "George, you've been a member of the Friars Club practically all your life. It doesn't seem right that you're not doing a scene here at the club. Why don't you tell Neil Simon to write one for you?"

Jesse seemed to have the notion that all I had to do was snap my fingers and Neil Simon would rush to his typewriter. I didn't want to embarrass him, so I said, "Jesse, it's a great idea, I'll ask him."

Well, that didn't stop Jesse. He said, "George, in the scene I'm sure you'll be working with somebody, so why don't you have Neil write me in."

I said, "Jesse, that's a great idea, I'll ask him."

He went right on. "And as long as he's writing me in, why don't you have him write a few lines for Eva?"

I said, "Jesse, that's a great idea, I'll ask him."

By now Jesse was all excited. He said, "George, do you think he'll do it?"

226

I said, "Jesse, I'll let you know as soon as Neil Simon throws me out of his office."

Well, a week later was the last day of the picture. Now, when you wind up shooting on a picture that ran as smoothly as *The Sunshine Boys*, you can't help but have mixed emotions. On one hand you're happy it's finished, and on the other you wish you were just starting again. When Herb Ross said, "That's it, boys, wrap it up!" nobody wanted to leave the set. I looked over at Walter Matthau, who was slumped down in a chair. He had on that old-man makeup and really looked tired. Ray Stark was on the set that day, so I pointed to Walter and said, "Ray, there's one thing I'll never understand. How did you talk the insurance company into letting a man that age make this picture?"

Although the actual filming of the picture was finished, another phase of the operation was just beginning. Dick Kahn, vice-president in charge of MGM's publicity and advertising department, and the United Artists publicity gang outlined an intensive campaign for Walter and myself to publicize the film. They worked in conjunction with my personal public relations people, Steinberg, Lipsman, and Brokaw. This involved countless magazine and newspaper interviews and appearances on talk shows from coast to coast. All of this was coordinated by one of the brightest and most capable publicists I've ever met. Her name is Regina Gruss, she works for MGM, and she is every bit as nice as she is talented. In spite of the heavy pressures of Regina's job, I never knew her to be rude, lose her temper, or be anything but pleasant through the entire campaign.

Regina had everything worked out on a very tight time schedule. There was one day when I had to give about six interviews. I was stopping at the Sherry-Netherland Hotel in New York, and my first interview was at ten o'clock in the morning. Regina cautioned me I could only give the columnist exactly ten minutes because we had to rush right over to NBC. Well, asking me to do ten minutes is embarrassing. Acrobats do ten minutes. Anyway, the interview was going very well, and I was really rolling. At the end of ten minutes I was right in the middle of my story about how Sid Gary and I put the two live chickens in the icebox, and Regina was getting very nervous. She was standing by the door, holding my hat and coat and making little motions that we had to leave. Well, I certainly wasn't going to stop in the middle of a classic story like the one about the two live chickens in the icebox, so by the time I finished, the interview had lasted about a half hour.

In the taxi on our way to NBC Regina gave me a little lecture. She said, "George, you've upset our schedule for the whole day. In the first place I didn't believe one word of that story about the chickens in the icebox. In fact, I don't believe any of your stories. So from now on you're just going to have to start telling shorter lies."

I let that little statement sink in, then I looked at Regina and said, "Teacher, when we get to NBC do I have time to go to the men's room?"

Regina laughed and said, "All right, George, but try to make it shorter than the chicken story."

My relationship with Regina during the promotion for the picture was perfect. She went with Walter and me for the opening of the picture in Chicago, in London, and even all the way to Australia. And boy, did we need her! I don't think we could have done it without her.

For me, the most exciting opening was when the picture premiered at Radio City Music Hall in New York. Now, my name had been up in lights before, but I felt an extra something special when I saw it on the marquee of Radio City Music Hall. It meant I had made it as an actor. Since New York was my hometown, I'd been to the Music Hall many times, but this night was different—they let me in for free.

All through the making of the movie I hadn't watched any of the rushes or gone to any of the previews. I wanted to see it for the first time in this magnificent theater with an audience. Well, opening night the picture started, and when it came to my first scene, there I was bigger than life—and bald! I was shocked! I never knew I wore a toupee before.

Well, that brings us right up to now. In my lifetime I've been lucky enough to experience a great many personal high points, but I can honestly say that making *The Sunshine Boys* was one of the highest.

Of course, the highest of all was the night I walked onto the stage of the Dorothy Chandler Pavilion and was presented the Academy Award for Best Supporting Actor of 1975. It would be impossible for me to put down on paper my feelings at that moment. At a time when most people are ending their career, there I stood, an eighty-year-old man, just beginning a new one. I think I'm gonna stay in show business!

Epilogue

In closing, I'd like to say I enjoyed writing this book. The last book I wrote was in 1955. That was twenty-one years ago, and I had so much fun doing this one that I think I'll write one every twenty-one years.

Now, since you've read this far you must have a pretty good idea what my life-style is. I've always believed that life is a lot easier if you're able to laugh at yourself. And it's a lot more fun, too. Whenever I do get serious, it doesn't last very long, because I'm always thinking of a humorous finish.

It's well known that I have a tendency to bend the truth a bit, but basically everything in this book is factual. There are many profound truths here, but they're not easy to find unless you read between the lies. I don't presume to tell anyone how to live their life, but there is one thing I am sure of: No matter what age you are—stay active!

In summing up my philosophy I'm reminded of an ancient Law of Physics that was told to me by the parking lot boy at Chasen's restaurant. It made sense. To him—not to me. Anyway, here's what he said:

> Once a body in motion,
> It tends to remain in motion;
> Once a body at rest,
> It tends to remain at rest.

What the kid meant was:

IF YOU DON'T USE IT, YOU'LL LOSE IT!

231

Things I Forgot to Put in My Book

When I finished writing this book I found out I had a lot of funny anecdotes left over. They were cluttering up my house. I kept stepping on them and tripping over them, and there's nothing messier than a houseful of funny old anecdotes. I called the Goodwill, and they wouldn't take them; I held a garage sale, and nobody showed up. I didn't know what to do with them. But then I got to thinking—I've been getting laughs with these anecdotes all my life, and even though they might be old to me, they're probably brand new to most of you readers. Anyway, here they are. If you think they're funny, laugh at them. If you don't, you can hold your own garage sale.

* * *

This is one of the greatest inside-show-business stories I have ever heard, and it really happened. Wilton LaKye was one of the finest legitimate actors on Broadway, and like all the other big stars of that time, each year he'd play in vaudeville for five or six weeks. He was headlining the Keith Theater in Cincinnati, and on the bill with him was a little dancing act that opened the show. They called themselves Dunbar and Dixon.

After Monday's rehearsal LaKye went into the bar next door to the theater to have a drink. Dunbar and Dixon happened to come in, and when they saw this big star, Wilton LaKye, they almost jumped out of their skins. They went over to their idol, and Dunbar said, "Mr. LaKye, we just wanted to tell you what a thrill it is for us to play on the same bill with you."

LaKye said, "Thank you, boys."

Then Dixon said, "Mr. LaKye, we would deem it an honor if we could buy you a drink."

LaKye said, "I'm sorry, boys, but I'd just as soon drink alone. I just got a wire saying that I lost my mother."

Dixon shook his head sadly and said, "We know just how you feel—our trunk is missing."

★ ★ ★

Another story in the same mood involved an act that called themselves The Seven Happy Fitzpatricks. After their father passed away, every year on the anniversary of his death they put an ad in *Variety* which read:

IN FOND MEMORY OF OUR DEAR DEPARTED FATHER,
THE SEVEN HAPPY FITZPATRICKS

★ ★ ★

Years ago in Philadelphia there was a hotel called the Hurley House, and all the small-time vaudeville actors used to stop there. The reason most of us stopped there was because of one waitress, a sexy little thing named Fritzi Watkins. Now, when you'd order breakfast, which consisted of doughnuts and coffee, Fritzi would bring it up to your room. And she'd always stay because she *loved* coffee.

Well, one morning I ordered breakfast, and when she brought it up I said, "Fritzi, how about a little coffee?"

She said, "I'd love to."

Naturally I locked the door, I didn't want the coffee to get cold. Well, five minutes later when I was dunking my doughnut there was a knock on the door and it was Hurley, the owner of the hotel. He hollered, "Is Fritzi in there?"

I got panicky. I had an adjoining room with a juggler

234

named Al Jacobi, so I knocked on the door, and when he opened it I pushed in Fritzi. I let Hurley in, he looked around and didn't see Fritzi, so he left. Then I knocked on Jacobi's door, but he wouldn't give me back Fritzi. So I phoned downstairs to Hurley and said, "If you're looking for Fritzi, she's next door in Al Jacobi's room."

Hurley came up, knocked on Jacobi's door, Jacobi opened my door and threw back Fritzi. But this story has a sad ending. In the meantime my coffee got cold.

* * *

In Vaudeville taking bows was an art in itself. The number of bows you took at the end of your act was an indication of how successful you were. Many performers had little gimmicks they used to trick the audience into applauding.

Let me start with Eddie Leonard, one of the great song and dance men. He always worked in blackface, and for years Eddie was one of the top headliners. When he was in his sixties, here's the gimmick he used.

After doing his last number he'd take about three bows, and then in sort of a tired voice he'd say, "Folks, old Eddie ain't gonna be with you much longer. This tired old body is comin' to the end of the road. And when I'm up there on that big stage in the sky, these old ears will always hear the applause you folks are givin' me here tonight. This may be old Eddie's last performance. So I love ya all, and good night, and good-bye."

Well, this brought the audience to their feet. They'd cheer, they'd cry, and they'd applaud. Eddie could have taken bows for four days. Oh, by the way, Eddie made that same speech for the next twenty years.

* * *

Herman Timberg was a comedy monologist who also danced and played the violin. This was his gimmick.

At the finish of his act he'd come out, and just as he was about to take his first bow he'd look into the wings as though somebody were calling him. Then he'd walk offstage as though he were going to find out what they wanted. Well, the audience resented this; they felt that somebody offstage didn't want to give this fine performer a chance to take his bows. So they'd applaud to bring him back.

Timberg would come back out and do the same thing again. And every time he walked offstage the applause got louder. After milking this gimmick for about five or six times he would finally take a legitimate bow. This time the audience would really go wild because they thought they had won. Timberg was a master at this, and it always worked.

*   *   *

The greatest bow for sustained applause was the one used by a tramp comedian who called himself Bilbo. He was a genius at pantomime, and the audience loved him. And this is how Bilbo finished his act.

On stage he wore oversized yellow shoes with big rounded toes. When the curtain came down Bilbo would stand in such a position that it would land on the tops of his shoes, leaving the toes extended in front so the audience could still see them. Then a baby spotlight would hit the shoes, and the audience would start to applaud. At this point Bilbo, behind the curtain, would step out of his shoes and go around and stand in the wings. Now, as long as the spotlight stayed on his shoes the audience kept applauding. Depending on his mood, when Bilbo thought the applause had gone on long enough he'd step onstage in his stocking feet and take a bow. The audience realized they had been fooled and they loved him for it.

Unfortunately, this story also has a sad ending. Bilbo was finally booked into Hammerstein's on 42nd Street and Broadway, which was the Palace Theater of the time. He

236

opened on a Monday and was never better. But what the audience didn't know was that Bilbo had a heart condition. At the end of that performance, when he stepped out of his shoes, he had a heart attack and died. The audience was wildly applauding his shoes, but Bilbo never came on for his last bow.

* * *

Gene Bedini was one of the few jugglers who became a headliner. Anything he could pick up he could juggle, and sometimes he'd have as many as ten or twelve objects in the air at the same time. For the finish of his act he'd have people in the audience throw apples and oranges and pears onto the stage, and he'd catch them on the end of a fork which he held in his mouth.

At the time, Bedini was headlining the Riverside Theater, and his publicity man came up with a stunt that he thought would get a lot of publicity for Bedini. The idea was for him to go up on the roof of a ten-story building, drop a cantaloupe, and Bedini, standing on the sidewalk below, would catch it on the end of a fork in his mouth. Bedini thought the publicity guy was out of his mind. He pointed out that if he tried to catch a cantaloupe dropped from that height it would not only knock his teeth out, it would probably kill him. But the publicity man told Bedini not to worry; his idea was to take the inside out of the cantaloupe, then put the two halves back together so that it would be hollow. That way it would be light and very easy to catch. Well, Bedini went for it.

Word got around, and when the day came for the stunt there was a big crowd gathered in front of his building, including a lot of newspaper people. Bedini got into position, and just before he put the fork in his mouth he hollered up, "I'm ready. Drop it!" The publicity man dropped the hollowed-out cantaloupe, a gust of wind caught it and blew it four blocks down the street.

237

Well, that's the end of that story, and I'm not sure, but I think it was the end of that publicity man, too.

* * *

One of my very close friends is Eddie Buzzell, who was one of our top motion-picture directors. He directed many movies, including *Honolulu*, the last motion picture Gracie and I made. Eddie told me a story that I think is worth passing on. When he first came to Hollywood he went to work for Columbia Pictures. At the end of his first year he had a verbal agreement with Harry Cohn, who was the president of the company, to get a $250 weekly raise. Now, I'm not going to say that Harry Cohn was a hard man to do business with—I don't have to, everybody else has said it. When the year was up, Eddie went into Cohn's office and asked for his raise. Cohn turned on his charm. He said, "Eddie, Sam Briskin is right across the hall. He's head of production, so go in and ask him for the raise. If he okays it, it's certainly all right with me." Cohn stood up and put a fatherly hand on Eddie's shoulder. "You know me, Eddie," he continued, "when I make somebody a promise, it's a promise."

So Eddie went across the hall. When he walked into Briskin's office Sam wasn't there, but the intercom was buzzing. Eddie pushed down the lever and said, "Yeah?"

Cohn's voice came over the intercom. "Sam, Buzzell is on his way in there to ask for a raise. Don't give it to him."

Eddie pushed down the lever just as Sam walked in. Sam said, "What can I do for you, Eddie?"

Trying to act nonchalant, Eddie said, "I just left Harry Cohn's office. I'm due for a raise, and he said if it's all right with you, it's all right with him."

"Well, he's the boss," Sam said. "If it's all right with him, you've got it."

Eddie Buzzell stayed with Columbia Pictures for years and got many raises, but Harry Cohn never knew that Eddie was always $250 ahead of him.

Years ago the great actor Louis Calhern got into a cab in New York City. The driver was Jewish and spoke with an accent. He recognized Calhern and said, "Mr. Calhern, I've seen you in a lot of movies."

Calhern was flattered and said, "Thank you."

As they drove along the driver said, "What are you doing in New York?"

Calhern answered, "I'm here to appear in Shakespeare's *King Lear*."

The driver was impressed. *King Lear*, he said. "I must have seen it a dozen times. I've seen it played by all the great actors—Jacob P. Adler, Boris Tomeshevsky, David Kessler, Maurice Schwartz." Then he thought a second. He said, "Tell me something, Mr. Calhern, do you think it'll go in English?"

* * *

In the early days of small-time vaudeville all the contracts had a cancellation clause in them. If the manager didn't like your act, after the first performance you'd be canceled. At that time there was a Russian dancing act called Petrov and Sonia. Petrov was bald. And in those days the toupees they made looked awful, so Petrov used to pencil in his hair. Before every performance he used to spend about two hours sitting in front of a mirror, drawing hair on his head with a heavy black pencil. And he was a master at it. When he came onstage he looked as though he had a full head of black wavy hair. Unfortunately his hair looked better than his dancing.

He and Sonia were booked for three days into the Myrtle Theater in Brooklyn, and after the first matinee the manager canceled them. So Petrov packed his wardrobe, collected his music and his picture, rubbed out his hair, and left.

239

* * *

Before Rudolph Valentino became famous he worked in New York City at a place called Rector's. Rector's was a high-class restaurant, and well-to-do women used to go there in the afternoon for tea and a sandwich, and perhaps a cocktail. Well, Valentino worked there, and his job was to dance with the unescorted women. He made $18 a week and whatever he could pick up in tips from the women he danced with.

At that time one of the biggest stars on Broadway was an actress named Valeska Suratt, and one afternoon she dropped into Rector's for tea. As soon as she saw the handsome Valentino she sent a waiter over to ask him to dance with her. Well, Valentino recognized this famous actress, so in the middle of a tango he mentioned to her that he was thinking of going to Hollywood to try to make it as an actor in the movies. Miss Suratt seemed interested, so she asked him his name. He told her it was Rudolph Valentino. She stopped right in the middle of the dance, and said, "If I were you, young man, the first thing I'd do is change that name!"

So I did, and I've been calling myself George Burns ever since.

* * *

In vaudeville the opening act on a bill was usually jugglers, acrobats, roller skaters, or something like that. Well, I remember one small-time opening act called Tower and Lee. They did a comedy bicycle act. Now, as I mentioned before, in those days if the manager didn't like you, after the first matinee he would cancel you.

Tower and Lee were playing the Odeon Theater on Clinton Street, and after their first matinee the manager came back and told them they were canceled. Well, Towers had a very short temper, and when he heard this he punched the

240

manager right in the mouth and knocked him to the floor. The manager groped around and finally found his glasses. Then, looking up at Tower, he said, "If I ever have to cancel you again, I'm gonna do it by telephone."

* * *

When I was about twenty-one or twenty-two I did an act called "Garfield and Smith—Singing, Dancing and Witty Remarks." My name was Smith. We were booked on the Pantages circuit, and headlining our unit was an act with eight beautiful girls called Sweet Sweeties. We were playing Oklahoma City, and on my way to the theater one morning I noticed a young fellow about my age sitting in a green Marmon convertible parked outside the theater—and he was crying. I couldn't figure out what he had to cry about, because a Marmon convertible in those days cost a fortune. So I started talking to him, and I found out the reason he was crying was because the girl he was in love with was having lunch in the restaurant across the street with another fellow. His named turned out to be Harold Spencer, Jr. He seemed like a nice guy, and I felt sorry for him. So I cooked up a little scheme that worked. I got one of the girls from Sweet Sweeties to have lunch with him in that same restaurant. Well, when his girlfriend saw him come in with a beautiful showgirl, she dumped the other guy and made up with Harold fast.

During that week in Oklahoma City, Harold and I became good friends, and he introduced me to a very beautiful Indian girl named Sally Trueblood. She was staying at the same hotel I was, and one night after the show she invited me down to her room to listen to some records on her Gramophone. Well, Sally was a real beauty, so I went all out and bought a bottle of scotch for two and a half dollars. And I wore my pongee robe, which I'd picked up in Vancouver a couple of weeks before. It was a beige Japanese robe

241

with very long, flowing sleeves and a red sash tied around the waist. On the back was embroidered a gold dragon with a big red tongue. I lived on the seventh floor and Sally lived on the fourth, and wearing that outfit I didn't dare take the elevator. So I walked down, holding my hands up over my head so I wouldn't step on my sleeves.

When I reached Sally's room I fixed a couple of drinks, and Sally put a record on the Gramophone. Her favorite was John McCormack singing "When Irish Eyes Are Smiling," and since it was twelve o'clock at night she stuck a towel into the Gramophone horn to muffle the sound. We no sooner got settled down when the door burst open and in came the house detective. Now, I want you to picture this: There we were; a full-blooded Indian girl and a twenty-one-year-old Jew wearing a kimono, drinking scotch, and listening to John McCormack sing "When Irish Eyes Are Smiling."

The house detective started giving me a hard time and wound up saying that he'd be willing to forget the whole thing if I'd give him $50. Well, all I had was $7, so I asked him to let me go up and talk to my partner, Garfield, to see if I could raise the rest of the money. He let me go but he made me leave my kimono as security.

Garfield only had about $7 himself, so that left me $35 short. Then I remembered that Harold Spencer lived upstairs in the penthouse. He was my last hope, so I went up to see him and told him my story. Harold's father was there, and after he heard what had happened he said, "Come on, let's go downstairs. I think I can handle this for you."

We walked into Sally's room and Harold's father fired the house detective. Harold Spencer, Sr., owned the hotel.

* * *

Novelty acts were very popular in vaudeville, and there was one act that was really a novelty. This fellow worked

242

with a chicken, and the chicken danced on one leg! The act was called Jackie Davis and Chick Fowler. The fellow's name was Chick Fowler.

Chick was a good entertainer, but he liked to drink a lot. Every once in a while he'd pour a little booze in a saucer for the chicken, and the chicken got to like it. He not only got to like it, he got to love it. Half of the time he was smashed. Well, it was tough enough for the chicken to dance on one leg when he was sober, but when he was smashed it was murder. Before you knew it, it got so they couldn't get a job.

I ran into Chick one day and said, "Chick, how are things going?"

He said, "Not good, George, things are so tough that last night I pretty near ate my partner."

I said, "Chick, you wouldn't do a thing like that!"

He shook his head and said, "Of course not. But I must admit I ate the leg he wasn't using!"

Another true story.

* * *

During the time I was doing the Burns and Allen show on radio most of the variety shows were using big bands. Our band leader was Artie Shaw. When we moved the show from New York to California, Artie had a problem with James Petrillo, who was then head of the musicians' union. One of the key men in Artie's band was his trumpet player, and naturally Artie wanted to bring him along to California. But Petrillo wouldn't allow it. Artie was very upset because this trumpet player was extremely important to him, but Petrillo wouldn't give in.

The day after we arrived in California I was on my way to the Brown Derby restaurant to have a drink, and there on the newsstand was a headline that read, LANA TURNER DIVORCES ARTIE SHAW. There was a picture of Lana in a sweater, and she looked absolutely beautiful. Inside the Derby, there was Artie at the bar having a drink. I knew how bad

243

he must have felt about losing a beautiful girl like Lana, so I put my arm around him and said, "Artie, don't take it too hard. Things like that happen to everybody."

Artie looked at me and said, "To hell with Petrillo—I'll find myself a trumpet player out here!"

* * *

One of our really big stars in the twenties was a lady named Blossom Seeley. She was not only an exciting personality onstage, but she created many innovations that were later used by other artists. Blossom was the first to snap her fingers when she sang. She was the first to put one foot over the footlights so she'd be closer to the audience. She was the first to use a baby spotlight over her head to give the effect of a halo. When she played nightclubs she was the first to use a small upright piano, which she wheeled from table to table. And she was the first performer to get down on one knee to sing a song.

Blossom was born in California, and at seventeen she was playing nightclubs in San Francisco on the Barbary Coast. She was known as Baby Blossom, and at seventeen she was the most voluptuous and sexy thing you've ever seen. In her act she'd come out wearing a skin-tight black leotard, and around her waist was strapped a tiger's head which hung in front of her. While she was singing, to show their appreciation the men would toss silver dollars at her. Blossom had a string attached to the tiger's head, and when the men tossed the silver dollars she'd pull the string and catch the money in the tiger's mouth. (Another first!) No matter where the men threw those silver dollars her little tiger's head was there to catch them. I once said to Blossom, "Did you ever miss catching one of those silver dollars?"

"Are you kidding" she said, "I not only never missed, I got so good at it I could even throw back change!"

It wasn't long before Blossom became famous, and she and Al Jolson were starring in a show at the Winter Garden

244

theater in New York. One of her big numbers was a song called "Toddling the Toddle-O." She was a sensation and took encore after encore. When she sang the last chorus she got down on one knee, and the audience went wild.

Well, Al Jolson watched this from the wings—and that man was no dummy. He came out onstage and got down on one knee with her. But Blossom made one mistake—she got up—but Jolson never did.

Later in her career Blossom married a talented young singer named Benny Fields. They worked together and became one of the great teams in vaudeville. Their closing number was a song called "In a Little Spanish Town," and Benny would stand behind Blossom, put his arms around her waist, and play his guitar in front of her. For an exit, as they were singing they would do a little side-shuffle step into the wings.

If it was a good audience, Blossom would snuggle back against Benny as they shuffled off. As I said, this little lady knew how to snuggle. The audience loved it, but not nearly as much as Benny.

That was, if it was a good audience. If it was a bad audience, Blossom always blamed it on Benny. There was no snuggling, and as they shuffled off she would stomp on Benny's toes with her high-spiked heels. Whenever I saw Benny limping to his dressing room I knew there was a bad audience out front.

* * *

When I lived on the Lower East Side there was a fellow in our neighborhood named Harry Farley, whose greatest ambition in life was to be on the police force. He tried and tried, but he couldn't make it. In those days you had to be at least 5'9" to be a New York City policeman, and Harry was only 5'8". Well, Harry was so desperate to make the police force that he rigged up a stretching machine in his basement and stretched himself every day for four months.

245

If Harry had lived, he would have been one of New York's finest!

* * *

Just for a change of mood I thought I'd throw in this next story for you readers who like tragedy. If you don't like tragedy, read the policeman story again.

There used to be a small-time dancing act called The Goldie Boys; two brothers named Jack and Phil Goldie. It was not the greatest act in the world, and they were getting nowhere. So Jack's wife, Nettie, talked him into giving up the act and opening a delicatessen. Jack had a friend, an East Side gangster known as Crazy Manny, and Manny agreed to lend Jack $2,000 to open the store. However, Jack had to promise to pay it back in three months.

Well, the delicatessen turned out to be just as bad as the Goldie Boys. At the end of three months Jack didn't have the money, so he went to Crazy Manny and asked for more time. But Crazy Manny wouldn't go for it. "Nothing doing," he said. "A deal is a deal. This is Friday—if you don't have the money by Monday morning at nine o'clock, I'll kill you!"

Jack tried everything possible, but he just couldn't come up with the money. So, after a sleepless night, at nine o'clock on Monday morning there was a knock on Jack's door. He knew this was it. There was nothing else he could do, so he took a gun and killed himself. What he didn't know was that the knock on the door was his brother Phil coming to tell him that Crazy Manny had been shot and killed the night before.

Isn't that a darling tragedy?

* * *

One of the vaudeville acts I did which I forgot to mention in the book was called "Ruby Delmar and Friend." I was

246

Friend. It wasn't great billing, but by that time I did so many acts I ran out of names. Ruby was a beautiful girl except that she was bowlegged. She always looked as though someone had stolen her cello. From her waist up, she was stunning. From her waist down, I was prettier.

In those days all the girls wore short skirts. But Ruby was self-conscious about her legs, so she always wore long skirts. Even on the stage her dress was right down to the floor. She was a great whirlwind dancer, but nobody knew it because everything she did was hidden by that skirt. When I was on the stage with her I'd look out at the audience, and they looked so confused—they knew something was going on under that skirt, but they didn't know what. So I had to explain to the audience that she was dancing. Once I had to explain it to the police.

Anyway, our agent said he couldn't get us any more work with Ruby wearing those long dresses. So I figured out the answer. I had Ruby wear a short skirt, changed the act to Latin music, and got Ruby a bongo drum. She was a sensation. She was the only girl who could do a whirlwind tango and still have room for the bongo. She was such a big hit that she teamed up with a bowlegged fellow and got rid of me. I really couldn't blame her; I had no place to hold my bongo.

There's a finish to this story. Ruby married her partner and I went to the wedding. It was a beautiful affair except for one thing—they had to walk down both aisles.

* * *

Years ago when Gracie and I were doing radio we hired Tony Martin as our singer. At that time Tony was very young and had been working as a saxophone player with a small band in Oakland. He sang with a saxophone around his neck, and he'd always play with the buttons on the sax while he was singing because he didn't know what to do with his hands.

247

When he came on our show he was just a singer and didn't need the saxophone. On his first show he sang "Begin the Beguine," and he was so used to playing with his buttons that when he got to the second chorus he lost his pants.

* * *

Several years ago I came up with an idea for a publicity stunt that I thought was tremendous. I was sure it would break into newpapers all over the country. Everybody always kids me about my singing, so I decided to take advantage of it and insure my voice for a million dollars. A brilliant idea, wasn't it?

I was so excited I couldn't wait to rush down to the insurance company, and I took a cassette and a tape recorder with me so the insurance man could hear my voice. I explained to him that I wanted to insure my voice for a million dollars and I played my cassette for him. It was one of my best numbers: a syncopated version of "Yankee Doodle Blues" with a yodeling finish. He sat there and listened patiently to the whole thing, then he just looked at me and said, "Mr. Burns, you should have come to us before you had the accident."

This kid made me kind of nervous. That was a very funny line and I couldn't think of a way to top it. But it didn't dull my enthusiasm any; I kept right on punching. I said, "Look, this is my natural way of singing, and you don't have to worry about having to pay any claims. Whatever is going to happen to my voice has already happened."

He sighed and said, "Mr. Burns, we're talking about a million-dollar policy. I could understand if you sang like Robert Goulet, or John Raitt, or Alfred Drake. They have trained voices."

I said, "Okay, so mine isn't even housebroken. But let me tell you the truth. This whole idea is a publicity stunt. I take out this big policy, it breaks in all the papers, I pay the first premium, and then we cancel."

He shook his head and said, "Mr. Burns, you're wasting your time. If my boss heard that cassette with that yodeling finish, there's no way in the world he'd approve the policy."

I said, "Do me a favor. Take the cassette inside, play it for your boss, and tell the truth. Tell him it's just a publicity stunt."

He smiled and said, "Mr. Burns, I know my boss, and it just won't work."

"I'll make a deal with you," I said. "If your boss doesn't okay that policy, I'll buy you a new suit of clothes."

He shrugged and took the cassette into the next office. Five minutes later he came out and said, "Mr. Burns, make that a blue suit with double vents in the jacket and dark-blue piping on the lapels."

Well, I never got the policy, but to show you what a sweet man I am, I threw in a monogrammed handkerchief for his breast pocket.

* * *

There was a very funny and zany act in vaudeville called Duffy and Sweeney. This particular time they were booked for a week into the Orpheum Theater in New Orleans. When they arrived they checked into the Roosevelt Hotel. Now, in those days you could get a double room for $3 a day, and that's what Duffy and Sweeney wanted. Somehow the hotel clerk got mixed up and instead of a double room gave them a whole suite. When they got upstairs and saw this elegant suite, Duffy picked up the phone and called down to the desk. He said, "How much is this suite?" And the clerk answered, "Twenty dollars a day."

"Well," Duffy said, "if we're going to pay twenty dollars a day, you better send up another Gideon Bible."

* * *

In reading over the galleys of this book I notice I didn't mention my friend Jack Haley. Jack and I have been very

249

close friends all of our lives, and if I don't mention his name, he may never talk to me again. So I better mention it. Here it is: Jack Haley!

* * *

In case you're wondering, let me tell you how this book got its subtitle, "They Still Love Me in Altoona!" When I was about eighteen I did a single and was using the name of Willie Saks. My billing was "Willie Saks and His Little Derby Hat." I don't say this was the worst act in show business, but if they'd taken a poll, I would have been right up there. Actually, I was what you called a disappointment act. I'd sit by the telephone with my grip packed, and in case an actor got sick or broke his leg, I was ready to jump in and take his place.

Well, after sitting in my room for about six weeks my phone rang, and it was a booking agent. An actor who was booked into Altoona had gotten sick and they needed somebody in a hurry. So off I went. I got there just in time to make the first matinee. My opening song went like this:

> You'll notice on the program where it mentions all the acts,
> If you take a look at Number 2, you'll see the name of Saks;
> It doesn't say company or anything like that,
> It simply says assisted by his little derby hat—
> Ohhhhhhhh,
> There is a little mystery what this little hat can do,
> It has a little history that I must tell to you;
> It doesn't sing, it doesn't dance or anything like that,
> It simply says assisted by his little derby hat—
> Ohhhhhhhh . . .

I sang about four more verses, then I told a few jokes, sang another song, and finished with an imitation of Pat Rooney. Don't ask me why, but I was a big hit. I took about six

250

bows. It scared me. I was so used to being a flop I figured I must be doing something wrong. After the matinee the manager came into my dressing room, and he was so happy about the way I had gone over that he asked me to stay and finish out the week. I was bowled over; I'd never played a full week anywhere before. Well, I finished the week, and after each show it was the same thing—I was a smash.

Three weeks later I was back waiting in my room again, and the phone rang. An actor had sprained an ankle and I was booked into Mechanicsville. I couldn't wait to get there; this time I was full of confidence. I swaggered out on the stage, did my act, and the people despised me.

And that's the way it went until I was twenty-seven. But whenever I got to feeling low, I could always look back and say to myself, *"They Still Love Me in Altoona"*!

Benny and Burns. *Photo by Trans Ocean Press.*

251

THE
THIRD TIME AROUND

CONTENTS

Every Chapter Must Have a Title	257
Me (Who Else?)	263
Every Family Should Have a Mother or Father	270
Never Trust Anyone Who Can't Sing Harmony	278
The Losing Breadwinner	286
Marriages Are Not Always Made in Heaven	292
All My Brothers Were Boys	300
It Takes Two People to Make a Marriage	309
They Paid Us in Pounds and Weighed Us in Stones	332
She Was Really Something	347
Titles Can Drive You Nuts	351
So We Stopped Working and Went into Radio	371
Some of My Best In-Laws Were Irish	382
I Never Like to Applaud Anything That Can't Applaud Back	392
Funny Routines Can Hurt Your Career	405
Screwballs, Oddballs, and Highballs	411
Please Pass the Hostess	420
Thanks for Letting Us Come into Your Living Room	443
A 79-Year-Old Star Is Born	458
W. Charles Emory Did It the Hard Way	470
If This Were a Serious Book, This Would Be the Last Chapter	473
Warm Leftovers	476
Roasted, Toasted, and Fried	487

EVERY CHAPTER MUST HAVE A TITLE

THIS IS MY third book. Twenty-two years ago I wrote my first one, in 1975 I wrote another, and here I am writing this one. Altogether I've written three books, which isn't bad for a guy who never read one. Well, that's show business.

Now don't misunderstand me, I think reading is a marvelous pastime, and it certainly can be exciting. For instance, if you're a man, try going to bed tonight with a good book and a cute blonde. If the blonde can't read, there's always television. And you women go to bed tonight with a good book and Robert Redford. You'll have a terrific time; they say he's the greatest reader in Hollywood.

Anyway, I've learned that when you write a book the most important factor is the basic overall construction; in other words, a book should have a beginning, a middle, and an end. If you've got that, you don't have to worry about the dull stuff in-between. Let me give you an example: In my book the beginning is page 1, the middle is page 128, and the end is page 256—it's that simple. When you know what you're doing there's nothing to it.

When my publisher, Putnam's, asked me to write another

book I thought to myself, why not write a bestseller. In the first place, more people buy them, more people read them, you make more money, and it doesn't take any more time to write a bestseller than it does to write a book that nobody buys. Since that was settled my only problem was what kind of bestseller should I write? I made my own little survey and spoke to Dave Lefcowitz—he's my milkman. Here's what Dave came up with. He said, "You better ask somebody else." When you're in a spot you can always depend on Dave.

Anyway, I took his advice and talked to my friends at the Friars Club and Hillcrest Country Club and found out that among the most popular types of books today are cookbooks, travel books, historical novels, and adventure stories. Well, I decided that of those four categories the easiest one for me would be to write a cookbook. After all, I've been eating all my life. In fact, I don't know anybody who's been eating longer.

Now I realized there were all kinds of cookbooks on the market, so I came up with an idea that was different—a cookbook of simple thrifty recipes for people with very little money to spend. My first recipe was a soup that was my favorite when I was a little boy. My family was extremely poor, and my mother used to make this delicious soup that cost practically nothing. Just thinking about it made my mouth water, so I fixed myself a bowl. I got a pan of water, put in some ketchup, added some black pepper and salt, and let it come to a slow boil. Then I poured it into a bowl and tasted it . . . .

So I decided to write a travel book. I figured everybody likes to travel, so I picked out the most exotic place I could think of. Why not write a book about Tahiti? This time I was so sure I was right I didn't even bother to consult Dave Lefcowitz. I put on my writer's coat, the one with the brown suede patches on the elbows, lit up a pipeful of aromatic tobacco, got myself a pad of paper and a half dozen sharp pencils, and I was ready to write. Well, I sat there . . . and I sat there . . . and I sat there.

Finally I figured out what my problem was—I'd never been to Tahiti.

This might have stopped an ordinary writer, but not a fellow who was dressed up like I was. Actually the solution was simple. The shelves are full of books about Paris, Rome, Tokyo, Athens, London, Cairo, Madrid, Helsinki, but those towns have been kicked. We've got dozens of places right here in the United States I could write about, beautiful places that you've probably never been to. In fact, I'm thinking of a place right now that I know all of you would love, and I think you should go there—Ronkonkoma, Long Island. During my days of vaudeville I played Ronkonkoma at least three or four times, and every night after the show I'd head straight for the town's most exciting spot, White's Cafeteria. And what made it exciting was the cashier. She was a sexy, well-built little redhead who . . . who . . . who . . . who must be about eighty years old by now.

It was then I decided to write a historical novel. So again I sat there, but nothing happened. The only historical event I remember is Washington crossing the Delaware. The reason I remember it so well, halfway across the General said to me, "Will you stop singing and row faster" . . .

Then I thought I'd write an adventure story . . .

Maybe I'd write a mystery story . . .

Why not science fiction . . .

Anthropology? . . . No, not anthropology. I knew less about anthropology than I did about Tahiti. I'd never been to either one of those places.

I was so depressed I planned to give up the whole thing. I poured myself a cup of hot coffee, took off my writer's jacket, put out my pipe, and broke the points off my pencils. I was just about to tear up my pads when I glanced down, and there was that cup of coffee. That's when it came to me! I'll write a book about sex! Well, I'm at the stage now where the only thing that turns me on is a cup of hot coffee. What I couldn't figure out was why I didn't think of writing a book about sex in the first place. Sex is the Universal Language in which nobody speaks; they don't have to. As the well-known philosopher Dr. J. J. Cromwell once said, "Put an Eskimo man in bed with a Polynesian woman—" That's when he left the room, that's all he said. It so intrigued me I ran after him, but I was too late. He was going down the street on his skateboard.

When I made up my mind to write about sex I gave it a lot of thought and came to the conclusion that there's one thing that makes it so popular: You don't have to get dressed for it. Furthermore, writing about sex has become a very lucrative business. Look at Harold Robbins and Irving Wallace. Both of them made a fortune out of sex. The only one I know who made more is my sister Goldie. And sex should be a simple subject to write about. After all, it's been with us since time began, and always will be with us until somebody finds a substitute for it. Which incidentally I've been looking for for some time now. (If you readers hear of anything, please throw it my way.)

Anyway, once the decision was made to write about sex it was a great load off my mind. All I had to do was put it down on paper, and I figured I'd write a book of 250 or 300 pages. I knew I could do it, I had the paper.

I planned on starting the first thing in the morning, so I went to bed early and had a marvelous night's sleep. When I woke up the next morning I even had the title, *Sex Is a Many-Splendored Thing*! I jumped out of bed—well, didn't exactly jump, I made it out of bed—and opened the window. It was a gorgeous day. The sun was shining and the birds were singing—naturally, I harmonized with them. You know I love to sing. I did my deep breathing exercises, went into the bathroom, brushed my teeth, shaved, and stepped into a nice hot shower. As I was drying off I happened to glance at myself in the mirror. Then I took a look at myself in the mirror. Then I took a *lonnnnnng* look at myself in the mirror. That's when I decided to write about Tahiti again. My dreams of being another Harold Robbins or Irving Wallace were shattered. I put my robe on fast so I wouldn't get any more depressed than I was. I didn't know what to do, so I started combing my hair. It was lying there, so I figured why not comb it. I'd never felt so low in my life. This could be the end of my career as a writer.

Even breakfast didn't lift my spirits. Everything was taste-less. Over my second cup of coffee I got to thinking; whatever gave me the idea I could write a book about sex in the first place? Things are different today than when I was young. In those days a fellow would meet a girl, they'd keep company, they'd get engaged, they'd get married, they'd raise a family and stay that way. Today marriage is old-fashioned, it's like getting your spats cleaned. If a boy and girl like each other, they live together, have a couple of kids, and if they like the way the kids look, then they get married. And if the kids are ugly, the parents can always get a divorce, start living together, and be happy again.

Of course, things are different for me nowadays, too. When I was young, before I got married I had a very exciting sex life. In my neighborhood I was known as the "Romeo of Rivington Street." I had all kinds of girls. There was Big Rose Siegel, and there was Little Rose Siegel, and that's about it. Now I spend my evenings in a comfortable chair watching television and smoking a cigar. I found out that smoking a cigar is much easier for me than being a great lover. With a cigar I don't have to remember its birthday; I don't have to worry about meeting its mother; I don't have to take it out dancing; I don't have to get undressed to smoke a cigar; and when I'm through with a cigar I don't have to call a taxi to take it home. You want to know the truth, I've reached the point now where sex is a spectator sport.

Anyway, after struggling and knocking my brains out trying to figure out what kind of book to write I came to the obvious conclusion: Why not write a book about the subject I know best—me. I've known me for eighty-three years, and during that time I've become very well acquainted with myself. So that's what this book is going to be about, and as you read it I hope you learn to love me as much as I do.

With all humility, thank you,

G. B.

ME (WHO ELSE?)

To LOOK AT me now you might not believe it, but I was born. As I recall, it was at a very early age. Now most people can't remember back that far, but I must have a remarkable memory. I remember the very moment I was born. I made my entrance into the world singing. The doctor held me up by my heels and kept slapping me, but I wouldn't stop until I finished two choruses of "Red Rose Rag." Then when I started singing "My Gal Is a High-Toned Lady" he put me in the incubator and turned off the heat. If I hadn't been smoking a cigar, I might have frozen to death. This had a great effect on my life. To this day whenever anyone picks me up by the heels and starts slapping me I go right into "Red Rose Rag." It happened just last night during dinner. I'll never be able to eat at Chasen's again.

Well, everything you've read up to now is a lie, which proves what a truthful man I am. If I tell you something is a lie, you know it's the truth.

And now that you understand my character, let me tell you how it developed. I came from a very large family. There were seven sisters, five brothers, and no mother or father. We were so poor we couldn't afford parents. Look, I know that's an old joke, but I couldn't think of anything else. You're just going to have to get used to my writing style, I'm too old to change it.

I better start at the beginning. My father's name was Louis Phillip Birnbaum, and my mother's maiden name was Dorothy Bluth. They both came from Eastern Europe and their families knew each other even though they lived in different cities. My parents' marriage was prearranged practically from the day they were born, and it was the custom in those days that in a prearranged marriage the bride and groom didn't meet until the day of their marriage. When the day arrived my mother was fourteen and my father was sixteen. I understand my grandmother was very relieved, she was afraid my mother might become an old maid. Even though my mother and father had never met before, I guess they learned to like each other, because before they were through they had twelve of us. Can you imagine getting married at fourteen? When my son Ronnie was fourteen he was still selling hot hub caps. But he was a good boy, he not only sold them to me wholesale, but he gave me a professional discount because I was in show business.

When my parents got married, conditions in Eastern Europe were pretty grim, and it was everybody's dream to leave there and come to America. So two years and two children later my father arrived in New York City and began living with some friends on the lower East Side. And since they were all strangers in a strange country, they became a very close-knit community. My father was able to find a job working twelve hours a day in a sweatshop pressing pants. By scrimping and saving, and with the help of his friends, he finally had enough money to send for my mother and their two kids. It took them about two weeks to get here by steerage. I'm sure the only reason they came by steerage was that TWA was on strike at the time.

When they arrived my father had arranged for them to move in with another family, for which he paid the enormous sum of five dollars a month. I don't know whether the crowded conditions had anything to do with it, but the Birnbaum family started to grow. They already had Morris and Annie, and soon there was Isadore, and then Esther, Sarah, Sadie, Mamie, Goldie, Nathan (the author), Sammy, Theresa and Willy. My father should have been a watchmaker because the kids came like clockwork.

By the time Willy came along we had really come up in the world; we had our own apartment at 259 Rivington Street, four small rooms on the third floor of a tenement house. There was a coal-burning stove in the kitchen which was used for cooking and heating the rooms, and we had cold running water except in the winter when the pipes froze. If you had to go to the bathroom, you went down three flights and out into the yard where there were just three toilets for the whole building. Sometimes you had to wait five or ten minutes. But not me. I knew exactly when to come down so I never had to wait. That's where I learned my marvelous sense of timing.

We had gaslight but very little of it, because about once a week when the gas ran out you had to put a quarter in the meter. My mother always kept the flame turned down very low to make the quarter last as long as possible. In fact, the light was turned down so low I was eight years old before I knew what my sisters looked like. Then one night my mother turned up the light, I got a look at my sisters and blew it out. They were happy, too, because they weren't too hopped up about the way I looked either.

Our family entertainment was pretty limited. In those days there was no television or radio, and we certainly couldn't afford the movies. Our idea of a fun evening was to sit in the kitchen and look out the window at the neighbors' wash. Sometimes that wash was pretty exciting. One time my sister Mamie jumped up and said, "Look, Mrs. Mittleman got new bloomers!" And you could always tell when the Goldbergs on the fourth floor had a fight. Mrs. Goldberg would hang out the

family wash, and then Mr. Goldberg had to hang out his own.
Except on Wednesday. On Wednesday she'd hang his wash out
first because that's the day he brought home a paycheck.

Thursday was bath day for us Birnbaum kids, and it was
quite a project when you consider that we didn't have a bathtub.
In fact, nobody in the whole neighborhood had a bathtub.
Here's how the project worked. My mother would boil water on
the kitchen stove and pour it into a washtub. And that one tub
of water took care of all of us, because it was expensive to heat
water. When the tub was full all the boys had to leave while the
girls bathed. The oldest girl went first and the others followed
in order. Believe me, nobody had time to play with a rubber
duck. It was just into the tub and out, because we didn't want
the water to get cold. Then the girls would dress as fast as they
could and rush out and the boys would rush in. We moved
around so fast we looked like a Mack Sennett comedy. We had
to, that bath water was still cooling off. Like with the girls, the
oldest boy went first. This routine was pretty tough on my
youngest brother, Willy. By the time it was his turn he was
dirtier when he got out of that water than when he went in.

You know, when I look back on those days on Rivington
Street it makes me realize how lucky kids are today. They've got
organized playgrounds, Little League, field trips, and in the
summer they all get on buses and go to summer camps where
they have swimming pools, basketball courts, baseball diamonds, and even a counselor to hand them a Kleenex in case
they sneeze. When I was a kid we had none of those things. Our
playground was the middle of Rivington Street. We only played
games that needed very little equipment, games like kick-the-
can, hopscotch, hide-and-go-seek, follow-the-leader. When we
played baseball we used a broom handle and a rubber ball. A
manhole cover was home plate, a fire hydrant was first base,
second base was a lamp post, and Mr. Gitletz, who used to
bring a kitchen chair down to sit and watch us play, he was
third base. One time I slid into Mr. Gitletz; he caught the ball

and tagged me out. There was no such thing as a uniform. One kid on the block showed up with a baseball cap and we made him go home. We didn't want to lose our amateur standing.

Our swimming pool was the East River. When we got tired of playing baseball we'd wave goodbye to Mr. Gitletz, run down to the river, take off our clothes, and jump in. This took a pretty strong stomach because the East River was full of garbage. When we'd swim we had to use what we called the "overhand slap" stroke. We'd slap the water with our right hand, and this would clear a path through the garbage. Then we'd slap it with our left hand, and that's the way it worked. I'm not sure, but I don't think Mark Spitz would have enjoyed this.

Using the overhand slap you could swim about five yards in five minutes. But there was one advantage. If you got tired, you could always crawl up on the garbage and rest. And if you were lucky, sometimes you'd find an apple with only one bite out of it.

After a refreshing swim we'd all get up on the garbage and walk back to the pier. Then we'd put on our clothes and head for home. After that swim, believe me, people knew we were coming three blocks before we got there.

The big treat for the little girls in the neighborhood was when Luigi the organ grinder came around with his monkey. Luigi was a big, good-natured Italian fellow, and the monkey's name was Toto. Toto wore a red velvet pillbox hat and a red velvet suit with gold buttons and a green sash. That monkey looked so good all us kids thought Luigi was working for him. Now seeing a monkey caused a lot of excitement on Rivington Street; the only animals we saw were stray cats and dogs running around. I remember bringing a dog home once, but he only stayed a couple of days. He left when he found out he had to take his bath after Willy.

When Luigi played the organ all the little girls started to dance. Everybody gathered around, and people stuck their heads out of windows and threw pennies which Toto tried to catch in his hat. For us kids this was more fun than watching Mrs. Mittleman's new bloomers. And it was my first taste of show business. When I saw that audience I jumped right in and started dancing along with the girls. We improvised all sorts of steps as we went along. We'd leap and twirl and do high kicks, and if I do say so myself, I was more graceful than most of the girls. My toes were always pointed, my back was arched, and my wrists were very loose. In fact, my mother was getting worried about me. When I recall times like that it makes me think that maybe kids today aren't so lucky. I'd give anything to hear Luigi play that organ again. But I don't think I'd get up and dance. My back is still arched, but now it's in the other direction.

There was never any problem finding somebody to play with because the streets were loaded with kids. And it's not hard to figure out why. In our building alone there were sixteen families, and each family had between eight and ten kids. When we were all playing together in the street there were so many of us we'd get mixed up and forget which family we belonged to. At nine o'clock in the evening my mother would holler out the window, "Come on up, children, it's time to go to bed!" We'd all rush up, and my mother would stand there with the door open. When the house was full she'd close it. Sometimes I made it, sometimes I slept in the hall.

In the summer I used to sleep on the roof under the clothesline. My favorite spot was right under Mr. Rosenbloom's underwear. I always opened up the flap so in the morning when the sun came up it would shine through on my face. I was the only kid in the neighborhood who had a suntan with buttonholes in it.

That last part isn't true, but I was rolling so good I couldn't stop myself. Look, I may exaggerate now and then to try to be a little amusing, but basically this was the way we lived. We were poor, our neighbors were poor, we thought everybody in the world was poor. Our idea of somebody being rich was the Feingolds who lived on the corner. They had curtains in their windows. I remember I used to get up early in the morning and steal their garbage. Then I'd put it in our can. I wanted people to think we were doing well.

EVERY FAMILY SHOULD HAVE A MOTHER OR FATHER

To this day what amazes me is how my mother and father managed to raise twelve kids under the conditions we lived in. But whatever they did must have been right, because every one of us turned out fine. None of us wound up in jail, none of us were alcoholics, and none of us got mixed up with drugs. And there was a reason for this: We couldn't afford it. The only thing that turned us kids on was if there was a little meat in the gravy. Nobody made gravy like my mother. And it was a damned good thing because we had it seven days a week.

There was only one thing better than my mother's gravy and that was her coffee. Every morning one of us kids would go down to the grocery store, and for five cents we'd get a half gallon of milk. Now this was raw milk with no cream in it, so it was sort of a bluish color and very thin. My mother would pour this into a coffee pot and put it on the stove. Then she'd float some chicory on top, and when the milk came to a boil the chicory would sink to the bottom. This not only flavored the milk but changed the blue into a nice coffee color. Next she poured this through a strainer into our cups, and that was our morning coffee. If Maxwell House had tasted this coffee, they would have gone into some other business. In fact, on Rivington Street my mother was known as Mrs. Olson.

We were a very close family, and it wasn't just because of my mother's gravy and coffee. When you're twelve people living in four little rooms, you've got to be close. Now a highlight on the Birnbaum social calendar was when our relatives would come over and we'd all sit around and listen to my sister Sadie sing. Actually, Sadie hated to sing, and the rest of us kids hated to hear her, but my mother thought she had a beautiful voice. It was sheer torture for Sadie to stand up and sing in front of people, but when my mother said "Sing!" Sadie sang. So Sadie wouldn't be embarrassed my mother would allow her to go into the bedroom and leave the door open. Then standing in that dark bedroom Sadie would sing, and we'd all listen from the other room. I recall one night just as she was building up to her high note, my Uncle Frank got up and closed the bedroom door. I think that was the last time he was ever invited to one of our musicales. I'm sure you're wondering why my mother didn't ask me to sing; after all, that's what later made me famous. But you see, Sadie knew all the traditional Jewish folk songs and lullabys. All I knew was "Rufus Rastus Johnson Brown, Whatcha Gonna Do When De Rent Comes Roun'. " I sang that once for my Uncle Frank, but he was so religious I had to sing it with my hat on.

I think that one of the things that kept us kids pretty much in line was the respect we all had for our parents. It wasn't something that was forced on us; it was just there. It was natural, we were born that way. I never remember my mother slapping me, and I'm sure that went for my brothers and sisters. We may have deserved a good wallop once in a while, but that wasn't the way my mother operated. She was a very practical lady, and .she dealt with our problems with patience and understanding. Nothing ever seemed to fluster her.

A perfect example happened when I was seven years old. I was singing with three other Jewish kids from the neighbor-

hood. We called ourselves the Peewee Quartet. Now there was a
big department store, Siegel & Cooper, which threw an annual
picnic, and the highlight was an amateur contest with talent
representing all the churches in New York. Right around the
corner from where we lived was a little Presbyterian church.
How it got in that neighborhood I'll never know; it certainly
didn't do big business. Well, they had no one to enter in the
contest, so the minister asked us four kids to represent the
church. We jumped at the chance. So that Sunday there we
were, the Peewee Quartet—four Jewish boys sponsored by a
Presbyterian church—and our opening song was "When Irish
Eyes Are Smiling." We followed that with "Mother Machree"
and won first prize. The church got a purple velvet altar cloth,
and each of us kids got an Ingersoll watch which was worth
about eighty-five cents.

Well, I was so excited I ran all the way home to tell my
mother. When I got there she was on the roof hanging out the
wash. I rushed up to her and said, "Mama, I don't want to be a
Jew anymore!"

If this shocked her, she certainly didn't show it. She just
looked at me and calmly said, "Do you mind me asking why?"

I said, "Well, I've been a Jew for seven years and never got
anything. I was a Presbyterian for one day and I got a watch,"
and I held out my wrist and showed it to her. She glanced at it
and said, "First help me hang up the wash, then you can be a
Presbyterian." While I was hanging up the wash some water ran
down my arm and got inside the watch. It stopped running, so I
became a Jew again.

In situations where most mothers would have become very
upset and excited, mine took it in stride. She had a way of
solving a problem, and you didn't even know she was doing it.
When I was seventeen I started running around with a girl
named Jean DeFore who I thought was the greatest thing since
ketchup. And you didn't have to hit her on the bottom to get her
started. Jean DeFore was six years older than I was, and believe

me, nobody would mistake her for Mary Poppins. At that time if a girl wore a little bit of rouge, she was considered fast and loose. Well, Jean not only used rouge, she wore beaded eyelashes and lipstick. And to top it all, she penciled in a black beauty mark on her cheek. All she needed was a red lantern hanging around her neck. If you're wondering why a seventeen-year-old kid would get mixed up with a girl like that, stop and think about it. It's better than playing with a rusty knife and cutting yourself.

When Jean had all that makeup on she may have been twenty-three, but she looked more like thirty. But I was so proud that she'd go out with a seventeen-year-old kid that I couldn't wait to take her home to meet my mother. So one Sunday afternoon I did just that. As soon as we got in the door I said, "Mama, I want you to meet my sweetheart, Jean DeFore."

My mother was all smiles, not a hint that anything might be unusual. "Sit down, Jean," she said, indicating a chair. "Make yourself at home." Well, we all got comfortable, and in a very friendly manner my mother asked Jean if she were Jewish. Jean said she wasn't, and then my mother inquired, "Do you understand Jewish?" Again Jean said no. Turning to me and still smiling sweetly, my mother said in Jewish, "Is this lovely lady planning to adopt you?" Then looking directly at Jean, in a motherly tone she said, "I just told my son what a charming girl you are."

That's the way my mother operated. In a nice way she had made me realize how perfectly ridiculous I must have looked.

Where my mother was very realistic about things, my father was exactly the opposite. He was a dreamer. And being extremely religious he felt that life here on earth was just a stopover on our way to the hereafter. I didn't mind stopping over, but I thought it would be nice to have a little something in my stomach before continuing that trip. If I said my father was the worst provider in the world, I'd be lying. He wasn't that good. It wasn't that he didn't love us because he did very much, but trifles like food and rent and clothing never even crossed his mind.

There was an aura about my father. I don't know how to describe it, but there was something so impressive about him that with no particular effort he commanded love and respect. Not only his family, but the entire community looked up to him. He had long since given up his job as a pants presser and now spent most of his time at the synagogue reading religious books and discussing philosophy with other scholars. Occasionally he would bring a little money into the house which he earned as a *mashgiach*. Now being a *mashgiach* is not the kind of a job that's going to put one into a high-income tax bracket. You see, in an orthodox Jewish community if a family has an engagement party, a wedding or a bar mitzvah, they hire a *mashgiach* to make sure that everything is kosher. There was no set price for this service; the families paid what they could afford. Sometimes it was nothing. But when my father came home with nothing it didn't bother my mother; even when he got paid it was so close to nothing she could hardly tell the difference.

Being a *mashgiach* wasn't my father's only source of income. He was also a part-time cantor. And sometimes he'd sing at the services of one of the small synagogues. This didn't happen very often because his singing voice sounded a lot like mine. I remember one year he was asked to sing at a tiny synagogue on Clinton Street for the High Holidays. This was a very poor little synagogue, so my father agreed to do it for nothing. That night the period of fasting was over so all of us were gathered in the kitchen waiting for dinner. My father was laughing and joking and teasing us kids; he seemed unusually elated. My mother didn't exactly share his mood because she was busy trying to water down a stew to the point where it would feed a bunch of kids who hadn't eaten in twenty-four hours. She looked at my father and said, "What are you so happy about, that synagogue is paying you nothing." My father turned to her, and with a big broad smile said, "I know, but they asked me to come back again next year." Let's face it, my father was not handled by the William Morris Agency.

Although his religion was the most important thing in his life, my father did have a sense of humor. As I mentioned before, our house was always full of kids running in and out. Well, one night when my father came home and sat down in his favorite rocking chair, a little boy ran over to him and jumped into his lap. He held up the boy and said to my mother, "Dassah, which one is this?"

She turned from the stove and said, "Don't be silly, that's the Steiner's little boy."

"Thank goodness," my father sighed, "I've been gone all day, I thought maybe we had another one."

It's very difficult for me to write about my father, because my recollections of him are rather vague. I was only seven years old when he passed away, and he never allowed photographs of himself to be taken. He believed that having your picture taken was catering to your ego. But I do remember that he was a very gentle man, with kindly brown eyes and a long, full, impressive gray beard. That beard fascinated me. I used to pinch my face every day trying to make whiskers grow so I could have one just like it. And I don't think I ever saw my father unless he was wearing either his hat or his yarmulke. I often wondered if he took his hat off when he went to bed. Come to think of it, I guess he didn't have time.

My father never showed any favoritism to any of us children. He loved us all equally. My mother expressed her love the same way, so there was no such thing as a spoiled child in our family. When my mother told us to eat, we ate; when she told us to go to bed, we went; when she said it was time to go to school, we'd go. It was like being in the army, except for one thing. Our Commanding Officer kissed us good night.

The day my father died left a lasting impression me. Since I was only seven this was my first experience with death. I don't know what I expected, but I didn't realize it could be so quiet, so simple, and so sudden. It was a late Saturday afternoon, and my father was sitting in his rocking chair in the living room reading one of his religious books. My mother was looking out the window watching the kids dance to the organ grinder down in the street. I was on the floor playing. I heard my father call to my mother. "Dassah," he said, but she didn't hear him because of the music. "Mama," I said in a louder voice, "Papa's calling you." She looked around; his book had fallen to the floor and he was gone.

My father was only forty-seven years old when he left us, but as I said before he had the respect of the entire community, and his funeral certainly proved it. The whole Lower East Side turned out, and you couldn't move on Rivington Street. His death was almost more than my mother could cope with. She was only a child when she was married, so it was very difficult for her to imagine life without him. She had no choice but to continue her household duties, but every time the thought of my father being gone would come into her mind, she'd start to cry. We younger children didn't quite understand, but every time my mother cried, we cried. I don't know exactly how long this went on, but eventually life returned to normal and there were no more tears. However, my mother's tears may have stopped, but her thoughts of my father never did. Twenty-five years later after I'd married Gracie and was doing well, on one of my frequent visits home my mother and I had a cup of coffee, and she filled me in on the activities of the rest of the family. Just as I was about to leave she said to me, "Nattie, I want you to do me a favor."

I said, "Sure, Mama, anything you want."

"I think," she told me, "it's about time to put a new tombstone on your father's grave."

So the next day I took care of it. Up until then I didn't know tombstones wore out; I thought they lasted a lifetime.

I feel it's only right that I close this chapter with an observation. It's true that my father may not have provided me with too many material things, but he did give me a sense of responsibility, and he taught me the difference between right and wrong. For that I will always be grateful to him.

NEVER TRUST ANYONE WHO CAN'T SING HARMONY

As long as I can remember I always loved to sing. It was something inside me that just had to come out. If you had something like that inside you, you'd want it out, too.

Even to this day my whole life revolves around singing. For example, as I write this we're having a water shortage in California, and in order to help out I make my singing work for me. When I'm taking a shower I sing a very fast song. That way I'm out in no time and save a lot of water. Of course, I do miss not going back for an encore.

Another way my singing comes in handy is with Arlette, my cook. She knows exactly what I want for breakfast by what song I sing. When I come downstairs if I'm singing "I'm Tying the Leaves So They Won't Fall Down," that means matzos, eggs, and onions. If I'm singing "When Uncle Joe Plays a Rag on His Old Banjo," that's bran flakes and bananas. But if I come down yodeling, that means only coffee this morning, I'm late.

I never stop singing. Even when I get in my car to go to work I sing to myself as I'm driving along. Of course, I always close the windows so nobody can hear me. If people are going to hear me sing, I want to get paid.

Now Hollywood is a big party town. You can go to a party practically every night of the week. And when celebrities are there it's a common thing for the host to ask them to get up and entertain. But when I give a party I don't put my guests in that spot. I bring in my piano player who can only play in my key and I never stop singing. It's amazing to me how many of my friends seem to be out of town whenever I throw a party.

I recall one time I planned a party for twenty people and eight people showed up. I guess the other twelve didn't like the dessert I always served. After dinner, as usual I got up and sang, and sang, and sang. I finally looked up, and the only ones left were Jack and Mary Benny. They had to stay, Jack was my best friend. By five after ten they were gone too. I guess you can only push a friendship so far. After they left I sang four more songs to Gracie. Of course, I had to sing them without music. . . . my piano player sneaked out when Jack and Mary left.

If I do say so myself, I'm a marvelous guest to have at a party. If things get a little dull, I jump right in and do two or three numbers. Sometimes I jump in before it gets dull. Once, Sylvia and Danny Kaye gave a party, and I went there with my piano player. Danny opened the door, let my piano player in, then closed it. Well, I figured Danny must not have recognized me, so I rang the bell. When he opened the door, I said, "Danny, it's me, George Burns." He said, "I know," and closed the door again. Well, I can take a hint, I don't have to have a brick building fall on me. I got in my car, closed the windows, and sang to myself all the way home.

Singing first became an important part of my life when three other kids and myself formed the Peewee Quartet. I was seven years old and sang tenor. A kid we called Toda was our lead singer. His right name was Moishe Friedman, so naturally we called him Toda. Our baritone was Mortzy Weinberger. We were all about the same age except Heshy Weinberger, who was eight. Heshy not only sang bass, but being older he was our business manager. If the Peewee Quartet were around today, I don't think the Osmond Brothers would lose any sleep.

It all started in the basement of Rosenzweig's candy store. After school the four of us each got five cents a day mixing the syrup that Rosenzweig put in his ice cream sodas. And as a fringe benefit we got all the sodas we could drink. By the end of the first week we could have opened a pimple factory. Toda's kid brother who was five years old tried to get a job working with us, but our manager, Heshy, threw him out. He told him he was too young to work.

There were four big copper vats, and our job was to pour in the extract of chocolate, vanilla, strawberry, and lemon. Then we'd stir it until it came to a boil, and bottle it. Well, when you stand there stirring syrup for two and a half hours a day for six days a week, it gets pretty monotonous. So as we were stirring we started singing, and before we knew it we were harmonizing with each other. And we didn't sound bad. Our favorite song was called "Dear Old Girl." Now "Dear Old Girl" was a very slow ballad, and naturally when you sing slow, you stir slow. When Rosenzweig heard us singing that song he'd run out on the street and holler down into the basement, "If you kids gotta sing, sing something fast like 'Row, Row, Row Your Boat,' I'm running out of syrups!"

The longer we sang together the better we sounded. Then one day we noticed that people were stopping at the head of the basement steps and listening to us. Well, when we saw we had an audience we stopped stirring altogether, stood in the doorway, and sang to them. We not only got applause, but they threw down a few pennies. At the end of the day we counted it up and we had made forty-two cents. Our manager, Heshy, was no dum-dum. He said, "Fellas, we made forty-two cents with our singing. That's over twice what we're getting from Rosenzweig." Our stirring days were over. We rushed upstairs, and Heshy announced, "Mr. Rosenzweig, we quit, we're going into show business!" Rosenzweig just stood there with his mouth open. He couldn't say a word. I guess he was stunned being in the presence of us celebrities. When we got out on the street we divided up the forty-two cents. Each of us got a dime, but Heshy kept the extra two cents because he was our manager. Besides, he was bigger than any of us.

That was the day I fell in love with show business. And here it is seventy-six years later and the romance is still going strong. I can still harmonize "Dear Old Girl," but please, don't offer me an ice cream soda.

We decided to call ourselves the Peewee Quartet. Of course, some people decided to call us other things. Anyway, our show business career started the next day. Right after school the four of us rushed down to the corner of Columbia and Houston Streets. We stood there and sang from three-thirty to six, and made exactly four cents. This meant a penny apiece, and there was no commission for Heshy. Mortzy took this pretty hard. "Fellows," he said, "I don't know about you, but I'm giving up show business. Tomorrow I'm going back to Rosenzweig's."

As we started back home we were all very discouraged until Heshy came up with a brilliant idea that saved the Peewee Quartet. He said, "Kids, we made a mistake. Instead of standing on street corners, tomorrow we'll start singing in backyards. That way people can't walk by us." And that's exactly what we did. The following day we hit about ten backyards, and by six o'clock we had made fifty-eight cents. However, we soon found out when you sang in backyards you had to be fast on your feet. Some people would throw down pennies, and sometimes you'd get a face full of dishwater.

By the end of the first week we were wet, but we each wound up with $1.30. There was no stopping us now. I don't know which one of us it was, but somebody came up with the idea that we could make even more money singing in saloons. It didn't matter that we were all too young to even be allowed inside. The first saloon we went into, Heshy walked right up to the bartender and announced, "We're the Peewee Quartet, and we'd like to sing for you and your customers."

The bartender shouted, "Get outta here!" and took a swipe at Heshy with a wet bar rag. But he missed him. Heshy was fast on his feet from dodging dishwater.

Back out on the street it was my turn to save the day. I said, "Fellas, we've made another mistake. The next saloon we go into we sneak under the swinging doors, and as soon as we get inside we start singing before they know we're there. If they like our singing, they'll let us stay." Everybody agreed, and we decided that when we finished singing Heshy would pass his hat around. It had to be Heshy because he had the only hat without a hole in it.

Well, at the next saloon we ducked under the door and went right into our opening song, which was "Goodbye, Girlie, and Remember Me." Sure enough, the bartender started to yell and went for his bar rag, but a customer stopped him. "The kids sound good, let 'em sing," he called out. We sang three songs, and when Heshy passed the hat everybody at the bar put something in it. And as we left, the bartender gave us each a baloney sandwich from the free lunch counter.

When we got outside the first thing we did was count the money. It came to sixty-five cents. Then Heshy went to take a bite of his baloney sandwich and a dime popped out of his mouth. Heshy was learning fast how to be a business manager. After that, first we looked in Heshy's mouth, then we counted the money.

Now don't get the idea that we scored in every saloon. Most of the time they threw us out. But that didn't bother us, we'd just move on to the next saloon.

However, it wasn't long before we wore out our welcome in every saloon on the Lower East Side. What we needed was a new audience, so we took the show on the road. We started singing on the Staten Island ferry. For a nickel apiece we could get on the ferry, and if we didn't get off, we could ride back and forth all day long. It worked out perfectly; every trip we had a captive audience. The only way they could get away from us was to jump overboard.

Now the Staten Island ferry had two decks, and the passengers would sit on benches. So whenever we would see a group of four or five people we'd stand in front of them and sing. Then Heshy would pass the hat, we'd check his mouth, and move on to the next group. We didn't do badly, but Sunday turned out to be our best day. On Sunday fellows would bring their girls with a basket lunch, and they'd spend the whole day riding the ferry. Well, we took advantage of this. Whenever we'd see a fellow begin to make love to his girl we'd jump in front of them and start to sing harmony. Of course, this would annoy the guy, so he'd give us a dime to sing on the upper deck. This trick kept us running up and down all day Sunday. We were making more money from people who didn't want to hear us sing than from people who did. But we finally had to give up playing the ferry boat, because most of the time we were only a trio. Mortzy Weinberger used to get seasick, and while the rest of us were doing our number Mortzy would be at the rail doing his.

Most kids would have been pretty discouraged by then. The ferry boats made Mortzy sick, the saloons had heard all our stuff, and the backyards meant a face full of dishwater. But that didn't stop the Peewee Quartet. We had a meeting and it was agreed that we should move into new territory. The following day was St. Patrick's Day, so we all put on something green and went up into the Irish neighborhood around Eighteenth Street and Tenth Avenue. All the saloons were jumping that day. The first one we went into we started right off with "MacNamara's Band," and we were a smash. We hit every saloon in the neighborhood, and by the time we were finished we had made over seventeen dollars, which to us was a fortune. We were standing on a street corner counting the money, when we looked up and there were ten tough-looking Irish kids coming down the street towards us. We didn't wait to find out if they were friendly or not, we just ran. And they took off after us. All we wanted to do was get back to our own neighborhood with that seventeen dollars. We must have run about two miles until we spotted this Jewish Boys' Club, and in we went. Inside there was a bunch of sixteen- and seventeen-year-old boys shooting pool, so we told them our problem. We explained that we had made over seventeen dollars and these Irish kids outside were trying to take it away from us. The biggest one in the group patted me on the head and said, "You boys are lucky you came here, we'll take care of this." With that they went outside with their pool cues and chased the Irish kids home. Then they came back inside, took our seventeen dollars, and chased us home. Well, that taught me a lesson that's still with me: Never go to a Jewish Boys' Club on St. Patrick's Day.

The Peewee Quartet hung together until I was about nine years old, and then we all went our separate ways. Mortzy and Heshy Weinberger became successful in the taxicab business. They both got married and raised grandchildren, and the last I heard they're retired and living in Florida. Moishe Friedman isn't called Toda anymore. He's now T. Harold Friedman and is a retired insurance broker living in a very nice house in Scarsdale. I'm the only one who didn't make good; I'm still in show business.

Those two years I spent singing with the Peewee Quartet must have been a great help to me throughout my entire career. As I mentioned before, I was a small-time vaudeville actor until I was twenty-seven years old. And when I say small, I mean the smallest. But I loved show business and never let anything discourage me. I was a singer, a dancer, a yodeling juggler, I did a rollerskating act, an act with a seal, I worked with a dog . . . you name it, and I did it. In those days if the manager of the theater didn't like your act, he'd cancel you after the first performance. I remember one Monday morning at the Farley

Theater in Brooklyn I was rehearsing my songs, and the manager heard the rehearsal and canceled me. I think it was the first time in show business that an act was closed before it opened.

But these things didn't faze me. I'd just think of the Peewee Quartet, and in comparison to a face full of dishwater or being hit with a wet bar rag, anything else was a step up. Anyway, I went from one cancellation to another until I met this little Irish girl, Gracie Allen, and we teamed up. Before long we started to play some good theaters, and people finally discovered I had a big talent. And I did—Gracie!

THE LOSING BREADWINNER

WE WERE ALWAYS a close family, but after my father died we became even closer. We all missed him not being there, but our family routine stayed pretty much the same. My mother had always been the one who handled everything. Although the three oldest children had married and moved away, there were still nine of us kids living at home. How my mother managed with practically no money coming in I'll never know. But she did. When Jesus fed four thousand people with seven loaves of bread and a few small fishes, he must have gotten the idea from my mother.

All of us kids did whatever we could to try to help out. Even though I was only seven, I decided to become the breadwinner of the family. I figured I'd been bumming around long enough, and it was time for me to go out into the world and seek my fortune. Of course, this was before I made my tremendous success with the Peewee Quartet. As it turned out, I wasn't exactly a breadwinner. I was more like the crumbwinner of the family.

Like most kids, every day after school I started out selling newspapers. Then I branched into all kinds of things. I became sort of a one-man conglomerate. And that was before I became a man, or before I knew what conglomerate meant. Newspapers in those days sold for a penny apiece. I'd start out with thirty-five papers and stand on the corner of Delancey Street and Clinton, which was a busy intersection. If I sold all the papers, I'd make seven cents. Sometimes I'd have eight or nine papers left over, and to get rid of them I'd run through the streets hollering things like "Extra! Extra! Ferry Boat Sinks in East River!!" or "Big Gun Battle in Sharkey's Restaurant!!" One day when I was stuck with eleven papers I took off down the street yelling, "Extra! Extra! Huber's Museum Goes Down in Flames!!!" Well, I was selling newspapers like hotcakes, when all of a sudden I felt a hand on my shoulder. It turned out to be a disgruntled customer. He held the paper in front of my face and said, "What are you pulling, kid? There's nothing in this newspaper about a fire at Huber's Museum!"

For a split second I didn't know what to say. Then I blurted out, "I know, that's such an early edition the fire hasn't started yet!" and ran.

I managed to save enough out of my newspaper earnings to branch out into the shoeshine business. I bought a can of polish for a nickel and got myself a little wooden box that I hung on a strap over my shoulder. I'd walk along the street selling shines for either two or three cents. For three cents I'd use a little polish, for two cents I'd just spit and rub. All I had was black polish, so if a customer had brown shoes, I'd sell him a newspaper.

One of my many big business ventures lasted exactly two hours and twenty minutes. I thought there was money to be made by selling vanilla crackers. I'd go into a grocery store and buy a bunch of vanilla crackers at ten for a penny. Then on the street I'd sell them eight for a penny. This meant that every time I sold eight crackers I'd make two crackers profit. The problem here was by the time I sold eight crackers I'd eaten two crackers. It didn't take me long to realize that this was the wrong business for a kid who was hooked on vanilla crackers.

Up to now my contributions to the Birnbaum Survival Fund hadn't been the greatest. But I figured if I kept trying sooner or later I'd strike it rich. I'd always heard that all wealthy men started at the bottom, and if this were true, I had a better start than anybody. For me to get to the bottom would be a step up.

When summer vacation came along I hit upon what I thought was my greatest idea. In summertime everybody needs ice, so why not go into the ice business. I made myself a pull-cart out of an apple crate and two old baby-buggy wheels. I nailed a stick on the front to pull it by, and I'd haul my cart down to an ice house by the East River and buy a hundred-pound cake of ice for five cents. Then I'd pull it back to my neighborhood, split the cake into four quarters, and sell each one for five cents. I was making a fifteen-cent profit on every cake of ice. By hustling I was able to do this three times a day, which meant I could make a profit of $2.25 in a five-day week. Unfortunately, I never made it to the end of the first week. In order to get to the ice house I had to go right through the middle of this Italian neighborhood, and on the fourth day I was happily running along with my second cake of ice when these two rough-looking kids stopped me. Right away I knew I was in trouble when one of them said, "Hey, kid, I never saw you in this neighborhood! What's your name?"

I knew I had to think fast, my ice was melting, and so was I. I had to come up with an Italian name, so I blurted out the only one I could think of, "Enrico Caruso!"

The biggest of the two stuck his face right in front of mine and snarled, "Are you Catholic?" I looked right back at him and said, "Are you kidding, my father's a priest!"

That was the end of my ice business. They took my cart and my ice and chased me all the way back to Rivington Street.

Well, this was the low point in my life. Here I was seven

years old and I'd already failed in four different enterprises. There was only one avenue left for me to take—I turned to a life of crime! And in a big way. I started stealing seltzer bottles.

I know this may shock some of you readers, but when my publisher asked me to write this book I promised to tell it just like it was. Of course, this confession might destroy my image as an ancient Casanova, but what the hell—that's a chance us sex symbols have to take.

Let me tell you how this little ripoff of mine worked. In those days people used to buy seltzer water in bottles that had a heavy lead top, and before they returned the empty bottles to the store to get a two-cent refund they kept them out on the fire escape. Now the first step in this caper of mine was to get my hands on those bottles. This involved going up on the roof, lowering a string with a hook on the end of it, catching it on the handle of the seltzer bottle and pulling it up. I got quite good at it. If I worked fast, within a half hour I could probably pull up twenty or thirty seltzer bottles.

I suppose you think the next step would be to take those bottles back to the store for the two-cent refund. Not me. I wasn't the Willie Sutton of my day for nothing. When I got about ten bottles I'd take them down to the basement, unscrew the tops, melt them and sell the lead for a much bigger profit. It worked out so that instead of two cents I got six cents for each seltzer bottle top.

Once I got the plan worked out I couldn't wait to put it into operation. The next day I played hooky from school. With all the money I planned to make I thought who needs an education? Looking back, it's amazing to me how stupid a kid could get in only seven years.

Well, the next morning there I was on the roof pulling up seltzer bottles. Within twenty minutes I had ten bottles. This was working out even better than I planned. Ten bottle tops at six cents apiece, there was forty-eight cents right there. (You can see what playing hooky did to my arithmetic!) I was gathering up the bottles to take them down to the basement when I got the feeling I was not alone. I looked around and there stood my mother with her arms folded, staring down at me. For a few seconds there was complete silence. Finally, with a weak smile, I said, "Mama, I'm not in the ice business anymore."

More silence.

I said, "Mama, I'm now in the used bottle top business."

"I can see that," she said, without changing her expression, "with other people's bottles."

"Mama, are you mad at me?"

"No, I came up here to take a tap dancing lesson!"

"But how did you know I was up here on the roof?"

"Everybody in the building knows you're up here. How often do people see seltzer bottles flying past their windows?"

Trying to plead my case, I said, "But, Mama, I was just trying to make money for us. I could unscrew the heads of these bottles and sell them for six cents apiece."

This did not impress my mother. "If somebody unscrewed your head, I don't think it would even sell for two cents," she said. "You're going to return every one of those bottles to the people you took them from!"

I couldn't stand the thought of facing all our neighbors. "Mama," I cried, "I can't do that."

"Yes you can, and I'll show you how! How many bottles did you steal from Mrs. Mittleman on the fourth floor?"

"Three," I whimpered.

Then pointing, she said firmly, "Pick up three of those bottles and come with me."

I felt like a drowning man going down for the third time. As I picked up the bottles all of my seven years flashed in front of my eyes. Like a whipped puppy I followed her downstairs and waited while she knocked on Mrs. Mittleman's door. When the door opened my mother gestured toward me, and with exaggerated sweetness, said, "Mrs. Mittleman, I'd like you to meet my son, the criminal."

I just stood there with my arms full of evidence and kept staring at the floor. "Now you march over to that window," my mother continued, "and put Mrs. Mittleman's bottles back on her fire escape."

Well, I rushed to the window, put down the bottles and got out of there as fast as I could. When we were alone in the hall, my mother said, "Up on the roof you said you couldn't return those bottles. Well, now I've showed you how. So you get busy and return every one of them right now!"

That's one morning I'll never forget. Not only had I been thoroughly humiliated, but here I was seven years old and all washed up. How could I go into another business with a criminal record? One thing this little episode taught me was that crime doesn't pay—at least, not like it does nowadays.

MARRIAGES ARE NOT ALWAYS MADE IN HEAVEN

HAVE YOU NOTICED that marriage seems to be on the way out? Well, I have. Maybe you've been so interested in reading this book that you haven't noticed it, but it's happening. People are just not bothering with the tradition of marriage anymore. Nowadays when a young couple meet, if he's got a rear seat on his motorcycle, they start living together. And after they start living together if some night the girl doesn't feel sexy, she can't use that old excuse about having a headache. When you've been riding around on a motorcycle all day it isn't your head that aches.

But I'm not criticizing the way young people do things today, I don't know whether it's good or bad. However, there's one thing I'm sure of, it's fast. When I was young, a couple had to be formally introduced. Now a guy sees a girl, he says, "Hiya, Foxy," and she says, "Your place or mine?" What's their hurry? Sex has been around for a long time. You may not believe this, but it was around before I was.

With all due respect to the kids of today, I think my generation had more fun. We made it last longer. Once a fellow met a girl he'd start going out with her, and maybe on the fifth date he'd steal a little kiss. After eight or nine months of keeping company they'd decide to get married, and the fellow would go to the girl's father and ask for her hand in marriage. Well, it's not that way today. Why should a fellow ask a girl's father for her hand? What does he want with her hand, he's already had everything else.

Our whole attitude toward living today is speed. Everything has to be done right now. Look around you. There's instant coffee, instant tea, instant soup, frozen dinners, take-out chicken, take-out pizza . . . it goes on and on. Anything you want, you can have in a matter of minutes. Now I think this was all brought about for the benefit of the younger generation. They want to get all that dull stuff out of the way so they'll have more time to do what they do best. And if you think what they do best is playing backgammon, you must still be wearing high-button shoes. The young people never quit. Even when they have leisure time what do they do? They go to a drive-in movie. You know, there's a fellow out in North Hollywood who owns a drive-in movie and he's making a fortune. Every night the place is packed and he doesn't even show pictures.

That kind of pace is not for me, and it never was. All my life I've taken things nice and slow and easy. And it paid off. I'm eighty-three years old and if I want some excitement, I get myself a bowl of hot soup. Come to think of it, maybe my pace was a little too slow.

In the neighborhood where I grew up none of the mothers would let their young daughters out after dark. Personally, I thought it was a mistake. If you could have seen some of those girls, they would have had a better chance getting a fellow in the dark. Actually it didn't matter when they went out because when it came to marriage, most of the girls had nothing to say about it. It was all handled by what was called a matchmaker. If a family had a marriageable daughter, they would send for him. He'd look the girl over, and for a fee he'd try to find an eligible young man to marry her. His fee would vary according to how much he thought the family could afford. For fifteen dollars he'd just go out and grab the first fellow he saw; for twenty-five dollars he'd try to find a guy who had his own store; at seventy-five dollars he'd go for a fellow who was studying to be a doctor or a lawyer; and if you could afford a hundred dollars, he'd divorce his wife and marry the girl himself.

Well, at those prices my family couldn't afford anything like that. After all, there were seven girls to unload, so my mother had to become her own matchmaker. The system she developed was uncanny. I don't know how she did it, but when anybody in the neighborhood had a young nephew or cousin, or any relative, close or distant, coming over from Europe, it seemed that she knew about it before they did. The day he arrived she was there to help him unpack, and that night he'd be having dinner at our house. All us younger kids were always very happy when it came time for one of our older sisters to be peddled. My mother made sure that we had an extra good meal that night to impress the prospective victim. The rest of the week we might be eating ketchup soup, but on that night we had chicken.

The seating arrangement at the table was an important part of my mother's strategy. She always made sure that the young man sat in the chair furthest from the door. That was in case when he got a good look at this group he'd try to escape. The only way this poor kid could have gotten out of that room would have been to dive through the fourth story window.

After dinner the rest of us would stay at the table in the kitchen with the door closed while my mother took the young couple into the front room to get acquainted. She'd seat the two of them on the couch, and then she'd sit in a chair and begin her pitch. She didn't waste any time; she got right to the point. This guy's still punchy from the boat trip he'd just made, and here's my mother reeling off my sister's great qualifications as a wife: what a great cook she is, how she sews all her own clothes, a marvelous housekeeper, lovable disposition, extremely religious, and most important of all, ending up by assuring him she's as pure as the new-driven snow. My sister is listening to all this wondering who my mother is talking about. My mother never bothered to ask the fellow what his plans were. All she cared about was that he was single, breathing, and Jewish.

I have to admit it didn't happen exactly that way, but look, I'm a member of the Friars Club, so I try to make it amusing. But whether it's amusing or not, my mother's system worked. My seven sisters all got married, raised lovely families, and none of them was ever divorced.

But there was one close call. My mother had arranged what she thought was a perfect marriage between my sister Mamie and a young dental student named Max Salis. Everything went fine while Max was struggling to get his diploma. But when he finally got it and hung out his shingle, for two months absolutely nothing happened. Max had gone deeply into debt for dental equipment and office furnishings, and even though he and Mamie lived in a small apartment in back of the office, there was no money coming in. One day Mamie came to my mother in tears. She was extremely upset. If Max didn't get some patients soon, it could possibly ruin their marriage. With no patients coming in, by the end of the day he was in such a state of depression he was impossible to live with. He considered himself a failure, and Mamie didn't know how to cope with it.

Well, as usual the next day my mother came up with a solution. Her idea was to have all us younger kids still living at home sit in the waiting room of Max's office. His windows faced right onto the street, and she reasoned that people passing by would look in, see the crowded waiting room, and figure that Max must be a fine dentist. Max didn't have much hope for the success of this idea, but he was so low he was ready to try anything.

For three days I sat there with my sister Theresa and my brothers Sammy and Willy. Nothing happened. Just when we were about ready to give up the whole idea as a failure, a woman started up the steps to the office with her little boy. I raced into the inner office and said excitedly, "Uncle Max! A patient is coming!" I waited a few seconds until I was sure the woman was inside, then I opened the door and came out into the waiting room, saying in a loud voice, "Dr. Salis, you're the greatest dentist in the whole world. I never felt a thing!" And with that I left. After making that dramatic speech I knew it would be only a matter of seventy-three years before I would win the Academy Award.

Well, from then on Max started doing business. In fact, things got so good that one day he came to my mother and said, "Please, would you keep your kids out of the waiting room, there's no room for my patients." Max was happy, Mamie was happy, and my mother had done it again. But I've got a little secret for you. Whenever I got a toothache I didn't trust Max; I went to another dentist.

By the time my two younger sisters were ready to get married they didn't need my mother. Things had changed, and girls were finding their own fellows. When my sister Goldie first started keeping company, it was with a young fellow named Willie Schusterman. When he'd bring her home after a date, they'd stand in the downstairs hallway and do a little spooning. They were standing right under the hall light, but they were so wrapped up in each other they didn't even notice the neighbors in the building who kept coming in and out. Well, my mother knew what was going on, so one night she went out and hollered down the stairs, "Goldie, why don't you bring Willie upstairs and kiss him in the parlor! All the neighbors have been watching you, why shouldn't I have a look?!" Anyway, it wasn't long before Goldie became Mrs. Willie Schusterman. And Willie was considered quite a catch. He owned a little store in Newark, and all he sold was straw hats. Actually, Willie was quite prosperous; that is, in the summer he was prosperous. In the winter he and Goldie had to eat the hats he couldn't sell in the summer.

Next came my youngest sister Theresa. She married a

fellow named Charlie Kalender who was a window dresser in Leopold's Haberdashery on Second Avenue. Now, that romance didn't blossom overnight. At that time Theresa had a job as a salesgirl in Klein's Department Store, and on her way home she always passed Leopold's. When Charlie would be working in the window and Theresa passed by, he'd wave to her and she'd wave back. This went on for about three months, and although Theresa liked Charlie's looks, nothing further happened. Theresa was getting desperate, so one evening as she passed the store and Charlie waved, she held a note up to the window which read, "How about a date?" Old Charlie picked up on this subtle hint in a flash. He held up a note that read, "I thought you'd never ask me." That night they had their first date, and a month later they were married.

This marriage worked out great for me. I was still trying to make it in show business, and every once in a while Charlie would bring me a suit that had been on display in one of the windows at Leopold's. However, being on display in the sun for so long the suit was always faded in the front. I remember one suit I had was dark brown in the back and gray in the front. I looked much better going away from you than coming toward you. From the side I looked like two people bumping into each other.

You'll notice that I haven't mentioned my brothers getting married. And there's a reason for it. My mother didn't have time to bother with us boys; she had a full-time job just getting rid of all those girls. But even though my mother wasn't directly involved as a matchmaker with my brothers and me, none of us would think of getting married before my mother met the girl and gave her approval.

Let me tell you how it worked with my marriage to Gracie. The first time my mother met her was when we were playing the Green Point Theater in Brooklyn. My mother saw the show and afterwards she came backstage to meet Gracie.

Now before I go any further, there's something I should

explain about our act. Gracie was absolutely marvelous on the stage, and I was just the opposite. The act was called Burns and Allen, but it should have been Gracie Allen and What's-His-Name. But as a straight man I did have a few lines. One was, "Gracie, how's your brother?" Another was, "No kidding, Gracie, what happened next?" And of course, there was, "Oh yeah?" There were others, but they were unimportant. For the finish of the act Gracie did an Irish jig and I tapped my toe and pointed to her feet. Then she'd exit by walking off the stage and I'd follow her. And believe it or not, I had the nerve to call the act George Burns and Gracie Allen.

But in spite of me the act was a hit, and after I introduced my mother to Gracie, she said, "Gracie, you're a very talented girl, and I can't tell you how much I enjoyed watching you."

"Well, thank you, Mrs. Birnbaum," Gracie said, "but what did you think of your son?"

"The people just laughed at everything you said," my mother answered, "and that little dance you did at the end was so darling."

"Well thank you, Mrs. Birnbaum, but what did you think of your son?" Gracie persisted.

My mother said, "He's a nice boy."

And that about summed it up, because that was one of the nights when Gracie made her exit and I forgot to follow her.

After that my mother met Gracie many times, and when we decided to get married, naturally I went to my mother to tell her. I said, "Mama, Gracie and I are going to get married."

A happy smile came over her face, and she said, "Nattie, you're a very fortunate boy. Gracie's a charming young lady. She's beautiful and talented, and I'm sure she'll make you a wonderful wife."

"But, Mama," I said, "I think you oughta know, she's not Jewish, she's Catholic"

She looked up at me and replied, "Nattie, if they'll have you, that's fine."

I once asked Gracie what her mother said when she told her she was going to marry me, and that I was Jewish. Gracie told me her mother said, "Maybe he'll get over it!"

Well, that's the way people got married when I was young. As I said at the beginning of the chapter, things are a lot different nowadays. And since I always like to keep right up with the times, I'm thinking of buying myself a motorcycle and a black leather jacket, renting a pad with a water bed in Laurel Canyon, and cruising the discotheques. But now I'm going to lie down. I got tired just thinking about it.

ALL MY BROTHERS WERE BOYS

NOW I'VE TOLD quite a bit about my sisters, so in all fairness I think I should give equal billing to my brothers. In order of appearance they were: Morris, Isadore, Sammy, and Willy. I made my entrance between Isadore and Sammy. None of us kids had a middle name. We were lucky we had any name at all. By the time my mother got around to naming one, there was another on the way.

I'm going to give you a little rundown on each of them, and since Morris was the oldest, I'll start with him. He was quite a bit older than I was, and my earliest recollection of him was after he had left home and would pay us occasional visits. He always dressed in very expensive clothes, and to look at him one would think he was the president of a corporation. Actually, Morris was a gambler, and like most gamblers he was either riding high or wondering where his next buck was coming from. But high or low, good or bad, he still managed to look like his corporation had just declared a dividend.

I'll never forget when I was a small boy, and Morris dropped by in one of his flamboyant moods. He breezed into the kitchen with a beautifully wrapped package, which he handed to my mother. All of us kids were very excited and gathered around the table while she unwrapped it. When she finished, all of us kids looked at her, she looked at us, and then we all turned and looked at Morris.

"Morris, what is it?" my mother asked.

Excitedly Morris said, "Mama, that's Russian caviar! That two-pound jar cost a fortune!"

This was exactly what we needed. We were then on the third day of a batch of my mother's potato soup, and Morris shows up with caviar. My mother just stared at him for a couple of seconds in disbelief, then, "Morris, I imagine for what you paid for this I could buy twelve pairs of shoes."

"But, Mama," Morris protested, "caviar is a special delicacy. You put it on a cracker and eat it!"

My mother said, "Good, we'll all eat caviar barefooted and without the cracker."

With that Morris opened the jar and asked her to taste it. She took a little, and then screwing up her face said, "Morris, you should return this and get your money back, it's spoiled. Look, it's already turned black."

I suppose you should be able to gather from this little incident that being practical was not one of Morris's strong points. If you're not already convinced, here's a beauty. Morris once got a crush on a little girl, and one night he decided to take a taxi to go visit her. Now this doesn't sound like such a big deal until you consider that Morris was in New York and the girl lived in Boston. I don't know what the taxi fare was, but a minor detail like that wouldn't bother Morris.

Those were things he did when he was riding high. But there was another side to the coin.

Years later when Gracie and I were doing well we were living at the Edison Hotel in New York and one night we got a visit from Morris. When he arrived Gracie was in the other room getting dressed to go out to dinner, and after the usual small talk Morris finally got down to the real reason for him being there. It seemed that he was a little short of cash, and he borrowed fifty dollars from me. When Gracie came in I invited Morris to have dinner with us. He said, "If you haven't made any plans, I know the perfect place—a restaurant on Second Avenue called The Little Gypsy, and they serve marvelous Romanian food." He went on to say how wonderful the atmosphere was, that they had the greatest zither player in the world, and a Romanian girl who sang beautiful gypsy songs.

This all sounded fine to us, so off we went. And it turned out to be everything Morris had said it was. We had a delightful evening. When we were ready to leave I asked for the check, and when the waiter brought it, Morris said in very impressive tones, "I'm paying that check," and he handed the waiter the fifty-dollar bill. Then continuing in grand style he instructed him, "Give ten dollars to the singer, ten dollars to the zither player, pay the bill and keep the rest for yourself."

Gracie was very impressed with Morris. Of course, she didn't know it was my fifty. On our way out while Gracie stopped in the ladies' room Morris turned to me and said, "George, I'm a little short, could you let me have fifty dollars?"

As I removed another bill from my wallet I said, "Why don't I give this directly to the waiter."

Morris took the fifty out of my hand, folded it, and put it into his pocket, saying, "Let's not spoil him, George."

I really owe a debt of gratitude to my brother Morris. Many of his close friends were actors in the Jewish theater, so Morris loved show business. He was the only one in my family who encouraged me to stay in it. And in my early days it wasn't easy for me to stay in show business, because everybody who saw me on the stage wanted me to get off.

Next in line came my brother Isadore H. Birnbaum. I know I told you that none of us had a middle name, but when Izzie started doing well he added the H. I once asked him what the H. stood for, and he replied, "It stands for H."

Izzie was the solid, industrious one of the family. He started out as a traveling salesman selling ladies' dresses, and he must have done a hell of a job because by the time he was twenty-eight he owned a department store in Akron, Ohio. All Izzie thought about was making a success out of his business, and he worked at it day and night. Come to think of it, he must have taken a couple of nights off because he and his wife, Madge, had two beautiful children.

Izzie always worried about me. All I could think about was getting into show business, and to him show business was the bottom of the barrel. He kept trying to convince me that I had no future as a performer and would only wind up as a bum. He didn't make much of an impression on me, because what he couldn't understand was I'd be very happy being a bum if I could do it with makeup on.

Anyway, when he started doing well in Akron, during one of his business trips to New York, Izzie came by the house. He sat me down on the couch in the living room and told me it was time we had a serious talk. I figured here comes the bum routine again, but this time Izzie had a plan for me. "George," he said, "you're sixteen years old and it's time we gave serious thought to your future. To begin with, you've had no education, so I've arranged for you to attend the Manhattan Preparatory School." He let that sink in, then continued with, "After four months there you'll come to my store in Akron and start out as an elevator boy. Eventually you'll work your way up, and who knows—someday you might even be a buyer in my store. You could make as much as seventy . . . eighty . . . maybe even ninety dollars a week!"

And there it was. However, if he expected that speech of his to make me give up my show business career, he was wrong. I said, "But, Izzie, I just read in the paper there's a young girl named Blossom Seeley in a Broadway show who sings 'Toddling the Tooddloo'—and they pay her a thousand dollars a week!"

He looked directly at me and said, "I've never heard Blossom Seeley sing, but I've heard you. And my advice to you is that you toddle that little toddle of yours down to the Manhattan Preparatory School early Monday morning."

Well, I lasted in that school exactly four days. The only thing I remember from this episode was that my teacher was a fellow named Leon Trotsky. I believe he eventually opened very big in Russia and later was canceled in Mexico. In case you're worried that I was influenced by Leon Trotsky, I wasn't. He never sang any of my songs, and I never used any of his philosophy.

Anyway, I never made it to that elevator in Akron. But years later when Gracie and I were successful we were headlining the Colonial Theater in Akron, and one night we had dinner with Izzie and Madge. I said to him, "Izzie, is that elevator job still open?"

He leaned over toward me and said, "George, let me tell you something. If it wasn't for me, you might never have made it in show business."

I didn't know what he was getting at, so I asked, "Izzie, what are you getting at?"

And very seriously he said, "If I had offered you a better job than running an elevator, you might have taken it." But he was wrong. I wouldn't have taken it if he had offered me the entire store.

Izzie was a wonderful man. He was a devoted husband and father all his life, and I can truthfully say that I never met a man as honest as my brother Izzie. If it's true that George Washington became president because he never told a lie, then Isadore H. Birnbaum should have been president. Well, maybe he told one little lie. Look . . . Secretary of State isn't a bad job, either.

After Izzie I was the next boy in the family. My parents had decided that I would be their last child, but after taking a look at me, my mother said to my father, "We'd better try it again, maybe this time we'll get it right." So along came my sister Theresa and then my brother Sammy.

Sammy was quite a character even when he was a kid. When he was about eight years old he decided he wanted to be a detective. And who knows, he might have become one if it hadn't been for one little unfortunate incident. He was caught in a five-and-ten-cent store stealing a detective kit. That night after my mother got through paddling his backside, "the detective" had to eat his dinner standing up. He didn't have to stand too long; we had very little to eat.

When Sammy was about seventeen he got a job with the post office and was making the princely sum of fifteen dollars a week. Out of this he gave my mother thirteen dollars and kept two dollars for himself. Even though he wasn't making much money Sammy always looked absolutely elegant. This was because my brother Morris gave Sammy his old clothes, and being a gambler, Morris was a very flashy dresser. So when Sammy wore Morris's clothes he looked like a seventeen-year-old gambler. And as long as he looked like one, he decided to be one. His first venture was on a Friday after he picked up his paycheck. He got into a crap game, and before he even got his hands on the dice he lost the whole fifteen dollars. After that Sammy didn't look like a gambler anymore; he had to sell Morris's clothes to get the thirteen dollars for my mother.

Eventually Sammy settled down and wound up running his own novelty store in one of the large hotels in Brooklyn. He's now retired and living with his wife, Sarah, and they have two fine children who are both teaching school. Sarah and Sammy have been married a long, long time, and even after all these years they have stuck to an arrangement they made before their wedding. Sarah was Italian, and she stayed Italian; Sammy was Jewish, and he stayed Jewish. I ate dinner at their house one night, and it was delicious, if you happen to like spaghetti on a bagel.

Recently their daughter, Dottie, treated Sammy and Sarah

to their first trip out of the United States: a tour of Israel and Rome. Living up to their original arrangement, they agreed to spend half their time in Israel and the other half in Rome. Frank Sinatra and Golda Meir couldn't have worked it out any better. After they returned I got this glowing letter from Sammy describing what a wonderful country Israel was. He was so impressed with how friendly the people were, how they had made the desert bloom with vegetation, the great advances they had made in education, the awesome feeling of standing in places where the history of the world began, etc., etc. Anyway, he went on for fifteen pages about Israel and never even mentioned Rome. I called him on the phone and said, "Sammy, that was a wonderful letter, but all you wrote about was Israel. What about Rome?"

Sammy answered, "If you want to know about Rome, I'll have Sarah write you a letter."

Within a week I got a seventeen-page letter from Sarah. She not only didn't mention Israel, she didn't mention Sammy.

Six months ago I was in New York, and Sammy and I were having lunch. I asked him, "Sammy, you're now about seventy-five or seventy-six years old. Looking back on your life is there anything you would have changed?"

"Just one thing," Sammy said. "If I knew I wouldn't get caught, I'd still like to be a detective."

My brother Willy was the youngest of the family. Now there was such a gap between the ages of Willy and my oldest brother, Morris, that for years Willy thought Morris was his grandfather. Willy also always thought of himself as quite a ladies' man. At the ripe old age of twelve he used to take soot from the stove and rub it on his face. He wanted the girls to think he was old enough to shave. And he was very skinny, so he wore his tie pulled up real tight around his neck, and that made his cheeks puff out. He looked like a squirrel with five-o'clock shadow.

Anyway, when he reached thirteen, one day he came home and announced to my mother that he was getting married. My mother went right along with it. "Good," she said, "who are you marrying?"

Willy said, "A girl named Gertie Moskowitz."

"This Gertie Moskowitz . . . how old is she?"

"She's eleven," Willy replied. "But don't worry, Mama, she's Jewish."

"That's nice," my mother said, "then you can get married next Sunday. We'll have the rabbi meet us at the soda fountain."

Needless to say, that marriage didn't take place, and needless to say, I sound pretty silly telling you that. However, at the age of twenty-three Willy did marry a very lovely girl named Louise, and they had three charming daughters.

Willy was the only one of my family who joined me in show business. He had a good business head, and when Gracie and I started doing well he became our personal manager. He handled all our contracts, our bookings, and traveled with us. Eventually, when we went into radio and then television, Willy even doubled as one of our writers. I don't know why, but there was one particular joke that Willy came up with that has stuck in my mind through the years. I've always enjoyed telling it and in fact, I still use it. And so you won't think I'm lying to you, I'll use it again right now. I was speaking at a testimonial dinner for Judy Garland, and this is what I said:

When Judy Garland was nine years old, the Trocadero restaurant on the Sunset Strip gave young talent a chance to perform every Sunday night. The night that Judy Garland sang there Louis B. Mayer, who was then the head of MGM, was sitting in the audience. He loved the way she sang, signed her to a contract and made her a star. Well, the same thing could have happened to me, but the only problem was when I was nine years old, Louis B. Mayer was nine years old.

Well, that was Willy's joke, and I'm telling it again next Wednesday. I only wish that Willy was still around to hear it. He passed away in 1966, and I still miss him very much.

Now I've told you a little bit about all my brothers and sisters. They were all married and all had children. And their children had children. And their children's children had children. By now I figure in some way or another I must be related to everybody in the United States. Believe me, if Alex Haley had my family, he'd still be writing *Roots*.

IT TAKES TWO PEOPLE TO MAKE A MARRIAGE

JANUARY 7, 1926, was the most important day in my life. That's when audiences discovered I had this big talent, and I stayed married to her for thirty-eight years. At that time getting married was so simple. At seven-thirty in the morning Gracie and I went to the Justice of the Peace; she said, "I do"; I said, "I do"; and we did.

But it's certainly not like that now. Just the other day I went to a wedding that wasn't even a wedding, it was a business meeting; just a few close friends, two lawyers, the boy and girl and their baby. They were there to sign a Marriage Contract. They didn't even say "I do," because there was nobody there to ask them. When kids get married today I don't know what they say. I guess it could be, "Perhaps" . . . "Maybe" . . . "I will, if you will" . . . "I'll try" . . . "Speak to my attorney!" . . . I hate to mention this because it might upset some of you readers, but I don't think that's very romantic.

Anyway, it was quite a ceremony. The two lawyers argued about some of the points in the contract and eventually arrived at a compromise. Then the lovers signed it and shook hands. How they got that baby I'll never know.

309

Imagine the boy and girl going home after having just been joined together by two lawyers. Now this is their wedding night. The music is playing softly, the lights are low, she's in a beautiful black negligee, he's in his silk pajamas, and they jump into bed, turn up the lights and start to read the contract. They're afraid that the next thing they do might not be legal.

Well, the contract probably reads something like this:

Whereas the Party of the First Part, for and in consideration of the covenants and agreements hereinafter mentioned, and to be performed by the Party of the Second Part, does hereby agree and consent to the Party of the Second Part privileges and considerations known and described as follows, to wit: . . .

By the time the kids tried to figure out what that meant I imagine the Party of the First Part was telling the Party of the Second Part that if there were any other parties with any other party, the whole party's over. (I don't know what I just said, but one thing I'm sure of is, the Party of the First Part and the Party of the Second Part didn't.) Of course, there must be a loophole somewhere in the contract that states if he catches her fooling around, the whole deal is off unless she's a good cook.

And I'm sure it wouldn't be a binding agreement without a clause pointing out that Tuesdays and Thursdays are for conjugal obligations, except on national holidays. Friday is his night out, but he always looks forward to Tuesdays and Thursdays, because those are his nights in.

Now being an old vaudevillian and having signed a few contracts in my day I'm certain the last paragraph says that the agreement is subject to renewal at the end of every two years; that is, if the parties are still speaking to each other.

By now no doubt you've come to the conclusion that I haven't got a law degree. I was in the fourth grade so long I wound up dating my teacher.

But getting back to that so-called wedding. After I witnessed the signing of the paper I took the two kids aside and asked them, "What kind of a wedding is this? Why don't you two really get married?"

Without blinking an eye, the boy said, "Oh, we love each other too much for that." And the girl chimed in with, "Sure, marriage has broken up more friendships than anything!"

Well, there I was stuck with two pockets full of rice. So I went home and made myself some rice pudding. And it was delicious. I've never had rice pudding with pocket lint before.

Now let's talk about that important day in my life, January 7, 1926. The week before that Gracie and I were booked to play a split week in Steubenville and Ashtabula, Ohio. They were small-time theaters, and the reason we booked them was to break in some new material. After that we were to play the B.F. Keith Theater in Cleveland, which was the big-time.

Before we left New York for Steubenville I said to Gracie, "We've got two days off in Cleveland before we open, how about getting married then?" I'll admit this wasn't a great romantic proposal, but I want you to know that I had proposed to Gracie at least four times a week for the last year. So I had used up all my good proposal stuff.

In case you think Gracie immediately said "yes," you're wrong. What she said was, "George, I love you, and I love Benny Ryan. He wants to marry me, and you want to marry me. I'm sorry, but I've got a date with Benny tonight, and when I get home I'll make up my mind and phone you."

What's the use of kidding, it didn't look good for me. Benny Ryan was tough competition. He was a tremendous talent, one of our top songwriters, a great dancer, an exciting performer—he was all of show business wrapped up in one man. And besides that, he and Gracie had a lot in common. They were both Irish, they were both Catholic, and they both had their own hair. When I said that things didn't look good for me, believe me I was bragging.

Waiting for Gracie's phone call, I didn't get any sleep that night. I kept looking at the gold wedding ring that I had been carrying around for a year in case Gracie ever said "yes." I figured there was twenty dollars going down the drain.

Well, at two-thirty in the morning the phone finally rang. I rushed to the phone and picked it up. It was a wrong number. That's all I needed. I went back and had my ninth cup of coffee to calm my nerves. At four o'clock the phone rang, and this time it was Gracie. She said, "George, I've been sitting home for a couple of hours thinking about this, and I've made up my mind. I love you, and I think Cleveland would be a wonderful place for you and me to get married."

I said, "Thanks, kid, you just saved me twenty dollars."

We got our wedding license between shows in Steubenville. I had made a reservation for a two-room suite at the Statler Hotel in Cleveland. It cost seven dollars a day, but I figured it was going to be our honeymoon, why not go all out. But unfortunately we arrived at the Statler at five o'clock in the morning. Check-in time was seven o'clock, so Gracie and I sat in the lobby for two hours so we wouldn't have to pay for an extra day. We couldn't even go into the coffee shop; it wasn't open yet. So there we were, sitting in this big empty lobby holding hands among the potted palms.

At seven o'clock I went up to the desk and registered as Mr. and Mrs. George Burns. I told the clerk to send our bags up to our rooms, that we were on our way to get married and would be right back. He smiled and gave me an understanding wink.

Well, Gracie and I hopped into a cab for the justice of the peace. On the way I said to her, "Did you notice that the clerk winked at me?"

She smiled and patted my hand and said, "Why not, George, you're a very attractive man."

Just as we pulled up to the office of the justice of the peace, he and a friend came out the front door. They both carried

Right, George's mother, Dora, taken around 1902.

Below left, his sister, Sarah, about 1909.

Below right, his sister, Theresa (right), with two friends in 1913.

Right, his mother, Dora (right), with his sister, Mamie.

Below left, his oldest brother, Morris, the ladies' man of the family.

Below right, his sister, Sarah, with her husband, Sam Weiss, and their children, Louis and Evelyn.

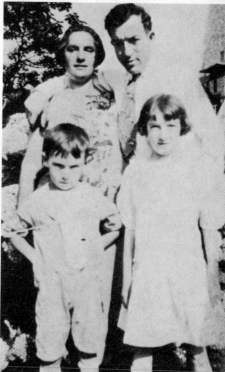

His darling mother, Dora, in a formal portrait, *above*, and in a snapshot taken around 1910, *right*.

Right, his sister, Goldie, with her daughter, Sally, holding Goldie's granddaughter, Karen, in the late 1940s.

His sister, Mamie, *below left*, when she was a kid of 70, and *right*, with George.

Above left, with his brother, Willie, and sister, Goldie, in the late 1950s.

Above right, his sister, Esther, taken early in 1959.

Below, his oldest brother, Isadore.

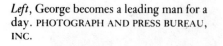

Left, George becomes a leading man for a day. PHOTOGRAPH AND PRESS BUREAU, INC.

Right, a vaudeville bill from Keith's Theatre, Philadelphia.

Burns and Allen in their early days of
vaudeville. WEISE STUDIO

Above, George breaks up as Gracie carries on a "perfectly normal" telephone conversation. *Facing page*, the proud parents with Ronnie and Sandra, 1936.

Above, with Ronnie and Sandra, 1940. METROPOLITAN PHOTO SERVICE

Right, Gracie and Sandra do a turnabout as George looks on, 1937. PARAMOUNT PICTURES, INC.

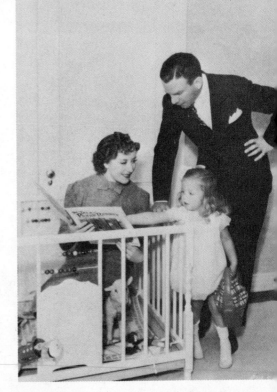

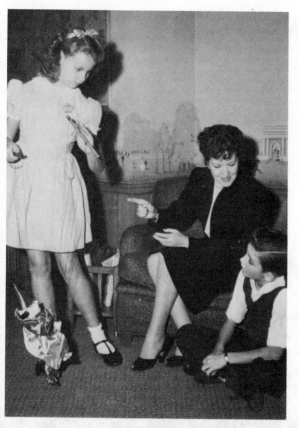

Left, Gracie and Ronnie are entertained by a budding puppeteer, Sandra, 1944. GENE LESTER

Below, with Ronnie and Sandra, 1950. HOLLYWOOD PICTORIAL SERVICE

Left, with Ronnie and Sandra at home posing for public pictures, 1952.

Below, with Ronnie, 1955.

With Ronnie and
Sandra. *Right*, CBS
PHOTO CREDIT BY
WALT DAVIS

Above, Gracie and W. C. Fields in *International House* at Paramount in the early 1930s.

Below, a studio publicity photo in 1934. PARAMOUNT PRODUCTIONS, INC.

Above, with Guy Lombardo on the set of *Many Happy Returns*, 1934.
PARAMOUNT PRODUCTIONS, INC.

Below, with Cary Grant. GENE LESTER

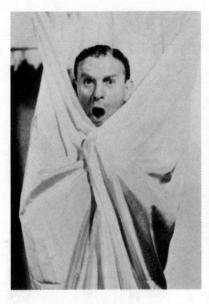

Above, George takes a shower—but no hot water, 1938. PARAMOUNT PICTURES, INC.

Right, George waiting impatiently for Gracie to get a laugh.

fishing gear and were obviously on their way to go fishing. I rushed up to them and said, "We'd like to get married!"

He gave me a look, and said, "Why don't you come back tomorrow?" As they started off I stopped them again. "Please, Mr. Justice of the Peace," I said, "we traveled all night, we've got our license, we've checked into a hotel, and we've got to get married right away. The fish can wait, but we can't!"

I could see that I had won, because he stopped putting worms on his hook. With a resigned sigh he said to his friend, "Come on, Joe, it'll only take a few minutes. You'll have to stand up for this couple."

With that we all went inside the office, with Gracie nervously clutching my arm. The justice called to his wife to be a witness. She came out from the living quarters in the rear wearing bedroom slippers, a wraparound kimono, and her hair up in pin curls. Believe me, this wedding picture would never have made the society page. The only romantic thing about it was the faded flowers on the woman's kimono.

I don't remember much of anything about the ceremony. All I know is the justice of the peace stood there with a book in one hand and his fishing pole in the other. He said something to Gracie, then he said something to me. Gracie said, "I do," I said, "I do," and the Justice said, "I now pronounce you man and wife." I gave him ten dollars, and he was out of the front door before we were. To give you an idea of how long this took, when we arrived there the meter on the cab read eighty-five cents; when we got back into the cab it read ninety-five cents.

On our way back to the hotel Gracie snuggled up to me and gave me a big kiss. "Honey, we really did it," she said.

"Yeah," I said, taking her hand, "you're finally Mrs. George Burns."

She looked at me with a funny little gleam in her eye and said, "I hope so. For a moment I thought we were getting a fishing license."

When we got back to the hotel and went up to the desk, Gracie deliberately held out her finger with the wedding ring on it, and in a voice just loud enough for the clerk to hear, said, "George, you have exquisite taste, the wedding ring is just beautiful."

I said, "Thanks, Gracie, I'm glad you like it, I made it myself."

With that Gracie laughed and turned to the clerk. Sweetly she said, "Mr. and Mrs. George Burns would like the key to their rooms."

Well, we went upstairs and unpacked, and then we did what every young newly married couple does—we went downstairs and had breakfast. A little later my older brother and his family came over from Akron, and that evening we had a lovely wedding party in the hotel's main dining room. After they left Gracie and I went back to our rooms and started out as Mr. and Mrs. George Burns. We turned out the lights. . . . At two o'clock in the morning the phone rang. It was my dearest friend, Jack Benny, calling from Omaha. I recognized his voice instantly. I picked up the phone, and Jack said, "Hello, George—" and I said, "Send up two orders of ham and eggs" and hung up. Ten minutes later the phone rang and it was Jack again. I picked up the phone, and he said, "Hello, George—" and I said, "You forgot the ketchup" and hung up.

Maybe you think that was the end of it, but it wasn't. A half hour later there was a knock on the door and it was the waiter with two orders of ham and eggs and a bottle of ketchup. Trying to keep a straight face, the waiter said, "Compliments of Mr. Jack Benny from Omaha."

I said, "That's very nice of him, and I don't want to hurt Mr. Benny's image, so don't tell anybody I'm giving you a tip."

Gracie got up and we had our breakfast at two-thirty in the morning. The ham and eggs were delicious, and when we were finished Gracie said, "George, this was the high point of the night!" I hope she was making a joke.

Now as I said at the beginning of this chapter, January 7, 1926, was the most important day in my life. And even though it was a short wedding, and a short honeymoon, it was a long and wonderful marriage.

THEY PAID US IN POUNDS AND WEIGHED US IN STONES

For Gracie and me it was much tougher getting married than staying married. The hardest thing was trying to ignore the advice from some of our well-meaning friends. Come to think of it, it wasn't difficult at all, I just didn't listen. To give you an example, one week after we were married, Jack Holloway, another vaudeville actor, sat me down and very seriously told me I had made a big mistake. He said, "George, you know I love you, and I love Gracie. I don't know whether I should say this, but I feel I must say it because I'm one of your closest friends. . . . Your marriage can't last."

"But, Jack," I protested, "we just got married."

He said, "So far you've been lucky. Let's be honest, you and Gracie both come from different backgrounds. She's very well educated, and you had no schooling at all. Gracie comes from an Irish Catholic family in San Francisco, and you're from an Orthodox Jewish family on the Lower East Side of New York."

"Jack," I said, "I imagine you're telling me this because you love me."

"Would I be saying it if I didn't?" he said. Then he put his arm around my shoulder and added, "George, don't forget, you'll have to eat fish every Friday night."

I put my arm around his shoulder and told him not to worry. I said, "Jack, coming from an Orthodox family, on Friday night when I eat fish I'll keep my hat on."

He gave me a look and said, "George, I hope you're not trying to be funny. Because now I have to tell you something that I didn't want to tell you.

"That's because you love me."

"Of course," he said. "The reason your marriage won't last is that you and Gracie work together, and your careers are bound to clash. That's why I've never allowed my wife to go into show business."

I'd had enough. Very calmly I said to him, "Jack, I know how hard it was for you to tell me all this, and to show my appreciation . . . you can kiss my ass."

Just as a footnote, Gracie and I were happily married for thirty-eight years. Jack Holloway and his wife were divorced a year and a half later. In fact, the last time I saw him he was having a problem with his fifth wife. I guess this kid never learned to eat fish with his hat on.

But Gracie and I had no problems with our careers, because we only had one—hers. We stood in the wings, the orchestra played "Love Nest," we made our entrance holding hands, and when we got to center stage I said to Gracie, "How's your brother?" and she spoke for thirty-eight years. And that's how I became a star. Believe me, it wasn't easy; sometimes I forgot to say, "Gracie, how's your brother?"

Here I am tearing myself down again, but I do that on purpose. I found out that if you tear yourself down, people feel sorry for you, and if they feel sorry for you, they like you. But don't feel too sorry for me. When I was on the stage I did more than just say, "Gracie, how's your brother?" I also used to find out which way the wind was blowing, and I'd make sure to stand on the opposite side of Gracie so my cigar smoke wouldn't blow in her face. That was my real talent. You feel sorry for me again? . . . you see, it works.

Well, you're not going to believe this, but it's true. Gracie and I were playing the Palace Theater in New York, and at that time the hit musical was *Show Boat*. It was produced by Charles Dillingham and he was putting together the cast for his London production. He came to the Palace because he was considering us for the Eva Puck and Sammy White parts. Puck and White were the comedy leads in *Show Boat*, and this would have been a tremendous break for us. But when I found out Dillingham was in the audience I got so nervous I forgot to check out which way the wind was blowing. So when we did our act my cigar smoke went into Gracie's face. The next day our agent, Tom Fitzpatrick, got a wire from Charles Dillingham. It read, "The team of Burns and Allen I'll pay $500 a week. For the girl alone I'll pay $750." As you've probably guessed, the London *Show Boat* sailed without us.

As long as I've mentioned Tom Fitzpatrick, I'd like to tell you a little anecdote involving him. Tom Fitzpatrick was one of the top vaudeville agents. He handled a lot of good standard vaudeville acts, such as Jack Benny, Barry and Whitledge, Block and Sully, Will Mahoney, Swift and Kelley, Burns and Allen, and many others. Tom was very religious, and one of the kindest, warmest, most considerate men I ever met. In those days it was the practice of the various acts to go into their agent's office to find out if they were booked somewhere. But Tom was so soft-hearted he couldn't tell an actor that he had nothing for him. It was just impossible for him to say, "You're not working next week." So when you came into his office and there was no job, Tom got very nervous and started opening and closing drawers of his desk like he was looking for something. He just couldn't bring himself to face you. The minute he started that bit you knew you were laying off. And because he was such a nice man and you didn't want to hurt his feelings, you'd back out of his office and quietly close the door.

Well, one day after backing clear down into the street, I ran into Jack Benny. Jack said, "George, are you and Gracie working next week?"

I answered, "No, I just left Tom Fitzpatrick and he was opening and closing drawers."

I don't know why, but that struck Jack funny, and he started to laugh. Now I don't mind making Jack Benny laugh when I'm booked, but not when I'm laying off. So I said, "Jack, what are you laughing at? You know that Tom Fitzpatrick's been doing that drawer bit for years."

That made him laugh even more. And the more he laughed, the angrier I got. Finally I stopped three strangers, pointed to Jack, and very innocently said, "Why is this man laughing?"

They looked bewildered and said, "Don't you know him?"

I said, "No." Then I turned to Jack and said, "Mister, why are you laughing?" Well, this really broke Jack up. He started to walk away, holding his sides, and every time he looked back I gathered more people. I must have had about forty or fifty, and the bigger the crowd the more he laughed. Finally he couldn't stand it any longer, fell down on the sidewalk, and crawled into a shoe store.

The next day Jack said to me, "George, that lousy joke of yours cost me twelve dollars yesterday."

"Jack," I said, "relax, the shoes look fine."

Here I am jumping around, talking about Jack Holloway, Tom Fitzpatrick, Jack Benny . . . my sense of continuity is pathetic. But come to think of it, Shakespeare had a problem with his continuity, too. Willy jumped from *The Merchant of Venice* to *Henry VIII*, to *Richard III*, to *Julius Caesar*. He didn't care about continuity, so why should I?

So let's take another little jump. The week after Gracie and I were married we played the Jefferson Theater on fourteenth

Street in New York City. We were doing a new act called Burns
and Allen in *Lamb Chops*, and all the bookers came to see us. We
were a very big hit, and we were signed for five years with the
Keith-Orpheum circuit. What a wedding present! And to make
it even more exciting, the contract called for us to play the
Palace Theater in New York. Right away I had my spats
cleaned, and to top it off I bought something I'd never owned
before . . . a cane with an engraved silver handle. I wanted to
look like I was a classy performer. Gracie didn't have to buy
anything; she always looked like a classy performer.

When you signed one of these contracts you worked a
minimum of forty weeks a year. That meant you had twelve
weeks open. But who wanted to lay off that long? Not me, I
layed off until I was twenty-seven years old. So at the end of
our first season when we were offered to play four weeks in
London, I ran home and told Gracie. "Gracie," I said, "they
want us to play four weeks in London!"

Gracie's eyes lit up, and she immediately started packing.

"Wait a minute," I said, "we're only offered four hundred
dollars a week. That means we'll only make sixteen hundred
dollars, and our passage on the *Leviathan* to London is twelve
hundred dollars, because we're going first class."

She just kept right on packing.

"So you see, Gracie, after we pay our hotel bill and all our
other expenses, we'll play four weeks," and laying it out, I said,
"and we will lose two hundred dollars!"

"George, I'm packed!" she said.

Well, we signed the contract, but I was wrong about losing
two hundred dollars. Gracie bought two evening gowns,
because you had to dress every night on the *Leviathan*. So we
were going to lose four hundred dollars.

Gracie and I were very excited about going to London
because neither one of us had ever been there. Now this being
my first trip out of the country, the one thing I didn't want to
look like was an American tourist. I didn't want to walk down a

London street and have people staring at me. I wanted to look like an Englishman looks. Now it happened that I had recently seen an English vaudeville act called The Ward Brothers, and they billed themselves as, "Two British Chaps from London." I said to myself, that's it. I'll dress the way they dress, and when I get to London I won't be noticed.

My outfit consisted of a pair of gray-striped pants, a double-breasted black coat, an ascot instead of a regular tie, and a black bowler hat. Naturally I wore my spats, and instead of my cane I carried an umbrella. When I tried it all on at the tailor's I looked so English the clerk was surprised I didn't pay him in pounds.

The *Leviathan* was the largest and most magnificent luxury liner in the world at that time. Gracie and I couldn't believe that we would spend five days traveling to London in such style. As the ship pulled away we stood at the rail waving to our friends who were seeing us off. Lined up on the dock were about a dozen and a half of our friends, including Jack Benny, Mary Kelly, Orry Kelly, Jesse Block, Eva Sully, and our agent Tom Fitzpatrick. They were all smiling happily and waving. Gracie turned to me and made a little joke. She said, "They all look so happy, they must be glad to see us leaving." And being a good husband, I laughed.

We stayed at the rail until we passed the Statue of Liberty, and then we did what everybody did. We found out where we were sitting in the dining room, rented a couple of deck chairs, and strolled around the ship checking everything out. After that we went to our cabin and unpacked. We couldn't wait to get into our evening clothes for our first dinner aboard the *Leviathan*. But we made a mistake. What we didn't know was that on the first and last night aboard a big liner you don't dress for dinner. Those are the nights you unpack and pack.

Anyway, we weren't able to get dressed fast enough, and just as we were about to leave our cabin, Gracie said to me, "George, in that tuxedo you look perfect."

And I said, "Gracie, I've never seen you look lovelier than you do in that dress."

She smiled and said, "Thanks, George, I was waiting for you to say that; that's why I mentioned your tuxedo." And being a good husband, I laughed again.

Well, we nonchalantly walked into the dining room, just as if we had made this trip a thousand times before. Suddenly we froze in our tracks. It seemed that all conversation had stopped, and hundreds of eyes were upon us. Everyone else in the room was dressed in casual clothes.

Somehow Gracie and I got to our table and sheepishly sat down. Fortunately, we had a table for four, and the other couple were charming, wonderful, and understanding people. They introduced themselves as Dr. and Mrs. Graham Hamilton from Philadelphia, and they gave no indication whatsoever that there was anything peculiar about us. After we ordered cocktails, Dr. Hamilton said, "Would you excuse us for a moment. We forgot to send a cable, we'll be right back." And they left. As soon as they were out of sight, Gracie and I looked at each other and made a beeline for our cabin, where we changed into casual clothes. When we got back to the dining room there were the Hamiltons sitting at our table in their evening clothes.

Isn't that a nice story? Too bad it's not true. But you know me, I'm a vaudeville actor and I always think I need a finish. What really happened was, when Gracie and I came into the dining room 250 people thought they had made a mistake and rushed to their cabins and changed into their evening clothes. Now that's true. But if I had told you that at the beginning, you never would have believed it.

Well, the trip over was marvelous. The food was excellent, the shipboard activities were fun, Gracie and I never missed a dance, and for us it was a smooth and romantic crossing. However, on the second day out I was in the bar, having a drink and minding my own business, when somebody tapped me on the shoulder. I turned around and staring down at me was a tall, well-dressed man. He said, "You're George Burns, aren't you?" I nodded, and he continued, "I'm Big Charlie. Remember Hunt's Point Palace about fifteen years ago? . . . You and a girl gave an exhibition dance."

As I looked at him the whole thing came back to me. . . . Let me tell you what happened then. I was about sixteen years old, and I used to dance with a little girl named Nettie Gold. Every Friday night we gave an exhibition dance at different dance halls. Sometimes we would dance the Peabody, or the Machiche, but our big number was an "eccentric fox trot" that we did to a popular instrumental number called "Raggin' the Scale!" Well, this one night we were going to dance at Hunt's Point Palace, and Big Charlie came over to me and said, "Kid, what do they pay you for this dance?"

I said, "Five dollars."

"How long does the dance last?" Big Charlie asked.

"Oh, about three minutes."

"If you can make it last six minutes, I'll give you an extra ten dollars," Big Charlie offered.

I said, "Of course," and he handed me a ten-dollar bill. I thought to myself, this guy must really love the fox trot.

Just then our number was announced. Nettie danced in from one side of the hall, I danced in from the other, and when we got to the center of the floor a spotlight hit us as they turned the house lights out. I made the dance last a full six minutes. Nettie was a little confused, but she followed right along. Nettie was good. But what I didn't know was, while Nettie and I were doing six minutes so was Big Charlie. When the lights were out he picked everybody's pocket.

Now I've got a little confession for you. I did not split the ten dollars with Nettie. I didn't want her to feel guilty for accepting tainted money. . . .

Meanwhile, back on the *Leviathan,* Big Charlie and I were still staring at each other. I said, "Well, Charlie, it was nice to see you again," and started off.

He stopped me with, "By the way, George, are you still dancing?"

I said, "Yeah, but I don't do the eccentric fox trot anymore."

Later that night I told Gracie the story, and for the rest of our voyage part of our fun was avoiding Big Charlie.

When we arrived in London I was surprised . . . nobody dressed like the Ward Brothers. But since I'd made one mistake getting into the wrong clothes on the *Leviathan,* I certainly wasn't going to make another. So I never even unpacked my black coat and my gray-striped pants. But it wasn't a complete loss, because years later I gave the whole outfit to Georgie Jessel. And when he wore it he was a smash at funerals doing eulogies.

We were in London four days before we opened at the Victoria Palace. That was the big variety theater at that time. Gracie was the typical tourist. She had to see everything. She saw the changing of the guard at Buckingham Palace, Westminster Abbey, the Tower of London, Madame Tussaud's wax museum, whatever London had Gracie saw it . . . twice.

But not me. I was the typical vaudevillian. I ran right down to the theater to find out about the lights, about how many musicians they had, what dressing room we would be using, what side of the stage we'd make our entrance and what side we'd make our exit, and of course, which way the wind was blowing. Anyway, after checking everything out at the theater I went to Henry Sherek's office. He was my London agent, and I was going to meet him for the first time. He turned out to be a tall, very big man weighing about three hundred pounds. Our conversation started out with me saying, "I'm George Burns," and with him saying, "I'm Henry Sherek." I followed that with "You look great, you look like you've lost some weight." Then there was a long pause, and he said, "I hope your stuff on the stage is funnier," and I said, "It is." We both laughed, and we knew that the relationship was going to be a good one.

Well, Henry invited me that Saturday to play golf with Val Parnell, who booked all the top theaters in London and in the provinces. I was very anxious to meet Val Parnell, because although Gracie and I were in London for five weeks, we were only booked for four. We had a week open in between. I figured if I could fill that week, that would give us an extra four hundred dollars and we would break even; that is, if Gracie didn't go shopping again.

Val Parnell turned out to be a very nice man, but a very bad golfer. For the first four or five holes he was slicing, hooking, he was in sand traps, he was in the rough, he was all over the golf course except on the fairway. I could see that this put him in a bad mood, and it was no time for me to try to fill that extra week.

At that time I was not a good golfer, and now I'm even worse. But I had taken so many lessons that I knew how to help other people, even if I couldn't help myself. So I had a thought. On the sixth tee I said, "Mr. Parnell, I can't understand why you're not playing better golf. The most important thing about playing golf is to keep your head down and your eye on the ball. And you're certainly doing that." He wasn't, but this time when he hit his drive, he did.

As we were walking down the fairway I said, "That was a pretty good shot, Mr. Parnell. And no wonder, you always keep that left arm of yours nice and stiff." He didn't. But on the next shot he kept his head down, his left arm nice and stiff, and he hit a beautiful shot right to the green. And then he two-putted the green and got a par.

On the seventh tee he was all smiles and couldn't wait to hit his next shot. But before he did, I said to him, "Mr. Parnell, Gracie and I are booked here in London for four weeks, and we've got a week open on the fifteenth. That week we'd love to play the Shepherd's Bush Empire."

He said, "George, I'll tell you what. If I hit a ball 200 yards or better and stay on the fairway, the week at Shepherd's Bush Empire is yours." Well, he teed off, and God hit the shot for him. He split the fairway in half for about 215 yards. He turned to me in amazement, and said, "George the week of the fifteenth you and Gracie are playing the Shepherd's Bush Empire!"

"Thanks," I said, "and now, Mr. Parnell, I'd like to tell you something. You're the lousiest golfer I ever played with."

Henry Sherek quickly turned to Parnell and said, "Val, his stuff on the stage is funnier!" Parnell laughed, Henry Sherek laughed, and I was hysterical.

Well, that Monday we opened at the Victoria Palace. It's difficult for me to tell you exactly how we felt as we waited in the wings. This was the first time we had ever played to an audience outside the United States. Finally our music started, the spotlight hit the stage, and ready to make our entrance I took Gracie by the hand. I could tell immediately that she was nervous. All talented people get nervous. My hand was very steady. We walked out and did our fourteen minutes, and the English people loved Gracie as much as the Americans. We were a big hit. In fact, after taking three bows, we had to do an encore.

Now I'm not going to tell you what we did for fourteen minutes, but this was our encore: It consisted of sort of a stage argument. I would talk to the audience, and then Gracie would start talking to the audience. Then we'd both be talking to the audience at the same time. And we kept on talking until finally Gracie out-talked me. Sound confusing? I'll show you how it went:

GEORGE

Ladies and gentlemen, thank you very much,
and it's very exciting for us to play here in

London. We'd love to do a little more, but
we're not prepared.

GRACIE

I am.

GEORGE
(Continuing to audience)

It's really a thrill for us to be so well accepted
by you people.

GRACIE

I am.

GEORGE	GRACIE
I must tell you what happened when we found out we had been booked to play the Victoria Palace. Our Agent, Tom Fitzpatrick, told us that we were booked to play London for four weeks. We were thrilled, because although we had played in vaudeville all over America, we never dreamed that one day we'd be—	I am. If my brother Willie was here, I could do something alone if my brother was here. But my brother isn't here so I'll have to do something by myself. *(Turning to George)* My poor brother Willie, he was held up last night. Willie . . . my brother . . . was held up . . . last night . . . Willie . . . held up . . . my brother.

GEORGE
(Turning to Gracie)

Your brother.

GRACIE

He was held up.

GEORGE

Your brother was held up?

GRACIE

Yeah, by two men.

GEORGE

Where?

GRACIE

All the way home.

GEORGE

Your brother must drink a lot.

GRACIE

So does my brother.

GEORGE

Hasn't your mother ever tried to do something about your brother Willie's drinking?

GRACIE

She sent him to a psychiatrist, and the psychiatrist worked and worked to get to the bottom of his drinking, and finally he found out Willie's problem.

GEORGE

What was it?

GRACIE

He likes to drink.

GEORGE

So does my brother.

GRACIE

Hasn't your mother ever sent him to a—

GEORGE

Say good night, Gracie.

GRACIE

Good night.

Well, that was our encore, but opening night it didn't go quite that way. In the middle of it while Gracie and I were talking at the same time, a man in the seventh row, he must have been about six feet four, slowly stood up. He kept snapping his fingers and calling out, "Young man! Young man!"

We stopped right in the middle of the routine. I couldn't figure out what was happening, and I said to him, "Yes, sir?" And pointing to me, in a firm voice he said, "I think it would be very nice if you would let that charming little lady carry on," and he sat down.

I was so stunned I didn't know what to say. Stammering, I said, "All right, I'll let this . . . this charming little lady carry on, but . . . but it won't do any good because I don't know where I am now."

Without missing a beat, Gracie said, "I do."

I said "What?!"

She continued, "I do."

I said, "You do?"

"Yeah," she said, "my brother. My poor brother Willie, he was held up last night by two men. . . ."

Yes, we finished the routine, and the audience loved it. In

fact, we were such a big hit I even made the man in the seventh row take a bow.

We played our five weeks, and London loved us! And we loved London! And I loved Gracie! And Gracie loved me! And we both loved show business! Now with all that love I think it's time to end this chapter.

SHE WAS REALLY SOMETHING

WHEN WE RETURNED from London we opened our season at the Majestic Theater in Chicago. And we were such a big hit at the opening matinee that the manager moved us from the No. 4 spot to the No. 7 spot on an eight-act vaudeville bill. A comedy act can't be paid a greater compliment than that. Everything seemed to be going right. Ahead of us was forty weeks of big-time vaudeville and then, out of the clear sky I got a wire saying that my mother had died. I told the manager to get another act to replace us, and that night Gracie and I got on a train for New York. It shouldn't have come as such a shock to me because my mother was sixty-nine years old and had been bedridden for three years. But no matter how you prepare yourself for the inevitable the shock is still there.

We had eight hours on the train before we reached New York and I thought I should prepare Gracie for what would be going on when we arrived at my mother's house. I told her, "Gracie, my mother was the backbone that held my family together all these years. And with seven sisters and five brothers, you're going to hear a lot of crying. And when you add all of their families, the weeping and wailing will be like

347

something you never heard before in your life. So when it happens be ready for it, that's the way we Jewish people express our grief."

She looked at me and patted my hand. "Don't worry, George," she said, "we Catholics shed a few loud tears ourselves."

I didn't get much sleep on the train that night. I kept thinking of how my mother's wisdom and strength had shaped my family. She had many wonderful qualities, but most of all I loved her sense of humor. It was never direct, it was always by inference. I remember one incident in particular. It was the first time Gracie and I played the Palace Theater in New York. My mother had then been bedridden for about two years. We had two more days left to finish the week, and early Saturday morning I went to visit her. The first thing she asked was, "How are you and Gracie doing at the Palace?"

"Just great, Mama," I answered.

She sort of sighed and said, "You know, Nattie, I've been waiting for years to see you play the Palace, and now you're there, and here I am."

Trying to cheer her up, I jokingly said, "Mama, I'll tell you what we'll do. Tomorrow I'll hire a limousine, and the girls can help you get ready. Then Sammy and Willy will help you to the car and go to the theater with you. We'll time it so you get there right after intermission. You'll see Gracie and me, and Elsie Janis who's the headliner, and then Sammy and Willy will get you back into the car and we'll all drive back to Brooklyn. How would you like that?"

"I'll wear my blue dress," she said.

I was knocked over: I didn't think she'd take me seriously. But I was delighted. I was also worried if she was strong enough to make it. But she made it. The next day at the Palace she saw Gracie and me, and Elsie Janis. And I must say, Gracie and I were never better. After the show Sammy, Willy, and I drove Mama back to Brooklyn. On our way, I proudly turned to her and said, "Mama, who was the best on that bill?"

She said, "First came Elsie Janis. Then came Gracie."

That wasn't exactly what I expected to hear. "But, Mama," I said, "what about me?"

She smiled and said, "Nattie, I said it before, and I'll say it again. You're a nice boy."

Lying there in my berth, with the train rolling towards New York, it made me feel good that my mother finally saw me at the Palace. But it saddened me to realize I would never again hear her say, "Nattie, you're a nice boy."

Well, the next morning Gracie and I arrived at my mother's house on Carroll Street in Brooklyn. As we were walking in Gracie took my hand. When I opened the door the house was full of all my brothers and sisters, and some relatives I'd never even seen before. But I got the surprise of my life. I looked at Gracie; I couldn't believe it. Nobody was crying. There was sadness and quiet conversation, but none of that weeping and wailing I had expected. After Gracie and I said hello to my family I took my sister Mamie aside. "Mamie," I said, "I'd like to ask you something."

She said, "I know exactly what you're going to ask me. Mama didn't want anyone to cry."

After the funeral I found out why. You see, my brothers Sammy and Willy were the only ones still living at home, and the night before my mother passed away she called them into her room and told them she was going to die. Naturally, they didn't believe her. But she insisted. "Boys," she said, "remember three years ago when I got very sick and everybody thought I was going to die. I didn't. I wasn't ready. Now I am."

There was a slight pause, then she continued. "Sammy, Willy, I want you both to sit down here on the bed and listen. All my life I prayed for one thing, that when it was time for me to leave this earth I wanted to be in my right mind. And my prayers have been answered." A little smile, then, "Now I want you to call your sisters and have them come over early in the morning. I want the house spic and span. And tell Goldie to make sure that the coffee is very hot. You know Uncle Frank, if the coffee isn't hot he won't go to the funeral." Another pause, "Now boys, this is very important. I don't want any crying. Be sure to tell everybody. I don't want any crying. And I know you'll all sit shiva* for a week. Nattie will be coming in from Chicago, and he's very busy and he's got to get back to work. I know he's not very religious, but tell him to sit shiva for a half hour, it won't hurt him. Now boys, do you understand?"

They both nodded yes, and Sammy said, "Here, Mama, take this medicine and rest a little. You'll feel better in the morning."

"All right, Sammy," Mama said, "I'll take the medicine."

In the morning when my brothers walked into her room it was just as she had said—Mama had left us.

Well, I sat shiva for four days. I wanted to sit shiva for a week, but I couldn't. Gracie and I had to open the following week in Milwaukee. On the train to Milwaukee I turned to Gracie and said, "My mother was really something, wasn't she?"

Gracie said, "Yes, she certainly was a great lady." Then she leaned over and gave me a little kiss. "And George, you're a nice boy."

---

*For those of you who may not know what "sitting shiva" means, in the Orthodox Jewish religion after the funeral the immediate family sits in the house of the deceased for seven days, giving up all comforts, as a token of respect.

TITLES CAN DRIVE YOU NUTS

I'VE SAID THIS before, but I'm going to say it again because I really believe it, and I think it's very important. And when something is important you can say it ten times, twenty times, fifty times, if you believe it. And I believe it, so I'll keep saying it and saying it. In fact, I've got to keep saying it because my publisher insists this book have at least three hundred pages.

What I'm trying to say is that if you're in love with what you're doing, failures can't stop you. When I was a kid I was always singing, but nobody liked it, so I started dancing, and nobody liked it. Then I started telling jokes, and nobody laughed. Then I tried to be dramatic, and everybody laughed. So I figured as long as I couldn't be a singer, or a dancer, or a comedian, or a dramatic actor, there was only one thing left for me to do. And I did it—I went into show business. By the time I found out I had no talent I was too big a star to do anything else.

I must admit that to make it, luck and timing are big factors, especially timing. I went from one failure to another until I was twenty-seven years old. And I hate to brag, but I wouldn't have had so many failures if my timing hadn't been perfect. But all those failures did teach me something. Eventually I must run out of them. And I did when I met Gracie. Now I'm not going to tell you how I met her, I've told that a thousand times. But if at the end of the book I'm short a few pages, I'll tell it again.

But now I want to tell you how luck played a big part in our career. It happened one night when Gracie and I were in the right place at the right time. It was at a party given by Arthur Lyons, one of our top theatrical agents in New York, who at that time represented Jack Benny. The only reason Gracie and I were invited was because we were friends of Jack. Well, during dinner Arthur came over to our table and told Jack that he had booked Fred Allen to make a short for Warner Brothers in Brooklyn the next day, but he just had a phone call telling him that Fred was sick and couldn't make it. He wound up saying, "Jack, I know you're busy, but can you suggest somebody? I need him right now."

While Jack was thinking I piped up with, "I can suggest somebody."

Arthur said, "Who?"

I said, "How about George Burns and Gracie Allen?"

Arthur thought about this for a moment. "Look," he said, "you have to be at Warner Brothers-Vitaphone in Brooklyn in your makeup at nine o'clock in the morning. You've got to do nine minutes, and you'll get seventeen hundred dollars. Do you think you can do it?"

"Arthur," I said, "for seventeen hundred dollars Gracie and I can not only do nine minutes, but we can drink a glass of water at the same time." As I said earlier, luck plays a big part. We were at the right place at the right time.

The next morning at eight o'clock we were at Warner Brothers putting on our makeup. There was a knock on our door and in came a man who looked very, very familiar. He told me he was Murray Roth. Well, I couldn't believe it. I hadn't seen Murray for years; we went to public school together, P.S. 22. After I introduced him to Gracie I asked him what he was doing there.

"The same thing you're doing," he said, "I'm in show business."

I said, "Murray, how could you be in show business? When we were in the fourth grade together you couldn't even sing harmony."

Murray laughed and said, "George, I'm a director. I'm directing you and Gracie in the short you're doing."

I said, "You're kidding. You, a director? You couldn't even find your way to the boys' room!"

"George," he said, "I've been directing shorts for two years now."

"Murray, I still don't believe it."

He said, "George, would I have my hat on backwards if I wasn't a director?"

That convinced me, and it also made me a little nervous. But then came the real problem. When we got on the stage I saw that the set they had built for Fred Allen was the interior of a living room. Well, that didn't fit Gracie and me at all, because the routine that we were going to do took place on a street corner. It took me a few minutes to solve the problem, and I'd like to show the way we did it.

Our director, Murray Roth, called, "Lights!" and the lights came up. Then he called, "Camera!" and the camera started clicking. Then he hollered, "Action!" and Gracie and I made our entrance into Fred Allen's living room. Gracie immediately started looking into the candy dish, the cigarette box, under the pillows, opening and closing drawers, etc.

GEORGE

Gracie, what are you looking for?

GRACIE

The audience.

GEORGE

You see that camera, you see the little lens sticking out. Well, you look right into that and that's where the audience is.

GRACIE

Oh? All right.

GEORGE

Now, Gracie, if we can talk for nine minutes, they'll pay us seventeen hundred dollars. Do you think you can do that?

GRACIE

George, just ask me what my brother Harvey is doing.

Well, that started her, and she talked for nine minutes. In the middle of a joke I stopped her:

GEORGE

Gracie, our nine minutes are up, and we just made seventeen hundred dollars. Now wave goodbye to the audience.

With that she waved, and I waved, and Murray Roth said, "Cut!" Murray was right, he was a director.

Don't ask me why, but that short for Warner Brothers was a big hit. It might have been because of our honest approach, or maybe it was Fred Allen's living room, or Murray Roth saying "Cut!" but before we knew it Paramount Pictures signed us for four shorts at thirty-five hundred dollars a short. That meant that Gracie and I made an extra fourteen thousand dollars a year. In comparison our vaudeville salary looked very small, even though we were getting five hundred dollars a week. But with this extra money coming in, and the short being such a big hit, I got very brave. I went to see Mr. Gottfried of the B.F. Keith office and told him that Gracie and I were very unhappy with our salary. Instead of five hundred dollars we now wanted seven hundred and fifty dollars a week. Gottfried stared right at me and said, "You and Gracie are not worth seven hundred and fifty dollars a week."

Full of our success, I stared right back and said, "Mr. Gottfried, you tell us why we're worth five hundred dollars a week and we'll forget the whole thing." He couldn't, so we got seven hundred and fifty dollars.

Well, Gracie and I were really moving up fast now. In fact, with all that money coming in I had my shoes shined whether they needed it or not. The first short was scheduled to be filmed at the end of our current road tour. So in between shows I started writing. I told Gracie I had a good idea for our first short where she played a salesgirl, but I just couldn't think of a title. For two days I sat there racking my brain, and then finally it came to me. I rushed into Gracie's dressing room and said, "Gracie, I've got the title!"

She stopped putting on her makeup and turned to me. "What is it?" she said.

"'The Salesgirl,'" I said proudly.

"George," Gracie said, "you're a nice boy," and she continued putting on her makeup.

Well, it wasn't easy for me to be a writer. I had to write everything in longhand. And as I said, I only went as far as the fourth grade in P.S. 22 and I was a very bad speller. And that was my best subject. So when I started being a screenwriter I had to spell everything phonetically. Then I would give what I had written to Gracie and she translated it back into English. Working out the idea and getting it down on paper, I was lucky if I finished a page a day. And to complete the short I needed at least twenty-five pages. So you see, Gracie had to do a lot of

correctıng, and not once did she ever mention my spelling. Now
that's true love.

We finished our tour and went to Astoria on Long Island,
where Paramount had their studio, to do our first short. And
who do you think was our director? Sid Garfield. No, Murray
Roth wasn't there anymore. Somebody turned his hat around
and he became one of the top producers.

Well, this is what I came up with. Here it is:

(The scene takes place at a cigar counter in a hotel lobby)

PARAMOUNT PICTURES

Presents

GEORGE BURNS AND GRACIE ALLEN

In

"THE SALESGIRL"

*(A telephone rings, and Gracie, behind the cigar counter, picks up the
phone)*

GRACIE

Hello. Oh hello, Mary, I was just going to
call you. When are you giving me the surprise party? . . . Tuesday night . . . Sure
I've got a new dress, I'm wearing it . . . What
time Tuesday night? . . . Oh, you can't tell
me, that's the surprise. . . . Sounds like fun.
Tuesday night, don't forget to be there. . . .
Goodbye.

(She hangs up as a customer comes up to the counter)

CUSTOMER

I'll have two of those cigars.

GRACIE

That'll be twenty cents.

CUSTOMER

Here's five dollars.

(She gives him the cigars and rings up the money)

GRACIE

Anything else?

CUSTOMER

Yes, four-eighty.

GRACIE

We haven't got cigars for four-eighty.

CUSTOMER

Who wants cigars for four-eighty? I want two cigars for twenty cents.

GRACIE

I think you're silly to pay four-eighty for cigars that only cost twenty cents.

CUSTOMER

(Exasperated)

Four-eighty! Twenty cents! I don't want any cigars! Here's your cigars, now give me back my five dollars!

GRACIE

Oh, we never refund money, and besides you had no right to leave the counter before counting your change.

CUSTOMER

Leave the counter, count my change!! I didn't leave the counter, I didn't get any change!!

GRACIE

Look, am I going to have the same trouble with you I had yesterday. I'm going to call the house detective.

(Calls)

Mr. Sweeney! Mr. Sweeney!
(Mr. Sweeney, a big, tall, burly man, enters)

SWEENEY

Yes, Miss Allen, what is it?

(She gives him the two cigars)

GRACIE

Here, have two cigars.

SWEENEY

Oh, I couldn't, Miss Allen.

GRACIE

Take them, they're paid for.
(He takes them)

SWEENEY

Thanks. Now, what's the problem?

GRACIE

Mr. Sweeney, this man bought two cigars for twenty cents and gave me five dollars. How much do I owe him?

SWEENEY

Four dollars and eighty cents.

GRACIE

And four-eighty from five dollars is how much?

SWEENEY

Twenty cents.

GRACIE

And how much are two cigars at ten cents apiece?

SWEENEY

Twenty cents.

GRACIE

Then doesn't that make us even?

SWEENEY

Yes, I guess it does.

GRACIE

Then throw this crook out. . . .

SWEENEY

Come on, get out of here.

(He drags the customer off)

GRACIE

(Calling after them)

I should have known yesterday I was going to
have trouble with you today!

(George enters)

GEORGE

Hello, Gracie.

GRACIE

Hello, George. Don't forget the party Tuesday night.

GEORGE

Gracie, it's supposed to be a surprise.

GRACIE

Oh, you spoiled it for me. . . .

GEORGE

I'm sorry. Let me have two cigars for twenty
cents.

(He gives her twenty cents. She rings it up and gives him the cigars)

GRACIE

Here's your four-eighty change.

GEORGE

Gracie, you're a little mixed up. I didn't give you five dollars. I gave you twenty cents.

GRACIE

Now listen, am I going to have the same trouble with you I had with that other fellow.

GEORGE

Not with me. I can use four-eighty. I haven't got a cent, I'm a pauper.

GRACIE

You're a what?

GEORGE

I'm a pauper.

GRACIE

Oh, congratulations, boy or girl?

GEORGE

I really don't know.

GRACIE

Well, you better find out. Your brother will want to know if he's an uncle or an aunt.

GEORGE

I'll phone him when I get home. . . . Say, Gracie, do you know who you remind me of?

GRACIE

I know, I was taken once for Clara Bow.

GEORGE

Well, that's show business. . . . You were taken once for Clara Bow, and I was taken for grand larceny.

GRACIE

George, don't be silly, you don't look a bit like him. . . .

GEORGE

He's sort of a big, tall blond fellow.

GRACIE

I know, and he's a very good dancer.

GEORGE

Say, you've got a pretty nice job here.

GRACIE

Job? I could have had two jobs. This one at ten dollars a week and another one at forty dollars a week.

GEORGE

Then why did you take this job?

GRACIE

Because I figure that if I lose a ten-dollar job instead of a forty-dollar job, I'll be saving thirty dollars.

GEORGE

Look, at thirty dollars a week, at the end of the year you'll have saved yourself fifteen hundred dollars.

GRACIE

Sure, if I'm out of work for ten years, I'll have enough money to retire.

GEORGE

Do you mind if I change the subject?

GRACIE

No, this is a free country.

GEORGE

That's a nice dress you have on.

GRACIE

I'm glad you like it. It's my party dress for Tuesday night. My sisters, Jean and Alice, are going, too. They're twins, you know.

GEORGE

I didn't know you had twin sisters.

GRACIE

They really should be triplets, because I think Alice is two-faced.

GEORGE

Do they look exactly alike?

GRACIE

Oh yeah.

GEORGE

Is it hard to tell them apart?

GRACIE

Standing up or sitting down?

GEORGE

What difference does that make?

GRACIE

Well, we noticed when Alice sits down and Jean stands up—

GEORGE

Jean seems taller.

GRACIE

Yeah. . . . Even though they look exactly alike it's easy to tell them apart because Alice is married.

GEORGE

And Jean is single.

GRACIE

No, Jean is married, too.

GEORGE

Well, how do you tell them apart?

GRACIE

Jean is the one who has a swimming pool.

GEORGE

And Alice?

GRACIE

She sleeps on the floor.

GEORGE

She sleeps on the floor?

GRACIE

She's got high blood pressure and she's trying to keep it down.

GEORGE

But Jean is the one with the swimming pool.

GRACIE

Yeah, we were there yesterday and we had such fun. We were diving, and doing back flips, and we'll even have more fun tomorrow when they put water in it.

GEORGE

Well, exercise is good for you.

GRACIE

That's why we took the old woman with us.

GEORGE

Your mother?

GRACIE

No, the old woman who lives with us. She's been with us for five weeks now.

GEORGE

Is it your aunt?

GRACIE

We don't even know her. She just wanders around the house and does anything she wants.

GEORGE

Now let me get this. There's an old woman who wanders around your house and does anything she wants, and you don't even know her?

GRACIE

Sure. You see, my sister bought a ticket.

GEORGE

A ticket?

GRACIE

You see, they ran a raffle for a poor old woman, and—

GEORGE

Your sister won.

GRACIE

Yeah. . . .

GEORGE

Gracie, let's talk about anything except your family.

GRACIE

Then you don't want to talk about my brother.

GEORGE

No.

GRACIE

You're sure.

GEORGE

Yeah.

GRACIE

He's very tall, you know.

GEORGE

Gracie, I don't want to talk about your brother.

GRACIE

He's an undercover agent.

GEORGE

An undercover agent? Is he in the secret service?

GRACIE

No, he knows about it.

GEORGE

Maybe I shouldn't have asked.

GRACIE

Last week he went out on a murder case, and do you know he found that man in an hour.

GEORGE

He found the murderer in an hour?

GRACIE

No, the man who was killed.

GEORGE

Not only is your brother tall, but he's fast.

GRACIE

Oh yeah . . . And then Mr. & Mrs. Jones were having matrimonial trouble, and my brother was hired to watch Mrs. Jones.

GEORGE

Well, I imagine she was a very attractive woman.

GRACIE

She was, and my brother watched her day and night for six months.

GEORGE

Well, what happened?

GRACIE

She finally got a divorce.

GEORGE

Mrs. Jones?

GRACIE

No, my brother's wife.

GEORGE

Gracie, I've enjoyed every minute of it, but we've run out of time. So just wave goodbye to everybody.

GRACIE

Don't you want to hear about my Aunt Clara?

GEORGE

No.

GRACIE

She's not only tall, but she's fat.

GEORGE

I don't want to hear about her.

GRACIE

She's the one who collects all the clothes.

GEORGE

Gracie, we'll do that in our next short.

GRACIE

Do you promise?

GEORGE

I promise.

GRACIE

Good. Then I'll wave and say goodbye to everybody. Goodbye, everybody.

(As Gracie waves into camera, the picture fades out as music comes up)

THE END

*(Written by George Burns, "Whiz Bang"
and "College Humor")*

Well, we kept making shorts for Paramount. And during this time we also went into radio, and we did very well. Then in 1932 Paramount brought us to Hollywood for our first feature film, *The Big Broadcast*. And all this happened because we were in the right place at the right time. So all of you young kids who are trying to make it in show business, here's the way to do it. Wait until vaudeville comes back, work up an act with a very talented Irish girl who can spell, and make sure you're invited to an Arthur Lyons party.

SO WE STOPPED WORKING AND WENT INTO RADIO

In the last couple of years I've been interviewed a lot. Now some of these interviews turn out good, and some of them don't. A lot of it depends on the questions. If the questions are stale, the answers are stale, and if the questions are fresh, the answers are fresh. Sometimes when you hear some of my fresh answers you're better off with the stale questions.

A few years ago Henry Edwards of *The New York Times* asked me an interesting question. He wanted to know if during our careers did Gracie and I have a problem going from one medium to the other. I told him I hadn't thought of it before. When Gracie and I were in vaudeville we did a man and woman talking act, and when we went into radio, although you didn't see us, we were still talking. Then on television where you did see us, we were still talking. And in motion pictures where we were ten times the size, we were still talking. I wound up by saying, "So Henry, for Gracie and me it was very easy to go from one medium to the other; we just kept talking. And now I'll let you in on a little secret, but this is off the record. I found out there's quite a lot of money in talking."

Anyway, it turned out to be a good interview because Henry

asked the right questions. The problem was we were both enjoying it so much that we didn't notice the time. I happened to look at my watch just as Henry asked this question, "George, you've been in show business all your life. How important are entrances and exits?"

"Very important," I said, "especially an exit." Then taking another look at my watch, "Henry, it's a quarter after seven, and I've got a date with a twenty-two-year-old girl. Now if you don't leave right now, that girl is going to be too old for me." That got a laugh from Henry. He picked up his hat, and as I walked him to the door, I said, "Henry, you are now making what I would call a great exit."

But Henry had brought up one very important point: the difficulty of going from vaudeville into radio. Some acts couldn't make it, like jugglers, acrobats, tight-rope walkers, Duncan's Collies, Power's Elephants, Madame Burkhardt's Cockatoos, Swain's Cats & Rats, Fink's Mules, and of course, Dainty Marie.

Radio was really revolutionary. For the first time people did not have to come to the theater to see you. You entertained them by coming right into their living rooms. We reached millions of people in one night. So overnight we performers got to be sensations; we all got to be stars. What I realize now is that it wasn't us at all, the invention was the sensation. If it wasn't for that little crystal set, I'd still be playing Altoona.

For instance, when Gracie and I had been on radio for a couple of weeks, we were walking down Broadway and a man stopped us. "Aren't you Burns and Allen?" he asked. We said we were, and he continued, "I heard you last night all the way from Cleveland," and he walked away. Gracie and I exchanged looks, and just then the man came back and added, "I can also get Philadelphia on my set."

I said, "Thank you, that's quite a compliment."

Another time Gracie and I were having breakfast at Lindy's restaurant, and after the waiter took our order, he said, "I heard your show last night on my new Atwater Kent." I said, "How'd you like it?" and he replied, "Like it, it's a great set! If I were you, I'd get one." When he left I said to Gracie, "Remind me to give this kid a big tip."

One night Gracie and I went to see Victor Moore and Billy Gaxton in the Broadway show *Of Thee I Sing.* We loved it, and during the intermission we were standing in the lobby discussing it. Gracie was talking about how she was enjoying the show when there was a tap on her shoulder. She turned around, and this woman, bubbling with excitement, said, "You're Gracie Allen, right?"

"That's right," Gracie said.

Getting very friendly, the woman said, "I recognized your voice. Now you're not going to believe this story, it really is amazing. Last week I heard you on my radio set in Syracuse, and my sister in Denver heard you tell the same jokes on her set."

"Did you like that routine about Gracie's brother Harvey?" I ventured.

"Oh, I don't remember the jokes," she said, "but the most wonderful thing is that you both came through so clear."

When Gracie and I went back to see the second half of the show we still enjoyed Billy Gaxton and Victor Moore. And the reason we enjoyed them is they came through so clear.

In those days we never had a rating problem. We were all in the Top Ten—there were only eight shows. But eventually the newness of the machine wore off, the static cleared up, and people started to pay attention to the performers. A lot of new shows were developed, the quality of the writing improved, studio audiences were added to give it more excitement, broadcasting stations sprang up all over the country, and eventually radio became a fully developed form of entertainment. And before you knew it, the audience of millions and millions of people had created their radio stars.

With radio, success came so fast that it not only went to your head, it went to your neck, to your shoulders, to your chest, and I don't want to get risqué. People would now stop us on the street and ask for our autographs. When we went into restaurants we always got the best table. There were fan clubs, radio columnists, articles in magazines, newspaper interviews. In fact, there were publications devoted exclusively to radio personalities. Within a short time we were known all over the United States.

When I look back, I was so full of myself, of my own importance, and I was taking credit for things I had nothing to do with. The writers would write the script, and I'd give it to the producer. The producer would read it and say, "George, a very funny script," and I'd take a bow and say "Thank you." Then there was the sound effects man. He opened doors, he closed doors, he rang the telephone, he picked up the receiver, he put back the receiver, he made it rain, he made it thunder, he cried like a baby, he barked like a dog, he neighed like a horse, he meowed like a cat, he made things fall out of a closet—and I kept taking bows.

It was so easy for Gracie and me. What did we actually do? Our announcer, Bill Goodwin, would say, "Here they are . . . George Burns and Gracie Allen!" Then they'd hold up the "applause" sign, the audience would applaud, and Gracie and I would keep taking bows. We stood there with scripts in our hands, and I'd read the first line. "Gracie, say hello to everybody." Then Gracie would read her line, "Hello," and that's the way it went. If the writers would think of any ad libs, we'd write them down on the script. If you got so you could read your ad libs without rattling the paper, you were a great performer.

But one day I came up with an idea that worked. I took the sound effects man and made him a character on our show. He was played by a fine actor, Eliott Lewis, who later turned out to be one of our top directors. The idea of the character was that this sound effects man was a college graduate, and he found the job beneath him. For instance, in the script he would open the door, but before he slammed it shut he'd mutter, "Here I am a Phi Beta Kappa and this is what I do for a living!" And then, Bang! he'd slam the door. Another time he would make the telephone ring, but before he would pick up the receiver he'd mumble, "Four years of political science and my kids have to tune in to hear me do this!" and then he'd pick up the receiver.

The character really caught on for us. But one of my favorite bits on the show was when he said, "Mr. Burns, I've been working very hard, and I finally came up with a brand new sound effect. Maybe you can use it. It's a Siamese cat walking across a Persian rug."

I said, "Let me hear it."

After ten seconds of absolute silence, he asked, "How'd you like it?"

"I didn't hear anything," I said.

"Then it works," he said. "Thanks, it took me a long time to perfect it."

Now that got a very big laugh. But when I just read it over it doesn't sound funny. However, as I said, this book needs three hundred pages.

There were things that happened in radio that are amusing when I think of them now, but they could have turned into a disaster then; that is, if it weren't for one thing. Gracie and I had an understanding between us. The minute I said, "Gracie, let's talk about your brother," that meant forget the script and go right into our vaudeville routine. Let me give you a few examples of how it worked. Once we were doing a radio show in downtown Los Angeles, and about two minutes into the show for some reason the lights went out. Well, I immediately said, "Gracie, let's talk about your brother," and without missing a beat she answered, "Which brother do you want to talk about, the one who's in love or the one who sleeps on the floor?" We continued the routine until the lights came back on and then we started reading our scripts again.

Sometime later we were broadcasting from the CBS studios on Sunset Boulevard, and at that time Gracie and I used one microphone and read from the same script. Well, just as the show started someone in the control booth waved to Gracie. Gracie, who had the script in her hand, waved back and forty pages flew all over the place. Gracie turned to me and said, "Which brother do you want to talk about, the one who's in love or the one who sleeps on the floor?"

These two incidents were mild compared to what happened on the *Rudy Vallee Show* back in New York. Gracie and I were just beginning in radio and an appearance on the *Rudy Vallee Show*, which was one of the top shows, was a big break for us. Now just before the broadcast began my optometrist delivered my new pair of reading glasses. You guessed it; he gave me somebody else's glasses. I put them in my pocket and waited for our entrance. Well, we got this beautiful introduction from Rudy Vallee and walked out to the microphone with our scripts. I put on my glasses and of course I couldn't see a thing. I turned to Gracie and said, "Gracie, let's talk about your brother."

This time Gracie was stunned; she didn't know what had gone wrong. "Are you sure?" she whispered.

I took off my glasses and showed them to her. "I can't see a thing," I whispered back.

"Of course you can't," she murmured, "you've got your glasses off."

"Gracie," I whispered meaningfully, "the optometrist gave me the wrong glasses!"

With that Gracie said, "Which brother do you want to talk about, the one who's in love or the one who sleeps on the floor?" We did our six minutes and were a riot. But poor Rudy Vallee spent the entire time looking through the script trying to find out where we were.

Now let me backtrack a little and tell you how Gracie and I got started in radio. Oddly enough it wasn't in America, it was in London. We were playing the variety theaters and we got an

offer from the British Broadcasting Company to do five broadcasts. We didn't take radio too seriously then, so we weren't too
impressed. But what did impress us was that we would make an
extra hundred pounds so naturally we accepted. They wanted
us to do a routine lasting about six minutes. And the way it
worked we did the same routine for all five broadcasts. Since at
that time there was no network, our first broadcast, on a
Monday, was heard only in London. The second broadcast, on
Tuesday, was heard in Manchester, the third in Bristol, the
fourth in Blackpool, and I think the fifth was heard in Glasgow.
In those days you got a lot of mileage out of six minutes.

But what really amazed us was the number of people who
heard us on that one broadcast in London. And what was even
more pleasing, they all liked us. We may not have been
impressed with radio before these broadcasts, but we certainly
were afterwards. I couldn't wait to get back to New York. I
figured if they liked us in America as much as they did in
London, no telling how far Gracie and I could go in this new
thing called radio.

Now let's pause a minute. Before I take you back to
America, as long as I'm now in England, I'd like to stay here for
awhile and tell you what happened to me here in 1976. I know
you're just dying to find out how Gracie and I made out in
radio, but I'm sorry, you'll have to wait. I want the book to have
a little suspense.

Well, on June 13, 1976, I was invited to give a concert at the
London Palladium. It was a Royal Gala Charity Evening and
attended by Her Royal Highness Princess Margaret. It was a
very successful evening and raised a lot of money. At the finish
of my performance, Max Bygraves, one of the top English
comedians, presented me with a beautiful plaque. I thanked
him, and said, "It's an honor to receive this award, Max, and
when I get home I'm going to invite Douglas Fairbanks, Jr.,
over to see it, because he's the only Englishman in Hollywood I
know."

Following the concert, Jeffrey Kruger, who produced the show, ushered me up to the Royal Box to meet Princess Margaret. There were a number of people there, and seated in the center of the group was this charming lady. So I went up to her and said, "Your Highness, it's a pleasure for me to meet you. I'd curtsy, but if I got down, I wouldn't be able to get up again."

She laughed, and said, "I'm sorry, Mr. Burns, I'm not Princess Margaret, I'm the Lady-in-Waiting."

Just then the Princess came in. I turned to her and said, "Your Highness, it's a pleasure for me to meet you, and you just missed one of my big jokes."

The Princess gave me a puzzled look, and as she sat down she gestured for me to sit next to her. We had a very pleasant conversation, and then she said, "Mr. Burns, you sing so fast I practically missed the lyrics to your first song."

I said, "Your Highness, would you like to hear me sing it again?"

With a smile, she said, "No, once is enough." I had a funny comeback, but I'm not topping a princess.

Well, a few minutes later the Princess stood up, and I assumed that this was my cue to leave. As I said goodbye and started to go, she stopped me and whispered, "No, no, Mr. Burns, I'm supposed to leave first." I quickly stepped aside, and she left. Then as I started to leave again, the Lady-in-Waiting tapped me on the shoulder and said, "Mr. Burns, I'm supposed to leave next." After she left I sat down; I didn't want to start another war with England. I sat there until everybody had left. Finally an usher opened up the curtains to the box and said, "Mr. Burns, the theater is empty, and you can leave after I do."

Well, that's not exactly what happened. As a matter of fact, none of it is true. Oh, some of it is true. I might even say that most of it is true. I really did give the concert, I met Princess Margaret, and I was the last one to leave. That's because I curtsied and couldn't get up.

And now . . . back to the drama! This is how Gracie and I got into this new thing called radio. When we returned to New York from London we played a couple of weeks of vaudeville. About then Eddie Cantor and George Jessel were putting together a show to play the Palace Theater for a couple of weeks—I believe it was 1930—and they asked us to join it. We were thrilled because this was the tail end of vaudeville, and it looked like maybe there would be no more Palace. Anyway, the show was a smash and we stayed there for eleven weeks.

At that same time Eddie Cantor was also starring every Sunday night in radio on the *Chase and Sanborn Hour,* which was one of the top shows on the air. One day Eddie told me he'd like to use Gracie on his radio show. I said, "Sure, Eddie, we'd be delighted to do your show."

"I'm sorry, George," he said, "just Gracie."

"Okay, Eddie," I said, "under one condition. Providing you use our material."

"Fine, just write it up," Eddie nodded, "and I want Gracie to do about five minutes."

I said, "Eddie, there's nothing to write. All you say to Gracie is 'How's your brother?' and she'll talk for five minutes."

Eddie looked at me with those big eyes, and said, "That's all I do?"

"That's all I do," I said. "But if you feel like it, you can throw in some of my big ad libs like 'Really?' . . . 'Is that so.' . . . 'You don't say' . . . 'Oh?' . . . and 'Hmmmm.'"

So Gracie did the *Chase and Sanborn Hour* with Eddie Cantor and she was a very big hit. And that's how I got into radio.

The following week we were asked to do a guest spot on the *Rudy Vallee Fleischmann Hour* (remember, that's when I had the problem using the wrong reading glasses). After that we were booked to do two guest shots with Guy Lombardo. His show was called *Guy Lombardo and His Royal Canadians,* Thirty Minutes of the Sweetest Music This Side of Heaven. But our five minutes of comedy didn't dare interrupt the music. It was the first time we ever did our comedy routine with a musical background.

But they must have liked us, because we were booked for two more weeks. At the end of our third week, John Reber, who was then head of the Radio Department of the J. Walter Thompson Agency, got a letter signed by fifty-four members of an Ivy League college fraternity. He called me into his office and said, "George, sit down, I want to read this to you." I did, and then Reber read the following letter:

> Gentlemen:
> For the past two years every Monday night has been very special for us. It has become a tradition that on that night we invite our girlfriends over to the fraternity house and dance to the music of Guy Lombardo and His Royal Canadians, Thirty Minutes of the Sweetest Music This Side of Heaven. However, for the past three weeks out comes five minutes of these lousy jokes. May we point out that if we want lousy jokes, we can get them from the same joke book they get them from. Please, stick to the music, don't ruin our evening.

And then followed fifty-four signatures.

When he finished reading the letter, Reber looked up at me. I said, "John, I think you're trying to tell me something."

"That's right," he said. "George, anytime you can get fifty-four fellows to sign their names to a letter like that, you and Gracie must have something. You're booked for four more weeks."

I got up and said, "Thanks, John. I'm going out to buy another joke book."

In case you think that's the end of the story, it isn't. A couple of weeks later John Reber got another letter from the same fraternity. This time they said that after they were forced to listen to us they had learned to like us. But on this letter there were only fifty-three signatures; one kid still held out.

Well, we stayed with Guy Lombardo for the rest of the season, which was thirty-nine weeks. Our popularity kept growing and growing. Actually, we didn't realize how well known we'd become until one Sunday night after we had been on the air for about eight weeks, we went to the Club Richman. Every Sunday night there was celebrity night, and after Harry Richman entertained he would introduce all the celebrities who were in the audience. The night we were there, after all the introductions, Jay C. Flippen, the well-known monologist and a friend of ours, called Richman aside and said, "Harry, you forgot to introduce Burns and Allen."

Harry said, "Burns and Allen? What do the boys do?"

Flippen put his arm around Richman's shoulder. "It's George Burns and Gracie Allen. Harry, do me a favor, just introduce them." And Harry Richman did. With that the place came apart, we got the biggest reception of anybody there. But as I said before, we'll take some of the credit, but most of it goes to the fellow who invented the little talking box.

Eventually Guy Lombardo left the show and they asked us to take over. The following season it was *The George Burns and Gracie Allen Show*, and we stayed in radio for nineteen years.

SOME OF MY BEST IN-LAWS WERE IRISH

NOW I'VE TOLD you a lot about my family, I think it's time to tell you a little about Gracie's family. They were Irish Catholic and lived in San Francisco. She had a brother named George, and three sisters, Bessie, Pearl, and Hazel. Gracie was the baby of the family. She was the youngest by seven years, and of course, her mother and father were the oldest. They were a close, happy family, and most of them were in show business. I never had the chance to meet Gracie's father, but she told me he was in vaudeville, but only played the West Coast. These acts who played just the West Coast were called "Coast Defenders." Why they were called Defenders I don't know, unless they had to defend themselves once in a while from the audience. Anyway, that's the best I can come up with.

Now here's the way Gracie described her father's act to me. He sang Irish songs, told stories, and did clog dancing. And for the finish of his act they would bring out this contraption consisting of four posts and a wooden ceiling attached to it. Hanging from the ceiling were two straps, and he would grab hold of the straps, turn himself upside down, and do a fast Irish jig on the ceiling. I think I was right about why they called them Defenders.

382

Gracie's mother was a tiny, charming little lady. Everybody loved her. Although she herself was never in show business, she was crazy about it and encouraged all of her children to go into it. And they did, with the exception of Gracie's brother, George. I once asked him, "George, how come all your sisters are in show business and you're not?"

He thought about this for a moment, then answered, "I guess I just came to the conclusion that I have no talent."

I said, "Well, I came to that same conclusion years ago and just ignored it."

Gracie's three sisters were the greatest Irish dancers in the San Francisco Bay area. They were continually hired to dance at the various fairs and social functions up and down the entire Pacific Coast. And in between they entered every Irish dancing contest they could find. And they always came home with medals, blue ribbons, trophies, and sometimes even money. The only reason Gracie wasn't with them was that she was still a little girl going to school.

Now at that time there was a very large Irish community in San Francisco, and they could all dance and loved it. And every time the Allen girls would learn a new step they would name it after the person who taught it to them. So when they were sitting on the cable car on their way to enter a contest, their conversation would go something like this: "We make our entrance by opening with a Fitzpatrick, then we'll do a Sullivan, and then into an O'Neil. And, Bessie, you'll do a Kelly with a Ryan twist. Then following that, Pearl, you'll do a fast Flannagan, and I'll do a gliding Sweeney. And for the finish we'll all do a triple Mahoney." Their dancing routines always looked fresh because every time they made an appearance they would change the names around.

Now these Irish contests were not easy. Granted, the performers' costumes and their cuteness and their personalities would influence the audience, but not the judges. The judges sat under the stage completely isolated from the performers and the audience. They judged entirely by listening to the taps. And these judges were old great Irish dancers, and if somebody so much as missed just one tap while doing a MacNamara he was out. So Gracie's sisters must have been fabulous Irish dancers. To win all those contests under those conditions they had to be.

These three girls were a riot. Hazel never stopped talking, Pearl never said a word, and Bessie never listened. It worked for Bessie. She never got involved, she never got into an argument, she couldn't be bothered—which reminds me of an old joke, about sixty years old. Now a sixty-year-old joke might be an old joke to you, but at my age a sixty-year-old joke is brand new. Anyway, joke:

> This married couple had her brother-in-law living with them for about five years. So Sam said to Sarah, "We've got to get rid of your brother Joe. At dinner tonight I'll say, 'the soup is hot,' you say, 'the soup is cold,' and if he agrees with me, I'll throw him out, and if he agrees with you, you throw him out."
>
> At dinner that night Sam said to Joe, "Is the soup hot or cold?" and Joe said, "I'm not answering, I'm staying five more years."

That was Bessie.

As I told you, Hazel loved to talk. She was a very outgoing, friendly person. She talked to people on the street, she talked to everybody. When she went to the market to buy some tomatoes, by the time she stopped talking to the grocer the tomatoes were out of season. She even went so far as to learn to speak Gaelic so she could talk to more people.

While Pearl was a fine Irish dancer, I don't think she loved it like her sisters did. In fact, I feel that she resented being a good dancer. Her sisters told me that Pearl wore out four pairs of dancing shoes to their one. I guess she was so angry she had talent that she took it out on the floor.

Once when the three Allen sisters were playing in Santa Cruz we had one of our famous California earthquakes. While nothing happened to the girls, Mrs. Allen up in San Francisco didn't know that. All she knew was what she had heard on the radio. She got all excited and ran to the neighbor next door. She said, frightened, "Pearl, Bessie, and Hazel are in Santa Cruz, and there's an earthquake there! What should I do?!"

The neighbor quipped, "Relax, they were a noisy bunch anyway."

I don't think Mrs. Allen ever borrowed sugar from her again.

Gracie told me another story about her mother that I think is amusing and rather revealing. While Gracie was in school and the other girls were on the road, Mrs. Allen was having her living room repainted. And naturally she hired an Irish painter. As he worked he sang *comailes*, what she called slow Irish ballads. The problem was he painted in time to his singing. Whenever he'd hold a long note he never moved the brush. It went something like this:

'Twas on the thirty-first of August in the middle of
   July-y-y-y-y-y-y

And during July-y-y-y-y-y-y-y that brush didn't move for twenty seconds. Then he'd continue singing.

The afternoon was wet and the mornin' it was
   dry-y-y-y-y-y
I met a fair young lady sittin' under an old oak
   tre-e-e-e-e-e
The divil a word I said to her-r-r-r-r-r-r
And the same she said to me-e-e-e-e-e-e!

After the third *comaile* Mrs. Allen walked into the room, looked around, and said, "Look, John McCormack, if you insist on singing while you're working, sing fast Irish jigs, and you might get the room done by Christmas."

The painter said, "But, Mrs. Allen, I don't know any fast Irish jigs."

"Very well," responded Mrs. Allen, "then you paint and I'll sing!" And sing she did. (I'm not sure, but I think Gracie's mother stole the bit from the Pee Wee Quartet.)

During this time Gracie was getting her education at The Star of the Sea Academy, a Catholic girls' school. Now Gracie's best friend was a girl she had grown up with. They did everything together and when they were about fourteen they were in the same class at the Academy. One day in art class the assignment was to draw whatever came to mind first. Gracie drew pictures of various stage costumes, but her girlfriend drew nothing but religious pictures. Right then and there one could see that these close friends were going in different directions. And they did. Gracie went into show business, and her friend stayed in the Church, became Sister Agnes and eventually a Mother Superior. Years later after Gracie and I were married we were making a movie at Paramount and Gracie invited Sister Agnes to come on the set and watch us. In between scenes I was sitting with the two of them, and I said, "Isn't it funny, Sister, you and Gracie were brought up together, but as close as you were you went in entirely opposite directions. You joined the Church, and Gracie went into show business. Just imagine, if that had been reversed, right now you'd be sleeping with me."

Gracie just fell apart with laughter, and so did Sister Agnes. That was one of my biggest laughs, and it was a novelty because at that time I was a dead-on straight man.

Well, Gracie couldn't wait to get started in show business. The ink was hardly dry on her diploma and there she was doing a single around the San Francisco area, with Mrs. Allen traveling with her. Naturally, her act consisted of Irish songs, Irish dances, and for the finish she did a dramatic recitation

about a poor Irish waif lost on the moors of Ireland. It's too bad
Barry Fitzgerald never saw her act; he would have loved it.

While Gracie was doing her act, the Allen Sisters were still
dancing up and down the coast. But Gracie and her sisters never
worked together until they met an actor named Larry Reilly.
I'm not sure, but I think Larry Reilly was Irish. He was
considered a headliner on the Pacific Coast vaudeville circuit, so
when he asked Gracie and her sisters to join him they were
delighted. It was a big break for them. The act was billed as
"Larry Reilly & Co.," and below in small print was "Featuring
the Allen Sisters." The act was so successful that they got an
offer to play ten weeks in the East. Well, Bessie, Hazel, and
Pearl wanted no part of this. They all had steady boyfriends in
San Francisco, so they decided to stay right there and open a
dancing school. But this was not for Gracie; she loved performing. So the girls opened their dancing school, and Gracie went
back east with Larry Reilly. He replaced the Allen Sisters with
an Irish bagpipe player and now called the act just "Larry Reilly
& Co." I don't know how the girls felt about being replaced by a
guy who blew into a bagpipe, but I guess they were in love, and
when you're in love who notices things like that?

"Larry Reilly & Co." did very well back east until they were
booked to play a split week at the Main Street Theater in
Mechanicsville. When Gracie arrived at the theater she noticed
that the billing was changed. Instead of "Larry Reilly & Co." it
just read "Larry Reilly." She didn't say a word, but on the train
back to New York she told Larry she was quitting the act for
good, the reason being the billboard in front of the theater just
read "Larry Reilly" and didn't even mention "& Co." She
wound up her little speech by firmly stating, "Mr. Reilly, I'll
never work with you again because I was humiliated, I didn't
get billing!"

Larry tried to make amends, but this kid didn't know
Gracie. When she said "No," she did *not* mean "maybe." It

wasn't too good for Larry, but it worked out perfectly for me. Two weeks later I met Gracie, and we never had a billing problem for thirty-eight years.

As the years went by, every time Gracie and I played San Francisco there was always a big family reunion at the Allen house. By now there was not only the Allen family but a room full of in-laws. These occasions were always very festive with lots of fun, a lot of singing, a lot of dancing. . . . In fact, the next-door neighbor was right, they were a noisy bunch. I remember at one of these parties in came a Mr. Callahan. He must have been about ninety years old; they even had to help him sit down. He was one of the original judges of those Irish dance contests. Well, the evening was full of gaiety and laughter, but the height of the evening was when all the Allen girls got up and did some of their old routines. Right in the middle of all this excitement, Mr. Callahan said, "Will somebody help me up!" They did, and do you know he danced two fast choruses of an Irish hornpipe without missing a beat. Then he took out his pillbox, put a nitroglycerin tablet under his tongue, and said, "Will somebody sit me down?"

All of Gracie's sisters were happily married, but Bessie's husband stands out in my memory as the most unforgettable eccentric character I ever met. He was a large, heavy-set German named Ed Myers. He was a scientist, he was an archeologist, he was an inventor; in fact, there was no subject on which he was not an authority. The man was an absolute genius, but he never worked at it. Money meant nothing to him. When he and Bessie lived in Glendale—of course, I'm now going back at least fifty years—Ed invented a new process for separating gold from ore. I can't go into detail about how it worked because after all I'm a singer, but this machine was revolutionary. Now he sold one of these contraptions for $420. However, the only time he'd sell one was when he needed $420. One day a mine owner came to him and said, "Mr. Myers, I'd like to buy six of your machines." But Ed answered, "I don't need that kind of money. The next time I'm short I'll call you and sell you one."

I always looked forward to having dinner with Bessie and Ed because I'd always leave with something to think about. One night he was philosophizing and said, "Do you realize that the human body is the greatest machine ever created? Imagine, your stomach can digest the stomach of any other animal, but no matter how hungry you get, it won't eat itself." I was glad to hear that because it had been on my mind for a long time.

Some of Ed's statements were even simpler. One Sunday afternoon I was sitting in his yard and he was working on some blueprint. He looked up and said, "George, you know I have a formula for settling all the debts in the world."

With a statement like that, I could only say, "Good, let's hear it, it might come in handy at the Friars Club."

"This will work with any amount of money," Ed continued, "but to make it simple let's start with ten dollars. Now there are ten people, and they all owe each other ten dollars. The problem is to get the first ten dollars, so you bring them together and they each put up one dollar apiece. Then they give the ten dollars to the first man, he pays the ten dollars to the second man, he pays it to the third man, and so on until the ten dollars gets back to the first man. He returns a dollar to everyone, and they're all out of debt."

I nearly swallowed my cigar. Later that evening when we were having some coffee after dinner, suddenly Ed looked up and said, "Well, it's nine o'clock."

"What made you say that?" I asked.

"The window rattled," he answered. "There's a train that passes ten miles from here exactly at that time, and the vibration causes the window to rattle."

I looked at my watch and said, "Ed, the window's five minutes slow tonight."

I didn't really say that to Ed. I didn't think of it then. How do you like that, it took me fifty years to come up with that line.

There wasn't a weekend that went by that a group of prominent men weren't sitting around in Ed's backyard trying to pick his brains. But Ed was amazing. He gave away ideas that could have made him millions. One of those afternoons the conversation of the group got around to airplanes. And one airline executive was telling about this difficulty the airlines were having. It seemed that the ice and snow would collect on the wings of the planes, and this extra weight was giving them problems. Ed stopped drinking his beer long enough to say, "Invent a defroster"—and they did.

When Ed was about nineteen and going to college back in Kansas City word got around that he was a young genius. That year they were having the State Fair in Kansas City, and a local lumber company contacted Ed and asked him if he could invent something that they could feature in their exhibit. Ed said, "Sure," and two weeks later he came up with a machine where you put in lumber and out came wooden boxes. But it was so successful they couldn't use it. There were so many boxes you couldn't get into Kansas City.

When Alaska was being developed, the government had a problem with one of their mining projects. It was necessary to pump water over a steep mountain, but the machinery they had was inadequate. The government engineers couldn't seem to find a solution, and somehow the name of Ed Myers came up and the government sent for him. So Ed packed his long underwear, hopped on a boat, and sailed for Anchorage. When he got there the engineers came aboard to meet him. Ed's first question was, "What's your problem, boys?"

They answered with, "We have to get water over a high mountain, but the water is so heavy and the incline so steep that our machinery can't handle it."

Ed leaned back in his chair and casually said, "Boys, don't pump all that water at once. Break it up with air. Pump once water, and twice air." He had solved that problem without even unpacking his long underwear.

In spite of Ed's eccentricities his marriage with Bessie was a good one. They must have had something in common because they stayed married all their lives. Bessie met a lot of interesting people whom she enjoyed, even though she didn't know what they were talking about. She used to sit there weekend after weekend hoping that someday the conversation would get around to Irish dancing. But it never did. Of course, Bessie had one big advantage that other women didn't have. . . . She always knew when it was nine o'clock.

Well, that about takes care of the Allen family. I enjoyed writing about them, and it brought back a lot of pleasant memories. Even though I know you can't live in the past, it's nice to have one.

I NEVER LIKE TO APPLAUD ANYTHING THAT CAN'T APPLAUD BACK

THE TROUBLE WITH vacations is you've got to go someplace. And I've been every place I wanted to go. Being an old vaudevillian, I've spent practically all my life traveling. When I arrived somewhere I'd perform, and when I performed I got paid. I'm not sure, but I don't think I'd enjoy spending two weeks seeing all the lovely sights of Ronkonkoma, Long Island. I never was much for vacations because I figured why should I go someplace where I have to pay.

However, on our fourth wedding anniversary the only thing Gracie wanted was a trip to Paris. Being a perfect husband, I said yes and tried to book a week there. But they turned me down. At that time I was thirty-four years old and Maurice Chevalier was forty-two, and the biggest thing in Paris. They didn't want anybody to hurt his career, and they thought I would because Maurice Chevalier and I wore the same size straw hat.

But I have to admit that after thinking it over I got very excited about Gracie and me spending a week in Paris. And we couldn't wait to get to Billy LaHiff's Tavern on forty-eighth Street to tell all our vaudeville friends. That's where we actors gathered after the shows were over. I said to Gracie, "Wait till we tell them we're vacationing in Paris; it'll knock them off their seats."

That night sitting at our usual table, I waited for just the right moment, and then in my best throwaway delivery I quietly said, "Gracie and I are going to Paris." But nobody heard me. So I threw away my throwaway delivery and in a loud voice said, "Gracie and I are vacationing in Paris."

I got about the same reaction as if I'd said, "Gracie and I are going to play three days in Altoona." Jesse Block of Block & Sully said, "You'll love it. Eva and I have been to Paris three times," and then turned to the waiter and said, "I want my roast beef rare." And Jack Benny came up with, "You've got to stay at the George V Hotel. Ask for Monsieur Philippe and mention my name, you'll get a rate," and then to the same waiter, "Make mine rare, too."

I looked at Gracie and Gracie looked at me. But I don't give up easy. I tapped the water glass for attention, and everybody turned to me. "You didn't let me finish," I said. "After Paris we're going to Vienna."

The only one who was impressed was Gracie. Jack Pearl, who was sitting with his wife Winnie, said, "Winnie has relatives in Vienna; we've been there six or seven times." And then Mary Kelly piped up with, "The last time I was in Vienna I couldn't walk past this little sweet shop in Ludwigstrasse. Eating those Viennese chocolate I must have put on ten pounds." And then Jack Benny added this, "George, when you and Gracie are in Vienna you must take in the opera house. It's absolutely breathtaking. And the acoustics are fantastic. The symphony was performing, and there I was sitting in the third balcony and heard every little note."

I just sat there thinking to myself, that takes care of Paris and Vienna. So I leaned over, and confidently said, "Has anybody at the table been to Budapest?"

"Yeah," Tom Fitzpatrick said, "I've been there." And the

waiter said, "So have I. It's beautiful." Tom followed that bit of information with, "Why? Are you thinking of going?"

"Not us," I blurted out, "we're just passing through Budapest on our way to Russia."

That finally did it. There was a moment of complete silence; then everybody at the table started talking at the same time. They were all excited about our trip to Russia—except me. I knew I wasn't going to Russia—and I wasn't going to Budapest—or Vienna. I was going to Paris, and the only reason I was going there was I liked to be with Gracie. But everybody at the table started congratulating us, and Gracie was so thrilled with the news that she threw her arms around me and gave me a big kiss. That's when I knew I had gone too far, and I better do something about it in a hurry. I tapped the water glass again and said, "I have another announcement to make."

With that, Winnie Pearl tapped her water glass and said, "So have I. My wonderful husband just told me that I can go to Russia with you and Gracie."

Gracie clapped her hands and said, "Oh, that's marvelous, Winnie," and the two girls hugged each other. "Now I'll have somebody to talk to, because George doesn't speak Russian."

I just sat there numb while I heard Winnie Pearl say to Gracie, "I understand we can buy sable coats there cheap." That's when I canceled my dessert.

And in the middle of all this hubbub Jack Benny tapped his water glass and said, "George, didn't you have an announcement to make?"

I said, "Yes. I just wanted to say that Gracie and I wanted to invite Winnie Pearl to go to Russia with us."

Well, a week later Winnie, Gracie, and I were on the *Île de France* on our way to Paris. Naturally, when we arrived we went right to the George V Hotel and asked for Monsieur Philippe. I mentioned Jack Benny's name, and he said, "I never heard of him." Anyway, we checked in and that night we decided to go to a Russian restaurant. You see, there's an old show-business tradition: if you do a new show, you break it in in New Haven before you bring it into New York. So we thought we'd better do the same thing with our stomachs. We'd break in the Russian food in Paris, and if we liked it, we'd take our stomachs to Russia.

It was a beautiful Russian restaurant, but when we sat down I noticed the dinners cost fifteen dollars apiece. And believe me, in 1930 that was a fortune. So I said, "Girls, our dinner is going to be forty-five dollars without any tips. This place is too expensive for us." The girls agreed and started to order.

That's when the waiter asked, "Would you like to begin your dinner with a little caviar?"

I said, "Certainly we want a little caviar," and after he left I turned to the girls, "What a question . . . do we want to begin our dinner with a little caviar? . . . For fifteen dollars I not only want caviar, I want a suit with two pairs of pants to go with it."

I must admit the food was excellent, so we decided to take our stomachs with us to Russia—until the bill came. They had charged us four dollars apiece extra for the caviar. That meant that dinner had amounted to nineteen dollars each. And I'm not going to tell you how much it came to with the tips or I'll start to cry again.

From there, like all good tourists, we went to the Folies Bergères to see the world-famous nudes. In the middle of the show, with forty beautiful nude girls on the stage, Gracie leaned over to me and whispered, "George, it's a little shocking, isn't it?"

I whispered back, "Shocking! It's outrageous! I'll never eat there again!"

Well, we stayed in Paris for five days and we really had a wonderful time. Of course, the girls did some shopping, and then we went to all the places the tourist books tell you to go. We saw the Left Bank, the Right Bank, we went to the top of the Eiffel Tower, took a trip down the Seine, we visited the Notre Dame cathedral (naturally I looked around for Lon

Chaney), and we took a guided tour of the Louvre. When we got to the *Mona Lisa* the guide very reverently announced, "You are now in the presence of one of the world's greatest art treasures . . . the *Mona Lisa* with her famous smile."

I piped up with, "She wouldn't be smiling if she ate in that Russian restaurant." Needless to say, Gracie and Winnie pretended they didn't know me for the rest of the tour.

From Paris we took the Orient Express to Vienna. I must say I was terribly disappointed; nobody was murdered on the train. As we got off in Vienna I said, "Girls, shall we take a taxi, or shall we waltz to the hotel?" After I got my laugh we compromised and waltzed to the cab.

We checked in at the Imperial Hotel, and Vienna proved to be everything we had expected. It was very exciting; the rolls were soft, the chocolate was sweet, the drinking water was ice cold, the streets were paved, and the towels were fluffy. This might not sound exciting to you, but I'm hooked on fluffy towels.

We spent three days in Vienna, and again we did what every tourist does. However, the girls insisted that one night we go to the Opera House and see a Wagnerian opera. That was the last thing I wanted to do. I'd never been to an opera, and I had never even wanted to go to one. But I had to go because at that time Gracie was getting all the laughs. My kind of music was Louis Armstrong singing "Ain't Misbehavin'," or Pinky Tomlin doing "The Object of My Affection Can Change My Complexion from White to Rosy Red." Me going to an opera. I always thought Caruso was one of the Marx Brothers: Groucho, Chico, Harpo, and Caruso.

That night the girls put on their evening gowns and I got into my tuxedo and off we went. The Opera House was gorgeous, the place was packed, and the audience looked very elegant. The opera itself was something to look at; the set was spectacular, the cast was enormous, the costumes were lavish, and the singing was loud and in German. And would you believe that at one point I got to be the center of attraction? Well, I did. The prima donna was singing one of her arias and when she hit this high note I started to applaud. I thought it was the finish of her act. The audience was horrified and everybody glared at me. How was I supposed to know that she was going to sing another thirty-two bars. But from then on I couldn't make another mistake because Gracie held onto one of my hands and Winnie held onto the other. And this wasn't easy, because I wasn't sitting between them.

This opera went on for about two and a half hours, but the finish knocked me out. The same prima donna was up there singing with the tenor and she must have hit a bad note or something, because suddenly he got mad at her, pulled out a dagger, and started stabbing her. And believe me, there were plenty of places to stab; she must have weighed about three hundred pounds. Well, he kept stabbing, and she kept singing. She finally hit her last high note, collapsed and died. When she hit the floor my cigar popped out of my holder. I'm sure when she landed it would have registered 8.2 on the Richter scale. And after dying she took twelve curtain calls. Now that really confused me. I'm a vaudeville actor, and in vaudeville when you died you were canceled.

The next morning we took the train to Budapest and checked in at the Gellert Hotel. I was amazed to find out that Budapest is really two cities divided by the Danube River. Buda is on one side and Pest is on the other. This caused some confusion for me, because when we had lunch the waiter said, "Would you like some wienerschnitzel?" and I answered, "I'll take the wiener and give the girls the schnitzel." You see, I thought everything was divided in Budapest. But that didn't get a laugh because the waiter didn't understand what I said, and the girls did.

At the next table there was a very attractive woman with three darling little blonde girls. I overheard the mother say to them, "If you don't eat your goulash, you'll all grow up to be very naughty girls," and the oldest one said, "But ve vant to be naughty girls!" I'm not sure, but I think those three little dolls turned out to be the Gabor sisters.

One of the biggest attractions in Budapest was right in our hotel. On the first floor was this enormous swimming pool with some sort of a machine that actually made real waves. On one side of the pool there was a large cocktail lounge where you could sit and have a drink while watching the swimmers. It was quite a gathering spot for all the young people. So Winnie, Gracie, and I went down to have a drink and take a look. Well, I don't mind telling you it was quite a sight. The girls around the pool wore very skimpy little bathing suits, but what really shocked me was the men. They all wore these tight little trunks with nothing on underneath. I shouldn't say nothing, because that's what shocked me. There they were—wieners without the schnitzel. Naturally, I was embarrassed for the girls, so I suggested that we leave. Winnie looked at Gracie, Gracie looked at Winnie, then they both turned to me and Winnie said, "Leave! We haven't looked at the waves yet!" So while the girls were looking at the waves and giggling I turned my back to the pool and finished my drink.

Look, don't get the idea that everybody in Budapest was swimming. Those who weren't were playing violins. I've never seen so many violins. Every time we left the hotel some kid would follow us and play the violin. The only way to get rid of him was to tip him. Well, this must have happened about twenty or thirty times, and I'm not crazy about the violin because I always had to listen to this friend of mine from Waukegan, I forget his name. But I did find a way to stop these kids from following me. I bought an old empty violin case and every time I left the hotel I carried it under my arm. It not only stopped the kids, but I got an offer from the A. & P. Gypsies.

We also made a point to see the famous Budapest Circus. What was so different about this circus was that it had a story line to it, and all the performers had speaking parts. It was amazing. The acrobats, the jugglers, the wire walkers, trapeze artists, animal trainers, clowns—while they were doing their tricks they spoke lines that were all part of the plot. And all this was done with musical numbers.

Well, I was so impressed with the whole idea that after we got back to New York I happened to mention it to Billy Rose, who at that time was one of our top Broadway producers. He must have been impressed with what I told him because he left immediately for Budapest, saw the show, and took the same idea and produced a big musical circus called *Jumbo* at the Hippodrome.

Three months later I said to Billy, "*Jumbo* is making a fortune for you, isn't it?"

"It certainly is," he said.

"Aren't you glad I told you to go to Budapest?"

"That's right," he smiled, "it was your idea. And George, to show my appreciation the seats to see *Jumbo* are seven dollars and fifty cents, but I'm going to give you and Gracie the house seats." And then he added, "But it's only going to cost you five dollars apiece." He made about $2 million on the show and I saved five dollars. But it was nice, we both came out ahead.

How I got into this Billy Rose story I'll never know, but I better get back to Budapest, because if we're going to Russia, we have to pick up our trunks. And that's exactly what we did.

As we drew near the Russian border I didn't know what to expect. Remember, I didn't expect to go there in the first place. However, at the border our two theatrical trunks proved to be a sensation with the Russian customs officers. They had never seen anything like them. The trunks were a bright yellow with heavy brass trimmings, and when you stood them up they were about five feet high. And on the top of the trunk it read "George Burns and Gracie Allen" in big, bold black letters. One of the inspectors pointed to the lettering and asked, "What's that?"

I indicated Gracie and me, and told him it was us.

He turned around to the other inspectors and said, "They

make trunks." Then he added to me, "You do beautiful job."

"Thank you," I said, "you should see our suitcases."

Wait, as long as I took time out in Budapest to tell you about Billy Rose, I must hold up the Russian customs inspection long enough to tell you about these trunks. They were the famous H & M theatrical trunks. They were enormous and beautiful, and they were a status symbol. If you were in vaudeville and owned one, that meant you were playing the bigtime. (I hope you noticed that Gracie and I had two.) Now one side of Gracie's trunk alone could hold at least twenty-five dresses and two or three coats. And these all hung on hangers so they never got creased. You could pull out these hangers and easily select anything you wanted. At the bottom of that same side was a drawer that held a dozen pairs of shoes. On the other side was a complete chest of drawers, an ironing board with a place for the iron, a small safe, a built-in radio, a special drawer that converted into a writing desk, and a deep drawer at the bottom that held ladies' hats. That was the H & M trunk. It was so big that if you weren't booked in a theater, you could play in your trunk for two weeks.

Well, when I opened these trunks for inspection at the Russian border they were a smash. Within minutes there were forty or fifty people gathered around gaping in wonder. Of course, I don't know if they were gaping or not because I don't speak Russian, but I know they were impressed. I remember saying to Gracie and Winnie, "I hope we enjoy Russia as much as they're enjoying our trunks."

After the trunks and we passed inspection, we got on a train and left for Moscow. This was almost fifty years ago so I don't remember much about the train ride, but I suppose we did what everybody does on trains; we ate something and looked out the window. However, we did reach Moscow, and when we got out at the station I was disappointed again. I looked around and didn't see Borrah Minnevitch & His Harmonica Rascals.

We checked into the Grand Hotel and met Natasha, our

Intourist guide, who drove us around and showed us the city. I have to admit the three of us were amazed. We had just come from Paris, Vienna, Budapest, where everything was lively, gay, exciting, and colorful. Here in Moscow everything appeared so drab and gray and somber. And the people all looked so serious. They looked a lot like the audience I played to in Schenectady.

For the next couple of days we saw all the sights one is supposed to see in Moscow, and they proved to be very interesting. But what we were really looking forward to was the Bolshoi Ballet. As it happened they were on tour and we were terribly disappointed. However, Natasha got us tickets to a concert of Russian folk dancing and it was a very exciting evening. They were absolutely marvelous. I'll let you in on a little secret: The Russians dance better sitting down than we do standing up.

Oh, I forgot to mention one of the first things Natasha told us was that giving or receiving tips in Russia was not allowed. (What's-his-name from Waukegan would have loved it here.) Well, that night we ate dinner in the dining room of the hotel. The food was fair, the soup was lukewarm, and the service was slow. There was a little orchestra playing, and they must have found out we were Americans because in our honor they played one of our folk songs, "Barney Google and His Goo-Goo-Googly Eyes," which was very difficult to dance to. After dinner we paid the check, and out of force of habit I left a five-dollar tip on the table. Back in our room I suddenly realized what I had done. I said to the girls, "My God, I forgot what Natasha told me and left a five-dollar tip. I might wind up in Siberia!"

I spent a restless night, but nothing happened. However, the next night when we went down to dinner the service was fast, the food was good, the soup was hot, and Gracie and I danced to "Dardanella."

When we were leaving Moscow I said to Natasha, "I've got a

confession to make. I left someone a tip, and he took it."

"Well, he wasn't supposed to," she warned me, "and he could get into a lot of trouble."

"What would happen if I gave you a tip?" I asked.

She answered, "I wouldn't accept it. I, too, would get into a lot of trouble."

"How about a half dozen pairs of silk stockings?"

There was silence for about half a minute, then she whispered, "That I wouldn't mind getting in trouble for."

And that's what the girls gave her.

Oh, by the way, her name wasn't Natasha. It was really Elsie. But if I called her Elsie, it wouldn't sound Russian and that would have been a terrible letdown for you. And that's the last thing I would do to my readers.

Anyway, we took a train to the Polish border, changed to a German train, and spent three days traveling through Poland and Germany and wound up in Paris. A very funny thing happened to us going through Warsaw, but I don't tell Polish jokes.

But we did have a very strange experience on the train. For three days Winnie, Gracie, and I were the only ones traveling first class. We had this whole car to ourselves, but no service. Nobody cleaned our ashtrays, made up our beds, gave us clean towels; they completely ignored us. We would keep ringing the service bell and nobody would answer. I think it was because Hitler was just coming into power and it probably was beneath the porter's dignity to wait on anybody who wasn't a member of the super-race.

When we arrived in Paris we picked up our grips and started to leave our compartment. Suddenly there was our porter blocking the doorway. After three days we finally got to see what he looked like. And he looked very unfriendly, and very big. He growled, "You owe me five dollars apiece."

"For what?" I said.

"For service."

"We didn't get any service," I said, and moved toward the door.

Still blocking the doorway, he said, "You owe five dollars apiece for traveling first class."

Now I was standing in front of him with this heavy grip, and right behind me was Gracie, who was small but very Irish. She pushed my grip, and the corner of it banged him in a very tender spot, forcing superman to take a bow. And while he was bowing the three of us made a hasty exit, with me leading the way. I know that in case of danger it's supposed to be ladies first, but that doesn't count when you're a coward.

We were hurrying down the platform when Winnie suddenly exclaimed, "Wait! George, stop! I left my mink coat in the compartment on the train!"

"Go get it," I said, "I'll wait for you."

Gracie gave me a firm look and said, "George, go back and get Winnie's coat."

What could I do? Suddenly she makes me John Wayne. So I put on my glasses and slowly started back toward our car. Sure enough, there was the porter. But when he saw me coming he turned and ran the other way, he thought I was coming to get him. Well, when he ran, I ran, too. The faster I ran the faster he ran, only I ran right into the compartment, got Winnie's coat, and ran right back to the girls. This might not have made the history books, but it was the first American victory over the Nazis.

This was the end of our vacation, and an hour and a half later we were in Le Havre getting ready to board the *Île de France* for home. As we approached the gangplank a man in a trench coat, with his collar pulled up and his hat pulled down, came up to me and said, "Comrade Burns? I'm from Russian secret police. In Moscow you tipped waiter five dollars. That's against law." While I was putting on my glasses in case of trouble he handed me the five dollars and said, "Here, we don't take tips in Russia."

"How about a half dozen pairs of silk stockings?" I asked.

"That I'll take," he said.

That last story isn't true, but being the end of the chapter I thought it needed a little something.

FUNNY ROUTINES CAN HURT
YOUR CAREER

In 1932 GRACIE and I signed a two-year contract with Paramount to make feature pictures. So besides having our own weekly radio show, we were now going to be movie stars. The first thing we had to do was move to Hollywood. And the first mistake we made was to ask Gracie's sister Bessie to find a house for us. Remember, Bessie was the one who was married to Ed Myers who told time by the rattle of the window.

She not only found us a house, she found us an Italian villa on four and a half acres. It was so big we didn't have any next-door neighbors. It was located on Sunset Boulevard right in the middle of Beverly Hills. In fact, I had a chance to buy all that property for eighty thousand dollars, but I turned it down. When I was young I was a very shrewd businessman. I wasn't going to let them put anything over on me, so I leased it for two years.

What a place. The bird bath was so big you could drown in it. I guess it was for eagles. The regular pool was enormous. It was made of decorative Italian tile and marble, and it even had a bridge over it that was a replica of the Rialto Bridge in Venice. That pool came in handy because I wear water wings when I take a shower.

The house was huge with dozens of enormous rooms. Even the furniture was big and heavy. Every time Gracie wanted to sit in a chair I had to lift her up. We spent most of our time in the kitchen because that was the only room that didn't have an echo in it.

Of course, with a big house like that we needed plenty of help. I couldn't clean it; my back was always out from lifting Gracie. So we hired this husky couple. The butler was about six feet two with a big head of blond hair, and he never smiled. I'm not sure but I think he was the brother of the porter on that German train. His wife was no shrinking violet either. She looked like she could make a few yards on the football field. We also had a governess for our children, Ronnie and Sandy, an upstairs maid, and a gardener. But we did save a few dollars because the butler also doubled as the chauffeur.

Naturally we had to buy a big car. It was an extra-long, custom-built limousine with a glass partition between the driver and the passengers. We didn't buy this car to keep up with the Joneses; we got it to keep up with the house. But we had a problem with the car. The back seat was so deep that when Gracie sat down her feet didn't touch the floor. One day she said to me, "George, return the car and have them take six inches off the back seat."

I said, "Gracie, you can't do that. This car is designed by experts who get millions of dollars just to design back seats. This back seat is custom built."

"Well, mine isn't," she said.

There was a long pause, then I got very mad . . . because I hadn't thought of that line. But Gracie had won her point. We sent the car back and had six inches cut off the back seat. From then on Gracie was very comfortable, but when anyone else sat down on that seat they fell on the floor.

We were now living the life style of Hollywood movie stars. One day we were visited by Ben Blue, one of our top funnymen, and while I was showing him around the estate he suddenly stopped short. He pointed across the way, and in a voice that sounded very impressed he said, "George, you've got stables over there."

And very nonchalantly, like a movie star, I said, "Ben, would I live in a house without stables?"

Ben looked at me and said, "I didn't know you rode horses."

"Who rides horses, I just love stables," I added.

Now I'm glad Ben Blue noticed the stables, because I've got a very amusing story about him. Shortly before we came to Hollywood, Gracie and I took out a six-act vaudeville unit on a tour of eight weeks, and Ben Blue was one of the acts. We got a ten-thousand-dollar guarantee from each theater, out of which we paid each of the acts, and if the box office receipts were over a specified amount, the theater and Burns and Allen would split the difference. So if business was good we could make quite a bit of money.

We were doing four shows a day to capacity business, but we would do even better if we could just squeeze in an extra show. However, the only way that could be done was to cut Ben Blue's act from thirty-five minutes to thirteen minutes. And I'll tell you a little secret, it's very difficult to cut an actor, especially Ben Blue. Because as much as the audience loved Ben Blue's act, Ben Blue loved it even more. Now at that time I was paying Ben Blue $750 a week, so I called him into my dressing room and said, "Sit down . . . have a drink . . . here smoke a cigar. . . ."

"You can't cut my act," he cut in.

"Ben," I said, "now that you've brought it up let me tell you something. You're getting seven hundred fifty dollars a week and you're doing thirty-five minutes. If you cut your act down to thirteen minutes, we'll be able to do an extra show and I'll give you a thousand dollars a week. You'll be making two hundred fifty dollars a week more."

He stood up and indignantly said, "Who the hell do you think you're talking to? Thirteen minutes! That would mean I'd have to take out the 'Ten Cents a Dance' bit that I do with my wife, and that's the only thing she does in my act. If I cut that, she'd divorce me!"

I said, "Ben, forget it, I'm sorry I brought it up."

With that he stormed out of the room. I didn't even have time to powder my nose before he stuck his head back into the room and said, "Three hundred fifty dollars?"

"You got it," I said.

So we did five shows a day, Ben did thirteen minutes, and two weeks later his wife divorced him. Isn't that a good story? Aren't you glad that Ben Blue noticed my stables? But wait, there's more. His wife took him to court and sued him for six hundred dollars a month alimony. At the trial Ben defended himself. He said to the judge, "Your Honor, I can't afford to pay my wife six hundred dollars a month alimony. If I did that, I wouldn't have enough money to put gas in my Duesenberg."

The judge stared at him and said, "You've got a Duesenberg?"

There was a pause, then Ben quickly said, "But Your Honor, don't forget, I drive it myself."

The judge pounded his gavel and said, "The lady gets six hundred dollars a month alimony, and the case is dismissed!"

The moral of this story is if you can't afford a lawyer, you shouldn't drive a Duesenberg. Let's see, I didn't expect this story to go on so long. Now I've forgotten where I was living. Oh yeah, I remember, it's the house with the big bird bath.

Anyway, there we were, Gracie and I, anxiously awaiting the arrival of the script from Paramount. This was the script that was going to change our lives from vaudevillians and radio performers to actors. It was very exciting for me; I would never have to walk out again and say, "Gracie, how's your brother?" Well, the script finally arrived, and it was titled *The Big Broadcast*. It starred all the big radio personalities: Stuart Erwin, Bing Crosby, Burns and Allen, Kate Smith, The Mills Brothers, The Boswell Sisters, Cab Calloway and his Orchestra, and a dozen others. The plot was very intriguing. It was all about Stu Erwin and Bing Crosby fighting for control of this big radio station. And on page 40 Gracie and I came in. It read, "Burns and Allen now do four minutes of their stage routine," and then we were not mentioned for sixty-five pages, and on page 105 it read, "Burns and Allen do four more minutes of their stage routine." That was our acting debut in feature pictures. We were ashamed to use that big limousine we bought. From then on whenever we went to Paramount we hired a taxi.

Well, we continued doing our weekly radio show while waiting for our next movie script, and one day Eddie Sutherland, one of Hollywood's top directors, rushed over to our house. He was very enthusiastic and said, "George, I'm directing your next picture. It's called 'International House,' with W. C. Fields, Peggy Hopkins Joyce, Stu Erwin, and Bela Lugosi . . . and there are two wonderful parts in it for you and Gracie!" He went on to explain that I would be playing the house physician in this large Oriental hotel, and Gracie would play my nurse-receptionist. Then he said, "The story's full of intrigue, and it'll be quite a challenge for you and Gracie, but I'm sure you can handle it."

This was it. I'd be playing a doctor. I could see myself wearing a beard like Paul Muni. I offered Eddie a drink and asked him to tell me a little about the story. He said, "Well, the plot is full of twists and turns, and Dr. George Burns and Nurse Gracie Allen are right in the middle of them."

"Wait a minute," I said. "Why do we have to be Dr. George Burns and Nurse Gracie Allen?"

He said, "Well, how else would you be able to do four or five minutes of your stage routine?" With that I took back his drink, showed him to the door, and as he left I tripped him.

Well, we did *International House*, and followed that with *College Humor, Six of a Kind, We're Not Dressing, Many Happy Returns, Love in Bloom, Here Comes Cookie, Big Broadcast of 1936, Big Broadcast of 1937,* and *College Holiday.* And in every one of those pictures we were always George Burns and Gracie Allen. All I got to say was, "Gracie, how's your brother?" I never had a chance to say, "Ladies and gentlemen of the jury, is this the face of a killer?"

. . . or bang on the cell bars with my tin cup and yell, "Let me outta here!"

. . . or "Follow me, boys, we'll head 'em off at the pass!"

. . . or "Frankly, Scarlett, I don't give a damn!"

I don't know about the other lines, but I know I would have been great doing that last one.

SCREWBALLS, ODDBALLS, AND HIGHBALLS

YOU PROBABLY THINK because I ended that last chapter that you're finished with my movie career. I've got a 1 for you, you're not. While we were making all those movies some very amusing things happened that I'd like to tell you about. Well, they're amusing now, but they weren't all amusing then. They might not even be amusing now, but when you're a writer you write. Some of the stuff you write is good, and some of it is bad. I'd say that about 82 percent of what I write is bad, but don't go by me; I'm as bad a judge as I am a writer. Look, if it were all good, you'd be paying twice as much for this book. So relax, read it, and if you don't enjoy it, remember that you're saving money.

Gracie and I made a couple of pictures with W. C. Fields, who was one of the all-time greats, but he was not the easiest person to get close to. For weeks while we were making *International House* I'd come on the set every morning full of smiles and greet him with, "Good morning, Mr. Fields." He'd respond with a very small nod . . . about an inch and a half.

One day Bill Fields was doing a scene with Gracie where they were seated at a table in a restaurant. Gracie hit him with a very funny line, which I don't remember, and made an exit. That was the end of the scene, but Fields didn't like it. He felt he needed a line or a piece of business to top Gracie. So shooting stopped for about an hour or so while Fields, the director, and everybody else tried to think of something. Finally I went up to him and said, "Bill, I think I've got it. On the table you've got a glass of water, a cup of coffee, and a dry martini. When Gracie leaves, you take two pieces of sugar, drop them in the glass of water, stir the coffee, and drink the martini."

Fields was delighted. He said, "George, from now on I'll always say good morning to you . . . even if it isn't."

What he didn't know was that the piece of business I gave him was a switch on an old bit I did with Gracie many years before. During a restaurant scene Gracie hit me with a funny line and left. I then took out a cigar and my lighter, struck a match and lit the lighter, and with the lighter I lit my cigar. Then I threw the lighter and the cigar away and stuck the match in my mouth. That got a laugh when I did it with Gracie, it got a laugh with Fields, and it'll get just as big a laugh when I do it twenty years from now.

After that Bill and I became friends, and he came to our house for dinner once in a while. But the first time he came— (Wait, right here I'd better let you in on something. Bill Fields used to take a little drink now and then. And those now and thens were about five minutes apart. Whenever he was invited to anybody's home he always wore his vest, because in the pockets he carried four small bottles of gin. This was in case the host didn't have any . . . or enough.) So the first time he came to our house I said, "Bill, you don't need the vest, I've got all the gin you can drink."

He opened the front door, and in the typical Fields delivery, hollered out to his driver, "Clarence, my good man, take the vest. I'm getting my libation from another source."

As you know, Bill Fields had a very distinctive delivery, and there's a story about that which I heard in England years ago. It was told to me by Stan Stinelli of Stinelli and Douglas. It seems when Bill Fields first started in vaudeville he was a juggler. He juggled clubs and balls, and for the finish of his act he'd juggle cigar boxes. But he never said a word on the stage. Now his wife worked as an assistant in his act, and she was a very beautiful young girl. They were playing a London theater, and the star on the bill was a famous music hall comedian named Mike Donohue, who had a very funny way of speaking. The words seemed to slide out of the corner of his mouth. He spoke as though he were slightly tipsy. Anyway, Donohue made a play for Bill's wife, and she went for him, too. So when Bill came back to the United States he came alone. His wife stayed with Mike Donohue. But Bill figured that as long as Donohue could steal his wife, he could steal Donohue's delivery, and he did. Personally, I think Bill got the best of the deal. However, I'm not sure if this story is true, because Stinelli used to lie a lot.

Another big star around that time was Frank Fay. He was a vaudeville headliner, and eventually was a smash in the original Broadway production of *Harvey*. Frank Fay was one of the most talented comedians in show business. That was not just my opinion, it was also his. On stage he had class, poise, and a certain arrogant elegance. Offstage he was just plain mean. He hated everybody who was doing well. Why he hated me I'll never know.

I'll never forget when Gracie and I were just getting started and we played on the bill with him at B.F. Keith's Palace in Chicago. He was the star and the master of ceremonies, and at the end of our act he came out on the stage, ignored me completely, and started talking to Gracie. I was standing right between them, and he never even looked at me.

He said, "Miss Allen, I think that you're a great new talent. You're very pretty, you have taste, you have style, your comedy timing is impeccable, and I predict that someday you'll become a big star."

And Gracie said, "Thank you, Mr. Fay."

Then Fay leaned over to Gracie very confidentially, and Gracie, being a good actress, leaned towards him. There I was, practically hidden by those two faces. There was a long pause, and then in a loud stage whisper Fay said to Gracie, "But where did you get the man?"

Needless to say, "the man" was ready to kill himself. That wouldn't have been a novelty, I've died on the stage lots of times. After that every time I would run into Frank Fay he'd never say hello or goodbye, he'd just pass, and without looking at me he'd say, "Hold on to her."

But I finally found a way to get even with Fay. He always had lunch at the Hollywood Brown Derby and so did I. Now I knew he was a very devout Catholic, so I always arranged to sit in a booth near him. Just as his food arrived I'd go over to his booth and sit down next to him and say, "Frank, I just heard some sad news, Walter Catlett died."

Fay would put down his knife and fork, cross himself, and say a little prayer. Then just as he'd pick up his knife and fork again, I'd say, "And Tom Fitzpatrick passed away." Again he'd cross himself and say a little prayer. Then I told him, "Sam Bernard is not with us anymore." I kept on mentioning people who were dead until his food got cold, and then I'd leave. After two months of this he stopped eating at the Brown Derby. It was just in time, too, I was running out of dead people.

One of the stars that everybody loved and still do is Fred Astaire. And in 1937 when Gracie and I got an offer to appear in one of his pictures, *Damsel in Distress*, we were absolutely thrilled. But there was one little catch to it. Before we were signed to do an Astaire picture Fred had to approve our dancing. Now Gracie was a great dancer, so there was no problem with her, but "the man" was sort of a right-legged dancer. I could tap with my right foot, but my left foot wanted me to get into some other business.

But I wasn't going to lose a chance to work with Fred Astaire. After all, look what it did for Ginger Rogers. Anyway,

I remembered an act in vaudeville called Evans and Evans. They did a two-dance where they each used a whisk broom, and it always stopped the show. I figured if I could get Evans and Evans to come to California and teach us the dance, we'd do it for Fred Astaire and we would be in the picture.

Well, I located one Evans, but the other one had died. (Too bad I didn't know that when Frank Fay was still eating at the Brown Derby.) I made a deal with the living Evans to come out to the West Coast and teach us the dance, which he did. When the time came for us to audition for Fred Astaire we showed up with Evans, Gracie, and myself, my piano player, and three whisk brooms. We did the dance for him and Fred flipped over it. He said, "George, I'd love to do this dance with you and Gracie in the movie."

I looked at him and said, "Fred, it's yours." So instead of Fred Astaire teaching me how to dance, I taught him. And can I tell you something, he picked it up real fast; that boy's a pretty good dancer.

Well, the story I just told you about Fred Astaire had a nice finish, but now I'm going to tell you one about Judy Garland that didn't. It seems that I was asked to speak at a testimonial dinner given for one of the big stars in Hollywood, I forget who it was. It's hard to remember, because in Hollywood whenever there's a lull they give somebody a dinner. Anyway, at these dinners, before the dinner starts, all those who are going to sit on the dais wait together in a reception room until all the guests have been seated at the tables. This night I'm in the reception room sitting with Judy Garland, and Sid Luft, who Judy was married to at the time, took me aside and said, "George, you'll be sitting next to Judy on the dais, too, and you can do me a very, very big favor. Don't let her drink too much tonight because she has to sing."

I assured Sid I'd take care of it. When I went back to Judy there on the table were two dry martinis. I quickly drank half of mine, and when she wasn't looking I switched glasses. I did that in the reception room, and I did that when we were seated on the dais. I must have done it five or six times . . . maybe ten . . . I was so busy switching glasses I didn't have time to count.

About twenty olives later George Jessel, who was master of ceremonies, introduced me, saying, "Ladies and gentlemen, and now George Burns!"

I looked around and couldn't find him. Milton Berle, who was also on the dais, came over and picked me up. "That's you, you're George Burns," he said. I just stood there and started to make my speech without even going to the microphone. Naturally, nobody heard me, which is just as well since I wasn't making any sense. Milton quickly pushed me back into my seat, and Jessel explained to the audience, "George Burns' speech was written by that famous writing team of Haig & Haig."

Later Judy got up and sang "Over the Rainbow" and was a smash. She was over the rainbow, and I was under the table. On the way out after the dinner was over, Sid Luft said to me, "George, you were disgusting tonight."

Wait a minute, I'm getting away from movie making. My continuity isn't what it used to be. Neither is my . . . my . . . my . . . my skiing. Of course, Gracie and I were very excited about making movies, but I never thought there would come a time when we would ever try to get out of one. Well, it happened. I received this script from a producer, whose name I'm not going to mention. In fact, I'm not going to mention the studio, either. But our entrance into this picture had Gracie and me in a rowboat in the middle of the ocean trying to hitch a ride. Suddenly an iceberg appears in front of us and conveniently splits in the middle as I rowed through. It's true. I'm not going to tell you the rest of the plot because it's not as believable as the opening scene.

Now at that time I was handled by the William Morris office, and I told Abe Lastfogel, who was the head of the agency, that we didn't want to make the picture. So he set up an appointment with the producer, and Abe and I went to see him to try to get out of the contract. In a very nice way Abe told the producer, "You've got a fine script, it will make a funny musical and should make a lot of money. However, the parts just don't fit Burns and Allen, and they'd like to get out of it."

This producer, who had never done a picture before, and whose only claim to fame was he had written a couple of songs, looked at me and said, "Burns, have you got anything in your contract that says you have script approval?"

I shook my head, "No."

"Well, I have," he said, "and you and Gracie are staying in the picture. If I didn't think these parts were right for Burns and Allen, I wouldn't have had them written that way." He leaned back in his chair and stared at us.

Abe got up and said, "George, I guess the meeting is over. Let's go."

When we got out in the hall I said, "Abe, the meeting isn't over. Let's go back, I think I know how to get out of that contract." So in we went, and in a very nice calm tone I said, "Look, Mr. Producer, don't you like living in California? Aren't you happy out here?"

"Of course I am," he said curtly.

"Then why do you want us both to go back to New York where we came from?"

He raised an eyebrow. "Why would we go back to New York?" he asked.

Continuing in the same calm tone of voice, I said, "Because if we make this lousy picture, they'll run us out of town. This story is for Mickey Mouse. Gracie and I rowing through the middle of an iceberg . . . and W.C. Fields getting on a motorcycle that's able to fly to a golf course . . . you should be put away for okaying a script like that. This is your first picture and it's going to be your last. You'll be lucky if they let you write those crummy songs again."

There was silence for about a minute while I waited. I couldn't find Abe Lastfogel, he was hiding somewhere. Then the producer, his face slightly purple, got up from behind his desk, crossed over and opened the door. And in a voice barely able to control his anger, said, "Burns, nobody can talk to me that way and be in one of my movies!"

"Thank you," I said, and when we got out in the hall I said to Abe, "Now that's the way to get out of a contract."

But can I give you a little bit more. The movie was made, and it made a lot of money, which shows you how wrong Abe Lastfogel can be.

However, this was Hollywood, and I certainly was not one to hold a grudge. Two years later Gracie and I made a movie for that same producer. This was a musical, and the cast was made up of practically all the big radio personalities: Bing Crosby, Bob Hope, Edgar Bergen, Jack Benny, Burns and Allen, Martha Raye, Ben Blue, and also Betty Grable, Edward Everett Horton, Jackie Coogan, plus about thirty chorus girls. So you can see it was a very expensive movie.

Now this producer was making a play for the lead dancer in the chorus, so he was always on the set. He was producing, directing, rewriting, anything just to impress this beautiful girl. Well, one night we were shooting late, and at seven o'clock they brought in a catered dinner for the cast and crew. This gave our producer a chance to be alone with the girl, and he took her to a very chi-chi restaurant nearby. About eight o'clock we were all ready to go back to work, but there was no producer or lead dancer. About a quarter to nine they showed up. Have you any idea how much it cost the studio to keep a cast and crew that size sitting around doing nothing? And they were all on triple time. I don't know what the guy accomplished with the girl, but I don't think it was worth it.

Anyway, at nine o'clock the entire company was ready to shoot this big production number. But just as the camera started to roll the producer jumped up and hollered, "Cut!" and everything came to a halt. "I don't like the way the girls' legs look in white tights," he said. "Put them all in black tights "

"But we don't have any black tights," the wardrobe woman protested.

"Then dye these black!" he ordered. "I'm tired of making all these decisions!"

"Look, if you want black tights, we won't be able to shoot this until tomorrow," the director cautioned, "and this number will cost the studio a fortune."

Ignoring this, the producer said, "Wrap it up, boys, we'll shoot this in the morning." And then, just for the benefit of the lead dancer, he announced, "When I make a movie, money is no object." And then he left.

Crosby, Hope, Jack Benny, myself, Bergen, all of us, we just looked at each other. We couldn't believe what was happening that night. Finally, I said, "Look, don't underestimate our producer. Any man who can open a picture with Gracie and me rowing through an iceberg has to know what he's doing."

The next morning we shot the number, and all the girls wore black tights. The white tights looked better.

Well, there was another three days of shooting, which we completed in two weeks. The final scene was where Bob Hope and Martha Raye got married, and we're all down at the railroad station waving goodbye to them as they leave for Niagara Falls on their honeymoon. We all thought that was it until the producer said, "Wait, I just thought of a great ending. As the train pulls out, all you stars lock arms and walk into the camera."

For the first time I thought he made a little sense, until I noticed I was locking arms with Martha Raye, and next to her was Bob Hope. I went over to the producer and quietly pointed out, "Look, Bob and Martha can't be in the finish. They're not here, they're on the train to Niagara Falls."

"Don't be silly," he scoffed, "nobody's going to notice those little technicalities."

So we all locked arms and walked into the camera. That was the finish of the picture, the finish of the producer . . . and the finish of this chapter.

PLEASE PASS THE HOSTESS

OF COURSE, YOU'VE all heard about those famous Hollywood parties, so let me do a few minutes on them. Now that Gracie and I were working in the movies, we were invited to a lot of parties. One of the first big ones we went to was given by the head of Paramount Studio. It was an engagement party for Gary and Rocky Cooper. The invitation was for eight o'clock, so of course, we showed up at eight o'clock. I guess that's our vaudeville training. In vaudeville if you didn't show up on time, somebody sang your songs.

Well, we arrived at eight o'clock sharp, and as we drove through the gate we were greeted by five little barking dogs. One of the parking attendants took our car, a butler let us in, and there we were alone in this big living room that could hold at least 150 people. We were both served a martini, and I sat there looking at Gracie and she sat there looking at me. After about fifteen minutes of this I said to one of the butlers, "Where's the host?"

He answered, "Oh, he asked me to wake him at eight-thirty."

Ten minutes later Gracie, who never drank, started to feel

the effect of that martini. She left me, went into the powder room, put all the towels on the floor, and lay down and went to sleep. Now I was really alone, so I went outside and barked harmony with the dogs.

Eventually the guests arrived, and we had a fine time. Driving home that night, Gracie asked me, "Did you make any new friends?"

"Yeah," I said, "I met a cocker spaniel with a great sense of humor."

But that experience did teach us an important lesson about Hollywood parties: Don't arrive on time. The bigger the star, the later he gets there. In fact, we went to one party where Clark Gable was so late he never even showed up.

Our next party was at the James Masons. I told Gracie that the invitation was for eight o'clock, but we'd arrive at eight-thirty. We weren't big enough to show up at nine. When we arrived there, again, not a car. So I started to drive around the block. I said to Gracie, "We'll keep driving until about ten cars show up, then we'll go in." Well, we drove around that block until we both got dizzy, and at nine-thirty there were still no cars. Finally I said, "Let's skip the party and go home, I'm running out of gas." When we got home I phoned Pamela Mason. "Pamela," I said, "I'm sorry, but Gracie and I can't come to your party tonight, I've got a very bad headache."

She said, "Well, I hope it gets better by tomorrow, George, because that's when the party is."

Gracie and I stayed in Hollywood and made about seven or eight pictures in a row for Paramount. We finally were doing so well that we began showing up at parties at five minutes to eleven. But there was one party we went to that was a classic. I guess you could call it one of those "wild Hollywood" parties. Anyway, it was given by John P. Medbury. He was not only one of Hollywood's finest writers, but he had a mad sense of humor. The party was in honor of a comedy team named Olsen and Johnson who were experts in madness. They had a crazy vaudeville act, and also starred on Broadway in *Hellzapoppin'*.

There were a lot of things that happened at that party that I still haven't figured out. Medbury lived in a big house in the Hollywood Hills, and when you arrived you parked your car and walked about a hundred yards up a roadway to the house. Well, this night when we arrived there were no attendants to take your car, but instead there were four donkeys tied to a tree. So after we parked the car, we carefully stepped around the donkeys and headed toward the house. At the entrance to the roadway we had to go through a tent. Inside there was a man sitting on a toilet reading a newspaper. Without even looking up, he said, "Keep walking, you're heading in the right direction."

Well, we kept walking . . . fast. A little further on there was a man sitting in a big tree with a rifle. As we passed by he yelled, "This is private property, don't pick any of the oranges!"

By the time we recovered from this we were passing the garage. The door was open, and the interior had been converted into a gaudy bedroom. Over the door was a red light, and beneath it stood a sexy little girl soliciting business. In ten yards we had gone from private property to public property.

Finally we reached the house, and there to greet us was John Medbury and a charming lady whom he introduced as his wife. As I passed her she gave me a friendly little goose. And remember, this was in the 1930s when this gesture wasn't socially acceptable. As soon as we walked inside the butler came up to me and asked if he could borrow my matches. He said he had some candles to light. So I gave them to him. Later on I found out that he had done this to everyone. There were two hundred guests without matches. At first, this didn't seem to be a problem because there were plenty of matches lying around. However, they were trick matches, the minute you'd light them they'd go out. Wherever you looked there was somebody trying to light a cigarette. This was one of the things I couldn't figure out. The girl under the red light, that I understood.

Here are a few more highlights of the evening. The party took place in July, but there was a fully decorated Christmas tree with presents underneath it in the living room. And there was a big fat Santa Claus sitting there with a cane. Every time somebody would try to pick up a present Santa Claus would say, "Ho, ho, ho," and whack him with the cane.

Every half hour a kid dressed like a bellboy would walk through the room calling out, "It is now eight o'clock!" It was always eight o'clock, it never got any later.

The ladies' powder room was bugged, and anything that was said in there was heard on speakers placed all over the house. We heard one lady say, "What a stupid party, when the hell do we eat?" Then Medbury's voice came over the speakers, answering her, "We'll eat when I'm damned good and ready!" I never did find out whether Medbury was in the ladies' room or with us.

About ten o'clock at night Medbury introduced a Russian man who was dressed in full diplomatic attire complete with a red sash, and wearing more medals than Georgie Jessel. He got up and spoke for fifteen minutes in Russian and left.

Finally at eleven o'clock they served a beautiful and elegant sit-down dinner. About an hour and a half later in came a twelve-piece orchestra. They put up their music stands, took out their music and tuned up their instruments. After a few minutes of this the leader raised his baton, and the orchestra played a loud fanfare. With that Medbury stood up and proclaimed, "Ladies and gentlemen, the party's over." The musicians packed up their gear and left. And so did the guests. When Gracie and I went through the tent, the guy was still there, only now he was reading the morning paper.

Let's get out of Hollywood for a minute and jump to London. Actually, this story began in America, we jumped too soon. So I'm on a flight from Los Angeles to New York, and on the same plane was Anne Douglas, Kirk Douglas' wife, and she introduced me to a friend of hers, a very charming lady named

Olive Behrendt. We all laughed and talked on the flight and had a wonderful time. Now Mrs. Behrendt knew that I was recovering from open-heart surgery, and she asked me where I was stopping in New York. I told her the name of the hotel and that was that. The following day at my hotel I received a beautiful little gold pillbox. Of course, I wanted to thank her, but I didn't know how or where to get in touch with her.

Now we jump to London, and it's a year and a half later. I'm staying at the Inn-on-the-Park, and I'm walking through the lobby when who should I bump into but this charming friend of Anne Douglas. Naturally, I was delighted to see her, and this was my chance to repay her for the lovely gold pillbox she had given me in New York. We talked for a few minutes, and I told her I wanted to give a party for her and a dozen of her friends at Les Ambassadeurs. She said she wouldn't think of having me do a thing like that, but I insisted. I told her she would make me very unhappy if she didn't accept, so she finally gave in.

That Saturday night there were fourteen of us for dinner. I went for the whole bit, French wine, the works. Now Les Ambassadeurs is a private club, and the dinner did not come cheap. But the evening was a huge success, and as we were sipping our brandy I turned to our guest of honor and said to her, "You know, I never had a chance to thank you for that beautiful gold pillbox."

She looked blankly at me and said, "What pillbox?"

Never one to show my feelings, I took a puff on my cigar and blew the smoke out of my ears. "Don't you remember when we were on that plane together with your good friend Anne Douglas?" I asked.

"I don't know any Anne Douglas," she said.

"You don't. Then where did we meet?"

"Why I'm Mrs. Joe Fields," she smiled. "We've been neighbors for years, we live on the same block in Beverly Hills."

I sat there speechless. I couldn't do the cigar bit again because she had just seen it. Well, we all had a good laugh, and

Above, relaxing at home. NBC PHOTO BY EARL ZIEGLER

Right, in the early radio days. TED ALLEN

Left, four of a kind—clockwise, fr
left, Eddie Cantor, George Jes
Jack Benny and George Burns.
PHOTO BY ELMER HOLLOWAY

Below, celebrating an annivers
with Harry von Zell. Gracie's the
in the middle.

Above, with Jack Benny.
JOSEPH JASGUR

Right, George and Gracie . . . oops! . . . Jack Benny incognito.

Above, CBS's William Paley pays tribute to two of his stars, Burns and Allen. From left, Gracie, Paley, George Jessel, George and Jack Benny.

Below, at a Friar's Club Frolic. From left, Dore Schary, Danny Kaye, Gracie, George and Eddie Cantor.

Above, in the early '40s. Standing, left to right, Benny Fields, Blossom Seely, Harry Ruby, George, Jesse Block, Mrs. Leo Spitz; seated, left to right, Eve Sully, Ida and Eddie Cantor, Gracie, and Al Jolson.

Below, in the early '50s. Eve Sully, George, Gracie and Jesse Block.

George and his team. *Ab*
teaching his writers what ma
people laugh. Left to rig
Seamon Jacobs, Hal Goldm
Fred Fox and Lisa Miller. Nᴀ
CUTLER

Left, secretary Jack Langdon
the typewriter) and manager
ing Fein. NATE CUTLER

Left, at Carnegie Hall during a "One Man Show."

Below, celebrating his 100th Birthday Party, a TV special. CBS PHOTO DIVISION

With Walter Matthau, *above*, and Johnny Carson and friend, *below*, on a TV special. CBS PHOTO DIVISION

Above, with Bob Hope on a TV special. CBS PHOTO DIVISION

Below, watching Don Rickles get a laugh on *The Tonight Show*, George joins Angie Dickinson, Carroll O'Connor, and host Frank Sinatra.

Above, Goldie Hawn. CBS PHOTO DIVISION

Left and *below*, Carol Channing. SEAWELL

Above left, Ann-Margret. *Above right*, Gladys Knight.

Below, Madeline Kahn. CBS PHOTO DIVISION

"Man of the Hour." George with Gene Kelly at the Dean Martin "roast."
NBC PHOTO

Above, George gets "made up" by Walter Matthau in *The Sunshine Boys,* 1975. M-G-M, INC.

Below, John Denver and . . . *Oh! God,* 1978. WARNER BROTHERS, INC.

Top, George steps out with the Bee Gees and Peter Frampton (second from left) in *Sgt. Pepper's Lonely Hearts Club Band*, 1977. DAVE FRIEDMAN PHOTO

Left, in a scene from *Sgt. Pepper's Lonely Hearts Club Band*, 1977. DAVE FRIEDMAN PHOTO

Above, with Brooke Shields on the set of *Just You and Me, Kid*, 1979. COLUMBIA PICTURES

Above, with Burl Ives in a scene from *Just You and Me, Kid,* 1979. COLUMBIA
PICTURES

Below, with the "No Shirt Gang" from *Just You and Me, Kid,* left to right,
Keye Luke, Leon Ames, Carl Ballantine and Ray Bolger, 1979. COLUMBIA
PICTURES

The newest George Burns hit movie from Warner Brothers, *Going in Style*. *Above*, counting the ill-gotten gains with Art Carney and Lee Strasberg. *Left*, contemplating a little mischief. HOLLY BOWER

when I got back to my room at the hotel I did what anybody would do who made a mistake like that; I killed myself. So, Olive Behrendt, if you happen to be reading this, thanks for that lovely gold pillbox, and I'm sorry that you missed the beautiful party I gave you in London.

Come to think of it, I gave another party that cost me a fortune and didn't pay off. My mistake that time was that I tried to make Jack Benny laugh. I should have known better. With Jack you couldn't try, it had to be spontaneous.

Anyway, here's what happened. One night I called up Jack and Mary and invited them to our house for a party, and I told them it was going to be formal. I hired six musicians and had a small dance floor put down in my living room. I also brought in two extra butlers for the occasion, and outside I had a parking attendant to park the cars. Well, at seven-thirty Jack and Mary arrived. She had on a beautiful evening gown and Jack was in his tuxedo. Gracie and I greeted them in our evening clothes, and while we were having drinks and hors d'oeuvres the orchestra played softly in the background. Around eight o'clock one of the butlers announced that dinner was served. Jack gave Mary a look and then turned to me and asked, "Where are the guests?"

"This is it," I said. "It's a party just for the four of us." Then I waited for Jack to fall on the floor and scream laughing. Nothing. He just kept staring at me.

Let me ask you readers something. If you were put in a situation like that, wouldn't you laugh? Of course, you would. But not Jack. Not only didn't he laugh, but he was very mad at me. He said, "You mean to say that you rented a dance floor, hired an orchestra, two butlers, and an attendant to park one car just to make me laugh?!" He took a breath and added, "You must be out of your mind."

"But Jack," I said, "you can dance with Mary, and I'll dance with Gracie. Then you dance with Gracie, and I'll dance with Mary. And there's nobody else here so they won't bump into us." Not a snicker from Jack, he just kept staring at me. So I thought this might do it. I said, "And Jack, if you're in the mood, you and I can dance together."

That did it. He got up and said, "Mary, let's go home," and they left. I'd never seen him so furious. When he got outside I heard him yell at the parking attendant, "Don't touch my car, I'll get it myself!"

Gracie was always the perfect wife. After they left she laughed and said, "George, don't feel bad, I still think it was a funny idea." Well, we had dinner, then I danced with Gracie, Gracie danced with me, she went to bed, I sang six songs with the orchestra, they went home, and I went to bed.

But that's not the end of the story. It seems that Jack went around telling everybody what an idiot I was to give him that kind of party, but they all laughed and thought it was very funny. I guess they must have convinced him, because weeks later one night after dinner the doorbell rang. I opened the door, and there was Jack standing there laughing his head off. He finally made it into the living room and fell on the floor still laughing. "Jack, what's so funny?" I asked him.

He gasped, "That party you gave me four weeks ago, that's the funniest thing that ever happened to me!"

I couldn't believe it. I leaned down and said, "Then why didn't you laugh four weeks ago?"

"Because four weeks ago it wasn't funny, now it's hysterical," and he continued laughing. I just stepped over him and went to bed.

Now there are some real wild Hollywood parties I could tell you about, but at the beginning of this chapter I told you I'd only do a few minutes on parties. I'm sorry, but the few minutes are up.

THANKS FOR LETTING US COME INTO YOUR LIVING ROOM

LET'S SEE, I told you about Gracie and me in vaudeville, about our radio days, and about our feature movie careers. Oh my goodness, I forgot that we were in television. Well, that's understandable, we were only in it for eight years.

Now for many radio shows, going into television was a big problem. They were afraid that people wouldn't like them if they didn't look the way they sounded. But for Gracie and me it was easy. Gracie looked even better than she sounded, and with me it didn't matter. Who cares how a straight man looks or sounds. My public couldn't be disappointed.

Well, when we went on television in 1950 we did make one adjustment. And it worked very well on our show. The executives at CBS had meeting after meeting trying to come up with all sorts of formats to give us a new look. I asked them why give us a new look when nobody had seen us before. I said, "Gentlemen, supposing Gracie and I do the same thing we were doing in radio, with one slight change. Gracie and I are still married, we have our next-door neighbors Mr. and Mrs. Morton, and the same kind of situations. However, I can step out of the set and talk directly into the camera.

This way I can further the plot, or complicate it, and make any kind of comment I want." And CBS bought this idea immediately.

I must admit that in the play *Our Town* they had a narrator who used the same technique. But I switched that bit completely. He didn't smoke a cigar and I did, so you can see that makes it entirely different. I'm full of those great switches. I just thought of another one: Happy Christmas and Merry New Year. See?

Our first fifty television shows were live. For those of you who don't remember, those live shows were not easy. There was no taping or filming ahead of time. While the actors were performing the audience was at home watching. When the show started, whatever was said or done, that's what went on the air. If a joke didn't get a laugh, it just lay there, there was no laugh track to help you out. And if you made a mistake, everybody watching saw it. I remember one actor walked out with his fly open. It didn't help our show any, but he got a lot of fan mail. My fly was open once, and not a letter. I told you nobody watches a straight man.

And there were other problems. The show had to come out on time to the second. If it looked as if a show was running long, the producer held up a sign reading "Talk Faster." If it was running short, he held up a sign reading "Talk Slower." One time Gracie and I were in the middle of a routine, and Gracie had just said, "When I cook roast beef I always put two roasts in the oven, a big one and a little one." And my next line was supposed to be, "Gracie, why did you put two roasts in the oven?" But just then the producer held up the "Talk Slower" sign. So I asked that same question something like this: "Gracie, let me ask you something . . . not that I'm inquisitive . . . and I know I shouldn't ask you this . . . but if I didn't ask you this, I couldn't sleep . . . not that it's important . . . but there's something I'd like to know . . . why . . . why. . . and please tell the truth . . . now why did you put . . . I mean why in the world did you put . . . not one . . . and not three—" About that time I looked up, and there was the producer holding up the "Talk Faster" sign. So, very fast I said, "Graciewhydidyouput-tworoastsintheoven?" And in the same tempo Gracie answered, "Whenthelittleroastburnsthebigoneisdone."

In those days we all had to memorize our lines. This was especially tough on Gracie because of the offbeat character she played. Her crazy answers didn't always go with the questions. For example, I'd say, "Gracie, how do you feel?" and she'd answer, "I'm glad you asked. My Uncle Harvey fell down a flight of stairs again."

So Gracie not only had to memorize her lines, she had to memorize everybody else's. I hope you're not confused, but what I'm trying to say is that normally when two actors are doing a scene if the dialogue doesn't make sense, they can't remember it. But with Gracie it was just the opposite, if it made sense, she couldn't remember it. Anyway, she memorized the entire script, and the only way she remembered her answers was when you asked the question.

Where I'm going with this is that on one of our live shows Bill Goodwin, our announcer, was doing a scene with Gracie. She was supposed to make a false exit, and he had a line, "Wait, Gracie, there's something else I have to tell you." But he forgot to say that line, so she kept walking right back into her dressing room and started taking off her makeup. She thought the show was over. I had to do something, so I took advantage of our new gimmick and stepped out of the set and began talking to the audience. "Ladies and gentlemen, in case you're confused, let me tell you what happened. Bill Goodwin was supposed to call Gracie back, but he forgot his line, so right now Gracie is down in her dressing room taking off her makeup. So you're never going to see the finish of the show, which I thought was very funny. But now that I think of it, what I'm doing now might be even funnier. Good night, everybody." Can I tell you something, what I did got a big laugh. They thought it really was the finish.

Live television was fun and it was exciting, but it was very demanding. After two years we were tickled to death when they started to put television shows on film. On film if an actor would blow a line, there was no panic, you'd simply do it over. There were no signs "Talk Fast" or "Talk Slow," it was all done in the editing room. Let's face it, on film the shows weren't always funny, but they always came out on time. Now I don't want you to get the idea that putting a half hour television show on film was a breeze. After all, that had its problems, too. Actually you were making a small movie every week.

I'll never forget when Freddie de Cordova was producing and directing the Burns and Allen Show (he's been Johnny Carson's producer for years). At that time Freddie was still a bachelor and living in a duplex with his mother. She had one apartment and he had the other, and he was a very thoughtful and devoted son. Now Freddie was a fine director, but he and I were always arguing about the show. Sometimes it would be about the opening, other times about the closing, or the way a line was read, or anything. And every time we would get in one of these arguments it would end with Freddie shouting, "This is my last show, I quit! I'm not showing up tomorrow!" So that night I'd send his mother two dozen roses, and the next morning, there was Freddie again. I kept Freddie's mother in fresh roses for about two years.

One day I walked into his office and said, "Freddie, I want to talk to you about the way you staged the finish of that party scene." As soon as I said that, Freddie started drumming his fingers on the desk and his face began to turn red. Before he could say anything I said, "Freddie, I just want you to know that I already sent your mother two dozen roses." We both looked at each other and burst out laughing. But there's a footnote to this story. Later on I found out that Freddie owned the flower shop.

Would you like to hear another Freddie de Cordova story? Of course you would. On one of our shows there was an actor who had only one line. He was supposed to come to the door of our house, ring the bell, and I would open the door and say, "Yes?" Then he'd say his line, "Hello, I'm Dr. J. J. Crothers," and I would say, "Come in." And that was the whole bit.

Well, Freddie had hired an actor he knew who hadn't worked for a long time. This poor guy was a nervous wreck. When it came time for him to do his one line he blew it. He not only blew it once, he blew it seventeen times. Finally, I called Freddie aside and said, "Freddie, this is ridiculous, we could kill a whole season with this one line. Let's bring in another actor."

"Please, George," Freddie said, "the man needs the job."

"Okay," I agreed, "but before we do the scene again I want to talk to him." I went over to the actor and asked him, "Before we try this scene again, what's your real name?"

"Philip Manchester," he stated.

"Great. Now forget that you're Dr. J. J. Crothers. When I open the door and say 'Yes?' you just say, 'Hello, I'm Dr. Philip Manchester.'"

The actor assured me, "No, no, Mr. Burns, I promise I can do it. When you come to the door and say 'Yes?' I'll say, 'Hello, I'm Dr. J. J. Crothers.'"

"No, no," I said, "I don't like Dr. J. J. Crothers. I wouldn't go to a doctor whose name was J. J. Crothers. In fact, when I get to the office in the morning I'm going to fire the writer who thought of that name."

"But please, Mr. Burns," he pleaded, "it's no problem. I can say it. 'Hello, I'm Dr. J. J. Crothers.'"

"Okay." And we did the scene again. I opened the door and said "Yes?" and the actor said, "Hello, I'm Dr. George Burns."

I said, "No, you're not. And you're not Dr. J. J. Crothers,

either. You're Philip Manchester, that's the name on the check you're going to pick up when you leave."

Well, the poor fellow looked so depressed and crestfallen that I couldn't go through with it. "Wait, I've got an idea," I told him. "We'll do it again. You just come to the door, I ask you a question, and all you have to do is say 'Yes.' Can you do that?"

"Yes," he said.

"That's a good reading, remember that," I added.

So we did the scene again. He came to the door and rang the bell. I opened the door and said, "Hello, aren't you Dr. J. J. Crothers?," he said, "Yes," and I said "Come in." And we did it in one take.

All the situation comedy shows had one thing in common; somebody was always eavesdropping, either listening at a door, peeking through a keyhole, looking through a window or whatever, so they could find out what was going on and plan their counterattack. Week after week I was spying on Gracie, and it was getting pretty monotonous. Well, one day my writers and I came up with a new idea that we were all excited about. We decided that we should put a television set in my den. That way, instead of eavesdropping I could just turn on the television set and tune in Gracie and see what nutty things she was up to. To us this was the greatest innovation since I discovered the wheel. But our sponsor didn't like it. He objected, "It's out of reality, you can't be watching your own show."

"Mr. Thompson," I argued, "we think it's a great refreshing idea, and I'm going to do it."

"Well, if you do, you might have to find a new sponsor."

"Then I'll just have to turn in my new television set and find one," I stated.

We finally compromised and did it my way, and it turned out to be one of the highlights of my show. Now this device is being used in banks, hotels, department stores, all over. I turned out to be the father of closed circuit television. So you see, I'm not only an actor, a singer, a dancer, an author, a producer, and a director . . . I'm also an inventor.

As you know, situation comedies can go on for years and years, and in that time the audience gets very attached to the same characters. The Burns and Allen show was on for about eight years and we had five principal actors. There were Gracie and myself, Harry Von Zell, and our next-door neighbors Blanche and Harry Morton, played by Bea Benadaret and Fred Clark. The chemistry between the five of us was like magic, right from the opening show the audiences loved us. We were a very happy unit. Now back in 1953 there weren't so many television sets in use, so naturally they weren't paying the kind of salaries they do today. Anyway, when our option was picked up for the second season I gave everybody a two-hundred-dollar-a-week raise, which was considered very generous. Well, after we finished filming the second show of the new season Fred Clark came to my office and announced, "George, with that raise you gave me I'm now making a thousand dollars a week, but it's not enough. If you want me to stay, you'll have to pay me fifteen hundred."

"Fred," I said, "I think you're a fine actor, but if I paid you that, you'd be making a hundred dollars a week more than I am."

"I'm sorry, George, but that's it. That's what I want."

I said, "You realize, of course, that I've got a contract with you for another year." He just stared at me and I continued, "But I imagine if I held you to it, I'd have a very unhappy actor on my hands . . . an actor who on the day of the show just might get a bad case of laryngitis."

"Oh yeah," he said, "in fact, just talking about it my throat is tightening up."

"Well, your throat might be tightening up, but not as much as my wallet. Goodbye, Fred, and lots of luck on your next job." I don't think Fred expected it to turn out that way. I was sorry to lose him, but there just wasn't that kind of money around.

Well, it was panic time. Here we had a hit show and we had lost one of our main characters. The network, the advertising agency, the sponsor, none of them knew what to do. We all had a series of emergency meetings trying to come up with an idea of how to explain the sudden disappearance of our neighbor, Harry Morton. Some of the solutions they came up with were beauties, especially for a comedy show; like Harry falling to his death from an airplane—or drowning in a swimming pool— choking on a piece of steak (that suggestion got quite a few votes)—running away from his wife with another woman. . . . There were others, but I've just mentioned the good ones.

We went round and round and got no place. Finally I said, "Gentlemen, I've got an idea!" and this is how the problem was solved. On our next show the story line had Harry Morton buy his wife Blanche an iron deer for the front lawn. Well, she hated it, and she was standing at the door with a rolling pin held over her head ready to slug him as soon as he came into the house. At that point I walked into the picture and said, "Blanche, hold it, don't move," and she froze in that position while I talked directly to the audience. "Ladies and gentlemen," I said, "Fred Clark, the actor who has been playing the part of Harry Morton won't be with us anymore. I gave him a two-hundred-dollar-a-week raise, but he was very unhappy and wanted five hundred dollars a week more. I couldn't afford it, so I brought in a very fine actor, Larry Keating, who is now going to play that part."

Then I turned to Blanche, and said, "Blanche, put the rolling pin down and come over here." Then I brought out Larry Keating. I said, "Larry, this is Bea Benadaret . . . and Bea, this is Larry Keating. From now on you're going to be husband and wife."

They both started complimenting each other saying what great performers each thought the other was, etc., and I said, "Okay, that's enough compliments, let's get on with the show."

Bea went back to the door, held up the rolling pin, Larry made his entrance, she hit him over the head, and a new Harry Morton was christened. And it worked. Everybody accepted the new husband, and I never got one letter asking what happened to Fred Clark. The sponsor, the network, and the advertising agency were all delighted the way it turned out. In fact, it worked so well I almost fired Harry Von Zell.

Oh yes, when it came to money I always made the right decisions. I remember way back in radio I was offered Frank Sinatra for $250 a week, and at the same time I was offered a singing group, two boys and a girl called The Smoothies, for $250 a week. Well, I'm not stupid, I figured I could get three for the price of one, so there was no question, I took The Smoothies. And I certainly didn't make a mistake, because all of you know where The Smoothies are today.

Well, our television cast with Larry Keating stayed together for seven years until Gracie retired. The only major addition during that time was when my son, Ronnie, joined the show. My daughter, Sandy, also did a few commercials. But I thought Ronnie could have made it in show business. He had a nice relaxed manner, he was tall and good-looking and had all the instincts of a good actor. I even offered to send him to New York to study under Lee Strasberg at The Actors Studio, where some of our biggest stars came from. But Ronnie turned it down; he said he would miss all the girls at the Luau Restaurant.

I said to him, "Ronnie, they have restaurants in New York that also have pretty girls. And the pretty girls in New York have the same thing that the pretty girls have in California, and in the exact same spot." He appreciated this lesson in sex education. In fact, he called that night to thank me from the Luau.

But I never did quite understand why Ronnie wasn't in love with show business. On our show I always made sure he had good lines so he got big laughs, and every week there was a different actress playing his girlfriend. And they were all beautiful. Among them were Carla Borelli, Yvonne Lime, Adele Jergens, Suzanne Pleshette, Raquel Welch, Mary Tyler Moore—but Ronnie still liked the Luau. So, there was only one thing left for me to do, check out the Luau. And I did. I went there one night, and I must admit that the Luau did have something special—the noodles in the chow mein were really crisp.

One of the things I missed most after Gracie retired was the double routine she and I did at the end of each show. It had nothing to do with the plot, it was just sort of an afterpiece. Here's one I picked out at random, and I hope you enjoy it as much as we did:

GEORGE

Well, Gracie, any news from home?

GRACIE

Yes. I got a letter from my little niece, Jean.

GEORGE

What did she say?

GRACIE

She didn't say anything. She didn't phone. It
was a letter, and she wrote it.

GEORGE

I mean what did she write?

GRACIE

It's Spring again, and my family is putting on
a backyard circus, just like we did when I
was a kid.

GEORGE

Every Spring you kids used to put on your own circus?

GRACIE

Yes. Of course, admission was free, but that was only for people who could afford it.

GEORGE

Well, that's because we're living in a democracy.

GRACIE

Oh yes, isn't it nice. . . . Anyway, my Cousin Barney was the sword swallower, and what a performance he put on. The kids would cheer when he put a sword four feet long down his throat.

GEORGE

Could Barney really swallow a sword?

GRACIE

Oh, George, don't be silly, it was a trick. You know the scabbard that the sword fits into?

GEORGE

Yeah.

GRACIE

Well, before the show he would stick that down his throat.

GEORGE

I see.

GRACIE

Then when he'd slip the sword into it . . .

GEORGE JOINING GRACIE

. . . everybody thought he was swallowing it.

GRACIE

Yeah.

GEORGE

It's a shame to fool the public like that.

GRACIE

But the admission was free.

GEORGE

Oh, I forgot.

GRACIE

And Uncle Otis was the strong man. He'd come out in a leopard skin and put big nails in his mouth and twist them between his teeth until they'd bend.

GEORGE

That's quite a trick.

GRACIE

Yes, but he looked pretty ridiculous walking around with all those bent teeth.

GEORGE

Well, they'd come in handy if he happened to get a crooked ear of corn.

GRACIE

Oh, you live and learn. . . . And Aunt Gertrude was the snake charmer.

GEORGE

Aunt Gertrude? The one who's so near-sighted?

GRACIE

Yes. She had a little snake and she was supposed to put it in a basket and then blow on a flute until the snake stuck its head up. And what do you suppose happened one Saturday afternoon?

GEORGE

She put the flute in the basket and blew on the snake.

GRACIE

Wasn't that awful!

GEORGE

That must have upset her.

GRACIE

Oh, George, it wasn't a real snake. It was just a few worms tied together.

GEORGE

Well, that's better. Who else was in the side show?

GRACIE

One of the big hits was Uncle Harvey and Aunt Clara.

GEORGE

What was their act?

GRACIE

Half man . . . half woman.

GEORGE

But didn't you have two halves left over?

GRACIE

Oh no, they both got into one costume.

GEORGE

Now I get the picture.

GRACIE

George, it wasn't a picture, they did it in person.

GEORGE

What was your part in the circus?

GRACIE

I was the lion tamer.

GEORGE

You were the lion tamer?

GRACIE

Of course I just used our house cat. For two
weeks before the circus I taught her all kinds
of tricks . . . to sit on a pedestal, to roll over,
to play dead.

GEORGE

Sounds like a pretty smart cat.

GRACIE

Yes, but when she got in front of the
audience she forgot all her tricks and just had
kittens.

GEORGE

That must have caused a sensation.

GRACIE

It was . . . but what good was it? The silly
cat wouldn't do it again for the second
performance.

GEORGE

Say good night, Gracie.

GRACIE

Good night, Gracie.

You know, that was quite a while ago. I still miss those
routines, and I always will.

A 79-YEAR-OLD STAR IS BORN

I HOPE THE title of this chapter doesn't make you think I'm egotistical calling myself a star, but I can't help it. That's what it says on my stationery. But it is true, I was seventy-nine years old when they asked me to play the part of Al Lewis in *The Sunshine Boys*. And it did start a whole new career for me. I'm not going to tell the story of how I got the part because I must have told it a thousand times. But if you haven't heard it, buy my last book, *Living It Up*, it's on page 213. Don't read just that page, read the whole book; it's very informative.

But there is one thing that happened as a result of *The Sunshine Boys* that I will mention again. I won an Oscar for the Best Supporting Actor. After being a straight man for sixty years I thought becoming an award-winning actor would change everything. But nothing changed. The following day I went to the Hillcrest Country Club and had lunch with Milton Berle. He looked just the same to me. And there was Georgie Jessel wearing the same medals. When I ordered matzos, eggs, and onions they tasted the same as they did when I was a straight man. Incidentally, there's a reason why I always order matzos, eggs, and onions. They sound like the name of a vaudeville act.

458

And for the same reason I order finn 'n haddie. I worked with them. Finn stole one of my orchestrations.

Anyway, that award changed nothing. I still get up at eight o'clock, I still brush my teeth with my right hand (sometimes I use a brush), I still do my same morning exercises, I still drive the same car, I still live in the same house, I still put my coat on with my right hand and put my hair on with my left. So you see, everything is exactly the same except for one thing—my stationery.

After *The Sunshine Boys* I got a few movie offers, but the one that amazed me was when Warner Brothers wanted me to play God in a new film they were making. And they weren't kidding. They had a script called *Oh God!* by Larry Gelbart, produced by Jerry Weintraub, directed by Carl Reiner, and starring John Denver and myself. It sounded very exciting, these were all very talented people. But after I accepted, I started to worry. I asked myself what am I doing? What am I doing playing God? How do you play God? What does God look like? So I looked in the mirror, and I didn't look like God, I looked like Al Lewis in *The Sunshine Boys*." I was very confused, so I looked up and hollered, "How do you play God?!" But there was no answer.

I sat down and thought to myself, "Why would they pick me to play God?" Then I realized it made a little sense. I was the closest one to His age. Since Moses wasn't around, I suppose I was next in line.

The whole thing really bothered me. If I played Him, what would be my attitude? What would be my motivation? Should I play Him tall, should I play Him short? What kind of voice should I use? Could I handle a role like this? I finally called my manager Irving Fein, and said, "Irving, maybe I'm making a mistake playing God."

"How can you make a mistake?" Irving replied. "They're paying you a fortune. If there's anybody who might be making a mistake, it's Warner Brothers," and he hung up. Now during my career I've had a number of managers, but in all fairness to

Irving I must pay him a compliment. Nobody can hang up a phone like he does.

However, I still needed help, so I turned to some of my actor friends. First, I went to Jimmy Stewart and asked him how he thought I should play God. He thought a second, and then he said, "Well . . . uh . . . well, uh . . . George, you . . . you . . . see, if . . . if . . . I . . . I . . . were you, I'd . . . I'd . . . play him . . . uh . . . slow . . . uh . . . uh . . . relaxed . . . uh . . . uh . . . uh . . . soft, easy and . . . and . . . whatever you do, don't . . . uh, don't . . . uh, don't rush it." All I know is if God worked as slow as that, He never could have created the earth in six days. He'd still be at it.

I talked to Lucille Ball next. "Lucy," I said, "you're a fine actress, and I've got a problem and need your help. How should I play God?"

She answered, "If I were you, George, I'd play her very motherly."

After that I turned to one of the top actors in our industry, Orson Welles. "Orson," I asked, "if you played God, how would you play him?"

"Sitting down," was his answer.

So far I wasn't getting very far. If I took the advice I had received, my God would be a very slow mother sitting down. But then I got an inspiration. There was one person who could impersonate anybody. Rich Little. So I asked him, "I'm playing God, Rich. What kind of voice should I use?

"That's simple," he said, and he did a voice for me.

I said, "Rich, that sounds like Danny Thomas."

"That's right," he said, "God stole his delivery."

Well, everyone had a different idea, so I finally turned to the one man who could tell me how to do it—me. I used all my own instincts and played Him as honestly as I could. And it worked. It had to work. I couldn't be criticized. Nobody has ever seen Him, so they didn't know whether I was good or bad.

We finally started shooting the movie, and John Denver was

a delight to work with. It was his first movie and he turned out to be an excellent actor. In one of our early scenes he asks me to perform a miracle to prove to him that I'm God. What he didn't realize was that the real miracle was that I was able to get to the studio every morning.

We all worked together easily, but every once in a while Carl Reiner would have an objection to my interpretation of the role. He'd take me aside and say, "Look, George, this scene isn't moving, it needs a little more God-stuff." Another time he said, "George, we're going to do that scene over, it needs more Goddishness." Once he stopped a scene right in the middle by saying, "Hold it! George, you read that speech all wrong. God would never say it that way."

"Look, Carl," I said, "the last time you had lunch with Him did He have any other suggestions?"

Carl paused for a second, then started to laugh. "Okay, George, do it your way."

Carl Reiner and I had a very delightful relationship. One day just before lunch he came up to me a little worried and said, "George, I'm in trouble. I'm supposed to speak at a luncheon today at the Sportsmen's Lodge, and I forgot my toupee. Can I borrow yours?"

"Of course, Carl, what are friends for?" So he put on my toupee and left. When he returned I asked him, "How did your speech go, Carl?"

"Your hair was a riot," he said.

Now when I play a role I really throw myself into it. I've always been that way. Even in small-time vaudeville, doing bad acts in broken-down theaters, when I walked on the stage I threw myself into the part. Sometimes the manager would take a look at me and throw me out. I remember one theater they threw me out before I had a chance to throw myself in.

But now that I'm an actor I really live the part. Before they started shooting *Oh God!* I rehearsed day and night. I rehearsed when I was driving my car, I rehearsed before dinner, I rehearsed after dinner, I rehearsed while I was doing my exercises, I never stopped. I finally got so carried away rehearsing the part that one night before I went to bed when I said my prayers, I realized I was talking to myself.

The next morning, to stay in the mood, when I came downstairs to breakfast I wore a flowing white robe and sandals. I ran into Daniel, the man who works for me, and gave him a long list of things I wanted done that day. He waited patiently until I was all through, and then said, "Mr. Burns, you may be God at the studio, but this is Thursday, my day off." That day God had to take his car to the gas station all by himself.

Well, the movie came out and was a tremendous hit. It made millions of dollars. I guess the reason for that was that John Denver attracted all his fans, and I brought in the kids. That's not true, it's just a little joke. Well, it's not exactly a little joke, it's a tiny joke. It's not even that, it's no joke. In fact, if it weren't already printed, I'd take it back.

Truthfully, in my opinion, the real reason the picture was such a big hit was the casting of John Denver. He was the perfect one for the part. He practically played himself; a kind, considerate, honest man who was concerned not only about his fellow man, but every living thing. If God actually came down to talk to one good man, it could have been John Denver. I don't think the picture would have worked if I had come down and talked to Milton Berle. Not that Milton isn't a good man, but he'd be standing there with a pad and pencil taking down all my good stuff. I wouldn't have enjoyed that. Besides, I don't think it would be believable to have Milton Berle jot down "Thou Shalt Not Steal."

After the movie had been out a couple of months I got hundreds of letters just addressed to "God," and they'd be delivered to my house. When I went to a restaurant, the maître d' would ask, "Where would God like to sit?" The cocktail waitress would come over and say, "Would God like it with one olive or two?" Even strangers on the street would wave to me and say, "Have a nice day, God!" It was great for my ego but did nothing for my sex life.

To this day people still keep asking me, "Was there a message in the picture?" There certainly was, and this is it: If you make a lot of money for Warner Brothers, you'll continue making pictures for them. And it's true, I am doing several more for them which I'll talk about later.

After the picture with John Denver I played a cameo role in *Sergeant Pepper's Lonely Hearts Club Band*. What a shock it was for me to go from *The Sunshine Boys* and *Oh God!*, two nice warm intimate movies, to this raucous rock musical. When I walked on the set I couldn't believe my eyes. They had built an entire town called Heartland, U.S.A., that cost $750,000. I played in towns like Altoona that didn't cost that much.

The cast was loaded with all the high-priced young rock stars, and instead of dressing rooms every one of them was furnished with a luxurious motor home. Now I'd seen a plush motor home before, but I'd never seen forty of them lined up in a row. It looked like a millionaire's Leisure World. These homes had everything; a wet bar, a complete kitchen, tub and shower, a television set, everything but a swimming pool. The refrigerator was stocked with gourmet delicacies of every kind, and the liquor cabinet looked like the wine cellar of the 21 Club. After spending the first day in my motor home, when I went back to my Beverly Hills house and looked around I got the impression I wasn't doing well. In fact, I sent my butler out for food stamps.

The first day I was on the set, aside from the expensive cast and the large crew, there were 30 dancers and 450 extras. I have no idea what this picture cost Robert Stigwood, the producer, but I hope his mother and father are very rich. And if they were rich, they're not anymore.

It was a new world for me, working with all these kids. There were The BeeGees, Peter Frampton, Aerosmith, and then there was a group whose name sounded like a weather report. What was it again? Oh, yeah, Earth, Wind and Fire. And then there was— Wait, I've got to stop and tell you about Peter Frampton. I was talking to his manager, while we were sitting in the foyer of my motor home, and he told me that the year before when Peter was twenty-four years old, that little kid made $52 million. I was so shocked I nearly fell out of my Louis XIV rocking chair. Then his manager told me how he made it. That year Peter Frampton made one album that sold sixteen million copies, from which he received $3.00 each. Right there you've got $48 million. The other $4 million he made playing concerts.

Twenty-four years old . . . $52 million . . . I couldn't get over it. As soon as I was alone I called Irving Fein. "Irving," I said, "you're supposed to be a great manager, so explain something to me. Last year Peter Frampton made fifty-two million dollars. Now I'm nearly four times older than he is, and last year I didn't even make fifty-one million dollars." He hung up on me.

I've got to confess this was all a little upsetting, because I had made an album, too. My sister Goldie bought it. But this album goes back a lot of years. I did it for Victor Records. Remember His Master's Voice, with a dog sitting under the phonograph horn? Well, while I was recording, when I got to the second chorus the dog bit me. And on the flip side of the record there was an apology by Thomas Edison.

But getting back to Peter Frampton, let's say he paid his manager 25 percent of his earnings. That means that year his manager made $13 million. Now Al Jolson was the world's greatest entertainer, and Peter Frampton's manager made more money in one year than Jolson made in his lifetime. I heard Frampton's manager sing. The dog would have bitten him, too.

All these rock stars in the cast made fabulous money, and I thought this was why they looked so happy. But it wasn't that at all. I found out it was because some of them smoked grass. Well, I wanted to be happy, too, so one day when nobody was looking I walked out on the lawn and grabbed a handful of grass. I sneaked back into my motor home and locked the door and pulled down the curtains. Then I stuffed the grass into my cigar holder and lit it. It was nothing! But the fertilizer was murder. It took the varnish off my Louis XIV rocking chair.

I enjoyed working with all those kids, and I learned something from them. I ordered longer hair and I'm taking up the guitar. Actually I was doing pretty well without the guitar. Not that I'm the hottest thing in Hollywood, but look, at my age lukewarm is not bad either. I was getting a lot of scripts, but finally Columbia Pictures sent me one that I fell in love with. It was called *Just You and Me, Kid*, and my costar was Brooke Shields, a fourteen-year-old girl who is absolutely gorgeous. She gave a fabulous performance, and so did I. I know you're going to hate me for my modesty, but I really think it's the best thing I've ever done. And I'll let you in on a little secret; I'm going to say the same thing about my next picture.

Now I'd like to tell you a little about the story of *Just You and Me, Kid*. Those of you who have seen it can go out and see it again while I'm telling it to those of you who haven't. I play a retired old vaudevillian who saved his money and lives in a beautiful house. Brooke plays a runaway orphan who has bounced around from one foster home to another. When I first meet her she's running away from a small-time crook (William Russ), and in order to help her I let her hide in my house. Now this makes my daughter (Lorraine Gary) very suspicious. She figures something is going on between her old daddy and this young chick. But the only thing that's going on is a very warm relationship that develops between these two. We see how young and old can change each other's lives. I finally save Brooke from the bad guys with the help of my old vaudeville pals (Ray Bolger, Keye Luke, Leon Ames, and Carl Ballantine). And while this is going on, Brooke helps solve a problem with my closest friend (Burl Ives), so bitter against the world that he hasn't said a word for seven years. It all adds up to a warm, funny, and suspenseful movie. And I ought to know, I've seen it four times. I'd like to see it again; too bad I know the ending.

Now I enjoyed making my other pictures, but there was something special about *Just You and Me, Kid.* Everything seemed to fall into place right from the beginning. Everybody liked everybody. The crew liked the actors, the actors liked the crew, we all loved the director, Leonard Stern, we were all crazy about the script, the words just seemed to fit everyone's mouth, even the food in the commissary seemed to taste better. One day on location we got caught in a cloudburst. We all looked up and exclaimed, "What a beautiful rain!" Another day it was 114 degrees in the shade, and nobody perspired. I don't know what it was. I'd say it was the chemistry, but I'm not a chemist. Look, in the last chapter I became an inventor. What do you expect from me, an author can only do so much.

And the strange thing is that when I first got the script I was worried. I was all the way through it. I had to memorize 88 pages out of 114. Even God didn't get that much. But I know one thing, I couldn't have memorized 88 pages when I was young. When I was young my mind was on food, booze, and girls. Now I never think of food.

Working with Brooke Shields was quite an experience. We could only shoot four hours a day; the rest of the time was devoted to school. Then they'd let me out and I'd rush right back to work. But I really had a lot of fun working with that little girl. She treated me like a teenager. One morning she came up to me on the set and said, "George, are you ticklish?"

"I really don't remember," I said, "I haven't been tickled in sixty-five years."

"Oh, George," Brooke laughed, "I'll bet you are," and she tickled me.

Now I'm not really ticklish, but I giggled. That shows you how much I thought of her, I don't giggle for everybody. It sounds silly, but that's the way we were. We played jacks together, we played hopscotch, exchanged autographs, she gave me her "John Travolta" and I gave her my "Marie Dressler."

Oh, I just remembered something that happened while making the movie that should go in this book. There was a dramatic scene near the end of the picture where Burl Ives rushes across the lawn and gives me a big hug. It's very emotional. Well, we did the scene, but Leonard Stern, our director, didn't like it. He said, "Burl, this is the way I want it done," and he ran across the lawn and hugged me. Then Burl hugged me again, but Leonard still wasn't satisfied. He said, "No, no, like this," and hugged me again. I must confess I enjoyed Leonard's hug more than I did Burl's. In fact, the next day I sent him flowers. I told you it was a very friendly group.

Leonard Stern was a delight to work with. He was creative, considerate, and open to suggestions from everybody. And I'm not saying this because he always photographed me from my best side.

Now at the finish of shooting a movie it's customary to have a wrap party, where everybody involved with the picture gets together one last time before they go their separate ways. While our party was sentimental, it was also a lot of fun. We sang, we danced, we ate, Leonard hugged me again, and Burl Ives got jealous. I gave Brooke Shields a farewell gift of a gold charm bracelet, and she gave me a pair of roller skates. How she knew I needed another pair of roller skates, I'll never know. For me this party was a perfect way to end a wonderful experience.

Now my next movie will be filmed in New York, and— Wait, wait, wait, I just realized I mentioned everybody in *Just You and Me, Kid* except the producers, Jerry Zeitman and Irving Fein. So I better mention them: Jerry Zeitman and Irving Fein. I feel so bad about forgetting them that I'll mention them again: Jerry Zeitman and Irving Fein.

I started to tell you about my newest picture for Warner Brothers. Well, it takes place in New York, and it's about three old guys living on social security. It's called *Going in Style*. By the time you read this it might not be called *Going in Style*, it might be called something else. It might not even take place in New York. In fact, I might not be in the movie. But who cares, as long as I get paid. That's not true; I did make the movie, and it will be shot in New York. You know me, money means nothing. If a director hugs me, I'll work my heart out for him.

This picture stars Art Carney, Lee Strasberg, and myself. We live our dull lives together, sort of waiting out our last years. It's not a musical. And it was a challenge for me because I had to play an old man. I had to learn how to walk slow, how to drop food on my tie, how to remember to forget things, and I had to get to the studio an hour early every morning. It took time for the makeup man to put on wrinkles. You see, I haven't got any wrinkles on the outside, all my wrinkles are on the inside. If any of you would like to buy some inside wrinkles, I'll give them to you wholesale.

I'm really looking forward to making this picture. It's a fine script, and very exciting, too. These three old guys aren't just sitting around, they're up to something . . . which I could tell you, but won't. I want my book to have a little suspense, too. The script was written by a young new talent, Martin Brest, who's also directing. I can tell you one thing, this kid is a perfectionist. He called me up one day and said, "Mr. Burns, I want you to wear different glasses in this movie. Can I stop by and have you try on a few pair?"

"Sure, why not."

Well, he came in on a Thursday with a photographer, a lighting man, three suitcases full of eyeglasses, and a consulting optometrist. They set up the lights, I put on glasses, I took off glasses, and they kept taking pictures. Well, it didn't take long; by the following Wednesday Martin was satisfied. Then he decided that I would need a different hair style. He wanted me to look like somebody else. That seemed strange, if he wanted me to look like somebody else, why didn't he hire somebody else? But I guess that's show business. When he asked me to go to the wig-maker I told him I'd be glad to but he'd have to wait for a few days until my eyes got back in focus.

But when it was all over, I did look entirely different. With my new hair, my new glasses, my new wrinkles, and walking with the spots on my tie, I looked so different that when I called up my manager Irving Fein, he didn't hang up on me.

As soon as I'm finished with this movie I'll be playing myself again, I'll be doing a sequel to *Oh God!* Now I'm sure some of you are wondering why God would come down a second time. Well, there's a very good reason. The first time He came down He made the studio $65 million. Who knows, if the box office holds up, I might come down another seven or eight times. This could turn out to be bigger than *Charlie Chan.*

Well, that about brings you up to date on my new career. I've made five pictures and have one coming up. There's one very important thing I've learned about acting, and I'd like to pass it on to any young aspiring actor who might be reading this. And remember this for the rest of your life: To be a fine actor, when you're playing a role you've got to be honest. And if you can fake that, you've got it made.

W. CHARLES EMORY DID IT THE HARD WAY

ALL WRITERS HAVE their own way of working. Take Ernest Hemingway, he did all his writing standing up at his typewriter. I tried that, but I couldn't type standing up . . . and I couldn't type sitting down . . . I can't type.

Now F. Scott Fitzgerald did his best work while he was drinking. So I tried that, too. I fixed a martini, but nothing came to me, so I fixed myself another one. Then after the fourth martini I started writing. Well, I kept writing and drinking, and drinking and writing, and when I woke up the next afternoon I couldn't wait to see some of the great stuff I had written. But there was one thing wrong with it: I could read it but I couldn't understand it.

I also heard that W. Charles Emory locked himself in his bedroom naked to do his writing. I didn't even try that. If I'm naked in a bedroom, I'm not writing.

So I finally developed my own method. I don't write a book, I talk it. At first I talked into a tape recorder, but there was no reaction. I was telling all these funny anecdotes and wasn't getting any laughs. It threw my timing off. So I got rid of the tape recorder and started interviewing writers. The one who laughed the loudest got the job.

When I started this book I only had one writer, Elon Packard, who had been with me fourteen years, and Jack Langdon, my secretary, who's been with me for nineteen. Jack doesn't type very well, screws up all my appointments, and he can't make a good cup of coffee. Now this isn't going to hurt his feelings because he can't read either. But he's got one admirable quality that makes him indispensable to me: he knows just when I need a laugh.

But there was one day when there was nothing to laugh about. Jack and I came to work one morning as usual, but Packy never showed up. A little later we learned that he had died in his sleep the night before. It was a terrible shock and I felt awful. In fact, for some time I couldn't bring myself to work on the book. But what can you do about those things. We all have to make the same exit. Like in the early days of vaudeville, if the manager didn't like your act, he'd give you back your pictures and that meant you were canceled. Packy got back his pictures. Eventually I'll get mine.

Around this same time I was signed to do a TV special for CBS, so I brought in four writers to work on it. They not only could write, but more important, they were very loud laughers. In fact, they were so good that after the special I signed them to laugh through this book with me. You see, it doesn't matter to me how many writers I have writing this book, I might have thousands before I'm through. That way I don't have to worry about the public. If each writer buys a copy, I've got a best seller. Imagine Hemingway standing there writing a book all by himself. What a dumb businessman.

Actually, I have always believed in giving credit where credit is due. From page 59 on this book has been written with the considerable help of the team of Fred Fox and Seaman Jacobs. Each of them has a nice sense of humor and is a very clever writer. And then there's Hal Goldman. He has a nice sense of humor and is a very clever writer. The fourth is Lisa Miller. She has a nice sense of humor and is a very clever writer.

You'll notice that in the above paragraph I said the same thing about each of them. Well, I'm not stupid; the four of them are sitting right here in the room with me. The truth is we all get along fine. No one worries about who says what. There's no credit, and no blame. Five mornings a week I meet with them for exactly two hours. This is enough time to accomplish something, but not enough for us to get sick of each other. When the two hours are up, that's it. They can go about their business, and I can go roller skating. It's a very pleasant arrangement. We have lots of laughs, and I enjoy working with them. And I think Seaman, Fred, Hal and Lisa enjoy working with me. Why shouldn't they? After all, I have a nice sense of humor and I'm a very clever writer—I mean, a very clever talker!

IF THIS WERE A SERIOUS BOOK, THIS WOULD BE THE LAST CHAPTER

WELL, YOU'VE COME a long way with me. The Peewee Quartet wasn't yesterday. Looking back over all those years since then, there were ups and downs, and some tears, but there were also lots of laughs, lots of love, lots of wonderful memories, and it was never boring. If you can think of anything better, let me know. But hurry.

My friends keep telling me I've mellowed, that things don't upset me like they used to ten or twenty years ago. That's what they tell me, and I'm convinced. Now if they can just convince the guys I play bridge with. But it's true, people do change. Each day you're a different person. Who knows, tomorrow I may be Cary Grant or Robert Redford. That wouldn't bother me too much as long as I could stay in show business.

I'm constantly asked which I preferred, vaudeville, radio, television, or movies. I could never answer that because I'm nuts about all of them. Of course, when you analyze it, each medium had its advantages. That was even true with silent pictures. John Gilbert, one of silent pictures' biggest stars, sounded like a chicken when he talked. Radio was just the opposite. In radio the voice was all that counted. It didn't matter what you looked

473

like. If they'd ever had a thing called silent radio, my brother Sammy would have been a smash.

As I said, if it's show business, I love it. And I love it as much today as when I first went into it. In fact, I can hardly wait for vaudeville to come back. I saved all my funny hats. But I don't think show business has changed that much. At least comedy hasn't. There may be variations in style and techniques, but if a joke is basically funny, it lives forever. And it's the same today as it was for Smith and Dale; if the audience laughs, you're a hit, and if they don't laugh, you can always take up singing like I did.

To me it's as simple as that. You do the best you can, and you don't overanalyze, because things rarely work out the way you would expect. Take these movies I've been doing lately. Each time they put me with a younger co-star. First it was Walter Matthau in *The Sunshine Boys*. Then in *Oh God!* I played opposite John Denver. In *Just You and Me, Kid* it was fourteen-year-old Brooke Shields, and in the sequel to *Oh God!* my co-star will be a girl who's eleven years old. I don't know who they have in mind for me after that, but I'm not taking any chances; I'm learning how to change a diaper.

But I'm not complaining, because I really get a kick out of working with young people. I've never understood all this talk about the generation gap. I never knew what that meant. I guess it was the way I was brought up. There were fifteen of us crowded into three rooms; my grandmother, my mother and father, and seven sisters and five brothers, all different ages. And we got along just fine. There was no gap, we didn't have room for one. We were lucky to have room for my grandmother.

I do think young people are great. I've always enjoyed their company. Now that doesn't mean you can turn back the clock. I see some older people try that, with the medallions and the tight jeans, and it can get pretty ridiculous. I've never lied about my age. If you're going to lie, lie about something important; like telling your wife there's no other woman; or telling the other woman you don't have a wife.

In our youth-oriented society we tend to forget the advantages of my present stage of life. Now that I've seen eighty-three summers come and go, let me leave you with a few thoughts on a subject I know something about:

> I've been young and I've been old, but I never knew when young ended and old began. . . .
>
> Old people are healthier than a lot of young people who died with the same ailment *they* have. . . .
>
> Just because you're old that doesn't mean you're more forgetful. The same people whose names I can't remember now I couldn't remember fifty years ago. . . .
>
> They say you can't teach an old dog new tricks. Who needs new tricks? If you play it right, the old tricks still work. . . .
>
> Walter Matthau once asked me, "George, when did sex stop for you?" I told him, "At two o'clock this morning." . . .
>
> I enjoy being old. For one thing, I'm still here. I like being older than I was yesterday. And I'm looking forward to being older tomorrow than I am today. When you're young, if you're lucky, you get older. When you're middle-aged, if you're lucky you'll get to be old. But when you're old, you're in a holding pattern—that's it. It's sort of a reward for being young all that time.

WARM LEFTOVERS

For an author my sense of continuity is really pathetic. Here I thought I had finished my book, and I didn't include some of my favorite anecdotes. They don't belong back here, so put them anywhere you want . . . but don't shock me.

Al Jolson used to bill himself AL JOLSON, THE WORLD'S GREATEST ENTERTAINER. Can you imagine anyone billing himself like that and walking out on the stage and having to live up to it? Well, he did. He was the greatest. He might not have been the greatest talent, but he was the greatest entertainer. And he also had the greatest ego. When he was in his dressing room and another act was on the stage performing, Jolson always had the water running. He couldn't stand hearing any other act get applause. When I started in the business that couldn't have happened to me. The dressing room they gave me had no running water.

Now even though Jolson was the greatest and went from one hit show to another, there came a time in his life when there was a lull. He certainly wasn't starving, he always had millions, but the jobs he was offered weren't worthy of "The World's

476

Greatest Entertainer." During that time sturgeon, which is a very expensive fish, wasn't sold in California, but Jolson was very fond of this delicacy. So every week he used to fly in $150 worth of sturgeon and kept it in the refrigerator at the Hillcrest Country Club. I had lunch with him practically every day, and one day I paid him this tremendous compliment. I said, "Joley, to me you'll always be the greatest showman who ever lived. There will never be anything like you."

He was all smiles, and said, "Thanks, George, and how would you like a little sturgeon for lunch?"

"Sturgeon?" I said, "I'd love it." And it was absolutely delicious. After that every time I saw Jolson I paid him a compliment and I had sturgeon for lunch. It got to the point where I liked sturgeon even more than I did Jolson.

Then Columbia Pictures made *The Jolson Story*. Larry Parks played Jolson, but he didn't do the singing, Jolson did. He sang all the songs on the sound track, and it was the first time in movie history that a sound track was the star of a movie. I saw the film and was thrilled. The next day when I saw Jolson, I said, "Joley, I saw the movie, and that sound track is the greatest thing I've ever heard in my life."

He looked straight at me. "You can buy your own sturgeon, kid, I'm a hit again."

While I'm on Jolson let me tell you one more story. When his career first started taking off he sent his father to Miami for a vacation. Now his father was a very frugal, conservative man. There was a cold spell in Florida that year, so Joley sent his father a camel's hair coat that cost ninety dollars. Well, he couldn't tell the old man how much the coat cost because Joley knew his father would think it was too extravagant. So he called him on the phone and told him he was sending him a coat that cost twenty dollars, to wear it, keep warm, and have a nice vacation. Two days later his father phoned Joley and said, "Joley, send me ten more coats, I just sold this one for thirty-five dollars."

Eddie Cantor was also one of the show business giants. I'd like to do about a minute and a half of Cantor stories, if you read fast. When Eddie was doing his radio show he had four very good writers working for him. One afternoon there was a conflict about a certain joke. Eddie didn't think it was funny, but one of the writers thought it was. So in his very high voice, Eddie said, "Boys, there's a difference of opinion here. But you know me, I'm a very fair man, we'll vote on it."

Well, the four writers voted in favor of the joke. Then Eddie said, "That's four votes in favor of the joke, but it's my show and I get five votes. So write another joke, and if I don't like that one, we'll vote again."

Years ago Eddie Cantor and George Jessel were headlining the Palace Theater, and at the finish of the show they did a routine together. Well, one night Cantor ad-libbed a line that got a big laugh. Then Jessel topped him with an even bigger laugh. Cantor couldn't think of anything to say, so he took his shoe off and hit Jessel over the head with it, and that got a still bigger laugh.

But this really upset Jessel. He walked down to the footlights, and in a grand manner said, "Ladies and gentlemen. This so-called grown-up man, whom I have the misfortune to be working with, is so lacking in decorum, breeding and intelligence, that when he was unable to think of a clever retort he had to resort to the lowest form of cheap slapstick humor by taking off his shoe and striking me on the head. Only an insensitive oaf would stoop so low."

Cantor said, "Georgie, are you through?" Jessel said, "Yes," and with that Cantor hit him on the head with his shoe again, and that brought down the house. This proves one thing; you don't need an education, just get yourself a pair of funny shoes.

On the Eddie Cantor radio shows every week he used big guest stars. If he had a funny joke, it went into the show. It didn't matter who did it. He would give the same joke to Gracie, Gregory Peck, or even the Mad Russian.

I'll never forget one time Jack Benny was the guest star, and when Jack came to rehearsal he learned that the script called for him to play the cello. Jack couldn't believe it. "Eddie," he said, "how come you've got me playing the cello? For fifty years I've been playing the violin."

"But, Jack," Eddie said, "it's funny. Let's take a vote."

"Oh no, I know how you vote," Jack said. "You leave me with the writers and let me work on it." And Cantor did. Jack and the writers rewrote the script where Jack played the violin, and it was a big hit. But Cantor didn't waste anything. On his show three weeks later he had Charles Boyer playing the cello.

Jack Benny was a tremendous star for the last fifty years of his life. Big things like million-dollar contracts, changing networks, staying in the Top Ten, these big decisions he could handle. It was the little day-to-day things that threw him. The smaller they were, the bigger the problem for Jack. There was the time he and I were having lunch at the Brown Derby, and he couldn't decide whether or not to put butter on his bread. He said, "You know, I hate bread without butter."

"Well, put butter on it then," I said.

"I can't," he sighed. "Mary put me on a diet and she said no butter."

"Then eat it without butter."

"But I love butter. Bread is nothing without butter."

"So put butter on it."

"I better call Mary."

"Jack, please, make this one decision yourself!"

Well, he had butter, and when the check came for the lunch, I said, "Give it to Jack Benny."

"Why should I pay the check?" Jack asked.

"Because," I said, "if you don't, I'll tell Mary you had butter."

* * *

Another story about Jack was when Mary, Gracie, Jack, and I went to Honolulu for a vacation. The girls flew over, and Jack and I sailed on the S.S. *Lurline*. We thought we'd have a few days' rest. Now on the *Lurline* everybody dressed for dinner, so on the first night we were in our suite getting dressed, and Jack put on a yellow dinner jacket. "What do you think of this jacket?" he asked me.

"It's beautiful," I said.

"Mary doesn't like it."

I said, "Well, Mary's not wearing it."

Shaking his head, Jack said, "I can't understand it, why doesn't Mary like it?"

How was I supposed to know? Maybe it reminded her of butter. "Jack," I said, "you look darling in that jacket."

"Good," he said happily, "I'll wear it tonight and enjoy it."

"Of course," I muttered.

Then admiring himself in the mirror, Jack said, "I can't figure Mary out, what's wrong with it?"

"There's nothing wrong with it. C'mon, let's go to dinner."

"Maybe I should wear something else. What do you think?"

"I don't care what the hell you wear," I said, a little exasperated. "Let's go to dinner."

"George, take a good look at it, front and back." As he turned around I said, "I'll see you in the dining room," and left. Ten minutes later in came Jack wearing his blue dinner jacket. I never mentioned it all during dinner. The next night out came the yellow dinner jacket again. "George," he said, "I'm going to wear it tonight." I never answered him. He looked at himself in the mirror and said, "I think it looks great." I didn't even look at him. "Mary wears a lot of things I don't like," he went on, "and I don't tell her what to wear. . . . If Mary knew I was wearing this tonight, she'd kill me. . . . It drives me nuts, I don't know why she doesn't like it! I'm not a fool, I'm over twenty-one and I know what looks good on me! And this jacket happens to look great on me!"

While he was still talking I went up to dinner. I had a cocktail, finished my soup, and was in the middle of my entree, when in came my roommate from Waukegan wearing his blue dinner jacket. Every night it was the same routine: "Should I wear it? . . . Shouldn't I wear it? . . . Mary doesn't like it . . . But I like it! . . ." but the yellow jacket never made it to dinner.

Finally the last night out we were ready to go to dinner, and Jack was wearing his blue dinner jacket. I said, "Jack, you love that yellow dinner jacket but you haven't worn it once. Tonight is your last chance. Wear it! I'll take an oath that I won't tell Mary."

Just a bit annoyed, Jack said, "Look, I'm not afraid of Mary."

"Then why aren't you wearing it?"

"I'm saving it on purpose," he snapped. "I'm going to wear it when the four of us go out to dinner in Hawaii to prove to you that I'm not afraid of Mary."

Well, we had dinner, and the next day as we were getting off the boat, Jimmy, our steward, came up to Jack and said, "Mr. Benny, I want to thank you again for giving me that nice yellow dinner jacket." Jack never looked at me, he just kept walking.

"Jimmy," I said.

"Yes, Mr. Burns?"

"Don't ever wear that jacket in front of Mary Benny."

It seems as though I've known George Jessel all my life, but back in the twenties when I first met him he was starring in *The Jazz Singer* on Broadway. And Jessel was really a great actor. I saw the show one night and it affected me very deeply. The story was about the son of a Jewish cantor who goes into show business against his father's wishes. Just before the High Holidays the father dies, and the son gives up show business, comes into the synagogue, and takes his father's place. At the finish of the play he sings "Kol Nidre," the holiest of all Hebrew melodies. Well, when the curtain came down I was a wreck, I was crying like a baby. I felt I had seen my own life, because my father was a cantor. I ran backstage to congratulate Jessel on his marvelous performance, but Jessel's manager was standing at the dressing room door and told me I couldn't go in. "Why not?" I asked. "I want to tell him how much I enjoyed his performance."

He said, "I'm sorry, you can't go in, he's in there naked."

"So what?" I said. "I've seen a naked Jew before. I want to tell him how great he was."

"Mr. Burns," he insisted, "he's got a girl in there."

So I left. I was really shocked. I didn't think anything could follow "Kol Nidre."

Throughout George Jessel's life he always seemed to be involved in some emotional crisis. I'll never forget when he was married to Norma Talmadge and she left him. He learned that she was going around with some doctor in Florida and this really set him off. He bought a gun and chartered an open-cockpit plane and flew directly to Florida. He went straight to her hotel, knocked on the door, and when she opened it there was this doctor. Jessel pulled out his gun and took a shot at him. However, he missed the doctor, the bullet went through the window and hit a gardener two blocks away who was bent over picking up a daisy.

Well, the gardener took Jessel to court. The judge asked, "Mr. Jessel, how is it possible for you to take a shot at someone ten feet away from you and hit a gardener two blocks away?"

Jessel answered, "Your Honor, I'm an actor, not Buffalo Bill!"

I've mentioned my personal manager, Irving Fein, several

times in this book, and aside from hanging up the phone, he has other talents. I'm glad to say that if it weren't for Irving, I wouldn't have this new movie career. In fact, he keeps me so busy I hardly have time to talk about him. He's honest, enthusiastic, fearless, full of ideas, and a great businessman. So much for the compliments. Now let me tell you about the real Irving Fein.

I found out that if it concerns me, there's no problem, nothing is difficult. I'm eighty-three years old, and he has me running around like I'm just starting in show business. One morning he came bouncing into the office all smiles and said, "George, we're going to do another TV special for CBS."

I said, "Oh, are we? Good, then you can do those same songs and dances that you did in the last special."

Irving gave me a courtesy laugh and continued. "George, this will be a breeze. We'll have some kind of a big opening, then the orchestra will play 'Ain't Misbehavin',' then you'll come out and do five minutes of funny stuff . . . you know, great topical jokes or whatever, and then you sing two or three songs. So far it's easy, right?"

I didn't say anything, so he took another breath and continued. "Then you introduce your first guest star and let them do their own bit. Maybe then you do sort of a five-minute hunk with them . . . no, I'll make it even easier for you, just do four minutes. Then you do some show business stories which are always good for twenty or thirty big laughs, go into your sand dance, and before you know it we're up to the middle commercial."

I just sat there dying to learn how easy the second half was going to be. I didn't have to wait long.

"The second half," Irving went on, "we open with some-thing different, something that's never been done before, something that people don't expect from you. Right there we've got a good five minutes. Then we go into a production number with about eight or ten girls . . . you don't have to bother with that, but it would be better if you came in for the finish. But anyway, you do a few more songs, a few more sketches, bring on a couple more guest stars, then do a dramatic finish, and we've got our show."

I kept smoking my cigar and looking at him. Then very quietly I said, "Irving, it can't miss, that show is bound to win an Emmy."

He said, "All we've got left to do is come up with a clever title, like . . . like . . . uh . . . you know, it's easy . . . something clever."

"Irving," I said, "you've got it worked out so well I won't even have to hire writers."

"And, George, the best part is," he stated, "you've got ten weeks to prepare the special. While you're doing that you can finish your movie."

"How can I do a movie and prepare a special at the same time?" I inquired.

"George," he assured me, "they're both in Los Angeles."

"Well, now I feel better," I said. Then I added, "Irving, I might have one Sunday off, maybe you can book me for a concert."

Irving just smiled. "George," he said, "I know you're putting me on, but I forgot to tell you the best part. When you're doing the special you don't have to use makeup."

Now that's how Irving Fein operates—almost. I did do the special, I did do the movie, but I broke Irving's heart. I didn't do the Sunday concert.

There's a footnote to this story. As we finished writing this Irving happened to walk in the room, so we read it to him. I said, "Irving, if there's anything you don't like, we'll take it out."

He said, "No, no, it makes me look like a dope, but leave it in. It's more important that you finish the book, because we're leaving for London in two weeks to play the Palladium."

*   *   *

When I was about twenty-four or twenty-five and a small-time vaudeville actor, I used to hang out at a little restaurant called Wiennig and Sberber on Forty-fifth Street in New York. In those days one could get a full course dinner for thirty-five cents. When I wasn't working they would let me sign for the meal. I'd run up a bill for four or five dollars, and when I'd get a job I'd pay them. One time I owed them $163, which gives you an idea of how well I was doing.

Wiennig's was a popular hangout for actors, newspaper people, politicians, prizefighters, song pluggers and, late at night, prostitutes. Some of them were very pretty, but it turned out they didn't give credit like Wiennig.

Let me tell you something about the partners who owned this restaurant. They were a couple of real characters. Sberber had a habit of smelling anything before he bought it. This habit started out with cigars but it spread to everything else. One time a man came in to sell him napkins, Sberber put one to his nose, sniffed it, and said, "I'll take six dozen." Another time a chair collapsed under a customer sitting at my table. Sberber rushed over to help him up, and I said, "Sberber, you got a bad chair there. Didn't you smell it before you bought it?"

Sberber never stopped talking, but nobody ever knew what he was talking about. Harry Richman came in there one night for a late supper, and Sberber tried to impress him. He came up to the table and said, "Mr. Richman, thanks for coming in. It's a pleasure to see such a talent eating here. From the way you sing I can tell you must like music."

Richman didn't want to encourage the conversation, so he just said, "Thank you."

Sberber said, "I like music, too."

"You do?" Richman muttered.

"Do I like music?" Sberber went on, "I come from Chicago." While Richman was trying to figure that out Sberber said, "My daughter is even taking singing lessons. You'll never guess from who."

Making up a name, Richman asked, "It couldn't be Teresa La Guardia?"

Sberber said, "It couldn't, huh? She charges fifteen dollars a lesson."

By now Richman was eating very fast. Sberber said, "I love good music. I'm always at the opera. I've seen *Carmen* seventeen times, I know it by heart."

Richman couldn't resist this. He turned to Sberber and said, "You know *Carmen* by heart? How does it go?"

Sberber said, "Good."

And that was Sberber. Now let me tell you a little about Wiennig. He was a different type of character. He was the kind who only remembered his last conversation. If you asked him a question, he gave you the answer to the last customer's question. One night I came in and said to him, "Have you seen Manny Mannishaw?"

Wiennig said, "Look on the floor, maybe it fell down."

Another time I asked, "Wiennig, did I get any phone calls?"

His answer was, "How do you like that? You give a waiter a chance to go up and he goes down."

He never called the customers by their names. Al Jolson would come in, and Wiennig would say, "'April Showers,' would you like table two?" With Sophie Tucker he'd holler out, "Waiter, make room for 'Some of These Days'!" Me, he called "Lay Off." I don't know why he was upset, I only owed him $163.

When the restaurant was crowded Wiennig would help by waiting on the tables. Once while he was doing that a customer stopped him and asked, "Where's the men's room?"

Wiennig said, "Please, I've only got two hands!"

Well, I had a lot of happy times there, and it was a big kick for me to see all those big personalities who came. But the biggest kick was knowing Wiennig and Sberber. I wonder if Sberber smelled Wiennig before he made him a partner.

ROASTED, TOASTED, AND FRIED

THROUGHOUT MY BOOK I talked and talked and talked about myself. Now that you know what I think about me, maybe we should wind up this whole thing with a few honest opinions. I was the Guest of Honor on one of the Dean Martin Television Roasts, and this is what some of my lovable colleagues said about me. Now being honored at one of these roasts is a lot like the way General Custer was honored by the Indians at Little Big Horn. The only difference was I knew what was coming; a lot of age jokes . . . going out with young girls . . . my singing . . . my sex life . . . my toupee . . . and they didn't disappoint me.

Here are a few excerpts from their remarks, starting with the host of this unforgettable occasion:

Dean Martin

"Tonight we salute our Man of the Hour, George Burns. We are honoring George tonight by special request—*his*. . . .
Though George is recognized as one of our truly great comedians, he'd rather be recognized for his singing. The fact is he started out as a singer. I don't want to say *when* he started

singing, but that was the year the Top Ten were the Ten Commandments! . . .

Did you ever hear a voice like his? He sings like he makes love—a slow start and no finish! . . .

Funny thing, but women are always fascinated by George. Even when George was a kid he had a lot of charisma. Then he started dating girls, and his charisma cleared up!

> **(So far I was right, the jokes were about my age, my singing, and my sex life. Dean's wrong about that charisma, that didn't clear up until I was thirty-eight.)**

Milton Berle

"Ladies and gentlemen, it's a great thrill to be here tonight to honor George Burns! *Yes, it's a great thrill!!* I'm speaking loud so he can hear me. . . .

Look at him sitting there. He doesn't know this is a Roast. He thinks he's having sex. . . .

This man's back goes out more than he does. . . . It's the truth. The other day I gave him a copy of *The Joy of Sex*. He took out his crayons and colored it. . . .

Boy, what a beautiful life George Burns is leading right now. Luncheon every day at the Polo Lounge in Beverly Hills— dinner every night with a gorgeous young chick—he's already won an Oscar—he's written a best-selling book—and gets offers from every movie studio in town. Oh God . . . I can't wait until I get old! . . ."

> **(Being a good straight man I sat there and laughed at all the right spots. But after the roast I told Milton I loved his joke about my back going out more than I do. And I asked him if I could use it. Milton said, "Why not, I stole it from you.")**

Gene Kelly

"It's a great pleasure to be here to honor my old friend George Burns. Now I'm expected to say some awful things about him. But not me. After seeing some of the things he did in his movie *Oh God!* he might make it rain in my living room. . . . A little while back George was doing a television special and he asked me to be one of his guests. He wanted me to recreate a scene I did in the movie *An American In Paris*. That's the one where I sang and danced on the banks of the Seine with Leslie Caron. Well, I thought it was a marvelous idea and was all for it until George suggested that instead of doing a romantic Gershwin song he wanted me to sing one of *his* songs, 'The Monkey Rag.' . . . I told him if I had sung 'The Monkey Rag' to Leslie Caron in the picture, she would have thrown me right into the Seine. George told me not to worry, Leslie Caron wasn't on the show and I was going to sing it to Phyllis Diller. So I had no argument. 'The Monkey Rag' is a perfect song for Phyllis Diller. . . . George, I loved you in *The Sunshine Boys*, I loved you in *Oh God!*, and I even love you in between pictures."

(I love Gene as much as he loves me, but it never would have worked out. Eventually he would have found out I was Jewish.)

Red Buttons

"Ladies and gentlemen, the question tonight is why, why are we toasting this ancient comedian . . . a man old enough to be his own father. . . . A man who embarrassed everybody at The Last Supper by asking for seconds. . . . A man, who, when Rome was burning, requested Nero to play 'You Picked a Fine Time to Leave Me, Lucille'. . . . And this is the type of person we're honoring tonight? . . .

And thank you, George Burns, for just being you. I love you!"

(How fickle can you be? First he chops me to pieces, then he tells me he loves me. I like Red Buttons, he's a nice kid, but I'm not cheating on Gene Kelly.)

Tom Dreesen

"You know, you just can't imagine how it is for me, a new performer, to be on the same dais with all these famous stars. And it's especially exciting that the Guest of Honor is George Burns, who's been my idol since I was a child . . . since my mother was a child . . . since my grandmother was a child . . . since my great grandmother was a child. . . . Look, I'll keep going until I get a laugh. . . .
In closing, I want you to know that when I started out in show business, an old vaudevillian pulled me aside and said, 'Would you like to become a good comedian?' I said, 'Yes,' and he said, 'Well, study the masters. Watch George Burns. In fact, watch his every move.' Mr. Burns, I've been watching you all night long . . . you haven't moved once!"

(It's always a pleasure to watch a young comedian work. And I'm very happy when I see one of them make it big. It's when more than one makes it that I start to get a little nervous.)

Jimmy Stewart

"George Burns and I go back together a long while. We were both at the MGM studio at the same time . . . 1938. In those days I was a romantic juvenile and George was an old man. . . . And it's just amazing that now, forty years later, we're both still at it. Only now *I'm* the old man, and George is the romantic juvenile. . . ."

(I love to watch Jimmy work. He takes his time . . . he
stutters . . . and he stammers . . . he puckers his lips . . .
he drawls . . . he swallows and he gulps . . . he's amazing.
He gets more laughs not saying anything than most
comedians get saying it. . . . Even when he's not working
he talks slow, and he walks slow, and he eats slow. I asked
his wife Gloria, "Does Jimmy do everything slow?" She
paused and said, "I'm trying to remember.")

Ruth Buzzi

(Playing the old spinster, "Gladys Ormphby")
"Tonight, ladies and gentlemen, you're in for a surprise.
George Burns, the man you see sitting there, he and I used to
go around together. And let me tell you something, George
was not the greatest lover in the world. In fact, he had a mean
streak in him. Most men will cover your face with kisses. He
covered mine with a burlap bag. . . .
George Burns wasn't the same person you see today. He
didn't even like the smell of those big, fat cigars. So I stopped
smoking them. . . . We were poor in those days. We had no
car, but George had a bicycle to take him to auditions. He
used to let me ride in the basket of his bike. That's how I got
my nickname . . . Old Waffle-Bottom! . . ."

(You know, Ruth Buzzi is a very pretty girl. It must take a
lot of effort and hard work for her to make herself
look so unattractive. I know, because I have to work
just as hard not to look the way I look.)

Abe Vigoda

"I suppose I should say it's a great pleasure to be here tonight,
but it would be a lie. I'm an old, tired man, and I should be
home in bed—alone. . . .
In all the years I've been watching television, not once was I
able to stay up for the *Late Show* . . . Recently I've been falling

asleep during the *Early Show*. . . . Last week I could hardly make it through *News at Noon*. . . ."

(I was the Guest of Honor, he spoke for seven minutes and never even mentioned my name. That was the nicest thing that was said about me all night.)

Dom De Luise

(Playing the part of a psychiatrist)
"George Burns came to me, because after playing 'God,' he thought he was. So I put him on the couch and said, 'Mr. Burns, you came to the right doctor. I can cure anybody. I once cured a man who thought he was a rabbit. Of course, I must admit not before he and his wife had seventy-eight children.' . . .
And just to humor George, I said, 'I hope you don't make it rain again for forty days and forty nights.' What do you think he said? He said, 'If I do, you better build yourself an ark and fill it with pairs—with a pair of elephants . . . a pair of tigers . . . a pair of horses . . . Raquel Welch'. . . ."

(I've got to correct Dom's last remark. I never said that. I never even mentioned Raquel Welch. I said Dolly Parton. If you're going to do jokes like that, why not be subtle?)

Phyllis Diller

"You know, Dean Martin does know how to relax. It takes him an hour and a half to watch *Sixty Minutes*. . . .
You don't know what a thrill this is for me to be here with George Burns. I've had a crush on George for years. He's my kind of guy. He's handsome . . . he's successful . . . and he's breathing. . . .
I don't know how you feel about old age, George, but in my case I didn't even see it coming. It hit me from the rear. . . .

But, George, I just want to tell you this. After the show—I know it's your night, but I'd love to share it with you—somehow . . . we'll find a way. Come to my room if you want to see a real woman—I'll get one for you!"

(**Phyllis Diller is a great comedienne, and she's always putting herself down. But don't believe it. She's a very charming lady. And about her saying that she liked me because I'm handsome, successful, and breathing, every time I meet her to make that joke believable I start to breathe.**)

Frank Welker
(The Impressionist)
"Good evening, everyone, this is Walter Cronkite. Tonight we pay homage to a man who is celebrating his seventy-fifth anniversary in show business. George owes much to the miracles of modern medicine—just how much only Medicare knows for sure. . . . But through the miracles of modern medicine George Burns still chases pretty girls, and through the miracle of modern psychiatry he intends to find out why. . . . You see, when you're his age, the memory is the second thing to go. . . .
Good night, George. This is Walter Cronkite signing off with the words I told my wife on our wedding night, so many, many years ago: 'That's the way it is.'"

(**Frank Welker is a very talented young mimic. He not only does Walter Cronkite, he does everybody. He does me so well that one night I got confused and thought I was Frank Welker. I took this girl to dinner and then we went to my place. We had a couple of drinks, and at ten o'clock I suddenly found out I was George Burns and sent her home.**)

Jack Carter

"I'm delighted to be here for my dear, sweet friend George Burns. What an adorable man. The sweetheart of the Stone Age. . . . This wonderful Neil Sedaka reject singer. . . . This beautiful man who was the first performer to give a one-man concert at Carnegie Hall. Fortunately, the next night two men showed up! . . ."

(Jack, I hope you won't be upset because I didn't use any more of your stuff. But some of it was too risqué, some of it was too political, and let's face it, nine-tenths of it was just too funny.)

Connie Stevens

"I had a marvelous time last night, and who do you think was my date—George Burns. I picked him up right after his nap. . . . It was then that I discovered George's secret for staying young. He never overextends himself. He wouldn't even whistle for a cab. He figures when he finally gets up a pucker, why waste it on a taxi. . . . We were driving along and all of a sudden George leaned over and said, 'My leg's asleep. It's numb. I can't feel a thing.' I said, 'George, please relax . . . that's my knee you're holding.' . . . Anyway, when the evening was over he took me to my room and kissed me good night. Can I tell you something. It was a pretty hot kiss—he forgot to take the cigar out of his mouth. . . ."

(I love Connie. We did a television show together called *Wendy and Me*. It was really a good show. And Connie was a delight to work with. She was never late for rehearsals— except once. The morning after she got married she was ten minutes late.)

Orson Welles

"As for our honored guest, George Burns, he certainly deserves more respect than he's been getting here tonight. After all, how many men his age could listen to insults about their sex lives . . . without the use of a hearing aid? . . . All these slurs about George's amorous adventures remind me of the words of the poetess Elizabeth Barrett Browning: 'How do I love thee? Let me count the ways.' In your case, George, don't bother to count the ways, just count the times. . . .

As for you, George, in your long and glorious career you've been the recipient of a perfect plethora of honors and awards. You've triumphed on radio, conquered TV, and headlined at The Palace. You have known presidents and kings. You, more than any living mortal, should be cognizant that there is something more exciting in life than women and sex. And whoever finds out what it is will make a fortune. . . ."

(I love to listen to Orson Welles. That dramatic delivery, the beauty of his voice, his diction, his excellent vocabulary, I sit there spellbound. But the problem is I don't know what the hell he's talking about. I never went to college. I never went to high school. I never got past the fourth grade in grammar school. I was really stupid, and I was very good at it. In fact, in kindergarten I flunked sandbox. I didn't know a teeter from a totter.)

La Wanda Page

"George Burns, honey, you oughta be ashamed of yourself, datin' all them young foxes at your age. A man as old as you, honey, should be *re*-spected, *re*-warded, and *re*-tired—and *re*-treaded. . . .

George, you're too old to get married again. Not only can't you cut the mustard, honey, you're too old to open the jar. . . .

I know what I'm talkin' about, George Burns. I was once married to an old guy myself, honey. When we faced the preacher, he didn't say 'I do'—he said, 'I'll try'. . . ."

(I enjoyed watching LaWanda Page again, she's such a marvelous comedienne. And I want to thank her for saying all those things about me. Compared to what she used to hit Redd Foxx with on *Sanford and Son*, I consider myself complimented.)

Ronald Reagan

"I just couldn't turn down this opportunity to say a few words about our Man of the Hour . . . this Bionic Geriatric . . . this Sun-City Fonzie . . . George Burns . . . the only man I know who does fool Mother Nature. . . .

George, Nancy wanted me to tell you that you're her favorite singer. But then, Harry Truman was her favorite piano player. . . . Just the other night I thought she had one of your records on. It turned out to be a spoon caught in the garbage disposal. . . .

If you're wondering why we're honoring this man tonight, who else do you know who was an actual eyewitness to most of the history of our country? . . . It was George Burns who told Betsy Ross, 'Personally, I feel the pattern's a little busy, but let's run it up the flagpole and see if anyone salutes it.' . . ."

(I've known Ronnie Reagan for a long time. Years ago when he was just getting into show business, every time I met him at a party we'd get up and sing a song together. Since then he became President of the Screen Actors Guild, did a great job as Governor of California, was almost nominated for President of the United States, and still might be. I can't understand it, where did I go wrong. I know I sing better than he does.)

Charlie Callas

"Good evening, my name is Doctor Cooper, George Burns'
personal physician. But before I talk about my famous
patient, don't forget to buy my book, *Brain Surgery Self-
Taught*. . . .
The first time George Burns came to my office he complained
about a ringing in his ear. I cured him. I gave him an unlisted
ear. . . .
Mr. Burns is always bragging about his sex life. I happen to
know he's at the age now when he checks into a motel it's to
catch up on his Bible reading. . . . And he has to take
somebody with him, those Bibles are heavy. . . ."

**(Charlie Callas is a very talented comedian and gets very
big laughs. But can I tell you something. I read
his book, *Brain Surgery Self-Taught*. Don't try it unless
you've got steady hands.)**

Don Rickles

"George, we're both of the Jewish world. Not that that
matters to show business, but it matters to me. And on behalf
of the Jewish religion, we want you out. . . .
Last night George took a girl up to his room here at the hotel.
When they left he noticed a sign on the door, 'Have you
forgotten anything?' George said, 'Yeah . . . how?' . . .
George, you're beautiful. I'll give you five dollars if you'll
marry mother, and thirty dollars if you have a baby. I always
wanted a fifty-year-old baby brother. . . ."

**(Don was the last speaker. He's always the last speaker,
nobody can follow that guy.
Wait a minute, remember at the beginning of this chapter
I said they were all going to do jokes about my age . . . my**

going out with young girls . . . my singing . . . my sex life
. . . and my toupee? The thing I can't get over is that no
one mentioned my toupee. But I think I know the reason. I
turned out to be such a great actor that I've got them all
believing it's my own hair.)

Dean Martin

"Ladies and gentlemen, now we'll hear from our Man of the
Hour, the beautiful George Burns!!
Will somebody help him up!"

George Burns

"Thank you, thank you, ladies and gentlemen. You know,
I've really come a long way in show business. Here I am
eighty-two years old, and to think that all these lovely people
flew all the way to Las Vegas, got all dressed up and came
down here tonight just to insult me. I'm very touched. . . .
Let me tell you something. I was a small-time vaudeville actor
until I was twenty-seven years old, so I'm used to being
insulted. I've been insulted by some of the nicest audiences in
the country. People used to stand in line and pay thirty-five
cents just to come in and insult me. . . . I was insulted at the
Jefferson Theater on Fourteenth Street, at the Gaiety Theater
in Altoona, at the Farley Theater in Brooklyn, at the Colonial
in Akron . . . I can hardly remember a theater I haven't been
insulted in. . . .
Oh, I must tell you what happened at the Farley Theater. I
was in the middle of my act, singing 'In the Heart of a
Cherry,' and just before my yodeling finish the manager
walked out on the stage and canceled me. . . . And to make
matters worse, the audience applauded him. . . . And as he
dragged me off the stage the musicians gave him a standing
ovation. . . .

But nothing fazed me. I got so used to being disliked I thought I was doing well. . . .

When I played in a theater I didn't care if the whole audience hated me. As long as I was on that stage I knew there was one person there who loved me. . . .

So, ladies and gentlemen on the dais, your insults about me tonight meant nothing. I've been insulted by pros. . . . In fact, I played on the bill with Swain's Cats and Rats, and they refused to dress next door to me. . . .

Even when I was working with Gracie I got a notice in Oklahoma City that was a beauty. We were playing the Orpheum Theater and the next morning there was a review in the paper that said, 'Miss Allen is not only a beautiful young lady, but a great talent. Her dancing is exciting and her comedy timing is flawless. There is no telling how far Miss Allen could go if she worked alone'. . . . I saved that review, that was one of the good ones. . . .

But to show you what a nice man I am, I never got cocky. I never allowed these insults to go to my head. Just last year when Frank Sinatra played here in Las Vegas all the women threw their hotel keys up on the stage. The same thing happened to me. When I played Las Vegas women threw their hotel keys at me, too. But it was after they checked out. . . .

So in conclusion, I want to thank all of my friends up here for coming tonight, and I enjoyed the evening very much. You know, right now I'm at a very comfortable stage in my life. I was always taught to respect my elders. Well, I've finally reached the age where I don't have to respect anybody. . . . Thank you."

(Now I've had a few comments about everybody who spoke that night, so I feel I should have something to say about myself.

But I've used up all my good stuff,
so this is the end of the book.)

DR. BURNS' PRESCRIPTION FOR HAPPINESS*

*Buy Two Books and Call Me in the Morning

CONTENTS

Foreword		505
Preface		509
Introduction		510
About the Author		513
1.	Getting to the Bottom of It	517
2.	Has Happiness Had It?	519
	Monday's Prescription	528
	Nine Definitions of Happiness	530
3.	You Can't Get There With Shortcuts Unless You're a Butcher	532
	Tuesday's Prescription	543
4.	As the Saying Goes . . .	544
	Nine Happiest Men I've Known	547
	Nine Happiest Women I've Known	550
	Wednesday's Prescription	552
5.	Is Aggravation a No-No? Yes-Yes!	553
	Thursday's Prescription	561
6.	A Hobby Can Be Fun	562
	The Nine Happiest Animals	570
7.	Getting There Is Half the Fun	571
	Friday's Prescription	584
	More Definitions of Happiness	585
8.	You Can't Say I Didn't Try	586
	Saturday's Prescription	589

     Nine Ways to Make Your Wife Happy   591
     Nine Ways to Make Your Girlfriend Happy   592
  9. Happiness Is Offering a Helping Hand   593
     Sunday's Prescription   603
10. Work Only Works If the Work You Work at   605
    Isn't Work
11. . . . and in Conclusion   618
     One Last Definition of Happiness   626

FOREWORD

HERE I AM writing another book. It's my fifth book, but my first foreword. All my other books I just started with Chapter 1. I don't know whether I'm more excited about writing my fifth book or my first foreword. In fact, I couldn't sleep last night. I'm not sure if it was the fifth book, the first foreword or the Mexican dinner I had.

I did a lot of research on forewords, and the trick of a good foreword is that it shouldn't be too long a foreword or too short a foreword. Another thing, it shouldn't be too good a foreword, or it'll make the book look bad. The smart thing would be for me to write a bad foreword. But it's not easy to sit down and try to write a bad foreword. I don't know how so many people have managed to do it. But then a lot of them just specialize in writing forewords; they don't write the rest of the book. No wonder they can write bad forewords—they've had a lot of practice. I haven't. Don't forget, this is my first foreword. And if it turns out to be good, it might be my last.

Wait a minute, there's something disturbing me. My friends Jim and Henny Backus recently wrote a book and asked me to do the foreword, and I wrote all this same stuff for them. I feel terrible. I just feel awful. My conscience is bothering me. Either that or it's that Mexican meal again. I don't know what to do. I can't use this foreword now. But then again, why not? If it was bad enough for their book, it's certainly bad enough for mine.

Hollywood Center Studios
Hollywood, CA.
May 20, 1984

Hollywood Center Studios.

Canyon Hotel, Palm Springs.

PREFACE

As LONG AS I'm doing my first foreword, I figured I'd do my first preface, too. But I had a problem. I didn't know the difference between a foreword and a preface. So I decided to ask my editor and publisher, Phyllis Grann. After all, she's a very intelligent lady, a college graduate and very well respected in the publishing business. I called her on the phone and said, "Phyllis, what's the difference between a foreword and a preface?"

She said, "Foreword starts with an F, preface starts with a P."

Now that she straightened me out I can go ahead with this preface. I feel great about it. Either that, or I've finally gotten over that Mexican meal.

I'm so confident right now about this preface that I'm going to put it in not only before I read my book, but before I write it. You've got to be willing to gamble a little to be a good author—take a few chances. After I read the book, if the preface doesn't fit, then I'll write a new book.

Canyon Hotel
Palm Springs
May 22, 1984

INTRODUCTION

YOU'RE PROBABLY ASKING yourself, "Why is he writing another book?" It's not healthy to talk to yourself, so I'll tell you. Actually, I was in the middle of writing a new country song, "There Are Cobwebs on My Mailbox 'Cause I Never Hear From You," when the phone rang. It was my publisher with an idea for another book, called *Dr. Burns' Prescription for Happiness.*

"Don't you want to do another book? The last one was so successful, this one will sell a million copies," she told me. "Will your song do that well?"

I looked at the song again, and now I'm doing another book. That's the way I am—quick decisions. Some people worry—did they do the right thing, did they do the wrong thing? Not me—I never look back. Boy, have I made mistakes.

So this book is going to be *Dr. Burns' Prescription for Happiness.* I don't know how I became a doctor so fast, especially since I never got past the fourth grade. But the publisher is giving me a nice advance, so if she wants me to be a doctor, I'll be a doctor. It might be fun. I can't wait to touch somebody's pulse.

Happiness is something everybody wants. We all pursue happiness, but catching it is the problem. It's not easy to come by; you don't go into a store and say, "I'll have a pound of happiness."

What is happiness, anyway? Where do you find it? If you find it, how do you hang on to it? If you can't find it, where do you look for it? If you lose it, how do you get it back? Why am I asking you

510

these questions? I'm the doctor. I just looked it up in the dictionary. It says, "Happiness is the enjoyment of pleasure." So I looked up pleasure. It said, "See Happiness."

Happiness is different things to different people. To some it's having great wealth, lots of possessions; to others it's having nothing. To some it's being in love; to others it's being married. A while back there was a popular song that decided "Happiness Is a Thing Called Joe." I always thought that happiness was a thing called Trixie . . . or Margie . . . or Gina . . . or LaVerne . . . or her mother. I'm not too fussy.

Happiness is a state of mind, it comes and goes. You can't be happy twenty-four hours a day . . . twenty-three maybe. You deserve an hour for lunch. It's also elusive, contradictory and inconsistent. Blondes don't always have more fun, not everyone adores canned salmon, and if what pleases some didn't make others miserable, you wouldn't have the world divided into "Smoking" and "No Smoking."

There are no rules, no guaranteed formulas, and if you—Wait, it just occurred to me if that preface I did doesn't fit, I don't have to write a new book, I'll just write a new preface. Hey, I better make a note of that. Why am I making notes? I can read it, I just wrote it.

Where were we? Oh yes, I was telling you about happiness. But what's the rush? This is just the introduction, we have lots of time for that. Stick around. We'll have a few laughs. Here and there you may come across something that makes sense to you. And two or three of you may even find that I helped you. As doctors go, that's not a bad percentage.

Carlos' Cantina
Tijuana
May 23, 1984

Carlos' Cantina, Tijuana.

ABOUT THE AUTHOR

NOW THAT I'VE introduced the book, I should probably introduce myself. It's always nice to know where your author is coming from. Right now your author is coming from Beverly Hills. Originally he came from Pitt Street on the Lower East Side of New York. Now Pitt Street is right next to Ridge Street, and Ridge is right next to Attorney, then comes Clinton, then Norfolk, Suffolk, Essex. This might mean nothing to you, but knowing that kept your author from getting lost.

And I wasn't always George Burns. I was born Nathan Birnbaum, and when I was a kid they called me Nat. That's not all they called me. Of course, in those days I wasn't your author, I was just starting out in vaudeville and I did all kinds of acts.

I was Harry Brown of BROWN & WILLIAMS, Singers, Dancers, & Rollerskaters. I was Joe Pierce of PIERCE & GIRLIE, The Whirlwind Dancers. I did a seal act, CAPTAIN BLUE & FLIPPER. I was Captain Blue. I was Jack Harris of DUNLAP & HARRIS. I was the straight man and Dunlap was the comedian, who also turned out to be a straight man. We were the first comedy team who ever had two straight men. I was Barney Darnell . . . Maxey Kline . . . Willy Bogart . . . Lily Delight (I was also a female impersonator).

I remember I was sitting in a small-time booking office, and a theater manager came in and said, "Where can I find Maurice Stinelli?" I said, "I'm Maurice Stinelli." I thought I was.

I changed my name every week; I couldn't get a job with the same name twice. It's not that I was committing any crime, although some of the audience who saw my act might dispute that. Fortunately, in those days not many people saw my act. I don't want to knock myself, but I considered it a successful engagement if I could get through my opening song.

There are a few things I should tell you here, things I'm sure you'd want to know about your author. I must admit, for example, my left leg is an eighth of an inch longer than my right leg. But then again my right leg is an eighth of an inch shorter than my left leg. So it balances.

I drink coffee with my right hand, and I smoke cigars with my left. But I talk with both hands. Incidentally, unlike my legs, my hands are both the same size. Although I do have one ingrown cuticle. I'm ashamed to tell you which finger.

What else can I tell you? Oh yes, my sleeping habits. I average about eight hours of sleep a night. When I travel it could be less, depending on how hard the pillow is, or what's going on in the next hotel room and whether or not I've been invited.

I'm also very fussy about my teeth. I brush them twice a day, and I use dental floss religiously. But not the waxed dental floss—I can't stand that wax. This is my fifth book and I've never revealed that fact before. But these days when you write you're expected to tell everything. And there's one more thing I've never revealed before. I can't bring myself to use a plastic shoehorn—it must be metal.

I could go on, but other people see you differently than you see yourself. So here are the opinions of some of my closest friends about your author:

BOB HOPE: "The first time I saw George Burns on the stage I could see he had what it takes to become a big star—Gracie Allen."

WALTER MATTHAU: "I did *The Sunshine Boys* with George, and everything I know about acting I learned from Jack Lemmon."

JOAN RIVERS: "Since I met him ten years ago there hasn't been a day that I didn't think of George Burns. And I didn't think of him again today."

STEVE ALLEN: "I was very excited about George's last book because I thought it was."

MILTON BERLE: "I have to say this about my friend George. He looks just the same today as he looked forty years ago—old."

CAROL CHANNING: "I never make a move without calling George Burns, and I just don't know what to say about him here because his line is busy."

DANNY THOMAS: "Even when he was a kid George had lots of charisma. Then he started dating girls and the charisma cleared up."

JOHNNY CARSON: "George Burns has been on my show twenty or thirty times, or maybe more. How can you turn down a guy that age?"

DON RICKLES: "When you talk about George Burns you're talking about a living legend . . . well, a legend, anyhow."

JACK CARTER: "There's one thing you can say about George, he wears well. But so do my army shoes."

RED BUTTONS: "George Burns, what a man. He read in the paper that it takes ten dollars a year to support a kid in India. So he sent his kids there."

PHYLLIS DILLER: "I've had a crush on George for years. He's my kind of guy. He's handsome, he's successful and he's breathing."

BOB NEWHART: "The way George Burns sings, even E. F. Hutton doesn't listen."

These comments turned out to be a little embarrassing, but remember they're close friends, so naturally they're prejudiced in my favor.

Well, I don't know about you, but I'm ready to start the book; that is, as soon as I get out of here. I can't understand it. All I had last night was a bowl of chili, a couple of burritos and some refried beans.

Cedars-Sinai Medical Center
Room 811
May 24, 1984

1. GETTING TO
THE BOTTOM OF IT
(Don't Worry, I'm Not That Kind of a Doctor)

BEFORE I START handing out my prescriptions for happiness, let's see if we can pin down the diagnosis. What do we know about it?

Well, for one thing, happiness is not a disease, although it can be contagious. You don't pick it up from drinking the water, it's not inherited and it doesn't seem to be confined to any one country, race or economic class. It can be seen anywhere, but probably less among the very poor. Some say it's not too common among the very rich, either, but I can't buy that one until I see more research on it.

I like to go by what I know or have personally observed. And I've noticed some interesting things about happiness. It can come on slowly, or you may suddenly break out with a dose of it—once you've had it doesn't mean you can't have it again—and what gives it to you now may not give it to you another time. I've also noticed that even though there are no telltale marks on the body, I can immediately tell when somebody has it. There's a certain look that's unmistakable.

As to what brings it on, it's been attributed to everything from winning a horserace to riding the ninth wave on a surfboard. There are those who insist that it's at its very best during sex. I think that also needs more research, and I personally volunteer for it.

Author fully recovered and ready for work.

Putting it all together, everything I see tells me that far from being a disease, happiness is an all-too-rare condition, of short or long duration, with wonderful symptoms and not one but many causes.

Not everyone could come up with this diagnosis. But I try to keep my eyes and my mind open. I'm always learning. In fact, I learned something from this diagnosis. I just realized that my prescriptions can't be for curing your happiness; they'll have to be for helping you get it.

2. HAS
HAPPINESS HAD IT?

WHEN I WAS starting this book I ran into a friend of mine, Barry Lefkowitz. You don't know Barry Lefkowitz. Why would you? He's my friend, not yours. I don't know why I even mentioned his name. Let me start this chapter over.

When I was starting this book I ran into a friend of mine, and I made the mistake of telling him about it. "You gotta be kidding!" he screamed. "In 1984?! With all that's going on in the world, you're giving out prescriptions for happiness? You're dead in the water, man! Who can be happy today? It's over. It's yesterday's mashed potatoes! Why don't you give them a book on something really helpful, like *How to Build a Bomb Shelter*?"

It was very upsetting. I don't like being dead in the water. I'm not even sure I'd like it on the land. I don't know where I'd like it. I'm hard to please.

But my friend is not alone. Everywhere you go you hear the same thing—how can you be happy in today's world? You can't blame them. When you look around it's not the kind of a picture my girlfriend Grandma Moses would have painted.

There's crime all over the place; people shooting people for the fun of it. There are wars going on in countries they don't even know the names of. There are terrorists taking hostages, blowing up embassies and sending letters that go off in your face. There are friendly nuclear warheads stacked across the street from

Happiness is reading a good book.

enemy warheads. There are laser weapons that can blind you, nerve gases that can wipe out entire cities—and there are even worse things, but I won't mention those. It's not that I don't want to scare you—I don't want to scare myself.

The thing is, you don't have to let all this get you down. There are ways to fight it. Listen to Old Doctor Burns here; he's got a few tips for you.

First of all, skip the bad parts of the newspaper: the headlines, the editorials and mostly the news. Just read the comics, the sports pages and "Dear Abby." Don't even look at your horoscope.

And don't watch the news on TV, either. Or those prime-time soaps like "Dallas" and "Dynasty," unless you can take murder, rape, incest, glamorous, conniving women, adultery and a lot of rough sex. The Old Doctor knows what he's talking about—he's never missed one of those shows.

Stay away from all those situation comedies, too. I saw one last night I couldn't believe. It was about this kid who gave a birthday party for his friend who's an orphan and has leukemia. There wasn't a laugh in it. If they wanted to make it really funny, why didn't they give the kid a limp, too? If you must watch television, watch something nice and cheerful like "Andy Williams' Christmas Show," "Perry Como's Christmas Show," my specials, "Johnny Cash's Christmas Show," "John Denver's Christmas Show," my specials, "Mac Davis' Christmas Show," my specials.

Oh yeah—and don't go to parties with all those intellectuals who sit around analyzing the problems of the world. Go to parties where they talk about each other's clothes, the "in" restaurants, the latest gossip, why Princess Di is having another baby, who's sleeping with your girlfriend . . . stuff that can't hurt you.

It just occurred to me that my friend Barry Lefkowitz is going to feel awful that I mentioned his name and then took it out. Maybe I should have left it in, he's such a good friend. But I had to take it out, it made no sense. Why am I so worried? He probably won't even read the book.

Where was I? Oh yes, I was going to say that things these days aren't all bad. The price of gas is coming down, the hemlines are going up and despite everything people are living longer today than ever before. Which is good and bad; I have a lot more

Just cut out the bad news.

relatives to deal with, but there are more people around to buy my book.

Look, there were always things to worry about. Do you think the caveman had it so good? Sometimes we were miserable— starting fires with sticks, wall-to-wall dinosaurs, and no martinis. Believe me, when a dinosaur stares at you, you can use a martini.

Everyone talks about the good old days. I happen to be an expert on them—I was there. And it's true, we didn't have today's problems. There were no highway accidents because there were no automobiles. And there was no television, no radio, no refrigerators, electric ovens or pop-up toasters. They weren't invented yet. And if they had been invented, I wouldn't have had them anyway, because as far as my family was concerned money hadn't been invented yet, either.

If it wasn't for my grandmother, we would have been in real trouble. She used to go around to all the weddings in the neighborhood whether she was invited or not. And she wore a petticoat under her skirt that had a big, deep pocket on the right side. At these weddings she'd fill that pocket full of food. When we'd see her coming home, if she tilted to the right, we knew we had something to eat. To this day I don't enjoy chicken unless it's got a little lint on it.

My father was a wonderful man, but I guess he figured after giving my mother twelve kids he'd provided enough. He was very religious. In fact, he was a part-time cantor. During the High Holidays if the cantor caught cold and couldn't sing, my father would take his place. One year it happened. The cantor got sick so my father did the singing. The following year that same cantor got sick. Instead of sending for my father they closed the synagogue. I think I inherited my voice from my father.

This reminds me of when I first saw *The Jazz Singer*, which was about a cantor, too. It was the original Broadway version starring Georgie Jessel. This cantor wants his son to follow in his footsteps, but the boy loves show business. And at the finish of the play the father dies, the boy gives up show business, takes his father's place in the synagogue and before the last curtain he sings "Kol Nidre," which is a very sacred song.

Author watching a situation comedy on TV.

I was in the audience watching, and it affected me deeply. I sat there and cried. I thought they were doing the story of my life. And after the show I went backstage with tears in my eyes to congratulate Jessel. But the doorman said, "You can't go into his dressing room, he's got his clothes off."

I said, "I've seen a naked Jew before, I just want to tell him how great he was."

The doorman whispered, "He's got a girl in there." I was shocked. I didn't think anything could follow "Kol Nidre."

Looking back at those days when I was growing up I can see now that it wasn't a bed of roses, but at the time I thought it was. Sure, there were plenty of things to be unhappy about, but nothing bothered me. I was in show business, I had orchestrations in my key, I had pictures of myself wearing a blue suit and yellow spats. I even had my own hair in those days. I was beautiful. Of course, I didn't have too many jobs, but I was ready. One time I was ready for seven to eight months. I laid off so long that my spats faded.

In those days even if you got a job there was a clause in the contract that you could be canceled after your first performance. I'll never forget once I was booked into the Farley Theater in Brooklyn. Monday morning at nine o'clock I was rehearsing my music. The manager heard my rehearsal and canceled me. I was the only actor in show business who was ever canceled before he opened.

Another time somehow I was booked into the Gem Theater on Houston Street, which was on the Lower East Side of New York. I got a contract to play three days for $15—$5 a day—and the contract had a no-cancellation clause in it.

Well, after the matinee when I came off the stage the manager was waiting for me. He said, "Look, kid, that act of yours can close my theater. You're booked here for three days for fifteen dollars. Here's the fifteen—go home."

I said, "Not me, I'm booked here for three days and I'm going to play the three days."

He said, "I'll give you twenty—go home."

I said, "All right, so you didn't like my first show. For the next show I'll change my songs. I'll open with 'Tiger Girl,' and then I'll

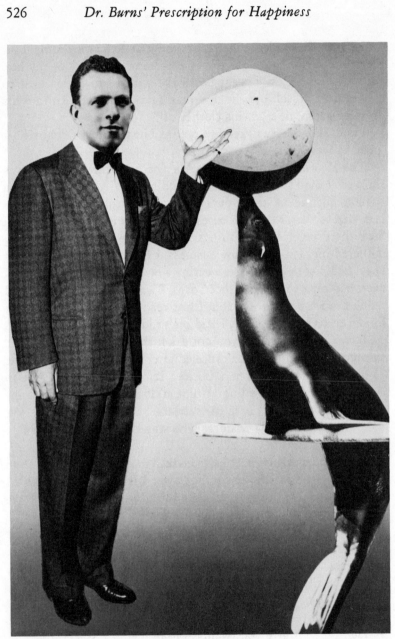

Author and partner in the "good old days."

sing 'In the Heart of a Cherry,' and then I'll do my big closing number, 'I'll Be Waiting for You, Bill, When You Come Back from San Juan Hill.'"

He said, "I'll make it twenty-five."

I said, "No, sir, I'm staying. I'm a performer and I can prove it. I've even got cards printed."

He said, "Okay, kid, you can stay, but give me back your key to the men's room."

I did, but that was kind of bad because that's where I was dressing. And let me tell you something. When you don't go to the men's room for three days it doesn't help your singing any. In fact, after the second day I didn't dare do my yodeling finish.

Oddly enough, for me those were happy times. And I have a hunch that fifty years from now they'll be saying, "Why can't we be happy like those lucky people in the good old 1980s?"

It's an interesting thought. I wonder if they'll really be saying that. I can hardly wait to find out.

Monday's Prescription

Dr. George Burns, H.S.
(HAPPINESS SPECIALIST)

DATE_____

NAME_____

ADDRESS_____

<u>One Hot Tub</u> *Monday*

Take with 1 blonde -- accompanied
by soft music and tall drink.

Repeat as desired.

If unable to get blonde, get
brunette.

If unable to get blonde or
brunette, take cold shower.

GB   R

Dr. Burns giving a patient a shot.

NINE DEFINITIONS OF HAPPINESS

Lists are very popular these days. There are lists on everything. And they're always ten—ten best this, ten best that. So to be a little different I decided to make my list nine. And it wasn't easy; it took me hours to figure out which one to leave out.

Anyway, here they are:
Happiness is:

1. Having a large, loving, caring, close-knit family; especially if they live in another city.
2. Hearing your proctologist say, "You can straighten up now."
3. Taking your car to the garage for a lube and oil, and getting it back with just a lube and oil.
4. Hearing your teenage kid say, "Dad, you're right." (My son Ronnie is forty-nine and I'm still waiting.)
5. Having a legitimate excuse for not attending a bar mitzvah.
6. Being stopped by a mean-looking 240-pound motorcycle cop and having him compliment you on your driving.
7. Telling your favorite joke without having Milton Berle beat you to the punch line.
8. A good martini, a good meal, a good cigar and a good woman . . . or a bad woman, depending on how much happiness you can stand.
9. Retaining your mental and physical powers despite advancing years. (I feel very fortunate. At eighty-eight I can do everything I could do when I was eighty-seven.)

Three more definitions of happiness.

3. YOU CAN'T GET THERE WITH SHORTCUTS UNLESS YOU'RE A BUTCHER

REMEMBER THAT SONG called "The Best Things in Life Are Free"? I sang it at the Odeon Theater on Pitt Street on the Lower East Side of New York. When I sang it I used to follow the bouncing ball. The manager at the Odeon didn't like my singing so he had the ball bounce out into the street. And when I followed it out to finish my song he wouldn't let me back in. That story isn't true. The Odeon Theater was not on Pitt Street, it was on Clinton Street.

Anyway, it was a good song and a nice thought, but it wasn't true then and it isn't true now. If a pair of jockey shorts can cost $4, how can the best things in life be free? Look, good health, a good marriage, good kids, self-respect, pride of accomplishment, they don't fall into your lap. You have to work at them a little.

It's a shame, but there are no shortcuts to happiness. Everyone's in a hurry these days. They want things prepackaged, precanned or prefabricated. It's called modern living. You go into the supermarket and buy boxes and plastic containers of artificially flavored, seasoned and colored food. Then you get into your car with the simulated leather seats and drive home to your prefabricated house. Everybody wants things instantly. Not me. I want things to last for a while. At my age if it's over too fast, I forget what it was I did, or why I did it, or whom I did it with.

It's amazing the routes some people take to get to happiness. Like drinking—and I'm not talking about drinking, I'm talking about DRINKING! The problem with that kind of drinking is, the people who do it usually don't know the condition they're in.

I remember I was on the Pantages circuit with Jack Whitehead, a monologist, and the opening act was a dancing team called The Gliding Gascoynes. And Gascoyne and Whitehead did a lot of drinking together. One night they really got bombed, and Gascoyne passed out in his dressing room. Whitehead sent for the doctor, and when Whitehead came out of the room, I said, "How's Gascoyne?"

He said, "He's really in bad shape. The doctor said to him, 'Do you see any pink elephants or green snakes?' and Gascoyne said, 'No.' And the room was full of 'em."

There have been some pretty good drinkers in show business: John Barrymore, Joe E. Lewis, Phil Harris, Dean Martin. The last time I saw Dean in a nightclub he staggered out on stage with a glass of booze in his hand, turned to his piano player and said, "How long have I been on?" It got a big laugh, but I don't think Dean drinks as much as he says he does. Nobody can drink that much. As a matter of fact, here's a true story. A woman jumped up on the stage one night, grabbed the drink out of Dean's hand and drank it. She said, "This isn't booze—you're drinking tea!" Dean looked at her and said, "Lady, you're drunker than I am." I hope I didn't just put the kid out of business.

Look, I drink a couple of martinis now and then. It's not to escape from anything—I enjoy it. If I come home at the end of the day and my help doesn't have a martini waiting for me, it's not the end of the world. It might be the end of my help, but that's a different story.

To some people it's not the drinking they enjoy, it's the ritual that goes with it. Some years ago José Ferrer moved into Beverly Hills, and one night I dropped in about nine o'clock to say hello. He asked me if I'd like a martini and I said sure. Now when I make a martini I take an old-fashioned glass, fill it with ice, then fill it

Author having his daily martini.

with gin, put in some vermouth, and in two seconds I've got a martini.

But not José. First he got a snifter glass big enough to swim in, took three jiggers of gin and slowly rolled them down the side of the glass. Then he took an eyedropper filled with vermouth and carefully rolled two drops down the other side of the snifter. Then he took one ice cube and a spoon and gently lowered it into the glass so as not to bruise the gin. Then he took the snifter glass in both hands and rocked it back and forth until the cube of ice melted. I went home at eleven o'clock and he was still making that martini.

I went back to pay him a visit three months later and he said, "George, can I make you a martini?" I said, "I haven't got time, I'm booked to play Vegas in two weeks."

Another shortcut that's being taken more and more these days is drugs: grass, acid, coke, speed, angel dust, 'ludes and heroin. Even prescription drugs like Valium, Percodan, Codeine, all sorts of amphetamines and barbiturates. People don't go to church anymore for peace of mind, they run to their pharmacy.

No one really knows how many people are on drugs these days. There are many surveys being taken, but they're unreliable—half the people taking the surveys are stoned. Our government is spending billions of dollars to put a few people into space. From what I can see the problem isn't getting people into space, it's getting them out of it. There are kids in school today on drugs. They can't have fire drills anymore—the minute a bell rings, the kids think they're being busted.

Some of our biggest athletes, the ones we should be looking up to and admiring, are users. It used to be that a good score meant you won the game by a comfortable margin. Now a good score means you made a hell of a "buy." I read about a quarterback who got caught using drugs before a game. Of course, if I had to go out there and face those 290-pound linemen, I'd probably want to be in another world, too. But what good is a drug that after you take it you can't find your fingers?

Look, I've been around a long time, and drugs have been around a long time. I don't use drugs, that's why I've been around a long time. I'm even afraid to take a laxative more than two days in a row.

When drugs became such a big thing out here on the West Coast I didn't know what they were talking about. A lot of people said they were smoking grass, so I thought I'd try it. I went out on the lawn, pulled up a handful of grass, pushed it into my cigar holder and lit it. It was nothing, but the fertilizer was murder.

I went to one of those parties without knowing it. I was hardly in the door when one of the guests came up to me and said, "George, have you got any junk on you?" I said, "No, I give it all to the Salvation Army." It was the first time I ever saw anyone with two heads look at me like I had three.

Later at dinner this attractive young girl sitting next to me leaned over and said, "George, do you ever use uppers?" I said, "What for, I've got my own teeth."

The woman on the other side of me started to laugh and said, "She's talking about those uppers and downers." I said, "Oh, 'The Uppers and Downers'? I've never seen them. Where are they playing?" They all thought I was trying to be funny. They didn't know I had never been to a party like that.

At the end of the meal out came a bowl of white powder surrounded by a lot of little silver spoons. Well, I like my coffee sweet, so I put in three or four spoonfuls. The next thing I knew the host was showing me to the door. And you won't believe this—I was never invited back.

These shortcuts to happiness all turn out to be dead ends. That's true not only of drinking and drugs, but also of gambling.

I see how you can get hooked on drugs or booze. Both are habit-forming and very difficult to give up. But compulsive gambling is something else again. How intelligent, often successful people can keep on losing and losing until they've lost everything is beyond me. I once heard a psychiatrist explain that the compulsive gambler has a subconscious desire to lose. What he really wants is not a big win, but a big loss.

I didn't believe that until the wife of a big gambler I know told me that when her husband comes home and mopes around she knows he's won a few thousand. If he comes home smiling, she knows he's lost the car or a bank account. And if he's laughing, it's time to start packing—the house is gone.

So maybe the psychiatrist was right. I do know that compulsive gamblers don't quit. This same fellow swore to me recently that he was all through—he'd promised his wife and there would be no more gambling. I said to him, "Come on, you said that same thing a dozen times."

"This time, George," he said, "it's different. I'm through gambling. I'm finished."

I said, "I'll bet you ten dollars you're not through gambling." And he said, "Okay, you got a bet."

This may come as a shock to you. Jack Benny gambled. I was standing right next to him at a table in Las Vegas one night when he held the dice for three-quarters of an hour. Finally I said, "Throw 'em, already!" So he did, crapped out, lost five dollars and we had to hold *him* for three-quarters of an hour.

After a while I went to bed, but Jack stayed there and gambled all night. When I came down to the casino the next morning there he was at the same table. By then he was out ten dollars. But it didn't bother him. He figured it was still cheaper than renting a room.

Actually, when you count all the free drinks and all the cigars they gave him, he wasn't out ten dollars, he was ahead twenty dollars. Wait a minute, he had to tip all those cocktail waitresses. So he was only ahead about $19.00 . . . maybe $18.50. I don't know—I was sleeping at the time.

I play Lake Tahoe and Las Vegas a lot. In fact, I just signed a contract with Caesars for five years. They wanted to make it twenty, but I wasn't sure Caesars would be around that long. I just played Tahoe and the gambling is unbelievable. People come in by the busload and head right for the casino. They're at the tables and slot machines night and day. I was the only one who knew there was a lake out there. Even young couples who come up there do nothing but gamble all day. Sex is like the lake; nobody knows it's there. I know it's there. At my age I'm stuck with the lake.

In the dining room if you see a young attractive couple, and if the man has his hand under the table, he's counting his chips. If her hand is under the table, she's counting his chips, too. It might be fun—I wouldn't know. I haven't had my hand under a table, January 20 will be thirty-one years. But if you're interested, the

That's me at one of those parties.

lake is 192 square miles, 1644 feet deep and has 71 miles of shoreline.

It's the same thing in Vegas. The last time I was there a honeymoon couple was staying in the room next to mine. They'd been there five days. They went down and played blackjack, lost all their money and couldn't afford to get married.

I don't even know why people bring their children there. Last year a man and wife arrived and the first thing they did was put their kids in the pool. They went straight to the dice table and won forty thousand dollars. Then they took a trip around the world, came back six months later, dried the kids off and took them home. They had two of the cleanest, most shriveled-up kids you've ever seen.

The thing about gambling is you can't beat Lady Luck. I knew a girl from Cleveland, she was a stripper who called herself Lady Luck. Believe me, she didn't give anything away for free. Well, she wasn't exactly from Cleveland, she was born in Akron and moved to Cleveland. I think that was the way it went. I was sleeping at the time—no, no, you're wrong. I was sleeping alone.

Anyway, what I've been trying to say is there are no shortcuts to happiness. I don't know any shortcuts to anything. If I did, this chapter wouldn't be so long.

You can't lose gambling like this. From *Going in Style* with Art Carney.

He must be a good doctor—he's got a stethoscope.

Tuesday's Prescription

Dr. George Burns, H.S.
(Happiness Specialist)

DATE_____

NAME_____

ADDRESS_____

Tuesday

For attacks of worry and anxiety --
1 hour brisk morning walk --
Stop 20 minutes to smell flowers.

May augment by singing in
shower, whistling in elevators
and dancing in the dark.

If still no relief, try mineral
oil.

GB   ℞

---

4. AS THE SAYING GOES . . .

THERE ARE A lot of highly respected, time-honored sayings and expressions about happiness, and may I tell you something, we'd be just as well off without them. They all sound good, but when you stop to analyze them they don't make any more sense than the ones on other subjects.

For example, how many times have you heard someone say, "He's happy as a clam"? You've probably said it yourself. I know I have. "Happy as a clam." Who knows how happy a clam is? He might be miserable. He might be very bored stuck in that same shell all his life. And maybe he can't stand all that sand up his bivalves. Yeah, bivalves—look it up like I did.

Or you'll hear: "I'm in a bad mood. I got up on the wrong side of the bed this morning." A bed is a bed. What's the difference which side you get up on? And if it bothers you to get up on one side, get up on the other. Personally, I don't care which side of the bed I get up on. I'm happy just getting up.

"Happy is as happy does." That's one I've been hearing all my life and I still don't know what it means. I wouldn't even put that in a fortune cookie.

And what about this piece of advice: "Let a smile be your umbrella." I tried that once. I had pneumonia for six weeks and shrunk a $450 suit.

And here's another beauty. "Laugh and the world laughs with

you." Try going around laughing all the time. Not only won't the world laugh with you, you'll end up doing your laughing in a straitjacket.

They make it sound so simple and so easy. Who are "they"? If they're so smart, why don't "they" identify themselves? "Laugh and the world laughs with you." When I do my next TV special, instead of hiring writers and a lot of guest stars, why don't I just stand there and laugh for an hour? It would be very entertaining; I'd be a riot. It's too bad I don't know who comes up with these great sayings. I don't know who to thank.

Now, "Money can't buy happiness"—that's not bad. The Rockefellers, the J. P. Morgans, the Fords, they're not happy— they just look happy. I can go along with the idea that just having money doesn't guarantee that you'll be happy. But then they tell us that "Money is the root of all evil." From just not buying happiness, money suddenly becomes the worst thing in the world. I mean, isn't that going pretty far? If money is the root of all evil, what happened to adultery and jealousy, and spoiled meat and all the other bad stuff?

But okay, let's say they're right: "Money is the root of all evil." Then we hear, "A fool and his money are soon parted." What are they talking about? If money is so evil, shouldn't it be, "A wise man and his money are soon parted"? And another thing, how does a fool get money in the first place? I know some fools who have a lot of money, but they won't tell me how they got it, and I won't tell them.

These sayings drive you crazy. What are you supposed to go by: "Look before you leap" or "He who hesitates is lost"? The other day I was crossing an intersection in Beverly Hills and stopped in the middle to decide whether to leap or hesitate, and a kid hit me in the rear end with a bicycle.

"Pride goeth before a fall." Wrong. A banana peel goeth before a fall. "You can't judge a book by its cover." What else are you going to judge it by? Suppose this book had a cover that said "Holy Bible." Wait, that's not such a bad idea. The Bible sells pretty good. It's the only thing I know that gets into more hotel rooms than Lily Delight.

"A penny saved is a penny earned." Big deal. You can put that one with "An ounce of prevention is worth a pound of cure." That was fine during the Depression when you could get a steak for a nickel. Today I don't know where you could get even a quarter of an ounce of prevention for a pound of cure.

I say we're better off ignoring all these one-line gems. So we won't make a stitch in time and save nine. We'll only save eight. And maybe we can't make a silk purse out of a sow's ear, but look at the fun we'll have trying.

Maybe you don't agree with me. Maybe you think this whole chapter was a waste of time. Well, so do I. But then again, it's not as though you laid out twenty or thirty dollars for the book. Don't forget—as that wise old saying goes, "You get what you pay for."

168 years of Happiness.

THE NINE HAPPIEST MEN I'VE KNOWN

1. JACK BENNY: That is, when he was with me. He never stopped laughing. If I said anything, he fell on the floor. If I didn't say anything, he fell on the floor. His suits were always at the cleaners.
2. ME: When I made Jack, one of the world's greatest comedians, laugh. He made me feel like I was nine feet tall. In fact, he had me so convinced I almost became a basketball player.
3. BOB HOPE: Bob has a knack for making the best of a bad situation. While we were all here with our families every Christmas, there was Bob, stuck in some camp 10,000 miles from home with only a Marilyn Monroe, Raquel Welch, Loni Anderson, assorted starlets and beauty queens to pass the time with. But Bob didn't complain, he was happy doing it for his country.
4. MILTON BERLE: It's no accident Milton Berle's so happy. He's got a reason, a good reason. I know, because I have the locker next to his at our club. Some of us get applause when we go onstage; Milton gets applause when he goes to the shower.
5. DON RICKLES: Contrary to his image, Don is one of the nicest, most cheerful, contented and well-adjusted guys I know. But if he asks me once more to marry his mother, I'm going to sew up that big mouth of his.
5. HOWARD COSELL: (alternate) Like Rickles, Howard is not what you see. He's a modest, soft-spoken, gentle soul who never criticizes and loves everything and everybody. He's also five inches taller with his shoes off and has a beautiful head of hair under that thing he's wearing.
6. AL JOLSON: Why wouldn't he be happy? He was the world's greatest entertainer in just about everyone's opinion, including his.
7. CALVIN COOLIDGE: Of all the Presidents I've known, Calvin Coolidge had the best sense of humor. I thought he was even funnier than Herbert Hoover.
8. BENJAMIN FRANKLIN: Ben was really something. He was always flying kites. He'd keep four or five kites on a string. That's not all he kept on a string. You don't think he spent all his time writing *Poor Richard's Almanack*, do you?

9. JULIUS CAESAR: There was a guy who appreciated good entertainment. If Julius liked you, there was nothing he wouldn't do for you. If he didn't, he'd throw you to the lions. I've got claw marks to prove it.

Spencer Tracy and Maurice Chevalier with two great actors.

THE NINE HAPPIEST WOMEN I'VE KNOWN

The Wives and Girlfriends of Milton Berle!

The doctor's caddy.

Wednesday's Prescription

DR. GEORGE BURNS, H.S.
(HAPPINESS SPECIALIST)

DATE_____

NAME_____

ADDRESS_____

Wednesday

No prescription today.

Doctor is on golf course.

℞

---

5. IS AGGRAVATION A NO-NO? YES-YES!

(It's Not Easy to Think of a Funny Title)

Do YOU KNOW the difference between irritation and aggravation? You don't? Well, I'm going to tell you. The other day I was sitting by my pool getting a little sun when the phone rang. I ran into the house, picked up the phone and a voice on the other end said, "Is Harry there?" So I said, "You've got the wrong number," and went back to the pool. Twenty minutes later the phone rang again. I ran in, grabbed the phone, again the same thing—"Is Harry there?" I said, "Listen, you've got the wrong number!" A half hour later the same thing happened. "Is Harry there?" That's irritation.

Now this is aggravation! Again the phone rang, and this time I heard, "This is Harry. Were there any messages for me?"

That didn't really happen to me. That's a story that was going around a few years ago. I told it because after that weak title I thought it would be nice to start off with something really funny, because the chapter's about irritation and aggravation, and because there happens to be a difference between the two. Ordinarily a comedian doesn't have to give three reasons for telling a funny story. But I'm not just a comedian now. In case you've forgotten, I'm also Dr. Burns—Old Dr. Burns.

Anyway, to me irritation is something that makes your skin red. Aggravation is paying the pharmacy $12.50 for something to cure the irritation, and when you get the bottle home you can't open it.

Right there we may have one of the major aggravations of 20th-century America. Nothing opens. Jars are impossible. Peanut butter, jam, pickles, those lids are on to stay. My thumb has never been the same since I tried to twist a new jar of peanut butter open. They tell you to put warm water over it and pound the lid. I tried that with a jar of mayonnaise. I pounded the lid on the kitchen sink, broke the jar, had mayonnaise all over the sink, but the lid stayed on.

In restaurants sugar used to be in a bowl. Pepper and salt were in shakers. Now it's all wrapped in cellophane. The crackers are wrapped, the mustard, the ketchup, the butter—the only thing that isn't wrapped is the check. Maybe you can get all that stuff open with your fingers, but I can't. I have to bite it and my teeth aren't that great. I'd like to save them for the food.

What I can't get over, they're even doing it with fertilizer. Not too many fertilizer bags come in cellophane, but try to undo the thick string they've woven through that heavy paper. Come on, it's fertilizer, it's not the Romanoff jewels! Let us at it!

Prescriptions are the worst of all. The regular bottles were bad enough, but when they started making them child-proof, did it ever occur to them they were also making them senior citizen-proof! Jack La Lanne couldn't open one of those bottles, what chance have I got! I realize we don't want the kiddies munching on our nitroglycerin pills, but if I'm having a heart attack I don't want to stand there for twenty minutes trying to figure out the combination.

There are a lot of other aggravations that we have to put up with these days. Just one by itself may not be too bad, but when you put them all together it spells MOTHER—No, no, that's a song I used to sing. What I meant to say was when you put them all together you begin to feel like Don Knotts looks. And when you're that upset and uptight you're anything but happy.

Probably the biggest single cause of tension headaches in America, and maybe in the world, is everyday city traffic. There's nothing like two hours of bumper-to-bumper on a Los Angeles freeway to send your blood pressure up fifty points. And that's when you're out there for pleasure. How about when you're a half hour late to your job, or an important meeting, or a doctor's appointment to check your blood pressure? And how do you calm yourself down when the greatest date of your life is ten miles away and you're moving two inches a minute? By the time you get there she's married and has two kids.

Some of our best inventions can be the most aggravating. Computers, for example. They save time, but has anybody ever added up the hours millions of people spend every day trying to correct the errors made by those computers? They shouldn't bother. Computer errors don't get corrected; they're there forever. There's a $185 charge that was added by mistake to one of my credit card statements. I've pointed it out to them, they've acknowledged it, but every month it's there. And the interest on it keeps increasing. But what am I complaining about, it's only been going on for sixty-two years. I have to admit that's a lie. I enjoy telling lies. You see, when I lie I tell you it's a lie. That means it's not a lie, which is not true.

And I don't know about you, but I could do without all those new telephone-answering machines. I happen to prefer being face to face with whomever I'm talking to. I like to see how my stuff is going over. I've never been comfortable with a telephone, and that dates all the way back to that first call when Alexander Graham Bell said, "George, can you hear me?"

So you can imagine how I feel talking to an answering machine. And what frustrates me even more is waiting for that wise guy on the cassette to finish his monologue. Why does everyone with an answering machine think he has to do ten minutes? And if he's going to be so funny, let him hire writers like I did for mine.

The latest thing is these gadgets that talk to you. You can now be awakened by a talking alarm clock and then go into the bathroom and have your talking scale tell you that you're overweight. In the kitchen a talking toaster asks you how you prefer your toast, the coffeemaker asks you how strong you want the coffee, and the refrigerator informs you you're out of bread and coffee. The only one not talking to you is your wife. You bought all this stuff and she wanted a fur coat.

Gadgets have their place, but we've OD'd on them. We used to need big houses because we had big families. Now we need them for all the equipment we own. I'm not knocking these inventions. They save steps and they make life easier and more enjoyable, but they also break down. Sometimes two or three at a time. And that's real aggravation, because they have yet to come up with the invention we need the most: a repairman who will show up the day he said he would.

A few years ago I got one of those automatic garage door openers. It still works, only lately it's been opening my neighbor's garage instead of mine. But then his started opening mine instead of his. So Daniel, the male half of the couple who works for me, offered to take both the openers and have them fixed.

"That's silly," I said. "Why don't I just put my car in his garage and let him put his car in mine? We'll trade garages."

"You could do that," he said. And then as I was wondering why I have to think of everything, he added, "But it would be simpler to just trade openers."

Sometimes I think I should be working for him. Sometimes I think he shares that opinion. Well, it would never work out. I couldn't live on what I pay him. And I could never do for Daniel and Arlette the things they do for me. Somehow they manage to handle most of the household problems that come up. That spares me a lot of the daily aggravation most of you probably experience.

Not that there isn't plenty left for me. It's very annoying to have to hold my own martini glass. Those things are heavy, especially with an olive in it. And how about putting a cigar into my holder fifteen times a day? It takes both hands. I've got to put down my martini glass to do it. And what good is getting a cigar into your holder if you run out of matches? I tried to use a lighter, but my thumb was still sore from trying to open that peanut butter jar.

Look, I don't believe in aggravation. I don't let it keep me up nights. When I go to bed nothing bothers me. If it does, I tell her to leave.

For most people, dealing with aggravation doesn't seem to be that simple. Almost everyone I know in Hollywood has been to at least one psychiatrist. But that's becoming old hat. There are all sorts of new ways to go. Jogging is still "in," and memberships in health clubs have skyrocketed. Pumping iron, riding exercise bicy-

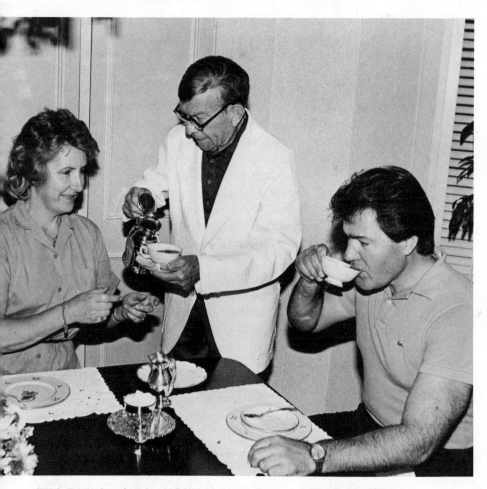

With Daniel and Arlette. It's not easy to keep good help these days.

cles that don't go anywhere, and jumping up and down to disco music are helping millions of people reduce the stress and tension in their lives, as well as the money in their wallets.

Then there's a thing called biofeedback. Don't ask me what that is. For all I know, biofeedback is what happens when your food repeats on you.

The other night I was watching one of those magazine shows on television, and they were demonstrating some other ways of escaping the aggravations in everyday life. One couple had built themselves a chamber in their garage for something called "primal screaming." You get into this big box, shut it tight and scream your lungs out until all the tension disappears or your neighbors ask you to move. This would do nothing for me. I take that back. It would probably hurt my vocal cords, and I'm a country singer.

Another group on the show was into something called "Somati tanks." They're all the rage in Los Angeles. They're also called sensory deprivation tanks. I thought Somati tanks were something they used to hold fresh fish for Japanese food. You float in this dark tank filled with water at body temperature. The idea is to remove yourself from the outside world and concentrate only on your inner self. The peace and quiet helps you relax and get in touch with yourself.

Being the adventurous soul that I am, I thought I'd try it. I filled my bathtub with lukewarm water, fixed myself a martini, lit a cigar, turned out the lights and got in. Then I had another martini, and then another. You know, I think Somati might really have something there.

I don't know if meditation is as big as it was a few years ago, but it still has lots of followers who practice it faithfully. Marsha Mason is one of the true believers. She says that meditation has changed her life, that it has given her spiritual strength and inner peace. As busy as she is with her career, she finds time for frequent trips to India to visit with her guru.

Which reminds me of the story about Mrs. Goldberg, who goes to her travel agent in Brooklyn and says she wants to fly to Nepal. He asks her if this is her first trip to Asia and she says it is. He tells her there are lots of other places there she would be better off seeing, but she insists on going to Nepal.

So she gets to Nepal, and right away she wants to go up the mountain where the guru is. They all tell her it's a tough trip up the mountain, but she doesn't care—that's where she wants to go. So they round up some donkeys, get her up the mountain, and she announces she wants to see the guru. They tell her this is not the guru's visiting hours; he's contemplating in privacy. She says she came all the way to see the guru and she wants to see the guru. She carries on so much they finally go and get the guru, and Mrs. Goldberg takes a look at him in his beard, robe and sandals, and says, "Sheldon, you look ridiculous. Put on a decent suit and come home already!"

I don't know why I'm suddenly so full of stories. I never tell other people's stories on the stage. I get my laughs the old-fashioned way, I *earn* them.

For those of you who believe in meditation, I didn't mean to offend you. I don't happen to believe in meditation, but I know something about it because a girl I went out with some time ago spent half the dinner talking about it. She told me she had been into it since it started in the sixties. I didn't have the heart to tell her meditation was actually a few thousand years old. I didn't want to give away my age.

She asked me if I had a mantra. I said no, but I had a cat. She explained that a mantra is something you hum when you're meditating, and she started humming. "Ommmmmmmmmmmmmmmm . . . Ommmmmmmmmmmmm . . . Ommmmmmmmmmmmm." It wasn't bad, but personally I'd rather listen to Julio Iglesias.

When we got back to my house she said if I got down on the floor she'd show me the lotus position and we'd do it together. It sounded exciting, but when we sat on the floor she explained this was meditation yoga style. She said I'd have to think of a word I could concentrate on, and she folded her legs like a pretzel and told me to do the same. I asked if she didn't think this was pretty silly. She said she didn't. And I said I didn't either, I thought it was stupid. That must have upset her, because before I could get up she was out the door and gone.

As long as I was on the floor I figured I might as well try it. Maybe there was something to this after all. So I folded my legs like a pretzel and tried to think of a word. After a half hour I tried to unfold my legs but I was stuck. Then the word came to me. It was "Help!" But nobody heard me—Daniel and Arlette were away for the weekend. So I dragged myself over to the telephone and called the fire department. They were just terrific. They rushed right over, smashed in the door, untangled my legs and the whole thing took only five minutes. The new door cost me $800.

Dr. Burns operating.

Thursday's Prescription

DR. GEORGE BURNS, H.S.
(HAPPINESS SPECIALIST)

DATE_____

NAME_____

ADDRESS_____

Thursday

Pay wife big compliment before bedtime.

If results indicate, repeat each night thereafter until out of compliments or strength.

GB

℞

6. A HOBBY CAN BE FUN

(Especially If Your Wife Doesn't Find Out)

I'VE ALWAYS SUSPECTED that people who have hobbies were happier than people who didn't. A few days ago to find out if I was right, I took my own private poll. I stood on the corner of Wilshire and Rodeo Drive, stopped ten people passing by and asked them if they had a hobby. Seven told me to mind my own business, and the other three didn't speak English. I guess Dr. Gallup must use a different corner.

But I still say, if you have something that holds your interest, something that you can throw yourself into and get your mind off your work for a few hours a day, it has to be good for you.

There's a famous old story, about a theater manager who comes out just before the curtain and says, "There'll be no show tonight, our leading man just passed away." Some guy in the balcony hollers, "Give him an enema!" The manager says, "He's dead, how would that help?" The guy shouts back, "It wouldn't hurt!"

It's the same with a hobby. It can't hurt and it might be very helpful. If you live by yourself, a hobby can give you something to occupy your time. If you're married, a hobby can be something for you and your wife to share. If you're happily married, you might not need a hobby. And if you're dating a different girl every night, you have enough hobbies as it is.

I have a daily routine that I never deviate from. I may have mentioned this in a previous book. One of these days I'm going to have to sit down and read my books so I'll know what I've said before. There may be stuff I've repeated. And if it was worth repeating once, I can certainly repeat it again. Anyway, I get to my office every day at ten in the morning, work with my writers as hard as I can on whatever has to be done, and at twelve sharp, no matter where we are, even if I'm in the middle of a sentence, I drop everything and head for the Hillcrest Country Club. I have lunch there, and then from one until three I play bridge. This is my hobby and it's been going on for years.

Not everyone at my golf club plays bridge. Some play gin rummy, some play poker, some play pinochle, some play casino. One or two even play golf.

I used to play golf. I took lessons, had expensive clubs, nice knickers, but it didn't work out. For one thing, nobody wanted to play with me. The problem was if I was playing well, I'd sing. That would annoy the other golfers. If I was playing badly, I'd sing even louder to keep my mind off my lousy game. So you see, I wasn't too popular to play with.

I played with Harpo Marx all the time, and I remember once when he parred the first hole, got a birdie on the second and parred the third. That was the best start he ever had. I didn't sing. I didn't smoke, I didn't breathe. I didn't want to do anything to upset him.

The next hole was a par 5 and his third shot went into a sand trap on top of a hill. And to keep out of his way I stayed at the bottom of the hill. He got all set for his next shot, then he stopped and looked down at me. He said, "Why are you standing down there?"

I said, "I didn't want to distract you."

"Well," he said, "that's exactly what you're doing. Come up here and just act natural."

So I went up there, but I was afraid even to look at him. Again he stopped his swing and said, "Why aren't you looking at me?"

So I looked at him. He swung and missed the ball completely. Then he came at me with his 9-iron and chased me into the clubhouse. When we got there we had coffee and cheesecake, I sang him a song, he harmonized with me and that was the end of it.

Another time I was playing with Lou Clayton of Clayton, Jackson and Durante. He was a very good golfer, but on the second nine he shanked a 2-iron into the lake. It upset him so much that he picked up his big bag with all those beautiful clubs and threw them into the lake, too. I couldn't believe it. I said to him, "Lou, why do you play golf?" And he said, "It relaxes me."

I was never a good golfer. It aggravated me that I couldn't break a hundred, that I couldn't come home and tell Gracie I shot an eighty. So one day I came home and told Gracie I shot an eighty and I felt better. And then I found out I didn't have to play golf at all, I could play bridge and come home and say I shot an eighty.

That's when I gave up golf as a hobby and took up bridge. And for me it's been the perfect outlet. Every hand's a new challenge, and it takes complete concentration. You forget everything else. Sometimes I forget I'm playing bridge I concentrate so hard.

One day I was on my way to the game and I passed one of our former club presidents. He said, "Hello, George," and I said, "Hello, kid." This annoyed him, and he said, "George, we've both been members of this club for over fifty years, and every time I see you I say, 'Hello, George.' and you say 'Hello, kid.' I'll bet you don't even know my name."

"Of course I do," I said. "I just don't know how to spell it."

He said, "S-C-H-I-F-F."

"Oh," I said, "so that's how you spell Schiff."

He said, "That's right, kid," and walked away.

Now I'm going to tell you about the fellows I play bridge with. You're not going to believe this so you better hold on to your book. I don't want you to fall down. It's quite a group. We're all about the same age, but some of the boys are hard of hearing and wear hearing aids. And one of them is very forgetful. He has that thing in his ear but keeps forgetting the battery. So I said to him, "Artie, a hearing aid without a battery isn't much of an aid." He said, "Thanks, George, and you look good, too."

One day we were playing and two of them forgot their hearing aids and the other one had a cold. I opened the first hand with a bid of one spade; the opponent to my left said a heart; my partner said one diamond; and the fourth guy said a club. I said, "Goodbye, gentlemen, we'll play tomorrow." And Artie said, "Thanks, George, and you look good, too."

Another time I was playing with the same group. They were all in great shape; they had their batteries, their hearing aids, they had cleaned their glasses and nobody had a cold. They were really ready. And Artie was my partner. Our opponents had a sensational hand and bid seven no-trump. Artie was in the lead and he laid down the ace of spades. I said, "Why the hell didn't you double?" He said, "I was afraid they would go into another suit." I said, "Thanks, Artie, and you look good, too."

Another tremendous hand I remember; this one was about eight or nine years ago when I was playing with three men who

Thought you'd like to see the three old guys I play with.

were much older than I was. One of the guys I was playing against opened with two spades, my partner passed, and his partner said four no-trump, asking for aces. The original bidder said five hearts, showing two aces. His partner had everything else, so he said, "Seven spades." Then very quietly I said, "Gentlemen, count your cards." There was silence for about a minute. The original bidder put a nitroglycerin pill under his tongue, and his partner said, "I'll take one, too." Then he very slowly counted his cards and said, "I've got thirteen." My partner said he had thirteen. The other opponent was shaking so I had to count his cards—he had thirteen. Then I counted mine, and said, "I've got thirteen, too, let's continue the game." And after the paramedics revived them, we did.

Incidentally, for those of you who don't understand bridge, I should tell you if you write to the publisher, you're not going to get your money back. But I'll make it up to you. Here's something you'll understand, it's a quickie. This ninety-year-old man was arrested and charged with rape. He was so flattered he pleaded guilty. That's the end of the joke.

Now back to hobbies. Wait—one more bridge story. Chico Marx, who loved to gamble, went into a bridge club in San Francisco, and except for four fellows playing bridge the place was empty. It was a game where you couldn't cut in unless one of the players quit. So Chico took one of them aside and whispered, "You're being cheated. That guy in the blue suit, when he holds his cigarette on the left side of his mouth that means he's got clubs. When he puts the cigarette in the center of his mouth that means he's got diamonds. If it's on the right side, he's got hearts, and when he doesn't put the cigarette in his mouth at all that means spades." The man thanked Chico profusely, quit the game, Chico took his place, lost $1200 and had a great afternoon.

Back to hobbies. To be a good hobby it should hold your interest. And if you get a sense of satisfaction from it, so much the better. Painting, sculpting, carving, furniture making, glass blowing—they all make great hobbies. The more you do them the better you get, and the better you get the more pleasure they give you.

Photography also makes an excellent hobby. It takes knowledge, patience and a sense of what makes an interesting composition. It also takes a camera. I'm not knocking photographers, but I've always felt that if I snapped a thousand pictures of a hummingbird, I too would end up with one that everybody would rave about. I must say photography is not for me. If I'm going into a dark room for three hours to see what develops, it certainly won't be with a lot of hummingbirds.

But that's me. Photography enthusiasts love their hobby. Some of them are in dark rooms so much they grow fungus. And there's nothing they won't do to get a good picture. I was in the men's room of the Beverly-Wilshire Hotel recently, doing what you do in men's rooms, when all of a sudden there was a flash. And there is this guy with a Polaroid taking my picture. I was very upset. I made him do it again—I wasn't smiling.

Cooking has become a big hobby lately. A lot of men are into cooking. In fact, some of the best cooks I know are men. Also some of the worst. Those are the ones I get invitations from. They love to have me over, and they always serve something they've had simmering for about three days, which means every time they pass the pot they throw something else in. Male cooks seem to pride themselves on not using recipe books. With them it's instinct. They cook by the seat of their pants, and usually that's what it tastes like. And when they serve it to you they announce this is their own concoction and don't ask how they made it because they're not telling. You're looking for a place to hide it and they're worried about someone stealing their secret. Look, it's their hobby. If they enjoy cooking, they should cook, but they should eat it, too. Leave me out of it.

It's nice to have a hobby you're enthused about, but you can get carried away. People with those elaborate model train sets have this tendency. I have a neighbor who is a real nut. We call him Engineer Bill. He's got more track in his house than Union Pacific. And he's adding to it. The set occupies three rooms, with a fortune in bridges, warehouses, little villages and tunnels for the trains to run through. Last year he re-created the entire state of Vermont in miniature, including two drunks passed out behind a bowling alley in Montpelier.

That train set is his life. Nothing else matters. He's always playing with his trains. And while he's playing with his trains, his wife is out playing with his friends. He has his hobby and she's got hers.

The most important thing about a hobby is that it be something you do because you want to, not because you have to. For years my cousin Louie was one of the best dress cutters in New York City. But the pressures of work were giving him ulcers, insomnia and heart palpitations. Everyone kept telling him he needed a hobby. So he decided to start collecting those painted wooden horses from amusement park carousels. I would have picked something more exciting, like antique door knockers. But for Louie it worked. Soon he not only felt great but he found that he was making good money trading his horses with other collectors. He did so well that he quit his job so he could pursue his hobby full time. But now the hobby became a business, and within a year his ulcers were so bad that he needed a hobby again. You guessed it—cutting dresses.

If you avoid Louie's mistake, you could do worse than have a hobby that involved collecting things. There is almost no limit to your choice. You can collect anything from butterflies to shrunken heads. And I've never understood why, but with a lot of collections the less the things are worth, the more valuable the collection is: beat-up bottle tops, old baseball cards, illegible writing on torn scraps of parchment, out-of-date stamps—a 2-cent stamp from the year 1721 is worth more than my house in Beverly Hills. I know someone who had that stamp. He's now divorced. He got the kids, the house and the car; she got the stamp. The last I heard he was contesting.

Another fellow I know collects guns. He's got pistols and rifles from all over the world from the time they were invented down to the present day. He has them stacked on every shelf and in every closet. About three months ago he and his wife were awakened by a burglar robbing their house. He told me later the thief got away with all his wife's jewelry.

"With all those guns," I asked, "why didn't you stop him?"

"Are you crazy?" he said. "I wouldn't touch those guns. They're too valuable."

I said, "You're lucky he didn't take your wife," and he said, "That's your opinion."

None of this should discourage you from starting some kind of a collection. However, I do have several warnings. First, don't collect big-game animals like lions or tigers if you live in an apartment, especially if the elevator operator doesn't have a sense of humor.

Second, make sure you don't go around collecting stuff that belongs to someone else, or you'll have ten years to think of a new hobby, that is if you get a kind judge.

Third, and most important of all, the worst mistake you can possibly make is to —————————

I'm sorry, it's twelve o'clock.

THE NINE HAPPIEST ANIMALS

1. THE HORSE: He sleeps standing up and doesn't know what it is to spend the night in a crummy hotel.
2. THE OSTRICH: He can be the happiest of all, but when he takes his head out of that sand he's in trouble like the rest of us.
3. THE RABBIT: Because he's always . . . (censored)
4. THE MINK: (Same as above)
5. THE ELEPHANT: He's been to just about every country and he has yet to lose his trunk.
6. THE MOOSE: No matter what, he'll always have a place to hang his hat.
7. THE HIPPOPOTAMUS: You'd be happy, too, if you could weigh four thousand pounds and not have to go on a diet.
8. THE PIGEON: Because it's not easy for us to do to him what he can do to us. (It's a good thing a hippopotamus can't fly.)
9. THE PENGUIN: He must be having fun, he's always dressed like he's ready to have dinner at Chasen's.

I don't know why I have to stick to 9, I'm going to do 10—I might even do 11 or 12. This is 10:

10. THE GNU: No matter how old he is he always looks gnu.

It sounded good when I thought of it, but on paper it's nothing. From now on I'm sticking to 9.

7. GETTING THERE IS HALF THE FUN

(But It's the Other Half That Keeps Me Home)

THE OLDER I get the more I realize there are some things in this world I'll never understand. One is how you can get to be my age and have so many things you don't understand. Another is why so many people are happiest when they are anyplace but home.

A man pays three million for a house in Bel Air or Beverly Hills, his wife lays out $500,000 to redecorate it exactly to their taste, they throw in another $100,000 redoing the pool and the landscaping and putting in a lighted tennis court, and after all that they move in and two weeks later they've locked it up and are off to enjoy the back alleys of Tangiers or the sights, sounds and smells of the lower Ganges.

What's amazing is that they're not the exception. They have company at every level of income; enough to make the travel business a billion-dollar industry. For some, getting away means the two weeks of the year that make the other fifty bearable. Others only come home long enough to pick up the mail, holler at the kids, get some clean underwear, feed the dog and leave again.

Everyone is someplace else. If you were planning to go to Tokyo to see the Japanese, forget it. They're all over here snapping pictures of Marineland. The Germans are in Spain; the Spaniards are in North Africa; the North Africans are in France;

the French are in Italy; the Italians are in Arabia; and the Arabs are everywhere. So are the Americans. If you want to see all your friends, go to London, Paris and Rome. If you want to meet interesting, exotic-looking foreigners, stay home.

I've seen lots of tourists in my time, and there are as many different kinds as there are countries. Some want everything done for them. They travel with groups on charters or organized tours where every detail is taken care of. When they get home they can't always tell you where they've been, but they'll do two hours on how smoothly things went.

Others are just the opposite. They wouldn't think of going with a group. And they don't even use travel agents, they do it themselves. I know a couple like that. Every time they go anywhere they spend months looking at maps, doing research, making up itineraries and writing away for reservations. They love planning their trip, and they love talking about it when they get back. The only thing they don't love is the trip itself. That they could do without.

Some people are only happy in out-of-the-way places, staying among the natives and living like they do. Others can be in France, India, Egypt or Tibet, it's all the same to them, because they're always in an American hotel where they eat only American food and stay in their room all day watching "I Love Lucy" reruns and sending local picture postcards to everyone they ever knew.

Then there are the shoppers. They don't go to see a country, they go to buy it. Wherever this year's bargains are is where you'll find them. One woman I know spent $10,000 dragging her husband all the way to Italy just to buy a pair of Italian alligator boots. They didn't tell her the alligator was from Florida. It was caught in a swamp about fifteen miles from their condominium in Fort Lauderdale.

And how about those happy travelers who only want to know three things about their trips: Where do we eat? What do we eat? and When do we eat? This is quite a large group, and they're getting larger by the meal. When they check into a hotel they don't want to see brochures on points of interest, they go right for the room-service menu. And they eat their way from country to country.

The other day I overheard two Jewish ladies in a restaurant in Beverly Hills. One had just returned from Paris and the other was asking about her trip. This was the conversation:

"So you liked the Champs?"

"Fantastic. Best crepes I ever had."

"And you got to the Eiffel?"

"Wouldn't have missed it. But the portions at the bottom don't compare to what they give you halfway up."

"And how about that Notre Dame!"

"They got a restaurant there?"

At least she enjoys herself. Some tourists complain from the minute they leave to the minute they get back: the bed's too hard, the bed's too soft, the room's filthy, the bus is too hot, the guide's rude, the château's a bore, the Riviera's a ripoff. If you give them the Seven Wonders of the World, they might be satisfied.

That's another thing I don't understand. What makes the Seven Wonders so wonderful, and who decided on them? I'm not putting down the Taj Mahal or the Great Wall of China, but when it comes to traveling these are some wonders I'd like to see:

A cabdriver who understands English, especially in America.

A place in the world where you can't get a Big Mac and a Coke.

A headwaiter who hides his scorn when you order the house wine.

A cruise ship that advertises "no gratuities" where you can actually skip the tip without running the risk of being thrown overboard.

And what about an airport, train station or bus terminal where you can understand the person announcing the departures and arrivals? That would really be a wonder of the world!

If you're getting the idea that travel is not my long suit, you're right. And yet I can understand why so many people can't wait to get away. For them it's an escape from the pressures of their daily life. I've never had that problem. I've always been able to turn it on and turn it off, although lately it seems to turn off easier than it turns on. And sometimes I don't have to turn it off, it turns off by itself.

The truth is I'm not a sightseer. I don't applaud anything that can't applaud back. And I'm not the kind to lie on a beach in the sun waiting for my skin to shrivel up. It does enough of that while I'm moving around.

I must say if I were the beach type and a year or two younger, I might give that Club Med a try. They have locations all over—the South Pacific, Mexico, the Caribbean—and their ads make it look very inviting. Lots of great-looking male and female bodies in lots of tan skin. And what activities! Tennis, golf, volleyball, sailing, scuba diving, surfing, dancing, drinking, and I think I left something out. Oh yes—investment counseling. I knew there was something I could do.

Actually, the only kind of travel I really enjoy is when it's a working trip. That gives it a purpose. When Gracie and I were in vaudeville we went all over the country to do our act. And when we traveled to England it wasn't to go through churches and museums, it was to play the Palladium or do a Command Performance for the Royal Family.

In 1982, years after I started working alone, they asked me to appear at the Royal Gala of the Barbican Centre in London. Prince Charles and Lady Diana were to attend. When I arrived in England the newspaper reporters met me, and one of them asked what I thought of Lady Di. I said, "She's a little too old for me." Not the biggest joke in the world, but it made all the papers.

After the show at the Centre all the performers stood in line to meet the Royal Couple. When they got to me, Lady Di said, "I understand I'm too old for you."

I said, "No, ma'am," and Prince Charles said, "And she's not too old for me, either." I had a funnier line than "No, ma'am" for Lady Di, but I don't go around topping royalty. I love playing England.

It reminds me of another time I appeared for the Royal Family. This event took place at the Palladium for one of Princess Margaret's favorite charities. After the show they took me up to the Royal Box to meet Princess Margaret. Well, this charming lady was sitting there, and I said to her, "Your Highness, I'd bow, but if I got down I wouldn't be able to get up again." She said, "Mr. Burns, I'm not Princess Margaret, I'm the lady-in-waiting."

Just then the Princess came in, and after we were introduced, I said, "Your Highness, I just told a funny joke and you missed it." She said she was sorry, and she was also sorry she missed some of the lyrics of my last song. I said, "Would you like to hear it again?" and she said, "No, once is enough."

I figured it was time to leave, but as I started to go the attendant stopped me. "No, no," he whispered, "the Princess leaves first." I sat down, and after the Princess left I got up and he stopped me again and whispered, "The lady-in-waiting goes next." So I just sat there—I was afraid to move. Finally the usher came in and said, "Mr. Burns, everybody has gone, we're ready to close the theater." So I got up to leave, and he said, "No, I go first." I said, "Oh, you do?" "Yes," he said, "and don't forget to lock up on your way out."

Just a few months ago I had a most enjoyable working vacation when I was invited to perform on the *Queen Elizabeth II*. The last time I entertained on a ship was the *Leviathan* in 1926. They must have liked me because here it was fifty-eight years later and I was back entertaining on a ship again.

Irving Fein, my manager, accepted their offer. We flew to Hong Kong, spent a few days there, boarded the ship and went on to Bangkok and Singapore. In our party besides Irving and his wife, Marion, were my piano player, Morty Jacobs, and his wife, Madeline, and Cathy Carr, the lovely, lively young lady from Dallas who came into my life four years ago and makes me feel like I'm eighty again.

We all had a great time. First of all, the *QE II* is not a ship, it's a floating city. There's a shopping mall selling items from all over the world, a movie theater, a post office and a country club with two swimming pools and a nine-hole golf course. It's so big they should have bus service just to get around the decks.

They've got every activity imaginable, but you can't do any of it because they're serving food every twenty minutes. Irving brought along his jogging suit. He told me he was going to jog around the

The QE II. That's me in the back waving.

deck three times a day. The only jogging I saw him do was around the buffet table to make sure he didn't miss anything. He'll deny that, but all I know is he bought a suit in Hong Kong, and when we got to Bangkok five days later he couldn't get into it.

Cathy doesn't eat, she shops. I couldn't get her out of that mall. And Hong Kong never had it so good. She had two staterooms, one for her and one for all the stuff she bought. She bought so many things in Hong Kong she had to sell it all in Bangkok to make room for what she intended to buy in Singapore.

Cathy doesn't buy one of anything, or five of anything. She shops like she's a buyer for Bloomingdale's. She came out of one shop in Hong Kong with four dozen handkerchiefs for me. I said, "This is it? This is all the handkerchiefs I get?"

"They're not for now," she explained. "They're for your birthdays. You get a dozen when you're eighty-nine, another when you're ninety, another when you're ninety-one and the fourth dozen when you're ninety-two."

I said, "Does this mean you're through with me when I'm ninety-three?"

"Oh no," she said, "When you're ninety-three we'll come back and buy more handkerchiefs."

She bought everything: silver place settings, jewelry, clothes, China (not the country, the plates). In Bangkok we went to see the famous Reclining Buddha. It's ninety feet long and made of gold. "George, isn't that magnificent," she whispered. "What do you think that Buddha weighs?"

I said, "Forget it, Cathy, it's not for sale."

All through the trip Cathy had been studying her Thai language book so she'd be ready when we got to Bangkok. The first store we went into there had everything. She saw some silver candlesticks she liked, so she took out her little book and tried to talk to the clerk about them. After a few minutes he gave up and walked away. I said, "Cathy, they all speak English."

"George," she said, "I'm having fun, let me enjoy myself. When in Rome do as the Romans do."

"They speak English, too," I said.

But she wanted to do it her way, and she went through the entire thing again with another clerk. He kept nodding, and she said, "You understand, don't you?"

Cathy and I in Bangkok. I think she just bought the building in back of us.

"Oh yes," he said, "except for one thing. What are you going to do with a live monkey?" That's when Cathy gave me the book.

But that wasn't the end of it. She had just decided on a pair of candlesticks when Irving came over. Now Irving Fein is not my manager for nothing. He said to Cathy, "Let me handle this, I'll get you a better price." He said it to her in English and she understood. So he asked the clerk how much the candlesticks were in American money, and the clerk said, "Thirty dollars apiece."

Irving said, "How much for cash?"

"Thirty dollars apiece."

"How much for four candlesticks?"

"Thirty dollars apiece."

The toes of the Reclining Buddha. I told you photography wasn't my hobby.

Irving said, "Down the street they're selling the same candlesticks for twenty dollars apiece."

The clerk said, "Why didn't you buy them there?"

"They were out of them," Irving replied.

The clerk said, "If I was out of them, I'd give them to you for fifteen dollars apiece."

"I like you," Irving said, "but thirty dollars is a lot for a candlestick."

And the clerk said, "I like you, too. I'll tell you what. If you buy them for thirty, I'll throw in the live monkey." Irving looked at me, and I said, "I'll explain it to you later."

Well, I don't know how he did it, but Irving ended up getting the candlesticks for $20 apiece. And to show you what a businessman he is, he went down the street and sold them to the guy who didn't have them for $35 apiece. But it turned out to be a losing proposition. With all that maneuvering we missed the last tender back to the ship, and hiring another boat to get us out there cost us three times what Irving made on the candlesticks.

A few days later we were in Singapore, where we stayed three nights at the Pavilion Intercontinental, one of their newest and finest hotels. I had been walking around and wanted to get back to the hotel, so I got on one of those bicycle rickshaws they have there. The native driver had pedaled me a few blocks when who did we run into but Irving. He asked the driver how much he was charging me, and when the driver told him, Irving said, "That's ridiculous!" But rather than have him go through that whole thing again I got on the bicycle, put the driver in the passenger compartment and pedaled us to my hotel.

Singapore was as fascinating in its own way as Hong Kong and Bangkok. And what amazed us was that in all of these places wherever I went the natives would wave or point at me and call my name. They knew me from my movies and TV shows. Outside the Pavilion Intercontinental a man asked me to autograph a book he had that was written in Japanese. I looked at it, and it was my last book, *How to Live to Be 100—Or More*. I must be a better author than I thought—I didn't know I could write in Japanese. I autographed it, gave it back to him, he bowed three times and left. I don't know why he was taking bows. I wrote a book in Japanese, I should be taking the bows.

I also found the people on board ship to be very fascinating. And very rich. To take an eighty-day trip around the world on the *QE II* with the best accommodations costs a quarter of a million dollars. One woman told me this was her twentieth trip. I had tea with her in the lounge one day, and she asked me where the bathroom was. Imagine that—her twentieth trip and she still didn't know. I guess the rich really are different.

Another lady that Cathy and I had coffee with had so much jewelry on she could hardly move. She had rings on every finger, and the jewels were so big she couldn't close her hands. I can't

With that rickshaw driver in Singapore.

I guess he doesn't realize he's being pedaled by a man who performed for the Queen.

close my hands, but it's arthritis. I go to a doctor; she goes to Tiffany's. I really haven't got arthritis, but if I can get a laugh, I'll even admit to an ingrown toenail.

Between performing and shopping, the sightseeing and having Cathy read me the daily papers in Thai, the two weeks went by like two days. I'm glad I went, but that takes care of the traveling for a while. That trip will last me until I'm ninety-three and need more handkerchiefs.

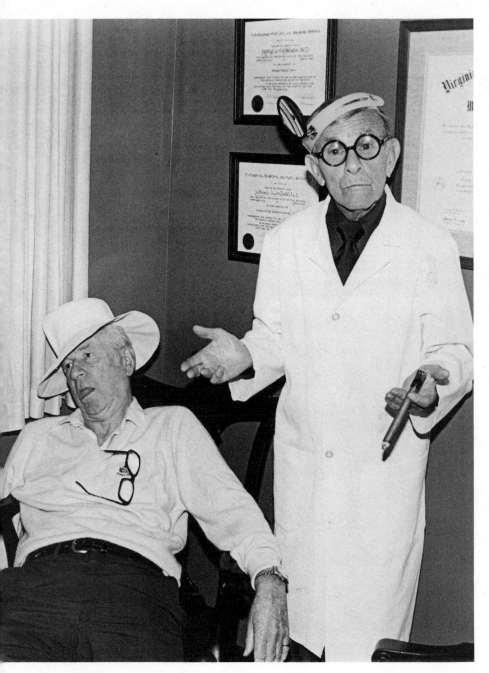

You win a few, you lose a few.

Friday's Prescription

DR. GEORGE BURNS, H.S.

(HAPPINESS SPECIALIST)

DATE_____

NAME_____

ADDRESS_____

Friday

For that all around good feeling--

1) Put neighbor's paper on porch.

2) Switch off headlights on unattended car.

3) Help little old lady across street.

Possible side effects

Being charged with:

1) Trespassing.

2) Car theft.

3) Attempted assault.

℞

GB

MORE DEFINITIONS OF HAPPINESS

Happiness is:

Getting a driver's license photo that doesn't look like you've passed away.

Being audited by the IRS and discovering that they owe *you* money.

Your mother-in-law developing an untreatable allergy to something in your house.

Your mistress coming down with morning sickness and finding out it's only from some bad sausage she ate.

8. YOU CAN'T SAY I DIDN'T TRY

WHEN YOU READ a book you see what's there on the page and you judge it accordingly. You have no way of knowing what went on behind the scenes, why certain things were put in and others left out, and that the writer may not always have the last word.

As an example of what we authors have to contend with, you might be interested in a phone conversation that took place a while back. I had just come up with a brilliant idea for getting forty or fifty hilarious pages for this book. In fact, when it came to me I got so excited I jumped up and did the Charleston. And I immediately put in a long-distance call to my publisher, Phyllis Grann. Since I happened to tape the whole thing, we don't even have to trust my memory. Here is our conversation, word for word:

Sound: Phone ringing . . . receiver up

PHYLLIS: Hello. Phyllis Grann here.
GEORGE: Phyllis . . . this is George Burns.
PHYLLIS: George! I've been thinking about you. How are you doing?
GEORGE: Great. Got a minute?
PHYLLIS: For you, anything.
GEORGE: I'll remember that. But I called about the book.

PHYLLIS: Oh good, you're done!

GEORGE: No, but it's going great, just great.

PHYLLIS: How far are you?

GEORGE: I'm starting the second chapter.

PHYLLIS: . . . I think we've got a bad connection. It sounded like you said you're starting the second chapter.

GEORGE: That's what I said.

PHYLLIS: I don't believe this. Two months and you're just starting the second chapter?

GEORGE: But I've got all my thoughts for it.

PHYLLIS: Congratulations. What happened to the George Burns who writes like he talks?

GEORGE: He's talking slower these days.

PHYLLIS: This is serious. You promised I'd have it in time to get it out for Christmas. Can't we do something to speed things up?

GEORGE: That's exactly why I called. You remember *How to Live to Be 100—Or More*?

PHYLLIS: Of course. You knocked that out for me in six weeks.

GEORGE: Seven. But you know, it just occurred to me, all those great chapters—the one on exercises, the one on diet, the positive attitude, the one about relatives—they would have worked in this book, too.

PHYLLIS: So what?

GEORGE: So I'll change it from longevity to happiness. A few words here, a few words there, and we got ourselves some fresh, funny stuff, right?

PHYLLIS: What are you talking about?

GEORGE: I'm talking about fifty pages. And if we look, I bet we can find another couple of chapters. That'll give us eighty pages and you'll have your book out by the Fourth of July.

PHYLLIS: You can't be serious.

GEORGE: This is long distance—I'm serious.

PHYLLIS: But, George, you can't just take from another book.

GEORGE: Why not? It's not Art Buchwald's book I'm taking from, it's mine. What am I gonna do, sue myself?

PHYLLIS: What about the person who bought the first book? Now he buys this one and suddenly he finds he's reading the same material all over again.

GEORGE: First of all, he must have liked the material in the first one or he wouldn't be buying the second one, so maybe he won't mind reading the same material over again. And how come you're so worried about him? What about the guy who just buys the second book and never bought the first one? Is it fair for me to deprive him of all that good stuff?

PHYLLIS: George, if it were all right to do what you are suggesting, everybody would be writing books.

GEORGE: Everybody is.

PHYLLIS: Why are we arguing? Take my word, George, it's never been done in the history of publishing.

GEORGE: Good, we'll have a first.

PHYLLIS: George, listen carefully. Are you listening?

GEORGE: I'm listening.

Sound: Click of phone being hung up

That ended that. I don't know why I even bothered calling her. She wasn't all that much help on the difference between a foreword and a preface.

Saturday's Prescription

DR. GEORGE BURNS, H.S.
(HAPPINESS SPECIALIST)

DATE_____

NAME_____

ADDRESS_____

Saturday

Repeat 3 times a day :

"Happiness is within me.
Material things mean nothing."

When convinced, give all your
money to charity.

But not before you pay
my bill.

GB   ℞

The doctor resting between patients.

NINE WAYS TO MAKE YOUR WIFE HAPPY

1. When you get home from work don't tell her about your problems at the office, let her talk about her problems. And if you're one of her problems, don't listen.
2. Surprise her with a sweater two sizes too small. She'll be flattered, she'll love you for it, and since she can't wear it, give it back to your secretary.
3. When you're with her watching a Bo Derek movie, say, "Come on, sweetheart, let's get out of here. I don't know what they see in her."
4. Instead of reading the newspaper at the kitchen table, try talking to your wife. You might learn a few things, like your kids have grown up and moved out.
5. Remember those important dates: her birthday, Valentine's Day, your anniversary, your first date together, your first trip together, and above all what happened the day you forgot one of those days you were supposed to remember.
6. Praise her in public. Let her hear you telling others how much you depend on her judgment and value her intelligence. What you say behind her back is up to you.
7. Call her from the office three or four times a day to chat. Take her to a long lunch once or twice a week. And never bring your work home with you. You might miss a promotion or lose your job, but your wife will be happy.
8. Take her on a second honeymoon. And this time it won't matter if she hides in the bathroom.
9. If all of the above have failed and you still want to make her happy, try leaving her.

(NOTE: If she's working, or if she's working and you aren't, Nos. 1 and 7 may not apply. If neither of you is working, you shouldn't be reading this book, you should be out looking for a job.)

NINE WAYS TO MAKE YOUR GIRLFRIEND HAPPY

Don't worry about it. Your girlfriend should make *you* happy. If she doesn't, you might as well be with your wife.

9. HAPPINESS IS OFFERING A HELPING HAND

(And Maybe the Rest of Your Body, Too)

IF YOU WERE to go around asking people what would make them happier, you'd get answers like a new car, a bigger house, a raise in pay, winning a lottery, a face-lift, more kids, less kids, a new restaurant to go to—probably not one in a hundred would say a chance to help people. And yet that may bring the most happiness of all.

I don't know Dr. Jonas Salk, but after what he's done for us with his polio vaccine, if he isn't happy, he should have that brilliant head of his examined. Of course, not all of us can do what he did. I know I can't do what he did; he beat me to it.

But the point is, it doesn't have to be anything that extraordinary. It can be working for a worthy cause, performing a needed service, or just doing something that helps another person.

I don't think there is any other profession that is as generous and unselfish as mine. Performers can count on each other for whatever is needed, be it money, advice or just moral support. If at the last minute some young actor gets sick and can't play a date, they can always count on me to take his place.

When it comes to doing "freebies" on telethons and benefits, the same people are called upon over and over again, and rarely do they fail to respond. Jan Murray does a great routine about his agent who doesn't get him paying jobs anymore, or even benefits. Now it's just parties. And even that's a struggle. If the agent doesn't answer his call, that means the Marvin Davis party fell through.

In all honesty I must say that most of the comedians I hang around with would be insulted if you invited them to your party and didn't ask them to get up and perform. Everyone gets up and performs. And it's always the same little game; they're asked by the host to get up and do something for the group, and invariably they'll say, "What? Again I gotta work for my supper? Forget it!" And then, with the host trying to pull him to the center of the room, "No, no! Come on, gimme a break! I got a sore throat. Please, not this time, ask Danny Thomas." And if the host lets go of his arm and asks Danny Thomas, that comedian will never set foot in that house again.

And it's important who comes off best. If Red Buttons is a bigger hit than Buddy Hackett, Buddy's evening is ruined. If it happens two parties in a row, Buddy could go looking for new writers. So even though everyone tries to make it look as if their routine just came to them, they work very hard preparing their party material. The trouble is the same comedians keep popping up at all the parties, and there are so many parties that there isn't always time to prepare new stuff, so you keep hearing the same old ad-lib bits over and over. It got so I knew Jack Carter's stuff better than my own. One night I forgot myself and was halfway through his routine before he came out of the bathroom and did what he had just done. It ruined my finish; I couldn't do my sand dance.

We all kid each other. That's the business. But we help each other, too. And I don't think there's one of us who wouldn't do what he could to give a newcomer a boost. I know it makes me feel good that I was able to help some very big talents get their careers going. Let me tell you about one of them.

When I was just starting to work alone I was looking for some talent to put together a show. I heard a record called "Splish Splash" by some kid named Bobby Darin, so I sent for him. Into my office came this middle-aged-looking man, about six feet two and weighing about 280 pounds. This was not what I expected. I said, "'Splish Splash'—you must have made a bigger splash than the record."

He said, "I'm not Bobby Darin, I'm his manager." Then he brought Bobby in, and I liked him the minute I saw him. Two weeks later he was part of my show in Lake Tahoe. As soon as Bobby walked on the stage the audience fell in love with him. After Tahoe I took him to Vegas with me, Bobby's recording of "Mack the Knife" came out and was a big hit, and things began happening fast for him. We got to be very close; he looked up to me like a father.

One night I heard that he had won $1500 at the crap table, so I went into his dressing room and said, "Bobby, what are you going to do with all the money?"

He said, "I'm on a roll, I'm going to win more."

"Give me thirteen hundred of it, and you gamble with the other two hundred," I said. "That's enough for you to lose. At the end of the date I'll give you back the thirteen hundred."

He said, "No, Mr. Burns. I'm not a kid—I'm twenty-two years old. I know what I'm doing."

Sure enough, he went back to the crap table and lost it all, plus another two hundred. When I heard about it I got very angry. I walked into his dressing room and said, "You ought to be ashamed of yourself, losing seventeen hundred dollars! That's a lot of money for a kid like you to lose!" Then I slapped him and walked out. I had to; if he had hit me back he would have killed me.

Ordinarily, before Bobby came on I gave him a very glowing introduction, but not that night. I just said, "Ladies and gentlemen, here he is, Bobby Darin," and started to walk off. Bobby ran out and grabbed me. He was very upset. "Mr. Burns," he said, "unless you give me that other introduction I won't be able to do my act!"

I said, "We'll let the audience decide." I told them the whole story and ended with, "Do you think a kid like this deserves a good introduction?" They all shouted "Yeah!" So I gave him the good introduction, Bobby and I hugged and he was a riot. He must have learned his lesson, because that night he stayed away from the crap table. I know; I was there. I lost $500.

Elvis Presley and Bobby Darin. I don't think they even knew I was there.

Bobby Darin was a tremendous talent and he came out on the stage with all the confidence in the world. Some people thought he was a brash, cocky kid. And in some ways he was. When he was twenty-two he told the press that at twenty-five he was going to be a living legend. The kid gave himself three years. I'm eighty-eight, and if I'm going to be a living legend by ninety-one, I better get busy.

Underneath all that bravado Bobby Darin was a very caring, sensitive person. I remember when Robert Kennedy was assassinated, Bobby was just shattered. Kennedy was his idol. It changed his whole attitude toward life. He gave up rock'n' roll to sing meaningful folk songs. Instead of a big orchestra he started using a four-piece combo. He stopped wearing his toupee, grew a beard and instead of that sharp tuxedo he came out wearing faded old blue jeans and a sweatshirt. He was playing nothing but small clubs and coffee houses.

One night I went to see him at the Troubadour, a little coffee house in West Hollywood. I couldn't get over it. After the show I went backstage to see him. I said, "Bobby, what are you doing? This isn't you. Get rid of that beard and those clothes. Get back into your tuxedo. And put on your toupee. If you haven't got one, I'll loan you one. You want to do something for Bobby Kennedy, do your old act, make a lot of money again and give half of it to the Kennedy Foundation." That's exactly what he did, and he was as big a smash as ever.

Bobby was like a son to me, and I still miss him.

Now I'd like to do a few minutes on Ann-Margret. When I first saw her she was only nineteen years old and she had just arrived from Chicago, where she had been attending Northwestern University. She came into my office with her piano player and said, "Mr. Burns, I'd like to sing for you."

I said, "Why for me?"

"Well," she said, "I heard what you did for Bobby Darin, and I thought you might do the same for me."

I asked her if she could sing like Bobby Darin, and she said, "I don't know whether I sing as good as Bobby Darin, but I certainly move better than he does." She should have said, "I don't know whether I sing as *well* as Bobby Darin," but I didn't notice at the time. Now that I'm an author I'm aware of those things.

Ann-Margret—1983.

Ann-Margret—1960.

Anway, there was a piano in the property room, so we all went back there. The place was covered with dust; it looked awful. But I wanted to hear her, so I said, "Okay, kid, let me hear you sing a song."

And she did. And she was right, she did move better than Bobby Darin. By the time she got to the second chorus she had dusted every piece of furniture in the place. Then she threw in a couple of little wiggles that even cleaned the ashtrays.

I put her in my stage show, took her to Vegas and she was just terrific. Six months later I sent for her and said, "Annie, how about playing Las Vegas again?"

She said, "Oh, I'd love to. Let me hear you sing a song." I sang a song, and she took me.

I always enjoyed working with Ann-Margret. One time we were playing Vegas over the holidays, and on opening night she came off the stage and started to cry. I said, "Annie, why are you crying? The audience loved you." She said it was Christmas Eve and she missed her mother. So I told her to go into my dressing room and phone her mother and charge it to me. Then I went out on the stage to entertain. An hour later I went back to my dressing room and she was still on the phone. I sat there and waited until she was finished, then I said, "Annie, you're not crying anymore. Your mother was glad to hear from you, huh?"

She said, "Oh yes, Mr. Burns. We had a wonderful conversation."

I asked her why she didn't invite her mother to Las Vegas, and she told me she couldn't, her mother lived in Sweden. Then I started to cry.

With all that talent and beauty nothing could have kept Ann-Margret from being the big star she's become. But the fact is I did give Annie her first important platform, and, knowing that, I still get a good feeling every time I look at her. Who am I kidding? I'd get a good feeling looking at Ann-Margret if I'd never done anything for her. That kid can dust my furniture anytime.

You won't believe it, but another kid I helped was Frank Sinatra. He was in his early twenties at the time, and he had just left Tommy Dorsey. I was looking for a singer for the Burns & Allen radio show, and I was offered Sinatra for $250 a week. I was about to sign him when I learned I could get an act called The Three Smoothies for the same money. Well, I wasn't born yesterday—if I could get three people for the same money, what would I want with that skinny kid? So I took The Smoothies. Frank has never forgotten that. Every Christmas I get a gift from him with a note thanking me for not doing for his career what I did for The Smoothies.

I'd like to tell you about some of the other stars that I helped, but I can't continue. I just remembered I'm invited to Steve Allen's house. He's giving a party tonight and I have to rehearse my ad-libs.

He still can't get over what I did for him

Sunday's Prescription

Dr. George Burns, H.S.
(HAPPINESS SPECIALIST)

DATE_____

NAME_____

ADDRESS_____

Sunday

If previous prescriptions haven't made you happy, get a second opinion.

If they have made you happy, get one anyway.

GB

Note: If you are getting a second opinion, don't forget Dr. Burns has two offices.

℞

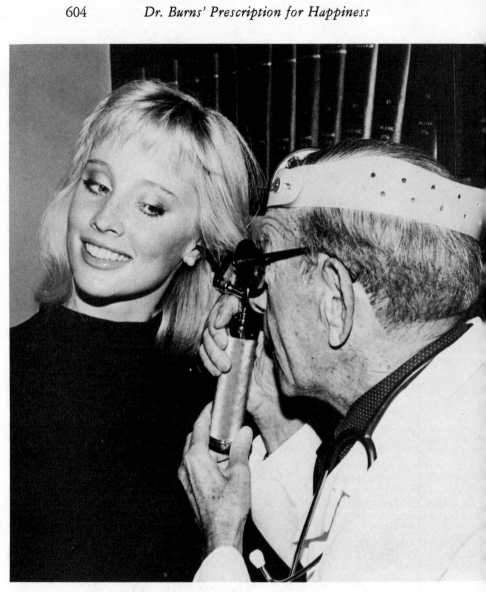

The doctor doing a little research.

10. WORK ONLY WORKS IF THE WORK YOU WORK AT ISN'T WORK

(I Get Paid by the Word, so I Threw in Two More "Works")

IF YOU WERE to ask me to name one thing above all others that makes for happiness, I would say without fear of contradiction that it's enjoying your work. Wait—why should I fear contradiction? I fear tough audiences, drafty dressing rooms, makeup that streaks, but not contradiction. Everybody gets contradicted. Maybe not as often as I do, but it's nothing to fear. It's nothing to brag about either.

Let me put it this way. You can't be happy if you don't enjoy your work. Actually, that's not true in all cases. There are people who don't have any work to enjoy, who are retired or rich enough to get along without it, and who are still happy. They enjoy not having a job to go to or any kind of steady work. I don't understand them, but I know they're out there. Just like I know there are people who enjoy sitting on flagpoles, or tearing a telephone book in half, or swimming in Lake Michigan in twenty-below weather.

Let me put it another way. If you enjoy your work, you can't be unhappy. No, there are exceptions to that, too. Your wife or husband could have just left you for someone else, or your car

605

radio could have been stolen, or your parrot could have laryngitis, in which case you'd be unhappy no matter how much you love your work.

Let me try again. I'd better decide how to put it, before you tell me where to put it. Okay, here goes. Generally speaking, there's nothing like enjoying your work to make you happy. I think we can all agree on that. It has certainly been true in my case.

For me, show business was always so exciting, so satisfying, so full of laughs and fun that it never seemed like work. And people sense that. Whenever I play Vegas or Lake Tahoe or give a concert they come backstage and tell me I looked like I was really enjoying myself out there. Why shouldn't I enjoy myself? I'm standing there smoking a cigar, hearing myself sing a dozen of my favorite songs in my key, giving a roomful of nice people some laughs and I'm getting paid.

It's all very relaxed, very easy. When I perform I don't sweat. Rodney Dangerfield sweats, Don Rickles sweats, Jackie Gleason sweats . . . I'm wrong, it's good to sweat. The next time I'm onstage I'll sweat a little.

I've always said I'd rather be a flop in show business than a success at something I didn't like. I'll admit I say it more often now than I did when I was barely making enough to keep that seal I worked with in mackerel. But that's the way I feel about it. I don't think you go into show business just for the money. It's not like selling dresses or making felt hats. You may do very well financially, but that's not what attracted you to it or keeps you in it.

Most of the performers I know would tell you the same thing. Danny Thomas, Bob Hope, Milton Berle, Phyllis Diller, Buddy Hackett, Bob Newhart, Red Buttons, Joan Rivers, Shecky Greene—they all love every minute of it. "The Johnny Carson Show" has been on five nights a week for twenty years, and Johnny still enjoys himself. He should. If you figure the nights he's had guest hosts, he's only been on about a year and three months.

Red Skelton always looked like he was having a blast out there. And I thought he was until I heard he was so nervous he threw up before every performance. Someone once asked Red if it were true that he always did that, and he said, "Sure, doesn't everyone?"

Walter Matthau has a different problem. He loves show busi-

Johnny, enjoying his work, too.

ness as much as any of us, and you could hardly be more successful. But like many big stars he's always worrying that it won't last. When we did *The Sunshine Boys* he had just come off three big hits in a row, including *The Odd Couple* with Jack Lemmon. We had a great time making *The Sunshine Boys*, and after we finished the picture Walter and I had lunch together. He'd been out of work maybe three hours. I noticed he was picking at his food, and said, "Walter, you're not eating." He said, "How can I eat? I just spoke to my agent, he's got nothing lined up for me." So I ate his lunch, too.

Actors are the worst of all. Once they get the bug they can't get it out of their system. Ronald Reagan's an exception. He was able to leave acting for politics, even with a smash like *Bedtime for Bonzo* under his belt. Some Democrats would dispute that; not the part about Bonzo, but that he's stopped acting. Personally, I've always liked and admired Ronald Reagan, and I think he's made a great President. In fact, I think he's the best President the Screen Actors Guild ever had.

When Irving Berlin said there's no business like show business he must have been thinking of my end of it. Between the writers, the comedians, the nutty vaudevillians and all the other characters around, you never stop laughing. At least I haven't. Let me give you a few small samples of what goes on.

There was this big comedian back in the radio days. He was very funny, very fast on the uptake and an incurable womanizer. I won't tell you his name, but he had his own show every week. I probably could tell you his name, but I won't. The show took place in a New York tavern. Anyway, this comedian got married to a very lovely lady, and the newlyweds immediately went on a honeymoon cruise. And right away, the first night out, he winds up in the cabin of another woman. After a few hours the wife goes looking for him, and sure enough, she bumps into him just as he's coming out of the other woman's cabin. And without batting an eye he says to her, "I forgot to tell you, I'm also a jewel thief."

Then there was the time John Barrymore was riding to his hotel in a cab, and the driver was Jewish. The cabbie said, "Mr. Barrymore, it's an honor for me to have you in my cab. What brings you to New York?" And Barrymore said, "I'm here to play

I told him he'd never amount to anything unless he learned the Time-Step.

Hamlet for the next six weeks." And the cabdriver said, "*Hamlet*? I've seen Jacob P. Adler play *Hamlet*, I've seen Aaron Kessler play *Hamlet*, I've seen Boris Thomashefsky play *Hamlet*. Will they understand it in English?"

Frank Fay was one of our great comedians, and for sarcasm he had no equal. One night he was master of ceremonies at the Mayfair Ball, a very swanky, black-tie affair. Practically every Hollywood star was there, and Fay was in top form. In the middle of one of his lines somebody at one of the tables said something. Fay stopped, looked over in that direction and said, "Who said that?" There was a long silence, then somebody from another table yelled, "Groucho Marx said that!" Fay looked at Groucho and said, "Groucho, why don't you come up here and we'll talk for a few minutes." Groucho just sat there; he wanted no part of Fay. Fay looked right through him and said, "So you do need Zeppo, don't you."

One more story. Look, I'm getting paid by the word. This one's about a comedy writer, John P. Medbury, one of the best. He used to sit in his office and write by the hour. In the little adjoining office was his assistant, a young kid named Harvey Helm. One day Medbury's wife happened to walk into his office while he was out. The top drawer of his desk was open, and she noticed a pair of silk panties. She gingerly held them up, and as Medbury came back into the office, she said, "John, what are these doing in your drawer?" Without missing a beat, Medbury hollered, "Harvey!" Harvey came in and Medbury said, "You're fired!" I don't think it worked, because the next day when Harvey got to the office he found Medbury sleeping on the couch.

I could go on and on, but that gives you an idea of why I've always gotten such a kick out of show business, and why I could never picture myself in any other profession. It bothers me when I see people who hate what they do for a living, or are bored with it and just go through the motions, getting no pleasure or satisfaction from it.

How do you go to a job every day that you can't stand? The only thing worse would be coming home to a wife you can't stand, or going to a job you can't stand and then coming home to a wife you can't stand.

You'd think someone in this position would do anything to get out of it. But that's seldom the case. People have a way of hanging on to what makes them miserable. At least they know what they've got. The thought of making a change is frightening. What if they can't handle it? What if they fail?

They underestimate themselves and their abilities, and when you think like that you're defeated before you start. Failing once in a while builds character. I should know, I have more character than I know what to do with. For years in the beginning failure was my middle name. It was only the first and the last names I kept changing. I was Harry "Failure" Pierce; I was Joe "Failure" Davis; I was Tom "Failure" Fitzpatrick; and then until I met Gracie I was George "Failure" Burns.

But I never underestimated myself. The audience did that for me. I'd go out on the stage and try something, and if it didn't work, I'd try something else. And when that didn't work I'd try something else. One theater manager suggested I try running an elevator, or running a drill press, or just running.

I shouldn't downgrade other lines of work. Just because something's not for me doesn't mean it's not for someone else. I'm sure there are some people who enjoy selling cemetery lots, although I never knew anyone who enjoyed buying one. As William Shakespeare once said, "How come you can't fill a theater on a Tuesday night?" That doesn't fit, but I figure if I quote Will, the next thing he writes he might quote me.

There was a good point I was about to make . . . oh yes . . . if you're going to accomplish anything worthwhile, you have to be willing to accept a challenge now and then. You can't always play it safe. There are times when you have to take a chance.

When Gracie retired I faced such a time. I had to make a big decision, and I did. I went into show business. Look, when I worked with Gracie, I was retired. I did nothing. We walked on the stage and I said, "Gracie, how's your brother?" and she talked for thirty-eight years.

Now when I suddenly had to go it alone, I didn't know if I could make it. What if they didn't like me alone? What if I didn't like me alone? And then I figured the only way I'd find out was to try it. So I did.

Bally's in Atlantic City. It's a tough job, but somebody has to do it.

I put a show together for Harrah's at Lake Tahoe, and I wasn't going to take any chances. I surrounded myself with the best: Bobby Darin, the DeCastro Sisters, Brascia & Tybee—they didn't need me. I went out there and I thought I did fine. That night when Gracie and I were in bed, I said, "Gracie, how'd you like the show?"

She said, "Bobby Darin was just fabulous." I waited, and then she said, "The audience just loved the DeCastro Sisters." I waited some more, then she said, "And Brascia and Tybee are the greatest dancing act I've ever seen." I couldn't wait any longer; it was starting to get light out. I said, "What did you think of me?" She said, "Bobby Darin was just fabulous."

"Come on, Gracie," I said. "I can take it."

She said, "George, I don't believe that you believe what you're saying. You're reciting all your monologues."

I didn't sleep that night, and can I tell you something, I never recited my monologues again. Now I'm out there on the stage for an hour, just me and my cigar, and it's one of the big pleasures in my life.

It turns out that some of the best things I've done were things I had to be talked into. When they brought me "I Wish I Was 18 Again" and asked me to record it, I thought they were kidding. Who was I to sing country? I can barely sing city. I'm not the country type; I'm from New York's East Side. I don't ride horses, I take cabs.

"The song's not for me," I said. "Give it to Kenny Rogers." They pointed out that it had to be sung by an older man. "Then give it to Kenny Rogers' father," I said.

Irving Fein thought I was crazy; he wanted me to do it. I said, "Nothing could make me do that song." Irving said, "They're not offering you nothing, they're offering you a lot of money." So I took it. It became a hit, and since then I've done several country albums, a TV special from Nashville, and I feel very comfortable with that music. Look, why shouldn't I be a country singer? I'm older than most countries.

Playing "Al Lewis" in *The Sunshine Boys* was another challenge. At the age of seventy-nine I had to become a dramatic actor. The big thing with acting is that you not only have to be able to feel the emotions you are to convey, but you have to feel them when the director yells "Action!"

This gave me trouble until one day it all came to me, and now it's a cinch. If the director wants me to cry, I think of my sex life. If he wants me to laugh, I think of my sex life. And if he wants me to laugh and cry at the same time, I look in the mirror. Olivier has his system, I have mine.

It must have worked, because they gave me an Oscar for *The Sunshine Boys*. But it's the *Oh God!* films that have had the biggest impact. When I go down the street people say, "There's God." They don't say, "There's Al Lewis."

I worried about playing God. We're about the same age, but we grew up in different neighborhoods. It didn't seem right for me to be God. Wouldn't they be better off with someone like Billy Graham? He's taller than I am. Then when they showed me the outfits I'd be wearing for the role, I figured they didn't have any more confidence in me than I did. I was expecting expensive white flowing robes and a halo or two. That stuff I wore must have cost about 12 cents. It looked like God was laying off.

But it worked out great. There was a sequel, and as I write this they're editing the third one, Warner Bros.' *Oh God! You Devil*. This time I've got a dual role. I play God and the Devil. As the Devil I go around with young girls, smoke a lot of cigars and drink martinis. It's the toughest role I ever had to play.

Looking back, I don't know what I would have done if I didn't have my work. And even now I'd be lost without it. People keep asking me when I'm going to retire. They say you're supposed to slow down and take it easy when you get old. Well, when that happens to me I'll think about it. Look, if I had started slowing down when I was sixty-five or seventy, by now I'd be stopped. A turtle would move faster. But I didn't slow down, I kept going. And now at eighty-eight there isn't a turtle around that can pass me.

Not that it matters. In my business the test isn't how fast you move. It's not the Olympics. I have an hour for my stage show, so if it takes a minute or two for me to shuffle out there, who cares? In fact, the longer it takes the more they applaud. They're pulling for me to make it to the center of the stage. So that's no problem. And when I record a country album I can do it sitting down. And if

That's me playing two parts: God and the Devil.

they want me to do a tap dance in a movie, they hire a double and I'm still sitting down.

So if I still love my work and I can still do it, why retire, especially now that I have it both ways? Not only am I making movies at eighty-eight, but as a senior citizen I only pay half price to see myself up there on the screen. I'd have to be crazy to retire. I'll never quit. I'm going to stay in show business until I'm the only one left.

11. . . . AND
IN CONCLUSION

WHEN I STARTED this book the very first thing I did was ask myself, "What is it that makes me happy?" After thinking about it I realized there are a lot of things that make me happy, which is good because I'd hate to have all my happiness in one basket.

As I explained in the last chapter, my work makes me happy. Being in reasonably good health for a man my age, or for that matter a woman my age, makes me happy. Cathy Carr makes me happy. Getting the most out of a tough bridge hand makes me happy. And I must admit a standing ovation makes me happy. Let's face it, a pat on the back is nice, providing the guy who does the patting isn't Larry Holmes.

I'd be lying if I told you I haven't enjoyed all the attention I've received, especially in recent years. The public has been very good to me, and it's not a one-way romance. If my fans appreciate me, I appreciate them just as much.

I've never understood why some performers resent their fans. What do they want, people who can't stand them? I've had both and I'll take the fans anytime. Those stars worry about going into a restaurant and having everyone notice them. They should eat at home. To me the time to worry is when you're in a restaurant and they don't notice you.

I don't mind it at all if they come over to my table while I'm eating dinner and ask for my autograph. I'll sign anything: napkins, menus, ties, just as long as it isn't the check. When that comes I ask Irving Fein for his autograph.

If a little kid comes over to me and calls me "God," what am I going to do, tell him to get lost? I'm too busy to say hello? I've got to go, I'm running behind on my miracles for the day? Would God do that? Of course not! I smile, offer the kid a cigar, make his father pay me for it and the three of us are happy.

You know something, I should ask my fans for their autographs. Sometimes they're funnier than I am, like when they mistake me for someone else. That's always happening. I never tell them they're wrong, I go along with it. It started when I worked with Gracie. Half the time they called me Mr. Allen. I didn't mind, Allen got all the laughs. It would have been worse if they had called me Mr. Smith or Mr. Dale. At least they got the right team.

One time a woman mistook me for Fred Allen. She asked me how my wife, Portland, was. I said, "She's fine, great little cook." She said, "It's amazing—you look the same in person. But how come you're not talking through your nose?" I said, "I only do that when I get paid."

I've even been mistaken for Bob Burns, the comedian who made the bazooka famous on the Bing Crosby radio show. This fellow came up to me and said, "Mr. Burns, I never miss you, you're my favorite. When are you going to play the bazooka again?"

Now Bob Burns had been dead for twenty-nine years, but I didn't want to tell him that. So I said, "I'm glad you reminded me. I haven't touched my bazooka in years, but as soon as I get home I'll take it out and try it."

You won't believe this, but once I was actually mistaken for Burt Reynolds. Last year I was in the lobby of the Sherry-Netherland hotel in New York, and some guy said to me, "Hey, Burt, are you still going around with Loni Anderson?" I said, "No, I'm dancing with Sally Fields again." How could he think I was Burt Reynolds? It's ridiculous. Burt's got black hair, mine is gray.

The one that tops all of these I think I've told before, but it's worth repeating. I was sitting in a doctor's office, and there was a lady sitting next to me. She said, "It's exciting to be sitting in a waiting room with a great celebrity." I said, "It certainly is. Who are you?"

She laughed and said, "I know who you are, Mr. Benny."
"Thanks," I said. "Everybody recognizes me."

"How's Mary?"

"She was fine when I left her in bed this morning."

She said, "Is it true everything George Burns says makes you laugh?"

"Oh yes, he's a scream," I said. "He's the funniest man I ever met."

Then the nurse came in and said to me, "Mr. Burns, the doctor's ready to see you now." The woman looked at me, and said, "Are you George Burns?"

"That's right."

"What were you doing in bed with Mary this morning?" she asked. I said, "At our age it takes both of us to keep her warm."

Some of the fans do strange things. I got a letter four or five months ago from a fan in Oklahoma City. He said his grandfather had seen Burns & Allen in vaudeville, then his father and mother listened to us on radio and he watched us on television, had seen all my movies, read all my books, saw all my TV specials and even had all my albums.

Then he wrote, "I'm getting married March twenty-fourth, and since I'm your biggest fan the least you can do is send us a nice sports car for a present. We'd prefer a Chevrolet Corvette, but if that's too expensive, a Pontiac Firebird will do—any color but yellow."

I didn't know what to do. I thought and thought about it, and I finally sent him a picture of myself and wished them a wonderful marriage and signed my name. I haven't heard from him since. Maybe he's not my biggest fan anymore.

I get all kinds of requests. After the first *Oh God!* picture came out I received a letter at my home from Milwaukee. It was addressed "God—Beverly Hills." It was from a six-year-old boy. It started out: "Dear Mr. God. I know you're very busy, but I have a big favor to ask. This Sunday is our championship baseball game, and I would be very happy if you would make it not rain. Don't forget, it's this Sunday." I guess it didn't rain, because I got another letter from that boy. It said, "Thanks, but we lost."

You never know when you're going to meet a fan. One morning I was driving to my office the same way I've been doing for years. I had to cross a busy intersection just before I got there, and I was almost through it when a guy ran a red light and smashed into the passenger side of my car. The car was a mess, but fortunately I was just shaken up. I got out and asked him what he thought he was doing, running a red light like that. He said, "You're George Burns." I said, "I almost wasn't." Then he told me what a great fan he was and how he loved everything I did. I said, "If you're such a big fan, why did you try to kill me?"

By then the police had arrived, and he started telling them what a big fan he was. After the police wrote out the report they took a picture of the two cars, and the guy said to them, "Would you mind getting one of George and me together? Is it okay with you, George?"

I said, "All right, just don't kiss me."

Another time I was at NBC on my way to do "The Johnny Carson Show" and a woman stopped me. She said, "You're George Burns, aren't you?" I said, "That's right." "I can't believe it," she said. "This is the first time I've ever seen you alive." I hope she wasn't disappointed.

Sometimes they get so excited they don't realize what they're saying. I don't know how many times I've had someone point their finger at me and say, "You're you, aren't you?" I say, "Yes," and they say, "I can't believe you're really you." I try to calm them down by saying, "Look, I've been 'you' for years."

Some people come up and test me. They say "Do you know who you are?" I say, "Give me a minute, I have to think about it."

This one is really a beauty. After my last TV special a woman rushed up to me the next day and said, "Mr. Burns, I saw your special last night." I said, "Thank you," and she continued with, "And I spoke to my sister in St. Louis and she saw it, too!"

I said, "That's very flattering," and she said, "Just imagine, I'm in Los Angeles and she's in St. Louis and we both saw the same thing. Isn't television amazing! What a world we live in!"

I thanked her again, why I don't know. All she did was compliment her television set.

And fans love to take pictures, especially at airports. I'll be sitting there waiting for my flight, and someone will rush over to me with a camera, put a baby in my lap and say, "Mr. Burns, do you mind smiling?" I must have had hundreds of pictures taken with babies. I don't dare travel unless I carry two or three extra pair of pants.

Here's a compliment I'll never forget. I was playing the Riviera Hotel in Las Vegas, and one day during lunch this attractive young couple came up to the table. The girl said, "Mr. Burns, we're on our honeymoon, and meeting you is the most exciting thing that's happened to us." Now that's what I call a fan.

Look, they may not always realize exactly what they're saying, but I love my fans. I'm grateful for every one of them.

Speaking of being grateful, it's time to thank the two fellows who helped me write this book. I know it's time for that, because they just told me. Contrary to the picture of them standing with me, they don't smoke cigars. They don't smoke at all. They put up with my cigars and I put up with their jokes.

The oldest is Hal Goldman and the youngest one is Harvey Berger. Actually, I'm the oldest. I'm older than both of them put together, and they can throw in their agents, too. Hal's an old hand in the business; he's forgotten more about comedy than most writers know. In fact, if he forgets any more, I may never be able to use him again. The other kid is a relative newcomer. He came into my office two years ago and couldn't write his own name. But after sitting at my feet for two years he can now write it easily. Look, if these kids don't learn, I don't keep them.

I also have to thank Jack Langdon, my secretary. I was going to say some glowing things about him, but he just asked for a raise, so that's the end of this paragraph.

Eric Butler is a new kid who's working for me. He's only been with me nine months, so I haven't had a chance to find out what he does.

Also, I should mention Cindy Delpit, Liz Slusher, Rieneke, Lori Garland and Tina Littlewood, the five models who posed for the

With my writers Hal and Harvey. I taught them everything they know.

pictures in this book. The girl who Johnny enjoyed with his work on page 607 is actress Inga Neilsen. I want to thank them for being so beautiful and cooperative. If I were a little younger, I might have more to thank them for.

Most of the pictures in the book were taken by that fine photographer, Peter Borsari. I wanted you to see what he looked like, but he doesn't have a picture of himself.

I mustn't forget my literary agents, Arthur and Richard Pine, who deserve credit for coming up with the idea for this book. Next time I'll come up with the idea and they can write the book.

With my secretary, Jack Langdon, in the middle, and Eric Butler—
whatever he does.

My manager, Irving Fein, telling me he renewed me for another year.

Again I want to thank Phyllis Grann, my editor and publisher, who has great editorial judgment, impeccable taste, unfailing literary instincts and dances close.

And now I come to my personal manager, Irving Fein. I appreciate the invaluable help Irving has given me, not just with this book but with everything I've been doing. He's my idea of what a good manager should be. Not only has he a good head for business, but when it comes to charity and giving, his heart is in the right place. I can't think of a single worthy cause he hasn't insisted I contribute to.

I'm also grateful to (in alphabetical order): Steve Allen, Milton Berle, Red Buttons, Johnny Carson, Jack Carter, Carol Channing, Phyllis Diller, Bob Hope, Walter Matthau, Bob Newhart, Don Rickles, Joan Rivers and Danny Thomas for those flattering comments about your author. It wasn't really necessary to mention them individually, but I'm still getting paid by the word.

ONE LAST DEFINITION OF HAPPINESS

Happiness is finally getting to write these two words—

THE END

After writing a book a man has to relax.

DEAR GEORGE

CONTENTS

Introduction 633
1. The First Ten Letters 637
2. The Second Ten Letters 646
3. Some Interesting Letters 654
4. More Interesting Letters 664
5. Short Letters With Short Answers 673
6. Short Letters With Long Answers 681
7. Short Letter With Very Long Answer 691
8. Intriguing Letters With Provocative Answers 712
9. Some Very Endearing Letters 722
10. Naughty Letters With Nice Answers 728
11. Naughty Letters With Naughty Answers and Nice Letters With Naughty Answers 736
12. Nice Letters With Nice Answers 744
13. Character Witness Letters 757
Dear Readers 777

INTRODUCTION

Dear Reader—

Wait a minute, that doesn't sound very positive.

Dear Readers—

Yeah, that looks better. You weren't expecting another book, were you. Neither was I. Let me tell you how it happened. A few days ago I was busy sitting in my office blowing smoke rings when the phone rang. It was Phyllis Grann, my editor and publisher at Putnam's, calling from New York to tell me how great my last book was doing.

"Do you realize," she said, "that *Dr. Burns' Prescription for Happiness* has been on the *New York Times* Best Seller list for eighteen straight weeks?"

I said I didn't believe it. She said neither did the *New York Times*, but we had to face it, I was a smash and when could she have my next book.

I told her to forget it. In the first place, I wouldn't know what to write about, and in the second place, I was too busy to do another book. "Look, I don't sit around here blowing smoke rings. I've got a TV special to do, concerts, personal appearances at Caesars Vegas, Tahoe and Atlantic City, and on top of that I'm reading a script for a new movie. I play this old detective who's retired, and I'm sitting around the park—"

"George," she interrupted, "I'd love to hear the plot, but I'm not taking no for an answer on the book. You've got two best sellers in a row. You're hot!"

"I'm hot?" I said. "Tell that to Trixie Hicks and Elsie Huber and Lily Delight." I waited for the laugh. Nothing. I tried again. "I'm hot? Tell that to my hands and feet. I wear gloves and socks in the steam room." Nothing again. "I'm hot? Tell that to—" I would have gone on but the operator cut us off.

However, Phyllis wasn't through. For the next three days I got big bouquets of flowers from her. And on the fourth day she was back on the phone.

"Phyllis," I said, "I love you, I love Putnam's, I love the *New York Times*, but the book is out. And stop with the flowers. At my age flowers scare me."

She started to laugh. "And laughing at that lousy joke won't do you any good, either," I said, "because I can't even see across my desk it's piled so high with letters that I can't find time to answer."

"That's it! That's it!" she shrieked. "I knew you'd come up with it!"

"What did I come up with?"

"The book! Letters from people who write you their problems and want your advice!"

"I just came up with that, huh?"

"You're a genius. I love it! Now if we can just think of a great title!"

"Hold it," I said. "You mean I'm supposed to come up with answers for all those people?"

"George, with that storehouse of wit and wisdom you have to draw from it'll be a breeze."

"But, Phyllis, giving advice—that's not for me. That's for 'Dear Abby.'"

"That's it!! That's it!!!"

"What's it?" I asked, switching the receiver to my other ear. (I didn't really do that, but it's nice writing. It sort of livens up the dialogue.)

"You got it, George! That's the title!"

"I did it again, huh? Okay, we'll call my book *Dear Abby*."

"No, no, no, it's *Dear George*! It can't miss!"

I said, "Good. I came up with the book and I came up with the title, now here's my first letter: 'Dear Phyllis—I can't do the book, I'm too busy.'"

"George," she whispered, "I'll give you twice what you got last time."

"Another letter: 'Dear Phyllis—I'll do the book.'"

Okay, so I was an author again. *Dear George* would be the sixth book I've written, which isn't bad for a guy who has only read two.

But after we hung up, I started thinking. What have I got myself into? Can I do it? Am I qualified to answer all those letters? It's true I have a storehouse of wit and wisdom to draw from, but I've been drawing on that storehouse for 89 years. It could be overdrawn.

I must be crazy. How can I do a book when I've got all these other things going on? But I said I'll do it, and when I say I'll do it, I do it! I haven't gone back on my word for the last three weeks.

Look, something will just have to go. What can I do, I'll give up my Tuesday-night bowling.

Author getting started.

1. THE FIRST TEN LETTERS

Dear George—

My boyfriend and I have never made love with the light on. I'm dying to try it and see what it's like. Do you think this is an unreasonable desire?

Pittsburgh Penny

Dear Pitts—

There's nothing wrong with making love with the light on. Just make sure the car door is closed.

• • •

Dear George—

Now that I'm getting up in years, my doctor keeps warning me to keep my weight down and eat the right foods. But who knows what's right to eat anymore? What do you think about all those natural food and high-fiber diets I'm always hearing about?

Aging Gracefully

Dear Aging—

I personally stay away from natural foods. At my age I need all the preservatives I can get. On the other hand, what could be wrong with a high-fiber diet? When was the last time you saw a fat moth?

. . .

Dear George—

My wife, who I loved and miss very much, passed away three weeks ago, and I have yearnings for the opposite sex again. I'd like to do something about it, but my kids say it's too soon. Actually, it's been three weeks and two days. I want to do the right thing, but how long does a man have to wait for sex after his wife dies?

Bereaved Husband

Dear Bereaved—

I'd say it depends on how long you had to wait for it when your wife was alive.

(This letter may seem like an exaggeration, but people are strange. Let me tell you what really happened to me one time. I was coming out of the Palace Theater Building and I ran into this actor I knew. He said, "George, I've got a big problem. My wife passed away, and there's this gorgeous tomato who wants to have an affair with me."

I said, "When did your wife die, Jim?" and he said, "Yesterday."

I couldn't believe my ears. I said, "How could you think of having an affair if your wife passed away yesterday?" and he said, "That's the problem, I'd have to miss the funeral.")

. . .

Dear George—

I'm involved with a much younger woman, but my mother doesn't approve. She says younger women are only out for one thing. I love my mother, but I think she's all wrong on this. Don't you?

Good Son

Dear Good—

I'm not sure what your mother is referring to. I'm taking out a young woman tonight, and I know what she's out for—a good meal. What she's in for remains to be seen.

• • •

Dear George—
   Last night I had a blind date with a wealthy doctor that my parents fixed up for me. He was nice, but ugly. Honest, George, he looked like a gorilla. I really believe I have found the missing link, and what's worse, he wants to go out with me again. My parents want me to marry him, and I know he would. But how could I eat breakfast every morning with that hideous monkey sitting across the table from me?

                                                                Apprehensive

Dear App—
   He's wealthy, he's a doctor, marry him, skip breakfast and eat a big lunch.

P.S. Let me know when you get married and I'll send you some peanuts.

• • •

Dear George—
   We're a young married couple considering starting a family. How far apart do you think children should be spaced?

                                                      Anxious to Get Started

Dear Anxious—
   About five miles.

• • •

Dear George—
   My fiancé dresses like Boy George, talks like Michael Jackson, but looks like Willie Nelson and walks like John Wayne. We're spending our honeymoon at Caesars Palace. Do you have any advice?

                                                                Engaged

Dear Engaged—
    Ask for group rates.

(I'm glad they're going to Caesars Palace. It's my favorite hotel, I play there all the time. Last time I played there I caught Tom Jones. He was working across the street. Women love him. During his act they throw their room keys up on the stage. They throw their room keys at me, too, but after they check out.)

• • •

This is what I have breakfast with every morning. And *she's* complaining.

Dear George—

I am a high school junior, and I'm in love with this girl in my French class. How can I tell if this is the real thing or just puppy love?

High School Hector

Dear High—

Feel your nose. If it's cold and it's damp, then it's just puppy love. Try not to soil the rug while you're getting over it.

Author beginning to make headway.

• • •

Dear George—

My marriage is just about on the rocks. The problem is that my husband and I don't know what to do about it. Should we take a vacation and try to put the marriage back together, or get a divorce and go our separate ways?

Up in the Air

Dear Up—

I don't know why you're having a problem deciding. It's simple. When a vacation is over, it's over. But a divorce is something you'll have forever.

• • •

Dear George—

I need therapy, but I'm a little suspicious of the psychiatrist who was recommended to me. I found out that instead of a couch he has a big double bed in his office. Should I go to him or not?

Paranoid

Dear Par—

Go to him. Why would a double bed make you suspicious? Maybe he likes to take a nap between patients. Maybe he's got a bad back. Maybe his nurse has a bad back. If you don't have faith in people, kid, you'll never get well.

(I've never gone to a psychiatrist, but I play bridge with one two or three times a week. One day I said to him, "Al, how can you stand that work of yours? How can you listen to people's problems eight hours a day?" He said, "Who listens?" Now I know why he's such a lousy bridge player.)

END OF CHAPTER

Dear George—

I love the material so far. Keep it up. Just one little thought. In your introduction you write, *"Dear George* would be the sixth book I've written, which isn't bad for a guy who has only read two."

Very funny, but if memory serves, you did that same gag about your last book.

Phyllis

Dear Phyllis—

Glad you like the stuff. However, on your little thought, memory doesn't serve you, because in the first place I didn't say it about my last book, I said it about *How to Live to Be 100—Or More.* And what I said was, "This is the fourth book I've written, which isn't bad for a guy who's only read two."

How is that the same? One is the sixth book, the other was the fourth book—that's a whole different joke. I'd never do the same joke twice.

You have to assemble the right secretarial staff. It could be a long project.

And they take shorthand, too.

2. THE SECOND TEN LETTERS

Dear George—

I'm 72 and a widower who is just getting back into the dating game. So far I've had some very nice evenings with girls in their twenties and thirties. But I've been told they're too young for me. So I thought I'd get it straight from the horse's mouth. Do you think I should date these young girls, or should I stick to women my age?

Puzzled

Dear Puzzled—

The mouth isn't the part of the horse I'm used to being associated with, but as to your question, I would definitely advise you to stick to women your age. That will leave more of the young ones for me.

Of course, age isn't everything. I'd even take a smart, beautiful, 25-year-old over a dumb, homely kid who's 23. I'm very flexible.

• • •

Dear George—

I'm addicted to gambling. I'll bet on anything, and I've lost more money than I can count. I want to have a normal life, settle

down and have a family, but I can't stop gambling long enough to
do that.

Crapped Out

Dear Crapped—

Get married. The odds on winning aren't any better. You'll still
have a lot of bad nights, but if it doesn't work out, your wife can
only get half of what you started with.

• • •

Dear George—

If good girls go to heaven, where do bad girls go?

Little Joe

Dear Little—

Anywhere they want.

*(If I'm not mistaken, Mae West answered that question the same
way. Mae and I had the same sense of humor, but different
deliveries. With that way of speaking she had, Mae could make
anything sound naughty. One time she ran into Gracie in Beverly
Hills, and said, "How's George?" Gracie came home and wanted
to divorce me.)*

• • •

Dear George—

I'm very superstitious. I don't walk under ladders or cross paths
of black cats. And I don't get out of bed on Friday the 13th. But
what about holidays? I heard it brings bad luck to have sex on
Ground Hog Day.

Worried

Dear Worried—

Don't worry. Unless you're planning to have it with a ground
hog. And it would probably be bad luck only for the ground hog.

(*Some people worry about everything. Not me, I never worry. If I have a problem, I don't take it to bed with me, I tell her to go home.*)

• • •

Dear George—

My wife has a fantastic job, and while she's away at work all day I'm home doing the housework and taking care of our three small children. Do you think this could confuse our kids about the mother-father roles, and if so, would that be harmful in later years?

Stay-at-Home Father

Dear Stay-At—

What you're saying is that your wife brings home the bacon and you cook it. I hear lots of talk these days about the effects of this kind of situation, and for every expert who says it's bad, it seems there's another who thinks it's good. All I know is that when I was growing up I had no trouble telling my father from my mother. He was the one with the beard, and she was the one with the mustache. Or was it the other way around? Wait, now I remember. My father had a beard, but it was my sister Goldie who had the mustache. We used to tell her to shave it off like mother did.

(*Actually, my mother didn't have a mustache, my sister didn't have a mustache, and neither did I. My father did have a beard, but if I just mentioned that, it would be a pretty dull answer. Did my father have a beard! It ran from the third floor down to the street. I never had to use the stairs, I used to shinny down his beard.*

Look, I like to throw in little things like this from time to time. It breaks the monotony—not yours, mine.)

• • •

Dear George—

I'm very nearsighted, and I have learned that men don't make passes at girls who wear glasses. Yesterday I was walking along

I like girls with glasses—especially if one is for me.

the beach in my bikini and took off my glasses. I couldn't tell if anybody made a pass at me or not, I couldn't see anything. What am I to do?

Out of Focus

Dear Focus—

Put on your glasses and take off your bikini. Or better yet, take off your glasses and your bikini. But you might catch cold, so you better wear a hat.

• • •

Dear George—

I seem to be having a hard time getting ahead in life. The other day I read that Thomas Edison once said, "Genius is 1% inspiration and 99% perspiration." Do you believe that?

Going Nowhere

Dear Going—

I'm not sure Edison ever said that. All I know is the last time I danced with him he could have used a can of Right Guard.

(That really deserves a better answer. To me, Genius is 1% inspiration and 99% good writers. I don't sweat.)

• • •

Dear George—

I'm in love with a wonderful girl, but she happens to be a professional. And I don't mean a dancer, I'm talking about the oldest profession. This worries me. Do you think I should marry her?

Unsigned

Dear Un—

Of course. She'll make you a rich man. She'll be saving you $200 a night. At the end of the year you'll be worth a fortune.

(These days it's not easy to tell a professional girl from a Vassar graduate. Come to think of it, it never was easy. I remember years ago Georgie Jessel and I were playing the B. F. Keith Theater in Philadelphia, and he couldn't stop bragging about this high-class girl he spent the night with in Cleveland. He said, "What a lady. She knows absolutely nothing about vaudeville. Her world is culture. All she can talk about is the opera, the ballet, the symphony, great works of art."

A week later he got a call from her, and she said, "Georgie, I've got bad news for you. You gave me Cupid's eczema."

Jessel said, "Wait a minute, I just came from the doctor. I didn't give it to you, you gave it to me."

"Oh," she said, "then the Three Stanley Brothers gave it to me.")

• • •

Dear George—

I own a good business, have a nice home and a wife whom I dearly love. But she always wants to have her way. And she has a habit that really bugs me. She always reminds me way ahead of time when her birthday is coming. And then she tells me exactly what she wants. Like this birthday she told me she wants a red convertible with white leather.

Before she even brought it up I was already thinking about getting her a car, but I had my eye on a snazzy, dark blue convertible. She takes the whole kick out of it for me. How can I explain that to her?

Farley in Fairfield

Dear Farley—

Don't explain. Give her what you want to give her. It's your gift. You have to start taking charge. Women like that. That's why he-men types like Gable, John Wayne, Clint Eastwood and the rest of us stay popular.

• • •

Author making real progress.

Dear George—

My boyfriend is a rock fan, but it's not what you'd think. I don't mean Mick Jagger or Rod Stewart. He loves to go rock climbing, and that's where we go on our dates, to different rock cliffs. When we get home he's always too pooped to make love. I just bought a new, extra, extra firm bed, and even that doesn't help. What should I do?

Upset

Dear Up—

Sorry, kid, it sounds like you're caught between a rock and a hard place.

(Some of you probably think I'm making up these letters just so I can have funny answers. I'm surprised at you, thinking a thing like that! I'm a nice, quiet, soft-spoken, 89-year-old man. I played "God"—three times—without makeup. And I got paid—three times. Making up letters! My older brother would be ashamed of me if I did a thing like that!)

END OF CHAPTER

3. SOME INTERESTING LETTERS

Dear George—

I've been trying to score with this gorgeous girl at work for over a year. But every time I try a squeeze play she's got some left-field excuse. I can't get to first base with her. It's not that I haven't tried. I keep coming up to bat, but I'm always striking out. I'm beginning to think it's time for a pinch hitter. If you're interested, I'll be happy to send you her phone number.

Bench Warmer

Dear Bench—

Don't bother. The season's over for me.

• • •

Dear George—

Last night my husband and I went to a masquerade party, and I went as a man and he went as a woman. And with my dress, blonde wig and makeup he looked very attractive. In fact, one fellow danced with him practically the whole night, and they ended up leaving together. Should I be worried?

Having Second Thoughts

Dear Having—
Only if you need the dress back by Tuesday.

(This reminds me of an incident that happened once with my close friend Jack Benny. We had to do a benefit performance, and I talked Jack into doing a Burns & Allen routine where he played Gracie. Now when Jack did something he went all out. He wouldn't play a woman like Milton Berle. He got hold of the dress Rita Hayworth wore in Gilda, *which fitted him like a glove, put on a beautiful black wig and even wore a garter belt and shaved his legs. He was a doll and the routine was a riot.*

After the show I went to his dressing room, and before I could congratulate him he started screaming. I said, "What are you so upset about?" He said, "I'll tell you what I'm upset about! When I was walking down the hall three guys whistled at me, that's why I'm upset!"

I said, "Jack, you've got beautiful legs." "Don't try to make up to me," he said. "I should never have let you talk me into this. It's embarrassing, it's humiliating!" And he stomped out of the dressing room.

Jack was my friend, now I was upset. I didn't know what to do. Finally, two days later I went over to his house to apologize for having him wear that outfit. And when he opened the door he was still in it. I didn't know whether to apologize or kiss him. So I did both.)

• • •

Dear George—
My wife keeps nagging me that it's time for me to have a talk with my 12-year-old son and tell him about the birds and the bees. To me he is still a little boy, and I feel awkward discussing this subject with him. What would you advise?

Reluctant

Dear Re—
Do what my father did when my mother nagged him to tell me about the birds and the bees. He took me to Coney Island, pointed

That's right, he shaved his legs.

to a couple making love under the boardwalk and said, "Your mother wants you to know that the birds and the bees do the same thing."

• • •

Dear George—

Now that I'm getting older, more and more of my friends are passing away, and I'm expected to go to each and every one of their funerals. But I really hate funerals. Am I wrong for not wanting to attend these depressing events?

Grave Situation

Dear Grave—

Just remember, if you don't go to their funerals, they won't come to yours.

• • •

Dear George—

My Uncle Jake recently died. After his funeral the family all gathered at my cousin's house to pay their respects. They not only had a catered buffet, but there in the middle of the table was a replica of Uncle Jake done in chopped liver. I found it tasteless and totally abhorrent. Don't you agree?

In from Outta Town

Dear In from Outta—

I agree. There's nothing worse than tasteless chopped liver.

(*That letter's like the story about old Sam who is passing away at home in his bed. The family is all gathered around, and in the middle of his good-byes this wonderful aroma hits him.*

"Becky," he says, "isn't that chopped liver I smell?"

She says, "Yes, Sam, it is."

And he says, "Becky, one last time I gotta have some of your chopped liver."

And she says, "You can't, it's for after."

I would have included this story in my letter to In from Outta, but she might have found it tasteless.)

• • •

Dear George—
My best friend has a dog who is very ill, and my friend tells me she is planning a big funeral, with a casket, services, eulogies and the whole bit. This seems a little eerie to me, but I suppose I'll have to attend. Am I also expected to send flowers?
                                        Friend's Next-Best Friend

Dear Next-Best—
Yes, and a contribution to the dog's favorite charity.

(People get attached to their pets. I know a woman who had a fancier funeral for her poodle than for her husband.
   And when Harpo Marx's cat passed away, he got George Jessel to do the eulogy. Jessel was never better. There wasn't a dry eye in the house as he eloquently recalled the deceased's loyalty, devotion and quiet generosity. But I thought he went a little too far when he said, "It would put you to shame if you knew what this cat did for Israel.")

• • •

Dear George—
I've got a new boyfriend. Neither of us is talking marriage, but things are going so great it scares me. What could ruin a casual affair?
                                                    Fingers Crossed

Dear Fingers—
You're writing to the wrong adviser. I've never had a casual affair. I don't believe in casual affairs, I'm very formal. I even wear spats and a tie when I take a shower.

• • •

With the King of Eulogies. I didn't like the way he was looking at me.

Dear George—

I've got a good business, a nice home, a lovely wife and wonderful kids, but I'm a compulsive liar. I lie to everybody about everything, and it's really bothering me. How can I change?

Two-Faced

Dear Two—

I don't know quite what to say here. If you're lying about your business, home, wife and kids, you've got to change. But if you're not, keep lying.

• • •

Dear George—

My husband is constantly humiliating me in public about my size. Like if I have a cold, he'll say, "Look at her, the elephant's trunk is all stopped up." The other night when somebody asked what he was giving me for my birthday, he said, "A cowbell to wear around her neck so I'll know where she is." This really bothers me. Am I oversensitive?

Feeling Hurt

Dear Feeling—

You're not oversensitive, you're overweight. You should do something about it. If you want to lose 170 pounds right away, get rid of that rude husband of yours.

(*I never had a weight problem. Nobody in my family did. We were seven sisters and five brothers, we were too poor to be fat. Our big Sunday-night dinner was bread and gravy. And you had to be very careful not to get your fingers in the gravy or somebody would eat them. To this day my brother Willy can't thumb a ride.*)

• • •

Dear George—

I got your advice. And I almost bought the blue convertible for my wife's birthday, but I couldn't quite bring myself to do it. Are you sure about this? What if she really gets upset?

Farley in Fairfield

Dear Farley—

Stop worrying. Just get her what you want to get her. She'll respect you more for it. Trust me. I've been around for a while. When I was a boy the Dead Sea was only sick.

END OF CHAPTER

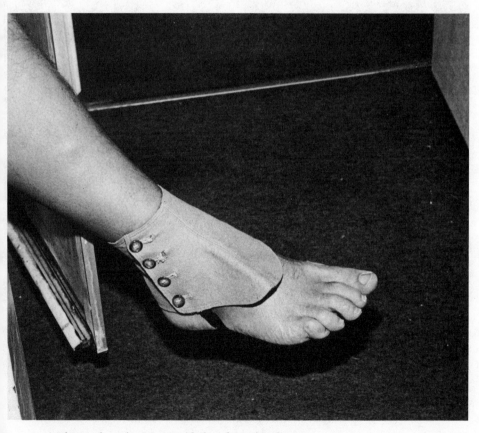

And you thought I just said that for a laugh.

Author getting away from secretary. You don't believe it? Then how about the next one?

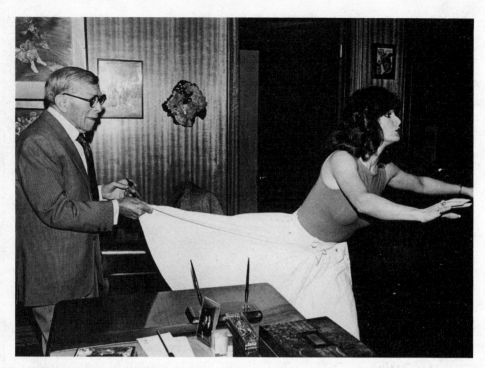

Secretary getting away from author.

4. MORE
INTERESTING LETTERS

Dear George—

The entire staff of *The Playboy Advisor* department wishes you success in your new field of endeavor and would like to contribute some information that might be helpful. From past experience we have found that over ninety percent of the problems presented to us by people writing in letters are related to sex. These letters contain the usage of many words and expressions that may be unfamiliar to you because of the tremendous generation gap between you and anyone who is still living.

Therefore, we are enclosing, under separate cover, a complete glossary of such words and expressions in alphabetical order, ranging all the way from "Amoral" to "Zipper Ripper." You will find certain words and phrases have taken on an entirely new meaning from the way a man of your age might interpret them.

For example:

"Getting off" no longer means stepping out of a stagecoach.

"Making out" does not mean hitting a pop fly to the shortstop.

"S and M" does not stand for the dancing vaudeville team of Smith & Mahoney.

"T and A" is not the logo of the defunct railroad line that once operated between Tennessee and Alabama.

"Doing a trick" is not pulling a rabbit out of a hat.

A man referred to as "well-endowed" does not mean his family left him a lot of money.

Best wishes, and we hope our glossary will be of help to you.
Playboy Advisor Staff

Dear Advisor Staff—
Thanks for trying to update my thinking, but I happen to be hip to what's going down these days. It may surprise you, but I know that a "boob" is not a cartoon character named McNutt. And I am also aware that "buns" are not something you fondle while marketing to see if they're fresh. (Although I've been slapped in several stores for trying it.)

P.S. I'd read your magazine more often, but my glasses keep steaming over.

• • •

Dear George—
My husband and I find that variety is the spice of marriage. But after three years we're running out of places to make love. We've tried the park, the car, restaurants, trains, hot tubs, even furniture store displays. Can you think of any other real good place for us to try it?
Panting in Pittsburgh

Dear Panting—
Your bedroom. On second thought, you kids are killing yourselves. You don't need any new places, you should rest for an hour.

• • •

Dear George—

I'm getting up there in years, but I still like to play tennis with the guys, dance with the gals and have a few snorts with both. But everyone says I should slow down and act my age. As one geriatric to another, maybe you can tell me—at what point does one graduate from *elderly* to *old*?

Another Geriatric

Dear Geri—

You'll know you're *old* when everything hurts, and what doesn't hurt, doesn't work; when you feel like the night after and you haven't been anywhere; when you get winded playing chess; when your favorite part of the newspaper is "25 Years Ago Today"; when you're still chasing women, but can't remember why; when you stoop to tie your shoelaces and ask yourself, "What else can I do while I'm down here?"; when everybody goes to your birthday party and stands around the cake just to get warm.

(These things really happen when you get old. I know, because that's what my father keeps telling me.)

• • •

Dear George—

You amaze me. Everywhere I look, there you are—TV shows, commercials, nightclubs, movies. At your age, how do you keep it up?

Flabbergasted

Dear Flabber—

My manager, Irving Fein, helps me.

• • •

Dear George—

We watch you all the time here at the Home. You're our very favorite. You always seem so chipper and full of pep. But just between you, me and my pacemaker, how does it really feel to be 89?

Can Keep a Secret

(What do they want from me? That's three of these letters in a row. That's all I hear—old, old, old! So I'm too old to win a Charleston contest! They don't even have Charleston contests anymore! Who cares? So I'm 89, what's the big deal?! I'm not even going to answer this, one of my secretaries can do it!)

Dear Can Keep a Secret—
Mr. Burns wants me to answer you. As his secretary I can assure you that day in and day out, no one feels better than he does. Or more often.

Black and Blue

(She's too funny. That's the last time she'll answer a letter for me.)

• • •

Dear George—
I'm 28 years old, and I must be attractive because I seem to turn guys on. The problem is they do the same thing for me—morning, noon and night. In high school I was known as Nina the Nympho. And it's not getting any better. If I'm with a man five minutes, I just can't control myself. I don't know what to do. Do you have any ideas?

In High Gear

Dear In High—
As a matter of fact I do have some ideas. But it's difficult going into them through the mail. However, I'm home after 8:00 P.M., Tuesdays and Thursdays, if you'd care to discuss your problem further.

P.S. Better make that Thursday. My couple is off that night, so we could really concentrate on the matter.

• • •

Thursday afternoon—author waving goodbye to his couple.

Thursday night—waiting for consultation.

Friday morning—exhausted from previous night's consultation.

Dear George—

When my husband and I got married I thought we'd be a very happy couple. Now that the honeymoon is over I realize he's not interested in the things I like to do, and I'm not interested in the things he likes to do. Is our marriage doomed?

Working At It

Dear Work—

Not necessarily. The fact that both of you are not interested in things the other one likes proves that you *do* have something in common. And that's a good beginning. Just be careful not to pressure one another into doing something you both like to do.

I suggest you find things neither of you like to do, and spend as much time as possible doing them together. For instance, not watching television together can be most enjoyable. And if you want a good, long, happy marriage, why don't you consider living in different towns together.

• • •

Dear George—

Maybe you can help. I'm in a quandary. Providing that an object in motion is under a constant force, is it true that the kinetics of the situation dictate that as the velocity of molecular friction resists the momentum of the shear component, an intolerable vector develops in a semi-rigid medium?

Stumped

Dear Stumped—

Only on Tuesdays.

• • •

Dear George—

My husband refuses to take care of the house repairs, so I have this problem with repairmen. Whenever I call one they come late, charge too much, drop cigar ashes on the floor and never fix anything right. How do you handle these kind of guys?

Fed Up

(I can't answer this letter, this sounds like a real problem. I don't answer real problems. If I'm going to solve real problems, I want more money. Come to think of it, I want more money even if I don't solve real problems. Maybe I should talk to my publisher about this, but that might create a problem neither of us could solve.)

END OF CHAPTER

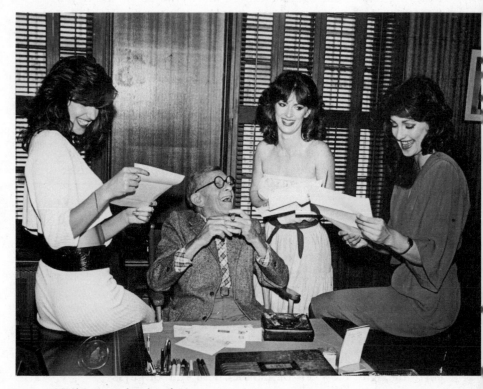

Nothing can be that funny.

5. SHORT LETTERS WITH SHORT ANSWERS

Dear George—
My husband and I are senior citizens and we still care about each other. Is it okay to make love in the 90s?

Getting Up There

Dear Getting—
I think it's best around 70 or 75. If it gets any hotter than that, I turn on the air conditioner.

• • •

Dear George—
I am a Senior Citizen, and they tell me I should be enjoying the Golden Years. How can I awake every morning with a song in my heart?

Still Kicking

Dear Still—
Try an AM-FM pacemaker.

• • •

Dear George—
   Has Dean Martin really done as much drinking during his career as he says?

                                                            An Imbiber

Dear Imbiber—
   Let me put it this way. If Dean Martin were to apply for a job as a professional wine taster, he would be considered overqualified.

(So Dean drinks a little. But don't forget—he never drinks when he's not working.)

• • •

Dear George—
   If you had your choice, what would you have for your epitaph?

                                                            Inquisitive

Dear In—
   Who cares as long as I'm standing there reading it.

(That wasn't my original answer. My first answer was a shrimp cocktail. Then my secretary explained to me, "An epitaph is not an appetizer. An epitaph is something that goes on a tombstone. How could you say a shrimp cocktail?" I said, "While I'm standing there reading my epitaph, I'd like to eat something.")

• • •

Dear George—
   I'm eighteen years old, and I want a motorcycle for my birthday. But my parents say it's too dangerous. Don't you think it's about time they stopped worrying about me getting hurt? After all, it's my body—right?

                                                            Grounded

Dear Ground—
From your parents' point of view it is *not* your body, they built it before you moved in—right?

• • •

Dear George—
After being married to the same woman for 42 years I have to admit that it's starting to go stale. Oh, we still do it now and then, but it's always the same. Why is that? I know her every move before she makes it.

Bored

Dear Bored—
Look, she moves, don't complain.

(*How about that guy, writing a letter like that. He's married 42 years and knows her every move. She knows his moves, too, and I didn't get a letter from her. He ought to be ashamed of himself. I'm sorry I answered him.*)

• • •

Dear George—
My boyfriend is very romantic about our dinner dates. But every time he invites me to an expensive restaurant he insists we go Dutch. How can I break him of this habit?

Busted

Dear Busted—
The next time he invites you to go Dutch, put on a pair of wooden shoes and kick him where it hurts—in his wallet.

(*That's not the world's greatest answer, but I'm still mad at that letter before this. Married 42 years and knows her every move! He's lucky somebody else doesn't know her every move. If he keeps complaining, somebody else will. I better stop getting so*

worked up about these things. It could keep your author up nights.
Look, if I'm going to be up all night, I want a better reason.)

• • •

Dear George—
    I don't understand today's kids. What do you think about young
girls who date older men?

                                                                Out of Step

Dear Out—
    I think about them 24 hours a day. Well, not exactly 24 hours, I
need at least an hour off for my nap.

• • •

Dear George—
    I recently read in a magazine that Wyatt Earp is buried in a
Jewish cemetery in Los Angeles. George, why did they bury Wyatt
Earp there?

                                                              A Fan of Earp

Dear Fan—
    Because he died.

• • •

Dear George—
    Three years ago I took up scuba diving, and now it's the
highlight of my life. I can't get enough of it. Have you ever tried
it?

                                                                   Estelle

Dear Estelle—
    I did, but I had to give it up. The cigar smoke kept fogging up
my mask.

• • •

Dear George—

I keep hearing about the sexual revolution. When did it start, and is it still going on?

Potential Volunteer

Dear Potent—

I wouldn't know. The last revolution I was in was the American Revolution. And from what I saw, sex didn't play too big a part in it. But maybe I was just in the wrong bunkers.

• • •

Dear George—

Thanks a lot! I got my wife that blue convertible for her birthday last week, and she hasn't talked to me since. Now I've got to apologize, take it back and get her what she wanted in the first place.

Farley in Fairfield

Dear Farley—

That's the worst thing you can do. Don't give in. She's testing you. Deep down she wants you to be strong. It may take a while, but she'll come around. I know what I'm talking about. I read Dr. Joyce Brothers faithfully.

• • •

Dear George—

I just turned 50, but I enjoy dressing like a 25-year-old girl. Is this a mistake?

Fabulous at Fifty

Dear Fab—

Only if your name is Irving. Or Seymour. Or Irving Seymour.

END OF CHAPTER

I have a feeling you still think I'm making up these letters. Be honest, that's what you're thinking, right? Well, it's very upsetting.

It's difficult enough to sit around and write a book, or even stand around to write a book, without having to worry about you worrying about me worrying about you.

There, you see, I just used three worries in one sentence. That's how upset you got me. If I was thinking straight, I could have written that sentence with one worry. Making up letters—if you're going to keep thinking that, I'm going to stop writing this book.

What am I saying? I'm getting paid twice as much as I did last time. I'm going to finish this book. You think what you want, I write what I want.

• • •

Dear George—
Do you think a daily massage does any good?—

—It must. They love it.

6. SHORT LETTERS WITH LONG ANSWERS

Dear George—

I have a ten-dollar bet about you. My friend said you once did an act with a seal. I said there's no way a classy performer like you would have ever worked with a seal. Tell me you didn't. I'll split with you.

Wagering Wally

Dear Wagering—

I could tell you I didn't, but I'd be lying, and for five dollars it's not worth it.

When I started in vaudeville it didn't take me long to figure out that if I wanted to eat, I'd have to work with a partner. But every time I'd find myself a partner who was good, he would start looking for a partner who was good and I'd be out of work again. Then I started to look for a partner who wouldn't leave me, and I found one—a very talented seal. And we called ourselves Captain Betz & Flipper. I was Captain Betz.

Flipper wasn't bad. He'd balance a ball on his nose, walk up a ladder and he'd take a mallet in his teeth and play a xylophone. And for a finish I would balance a ball on my nose, and Flipper would smoke a cigar.

We opened at the Hippodrome in Cleveland, and after the first performance the manager came back and said, "Captain, you've got a very talented seal there, you ought to give him first billing." I didn't mind him saying that, but he said it in front of the seal. It was embarrassing.

Everywhere we played, people would make comments like that. It got so I couldn't handle Flipper. Every time I'd throw him a fish he'd throw it back at me. Finally I had it with him.

Wally, you're right, a classy performer like me didn't have to work with seals. Two weeks after I dropped Flipper I opened at the Poli Theater in Wilkes-Barre with my new act, Captain Betz & Fido.

• • •

Dear George—

As Henny Youngman would say—take my grandson, please! It used to be he couldn't get enough of Gramps. Now at 10 he's through with me. Nothing I have to say seems to interest the little rascal. If this is the Generation Gap, you can have it.

Disillusioned Grand Pappy

Dear D.G.P.—

Forget the Generation Gap, relax and keep talking. He needs you as much as you need him. You should be like my friend Barry Lefkowitz, who thinks he's the greatest thing that's happened to his grandson.

Last Sunday the three of us were walking in Roxbury Park, and the kid said, "Grampa, what makes the tree have leaves?" And Barry said, "What am I, a horticulturist? How would I know why trees have leaves?"

Then after a moment the kid said, "Grampa, why is that dog walking sideways?" And my friend said, "If I knew why the dog is walking sideways I'd be a veterinarian."

A few minutes later, "Grampa, why do robins eat worms?"

"Why do robins eat worms—what am I, the Birdman of Alcatraz?"

We walked a little more, and the kid said, "Grampa, could I ask you another question?"

And my friend said, "Ask, ask. How else are you gonna learn?"

(*I have to be honest. That's a funny story, but it's not new. Then again, neither am I. I didn't have to tell you that's an old story. I could have said I made it up. But I don't lie. I don't say I never lied. If I never lied, I could be like George Washington, I could be President of the United States. Wait, I think I remember telling one lie. Well, Secretary of State isn't a bad job, either. That's an old line, too. Look, I'm 89, what do you want me to have—new stuff?*)

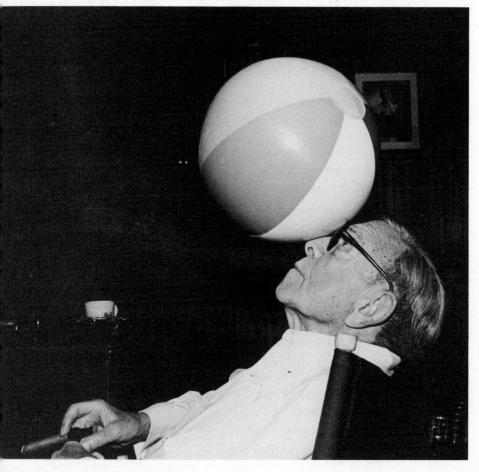

Some tricks you never forget.

• • •

Dear George—
I'm in trouble with the law and I need an attorney, but I can't afford one. Since I know that I'm innocent, I'm thinking about defending myself. Do you think this is a good idea?

On Trial in Tulsa

Dear On—
There's an old saying that anyone who defends himself has a fool for an attorney. I remember the time a friend of mine had a head-on collision with another car. He was so sloshed he was driving on the wrong side of the road. When the case went to court, my friend decided to defend himself.

The plaintiff's lawyer argued that the accident occurred because my friend had been drinking. My friend claimed that the accident was due to the fact that the other driver had NOT been drinking. He argued that if the other driver had been loaded, he, too, would have been driving on the wrong side of the road, and the two cars would have missed each other.

My friend told me this story while I was visiting him in jail.

(I just remembered, I never told you how I happened to find that seal, Flipper, that I worked with. I better tell you. It's an amusing story and it's true. That doesn't mean the other stuff I've been telling you isn't true . . . or amusing.

Anyway, this very close friend of mine, Jack Webber, who did an act with his wife, called Webber & Webber, wanted an exciting finish, so they added a seal at the end of their routine. And they were thrilled with their new finish.

But when the booker saw the act he told them to take the seal out and finish with a song and dance.

Webber said, "But the seal is a novelty. Everybody finishes with a song and dance."

And the booker said, "I know, and everybody's working but you."

And that's how I got possession of the seal. Now wasn't that worth waiting for?)

• • •

Dear George—

I am a financial consultant and I have always done well on my own, but my wife has been nagging me that I should get a partner. She keeps hitting me with that old bromide that "two heads are better than one." What do you think?

Henpecked

Dear Hen—

I have never believed that two heads are better than one. When I was going to school we had a kid on the block who had two heads. His parents named him Frankie and Johnny after a song they used to dance to when they were courting. But he wasn't any smarter than the rest of us. Everything you told him would go in one ear and out the other, and in one ear and out the other.

I had a brother who thought four heads were better than one, but he had a hat store.

Look, you have to take these sayings with a grain of salt. There's another one that makes no sense. Who wants to take sayings with salt? Salt is bad for you. I don't season my sayings. If I take a saying, I may sprinkle a little sugar on it, or pepper, but never salt.

Then there's that other one: "If the shoe fits, wear it." Until I heard that one I went around for 53 years in shoes that didn't fit me. Now, thanks to that saying I'm wearing shoes that fit me, but my feet hurt from the shoes I wore before.

Well, Hen, I hope this solves your problem. If it doesn't, maybe I should get a partner, maybe two heads *are* better than one.

• • •

Dear George—

I'm trying to break into television as a comedy writer, and it's not easy. Coming up with funny stuff every week is murder. Did you have that same problem when you started out?

Struggling Novice

Dear Strug—

I started in vaudeville, and we didn't have to come up with new stuff every week. If you had a good routine, you could use it for years and years. And if anybody stole one of your jokes, it was the end of the world, either for you or for him.

Strug, let me tell you a story about how important one joke could be. It must have been fifty years ago, and Gracie and I were doing very well. We were playing the Palace Theater, and before the show I ran into a friend of mine who said, "George, I've got a great joke for you. In that hunting routine you do, have Gracie say, 'This bird flies backwards. It's not interested in where it's going, it's interested in where it's been.'"

Gracie and I did it, and it was a tremendous laugh. The next day I got a call from Fred Allen telling me I couldn't use that joke, it belonged to him. I offered him $50 for the joke, and he said no. I offered him $100, and he said no. I offered him $200, and he still said no. I couldn't offer him any more, I wasn't making any more.

But I couldn't bear to take such a big laugh out of our act. So I called John P. Medbury, a very good writer I knew in Los Angeles, and explained my problem to him. Without taking a beat, he said, "Don't have the bird fly backwards, have the bird fly upside down. In case a hunter shoots it, it falls up."

Well, we did it, and it got just as big a laugh. In fact, I sold it to Fred Allen for $300.

Good luck with your career, Strug, and since you're just starting, if you want to use that joke, go ahead, it'll only cost you $100.

(I just remembered another argument over a joke that involved John P. Medbury.

At the time, he was writing a popular joke column in the newspaper, and Gracie and I used one of the jokes from his column. It went like this: I said to Gracie, "A funny thing happened to my mother in Cleveland." And she said, "I thought you were born in Buffalo."

The next day I got a call from Jesse Block of Block & Sully, another man/woman act. He said, "George, you can't use that joke. It's our joke, it belongs to us." I said, "How can it belong to

you? I got it out of Medbury's column yesterday." And Jesse said,
"But we got it out of the first edition."
I also sold that to Fred Allen for $300.)

• • •

Dear George—

Our family lives here in Hollywood, and my daughter, Pearl, who is quite beautiful, has her heart set on becoming a movie star. I know it's difficult, but I read where Robert Taylor was discovered working in a gas station; Lana Turner was discovered having an ice cream soda at Schwab's; and they discovered Cary Grant advertising a restaurant by walking up and down the street on stilts. What would be the best way for my daughter to get into pictures?

Pearl's Mother

Dear Mother of Pearl—

It's very simple. Just have her get a job at a gas station, order ice cream sodas at a local drugstore and walk back and forth to work on stilts. If that doesn't work, she can always marry a producer or two.

(It's not easy getting into motion pictures. Sometimes it's not easy getting out of a picture. That was my problem.

Back in the early thirties, when Gracie and I were doing our radio show, they brought us to Hollywood to do a movie. We were very excited about it until we got the script. The opening shot had us in a rowboat in the middle of the ocean trying to hitch a ride. And there was this iceberg that split apart to let us go through. It was a very believable opening. What Gracie and I were supposed to be doing stranded in the middle of the ocean, I never understood.

I told my agent Abe Lastfogel, who was the head of the William Morris Agency at that time, that I didn't think this picture would help our career, and I'd like to get out of it. Abe said, "Look, you don't get out of a picture just like that, but we'll go talk to the producer."

The next day we did. I said, "Go ahead, Abe, tell him."

He said, "I don't know what to do, you tell him."

So I said, "Look, Mr. Harris" (that wasn't his name, but I couldn't call him Mr. Lastfogel because Abe was standing next to me). Anyway, I said, "Mr. Harris, there's no way Gracie and I can do that opening scene, it doesn't make any sense. It's unbelievable."

He said, "For Burns and Allen it's believable."

I said, "What about that scene where you've got W. C. Fields flying on a motorcycle? A motorcycle doesn't fly, W. C. Fields flies."

"Don't tell me how to make pictures," he said, "you've got a pay-or-play contract, and we'll do it my way. And I don't want to see you again until you're going through that iceberg."

Abe pulled me out of the office. I said, "Abe, you're my agent, why didn't you say something?"

He said, "What could I say?"

"I'll show you how to get out of this picture," I told him.

We went back into the office and I said, "Mr. Harris, you have a beautiful big house in Bel Air."

He said, "Yes."

"And you'd like to continue to live there?"

He said, "Yes."

"Well, if you make this lousy movie, you won't. It's the worst thing I ever read. And anyone who will produce a movie like this knows nothing about show business. And if you do this, you'll be laughed right out of Hollywood!"

"No one can talk to me that way and work for me," he said, and tore up my contract.

Abe and I left, and out in the hall, I said, "Abe, that's the way to get out of a picture."

I don't remember the name of the movie, but it was a very big hit.)

END OF CHAPTER

Dear George—

How do you deal with those pesky salespeople who constantly knock at your door?—

—Some annoyances you just have to put up with.
I didn't even wait for this little salesgirl to ring my bell.
I bet she could, too.

7. SHORT LETTER WITH VERY LONG ANSWER

Dear George—

My grandfather always keeps talking about vaudeville. Who were some of the great vaudevillians you worked with? And what can you tell me about them?

Curious Yuppie

(I've been asked this question so many times, instead of just answering it for him, I'm going to answer it for all of you.

I can't mention all the stars I've worked with, but here are just a few you might enjoy reading about:)

Ethel Barrymore was one of the famous Barrymores, America's leading theatrical family. In the summertime she would play ten weeks of vaudeville in a sketch called "The Twelve-Pound Look." One week she was headlining in the Albee Theater in Brooklyn, and Gracie and I went on right after her.

The old people came to see Ethel before they died; the young people came to see Ethel before Ethel died. Ethel didn't die and the old people didn't die. Gracie and I died. We couldn't follow "The Twelve-Pound Look."

Houdini was the greatest escape artist in the world. He could get out of a locked steamer trunk in thirty seconds. He went into Mae West's dressing room once and couldn't get out for two days.

The four Marx brothers: Chico, Groucho, Zeppo and Harpo. The only way they could have been funnier was if there were five of them. Come to think of it, there was a fifth one—Gummo. But he wasn't funny. So they were funnier with four of them.

In our early days together I must have met them a dozen times, and they never remembered me. Maybe if I had changed my name to Burnso, they would have.

Eva Tanguay. They called her the "I Don't Care Girl." She did a
song where she claimed she couldn't sing, she couldn't dance, she
couldn't act, but she didn't care.

She was one of the top headliners. But that's show business. I
was starving, couldn't get a job, and I cared. She made a fortune,
and didn't care.

This is the one and only Will Rogers. It's amazing how far he got just standing on the stage, twirling a rope and talking. But that talk of his was pretty sharp. One of the things he said was that no one could be as funny as the politicians in Washington. He was wrong, he was funnier.

Sophie Tucker was billed as "The Last of the Red Hot Mamas."
She was a headliner for fifty years. That's a long time to be a Red
Hot Mama. I never knew a mama who could stay hot for fifty
years—lukewarm, maybe, but not hot.

Here's Clayton, Jackson & Durante with Ruby Keeler. I don't remember Ruby being with them very long, but I sure remember Lou Clayton, Eddie Jackson and Jimmy Durante. What an act they had! When they brought the house down it included the scenery, the piano and anything else they could lay their hands on. They did great business, but they had to . . . to pay for everything they destroyed.

Bill "Bojangles" Robinson. I worked with him many times. He was a great tap dancer and an even greater showman. When he did that routine of his dancing up and down the stairs, he always stopped the show.

People ask me why they called him "Bojangles." What should they have called him—Bo Derek?

A performer like Bill Robinson comes along once in a lifetime, and I'm glad he came along during mine.

This is an early Jack Benny. I don't know about the hair, but the violin is genuine.

That's Eddie Cantor in blackface. Cantor was one of the greatest. His biggest hit was a song called "Suzie." He sang "Suzie," but I knew Suzie. I knew Suzie better than he knew Suzie. Suzie wasn't bad, she sang in my key.

This is Mr. Berle before he became "Mr. Television." You can tell he was funny even then because his hat is turned up. But there's nothing I can say about Milton that he hasn't said about himself.

Fannie Brice was the first great stand-up comedienne. She got laughs, she sang, she danced, she took pratfalls, she could be broad, she could be subtle—and she did a great imitation of Barbra Streisand.

This is a team who worked in vaudeville for a lot of years. I think they called their act Burns & Allen. Miss Allen was a very talented comedienne. I always felt she could have done better with another guy.

W. C. Fields not only said things funny, he moved funny, he looked funny, everything he did was funny. He was funny on the stage, he was funny in the movies, he was even funny at funerals.

Gracie and I did several movies with Bill Fields. In one of them there was a scene in a café where Fields was sitting at a table with the beautiful Peggy Hopkins Joyce, and Gracie was the waitress. Toward the end of the scene, Gracie said, "After I wait on you I've got to rush right home. My sister just had a baby."

Fields asked, "Is it a boy or a girl?" and Gracie said, "I don't know. That's why I want to get home. I can't wait to find out if I'm an uncle or an aunt." And then she made her exit.

Well, Bill Fields felt he needed a laugh to top her, but nobody on the set could think of anything. So I walked over to Bill and said, "After Gracie hits you with that silly line, here's a funny thing you can do. There is a glass of water, a cup of coffee, a martini and a napkin in front of you. Why don't you take two lumps of sugar, put them in the water, stir the coffee, drink the martini and wipe Peggy Hopkins Joyce's mouth with your napkin."

Fields looked up at me and said, "Yeah. Thanks, George. This is the first time I've ever liked a straight man."

Vernon and Irene Castle. They were the top dancing team of the 1920s. They were ballroom dancers, and their finale was an exciting number called "The Castle Walk." It swept the country, everybody was doing it. Irene was a sensational dancer. I can't say how good Vernon was, because I never danced with him.

Al Jolson—I still think he was the world's greatest entertainer. I'll never forget a World War I bond rally. It was the biggest show ever put together. Every star you could think of was on it.

Finally, Enrico Caruso, the opera sensation of his time, came on. He sang an aria from *Pagliacci*, and then he introduced a new war song written by George M. Cohan, called "Over There." He brought the house down.

Then out came Jolson. He walked to the center of the stage, looked at the audience and said, "You ain't heard nothing yet!" Can I tell you something, he was right.

END OF CHAPTER

Dear George—
   Everyone's jogging these days. Would you advise it?—

—It helps me. I do this every morning.

8. INTRIGUING LETTERS WITH PROVOCATIVE ANSWERS

Dear George—

I am really looking forward to your new book. I've always loved your humor, and as a psychologist, what I appreciate even more is your straightforward, hide-nothing approach.

You admit your age, your lack of formal education, and you're the first to say that until Gracie came along you were a flop. I find this not only an endearing trait, but a very healthy one as well.

Some people are shocked by what I say, and how I say it on my radio and TV shows. I don't try to be shocking, it's the only way I can do it. I'm like you, George, I have to tell it like it is.

Dr. Ruth Westheimer

Dear Dr. Ruth—

It's true, I've always believed in telling it like it is. However, with your favorite topic, I've reached the point where I have to tell it like it was. That is, if I can remember what it was.

• • •

Dear George—

I heard that Michelangelo didn't start painting the ceiling of the Sistine Chapel until he was 70 years old. Is this true, and why did he wait so long to do it?

Artistic Alvin

Dear Art—

I happen to know all about this, because I held the ladder for him. I knew Mike very well. And it's true, Michelangelo started painting the ceiling when he was 70 years old. He would have started sooner, but he felt it only needed one coat.

• ፨ •

Dear George—

I love to play poker. But, George, I must be the worst card-player in the world. Last night I was dealt a hand that knocked my socks off, but I played it so bad I lost my shirt. And by the end of the night they beat the pants off me. Can you help me?

Plain Stupid

Dear Plain—

I can only help you if you wear clothes my size.

• • •

Dear George—

I have a sheep named Shirley, and I've been trying to teach her to dance. If she could, we'd be a hit in show business. I've played disco music for her, rock music, country music, even classical music, but she refuses to dance.

George, you've worked with animal acts. What advice can you give me?

Sheepish Sheldon

Dear Sheep—

I think Shirley's trying to pull the wool over your eyes. But don't give up, I can't believe that sheep won't dance. I've seen dogs that can dance. In fact, I danced with one last night.

• • •

Dear George—

I know you've been in show business practically all of your life and have a very wide acquaintance. One of my all-time favorites was John Barrymore. Did you know him?

Old, Old Fan

Dear Old, Old—

Did I know John Barrymore! I knew him very well. I was introduced to him by Minta Arbuckle, who was married to Fatty Arbuckle. Now Fatty Arbuckle was one of the great comedians in silent pictures. His first name was Roscoe, and they called him Fatty because he weighed about 300 pounds. He came to Hollywood as a stagehand and was discovered by Mack Sennett, who only weighed 145 pounds. He was the one who put Fatty Arbuckle in all those great comedies.

Fatty was a very good friend of Buster Keaton, who was also one of the greats. Keaton originally started in vaudeville with an act called "The Three Keatons." He worked with his mother and father. And he never smiled, he always kept that deadpan expression.

Now Keaton was a very good friend of Charlie Chaplin, who was the king of the silent pictures. At that time Charlie Chaplin was married to Lita Grey. This was before Paulette Goddard. And Lita Grey had her dresses made in a little shop on 45th St., right next door to Wienig's restaurant. And Al Jolson used to eat at Wienig's. And right above Wienig's was the Jack Mills Publishing Company. . . . So you see, I really knew John Barrymore!

(*It's a good thing he didn't ask me about George Arliss. I didn't know him nearly as well as John Barrymore.*)

• • •

Dear George—

I recently read an interview where you said that you can often tell right from the start if a performer is going to make it or not.

Could you tell that Bob Hope was destined to become a star the first time you saw his act?

Skeptical

Dear Skept—

No, it was not until the *second* time I saw Bob Hope's act that I knew he'd become a star. The first time I saw Bob Hope's act Milton Berle was doing it.

• • •

Dear George—

I'm from Dallas, and I'm going around with an elderly gentleman who's your age and looks exactly like you. He lives in Beverly Hills, too, and belongs to your country club. He used to phone me twice a day, now he phones me once a day. He tells me he's writing a book of silly letters. You must know him. The next time you see him at the club ask him if he's really writing that book or just trying to save the price of a phone call.

I'm so mad—not at you, at him. But you look so much like him, I'm mad at you, too! Of course, he hasn't got your sense of humor. His idea of a fun evening at Chasen's is flipping a spoon into a glass of water.

All he ever talks about is show business . . . all those stories about Al Jolson, Georgie Jessel and his best friend, Jack Benny. I'd rather watch the spoon trick again. And he's always got a cigar in his face, which really bothers me, especially when he's kissing me. And I know his heart belongs to me, but his hair belongs to Max Factor.

On second thought, I'm sure you'd be more fun than he is. Why don't we forget about him. You give me a call sometime and we'll get together.

Cathy from Dallas

Dear Cathy—

I happen to know this fellow you're talking about. In fact, I know him very well. Don't underestimate him. He's a wonderful man. He's much funnier than I am. Everything he says knocks me out. He's the funniest guy at our club. And I love his spoon trick.

I'm through with girls.

Look, I know his faults better than you do. So he smokes a few cigars a day. That doesn't bother me, but then again he's never kissed me.

I'm sure that even though he's working at that book now, he's thinking of you twice a day. You really should give the old guy another chance. But I like the idea of getting together. Why don't the three of us do it sometime.

• • •

Dear George—

I'm sorry I bothered you, but right after I received your answer I heard from my gentleman friend. And he couldn't have been nicer. He said he'd call me twice a day, and he's going to stop smoking cigars when he kisses me. He even promised me he'd start growing his own hair. So everything is fine again, and you were right, he is funnier than you are—much funnier.

Cathy from Dallas

(*You know something, I just figured it out. That's Cathy Carr, the girl I've been going with for the last four years. I know her mother and father, her whole family. I've been in her house a dozen times. How could it take me so long to figure it out? I must be losing my marbles. Maybe she is better off with the other guy.*)

• • •

Dear George—

I run a small market, and this lady brings in her little kid who has a new angle on shoplifting. Every time they go through the produce section I see him eating grapes, apples, peaches, everything in sight. But by the time I get to him he's already swallowed the evidence. How can I put a stop to this ripoff?

Victimized

Dear Vic—

The next time this lady and her little freeloader show up at your store, weigh the kid on the way in, and then weigh him on the way out. Charge her a flat fee for how much you figure he has eaten.

If she refuses to pay, stick your finger down his throat. If he eats your finger, add that to the original total.

• • •

Dear George—

For eighty years I've tried to live an exemplary life so that when I die I'll go to heaven. I've done the best I can, but quite

This is Cathy Carr from Dallas with the real George Burns.

honestly, it's been a little boring. I've never been married. In fact, I've never even been with a woman. Now that I'm old, I'm beginning to wonder what I've been missing, and what I have to look forward to in the afterlife. Is there sex after death?

Heaven Can Wait

Dear Heaven—

Is there sex after death? Why ask me, I'm still here. I may not be able to answer that for another 20 or 30 years. I know of some cases where there was death after sex. But that also applies to jogging, overeating and dueling.

END OF CHAPTER

Dear George—
   I'm bald and can't get dates. Do you think a toupee would make
me look better?—

—Of course it would.

9. SOME VERY ENDEARING LETTERS

Dear George—

Our Ladies' Club is holding a raffle, and I would like an autographed photo of you as first prize, if it's not too much trouble. Although maybe you could provide a dinner with you as first prize instead. Or maybe a weekend at Caesars Palace, because I know you play there a lot. But pick the weekend when Frank Sinatra is appearing there, as we are all big Frank Sinatra fans. And make sure the weekend includes tickets to Frank Sinatra's show.

On second thought, you don't have to bother sending that autographed photo of yourself.

Pauline in Portland

Dear Pauline—
Where can I buy a raffle ticket? I'd like to see Sinatra myself.

• • •

Dear George—

Next week I have to speak at a Rotary Club meeting, something I've never done before. I'd like ten minutes of surefire jokes from you. Nothing dirty, maybe a little risqué, but it has to get lots of laughs. None of your old stuff, just ten minutes of good, new, dynamite material.

Rotary Al

Dear Rot—

I only happen to have 9½ minutes of dynamite material, so I'll have to write another half minute. And if the half minute is as funny as the other 9½ minutes, I'll use it myself. Glad I could help.

• • •

Dear George—

My biggest form of entertainment is seeing your movies. I have seen every one of them. Some of them I've even seen twice. But I have one complaint. How come you never do any nude scenes in them? Come on, George, give us a nude scene.

Betty in Barstow

Dear Betty—

In *The Sunshine Boys* I appeared topless—no toupee.

In *Going in Style* I appeared bottomless—no shoes.

Sorry, kid, that's as far as I go. If I smoke my cigar without a holder on it, I catch cold.

• • •

Dear George—

I think you're the greatest. You ought to go into politics. How about running for Governor, or the Presidency, or something bigger?

Silent Citizen

Dear Si—

I'd consider walking for the Presidency, or strolling for the Presidency, or being pushed for the Presidency, but not running. I couldn't run if a bear chased me. Even if it comes to the bathroom, if I have to run, I just don't go.

. . .

Dear George—

I've seen your nightclub act, and to tell you the truth, it could be better. I think I know what it needs—riddles. You should tell riddles. Here are a couple that are surefire:

a) How far can a dog run into the forest? (Only halfway. Then he is running out!)

b) What position did Count Dracula play in Little League? (Batboy!)

c) When do one and one make six? (When one is a male and one is a female.)

I know these will save your act and push you into the big rooms.

Cal from the Catskills

Dear Cal—

I have a riddle for you. What's white, all crumpled up and is about to land in the bottom of my trash basket?

You got it!

. . .

Dear George—

You and your advice. I did everything you said, and you may be happy to know that my wife has now filed for divorce. And she's taking my house, my business, the dog and everything I've got but that lousy blue convertible, which I plan to sell so I can hire a lawyer and sue you for everything *you've* got.

Farley in Westport

(There's no point in even answering a letter like that. What can you do? You're bound to run into a few cranks now and then. Their bark is worse than their bite. Still, I don't want him to be upset with me. I know, I'll send him an autographed photo of myself. He'll like that.)

END OF CHAPTER

Dear George—

I'm your age and lately I notice I'm constantly looking back. Do you find yourself doing that?—

—I never look back.

10. NAUGHTY LETTERS WITH NICE ANSWERS

Dear George—

My wife seems to prefer the same old position, whereas I like variety in bed. What's your feeling about this?

Open-minded

Dear Open—

If you like *Variety*, read *Variety*. If you don't like *Variety*, read *The Hollywood Reporter*. And you can read them sitting up or lying down.

(I know that's not the answer he wanted. How do you answer a letter like that? That's a dirty letter. I don't answer dirty letters. I read them, I enjoy them, but I don't answer them. If you put dirty things on paper, you can get sued, unless you're a canary.)

• • •

Shocking! Anyone who would write a letter like this should be ashamed of himself.

Dear George—

I have been reading and hearing a lot about the G-Spot and how excited it makes you feel. I've asked all my friends about it, but so far none of us have been able to find it.

Searching

Dear Searching—

Don't ask me. I never touch anything unless it's in my key.

(Imagine asking me about finding a G-Spot. Although I did get excited once when I found a ten-spot in the men's room of the Earle Theater in Philadelphia.)

• • •

Dear George—
You've been around for a while. Where can I find Spanish Fly?
Ready for Fun

Dear Ready—
That's easy. I'll tell you where to find a Spanish fly—on Julio Iglesias' pants.

(After I wrote that answer my secretary explained to me what Spanish Fly is and what it does for you. I got so excited I gave her a raise. It wasn't much of a raise, but look, it's the best I could do.)

• • •

Dear George—
I've been thinking about joining a sperm bank. Which one do you recommend?
Ben from Altoona

Dear Ben—
One that doesn't have a drive-thru window.

• • •

Dear George—
   Every time my boyfriend takes me to a movie, all he wants to do is fool around in the balcony. I never get to watch the movie.
                                                                Cheated

Dear Cheated—
   Don't worry. They're not doing anything up there on the screen that you're not doing in the balcony.

END OF CHAPTER

Dear George—

We're all enthused here at Putnam's. This one can't miss. My secretary read the last batch you sent in three days ago and she's still laughing.

There's just one thing. I hesitate to even mention it. But I have this nagging feeling that you've been making up a lot of those letters. I'd hate to think you'd do a thing like that.

Phyllis

Dear Phyllis—

I'd hate to think so, too.

Dear George—
Are you really a country singer?—

—That ain't Willie Nelson, partner.

11. NAUGHTY LETTERS WITH NAUGHTY ANSWERS AND NICE LETTERS WITH NAUGHTY ANSWERS

Dear George—

It's the dead of winter and I'm sitting in my home in Juneau, Alaska, watching it snow. I know I'm supposed to learn something from everything that happens in my life, but what is there to learn about yet another snowstorm?

Snowbound

Dear Snow—

Let me answer you this way. When I was in vaudeville I knew a stripper who worked at the Globe Theater in Atlantic City. One winter night we were having supper together, and she said to me, "The way I see it, sex is like a snowstorm. You never know how much you're going to get, how long it's going to last, or how you're going to get out of it." She also said, "Sex can't hurt you if you don't inhale," and lots of other things I can't repeat. But it doesn't matter, because they have nothing to do with snow.

• • •

Dear George—

My business takes me out of town two or three weeks a month. I'm a married man, but being away so much I am constantly cheating with other women. However, when I return home I'm much thinner than when I went away. My wife is becoming suspicious of the way my weight keeps going up and down. What should I do?

Traveling Man

Dear Trav—

The only way to keep your weight from going up and down is for *you* to stop doing what your weight is doing.

• • •

Dear George—

I heard that if you lead an excessive sex life, it ruins your vision. Is this true?

Asking for a Friend

Dear Asking—

I'm sorry, I can't read this. The print's too small.

• • •

Dear George—
    Is it true that a lifetime of too much sex will affect your ability
to spell?

                                        Concerned in Connecticut

Dear Kansurned—
    Probablee knot.

*(I'm not sure, but I think the last two letters were written by the
same guy. I know the answers were written by the same guy.)*

*   *   *

Dear George—

Every night when we go to bed my wife complains of a splitting headache. She's fine during the day, but comes the night and she gets the headache. Do you think she should see a doctor?

Frustrated in Fresno

Dear Frustrated—

Should she see a doctor??? *You* should see a doctor. Or better yet, you should see my friend Ruby Bancroft. I don't have Ruby's number on hand, but her car is usually parked in front of the Happy Hour Motel on Sunset Blvd. You'll find the phone number on her bumper sticker.

P.S. Ruby has never had a headache in her life. Although sometimes her back hurts.

• • •

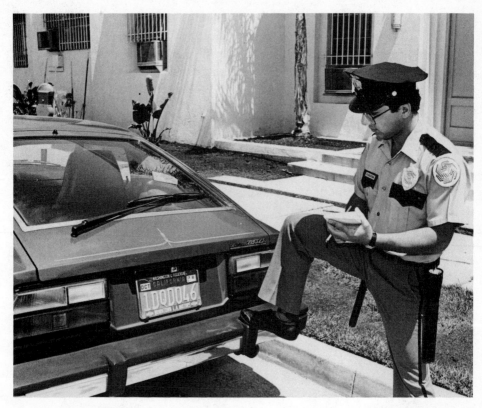

I don't know if he's giving Ruby a ticket or writing down her phone number.

Dear George—

I just read a survey that says 85% of American women have sex before they're married. Do you believe this?

Pre-Nuptial

Dear Pre—

No. But I don't believe that 85% of them have it after they're married, either.

• • •

Dear George—

I just married a wonderful girl. We're both from traditional families, so of course we abstained from making love until after the wedding. Although we both wanted children, we were planning to wait a few years. But to my surprise, my wife got pregnant on our wedding night. Is this unusual?

First-Timer

Dear First—

I guess you were just in the right place at the right time.

END OF CHAPTER

Dear George—

I've never tried it before, but do you think you can have fun on a double date?—

—As long as the girls don't mind sharing.

12. NICE LETTERS WITH NICE ANSWERS

Dear George—

At *Cosmopolitan* we salute solid achievement. So congratulations on a career that makes Bob Hope, Laurence Olivier and Helen Hayes look like late arrivals.

At *Cosmo* we also focus on the woman's point of view. And while you have become perhaps the leading exponent of older men keeping company with young women, we wonder how you feel about the reverse situation. What pleasures would you say are in store for a woman who goes with a man half her age?

Helen Gurley Brown

Dear Helen—

I wouldn't know. I've never gone with a man half my age.

OR:

I wouldn't know, but if you know a woman twice my age who wants to find out, send her around.

Incidentally, Helen, you may be interested in the lyrics of a song I do from time to time in my stage act. It was written by Billy Rose and Fred Fisher, and goes like this:

Oh, she looks like Helen Brown
She's the best-dressed gal in town
Got the skin you love to touch
Never lets you touch it much.
Oh, she won a beauty crown
In her new red satin gown
She knocked the boys dead
When she wore red
But she looked like Helen Brown.

This song always gets a laugh on the stage. Of course, those lyrics don't apply to you, because you look great in brown, black, blue, green, yellow and plaid. But not all at the same time.

• • •

Dear George—

I'm an old-time radio fan, and one time I remember Portland asking Fred Allen if it were true that Jack Benny had a burglar alarm on his garbage can. And Fred answered, "No, because Jack Benny never threw away anything." George, you were a very close friend of Jack Benny, was he really that cheap?

Old-Timer

Dear Old—

Yes, he was that cheap. But just in real life, not on the stage. I switched that to be funny, but it's not much of a switch. I don't feel well today.

(*The truth is that Jack Benny's cheapness was a made-up character for the show. And he wasn't just cheap, he was the cheapest. Back in those days radio was full of extreme characters, and that's what made them stars. Jim Backus' character "Hubert Updike" wasn't just rich, he was the richest.*

If you were the poorest, it was funny . . . or the skinniest . . . or the dumbest . . . and if you had no talent, you had it made. With a little talent you were in trouble, but with no talent you were a star. It took me a while, but I finally made it.)

• • •

Dear George—

I'm a minister and a long-time fan of yours. I could use some advice on how to keep my congregation awake during my sermons. They just don't seem to be interested in what I'm saying. You're so great with an audience, I wonder if you could give me a few pointers.

Man of the Cloth

My Dear Man—

The secret of a good sermon is having a good beginning and a good ending. And having them as close together as possible.

• • •

Dear George—

It was some time ago, but I still look back with pleasure to that bit you had me do on your last TV special. What I can't get over to this day is that of all the performers on the show you not only worked the hardest, but you used the least makeup.

George, you would be shocked if you knew how often I talk about you to my elderly patients in trying to bring them out of the depression, resignation and sense of futility that besets them. Some are considerably younger than you are, but they are convinced their life is over. You're my prime example, living proof of the benefits of a positive "up" attitude, and to be able to point out your continuing activity, popularity and success is invaluable.

So you see, you can't quit now, even if you wanted to.

Dr. Joyce Brothers

Dear Dr. J.—

Comedians don't quit. If they hear one laugh, they keep going. Which is exactly what I intend to do. I'm not quitting anything. I haven't quit working. I haven't quit smoking cigars. I haven't quit drinking martinis. Actually, there is one thing I've given up. I quit that last week.

By now I'm sure everyone knows my opinions about retiring. I've talked about it on the stage and in my recent books. To go into it here would mean just repeating myself, which I can't do, because that's the thing I gave up last week. You thought it was something else, didn't you? I couldn't quit *that*, it would ruin your example for those elderly patients of yours.

• • •

Dr. Joyce Brothers in that TV special of mine. The one in the middle is Arte Johnson. I'm not sure but I think he does have more makeup on than I have.

Dear George—

I've got a very attractive teenage daughter who has the idea that she wants to look like a movie star. Every day she makes herself up to look like a different Hollywood sex symbol. I try to discourage her. I think she should just be her own person. Since she won't listen to me, maybe she'll listen to you.

Concerned Mother

Dear Concerned—

What's wrong with her wanting to look like a Hollywood sex symbol? As long as it's Marilyn Monroe or Madonna and not Telly Savalas.

• • •

Dear George—

I'm a big fan of Carol Channing, and I understand that you and she are very close. Is it true that show business is her whole life, and that she even dresses and uses the same makeup on and off the stage?

A Loyal Fan

Dear A—

It's true. Carol is always on stage. When she comes to my house and uses the powder room, she won't come out unless I applaud her. One time she was in bed fast asleep, and a burglar broke into her house. When he shined a flashlight on her face she sat up in bed and sang two choruses of "Hello, Dolly!"

I finally got her out of the powder room—and just in time.

I know diamonds are her best friend, but this is ridiculous.

• • •

Dear George—

I am so mad at the phone company I would like to reach out and "slug" someone. Every since they split up they keep increasing local rates and lowering long-distance rates. When my girlfriend was living in Chicago I made a lot of long-distance calls. Now that she's living in town my phone bill is even higher. What would you advise me to do?

Furious

(*I know you readers all expect me to tell him to have his girlfriend move back to Chicago. Well, I won't disappoint you.*)

Dear Furious—

Have your girlfriend move back to Chicago.

• • •

Dear George—

I belong to a minority group that has no racial, political or social identification, but is nevertheless discriminated against. I happen to be left-handed.

At present I am in the army, and occasionally forget myself and acknowledge an officer by saluting with my left hand. For this I am constantly receiving demerits, put on latrine duty and having weekend passes revoked.

Is there some way I can call attention to this discrimination without getting myself into trouble with my commanding officer?

Southpaw

Dear South—

I would suggest that the next time you meet your commanding officer, instead of saluting, curtsy. It might get you into trouble, but it might also get you out of the army.

It's true, left-handed people have always been picked on. When you take an oath, they say, "Raise your right hand." What does that mean, that left-handed people are liars?

If you can't dance, they say you've got two left feet. If you had two right feet, could you dance any better? I've got a left foot and a right foot, but I still don't dance well. Maybe they're on the wrong side.

Even left-handed children are at a disadvantage. Whenever you see one on a merry-go-round, reaching for the brass ring, it's always on the wrong side. So the righty gets the ring, and the lefty gets dizzy.

And pantsmakers are prejudiced. They make the fly so that the opening to the vent of the zipper is located on the side where only right-handers can get to it in a hurry. What's a left-hander supposed to do, take a right-hander with him when he goes to the men's room?

Well, South, the reason I have devoted so much time to this subject is because being an actor, I live on applause, and since it takes both hands to applaud, I hate to see either hand discriminated against.

END OF CHAPTER

Dear George—
   You look great on TV. But I'm dying to know—how do you look when you get up in the morning?—

DAVID JAMES/CBS

—Like this. But I look much better after my morning coffee.

Dear George—

As your lawyer I have to inform you that this fellow Farley, formerly of Fairfield, now of Westport, has filed suit against you for bad and wrongful advice. I urge you not to take this lightly, as he wants both compensatory and punitive damages, and it could amount to big money. I suggest we start immediately lining up some character witnesses for you—the more the merrier.

H. Brown

P.S. He sent back your autographed picture.

13. CHARACTER WITNESS LETTERS

Dear George—

You didn't even have to ask. After all, George, we go back together to when you and Gracie first teamed up. I would have to say Gracie was one of the finest persons I ever knew. What values she had! Integrity was her middle name. If she gave her word, that was it. Gracie was totally honest. She was dependable. And she was generous to a fault.

You can count on me, George, and if there's anything else you want me to say about you, let me know.

Danny Thomas

• • •

Dear George—

Leave it to Uncle Miltie. I usually don't do courts, but I've got it worked out great.

There's no point tampering with success, so I'll open with "Good afternoon, ladies and germs." Then I say, "Let's not forget, when we talk about George Burns we're talking about a living legend. Well, a legend, anyhow." Big laugh.

Then I say, "There he is—actor, comedian, author, country singer. . . . Why shouldn't he be a country singer? He's older than

757

most countries." Another scream. Why am I telling you? It's your line.

Then I go into my regular proven stuff. Allowing for laughs and applause, plus my entrance and closing number, "Near You," you can figure me for a smash fifty minutes.

That's a lot, but what are friends for?

Milton Berle

P.S. Have your lawyer put me on the stand last. Because as you know, I always close the show.

• • •

Dear George—

I . . . I . . . uh . . . uh just got this call from your . . . lawyer . . . asking me to write a . . . write a . . . character . . . reference for you.

Well, George, I've . . . uh . . . I've . . . uh . . . known you a good long time. I knew Gracie, too, but that's not what this is about, is it. . . .

Anyway, I'd . . . uh . . . I'd . . . uh . . . be happy to . . . write you a . . . uh . . . letter stating whatever it is your lawyer called about. Just have . . . have——— Oh, forget it. By the time I get through with this, the trial will be over.

James Stewart

• • •

Dear George—

It never ceases to amaze me, the sheer audacity of some people. Who does this guy think he is suing . . . *you?* Rest assured when the time comes, if this goes to court, I will be there alongside you. You lie if you have to, and I will swear to it.

To me, it does not affect your credibility at all that you told me "The Gambler" was a nothing song and would not sell ten copies. Feel free to call on me if you need any additional help.

Your friend,
Kenny Rogers

P.S. Now that Christopher is born and is the light of my and Marianne's life, she is no longer upset by your rather off-the-wall advice on birth control.

• • •

Dear George—

Sweetie, I'd do anything for you. You're a real gentleman. Of all the times you've taken me out, not once did you try to take advantage of me.

But I still think you're wonderful.

Phyllis Diller

• • •

Dear George—

I'll be happy to do whatever I can. However, I doubt that I'd be much of a character witness for you. I really don't know you that well.

Your son,
Ronnie

P.S. Your daughter, Sandy, says she has the same problem I have.

• • •

Ronnie

Sandy

Dear George—

At a time when the incidence of malpractice suits—not to mention my gorge—is rising, I must say I was not surprised to be contacted by your lawyers about your present predicament. The first inkling I had that things were not going well was when I found out that Dear Abby and Ann Landers were calling you for advice.

But be that as it may—and I doubt that it is—Jayne and I will be happy to testify on your behalf.

I personally don't really understand why you're being attacked, anyway. As long as I've known you, I've been aware that you're a stickler for accuracy. Whenever they want accuracy, they send for you and you come in and you stickle.

Steve Allen

• • •

Dear George—

You know I'd do anything for you, but you see, I no longer make movies, I try not to appear on television, I don't write books and do my best to stay out of courtrooms.

Love,
Cary Grant

• • •

Dear George—

How could I refuse to write a character reference for you?! You are one of my favorite characters!

But let's be honest! You're not an easy person to do. It's not so much what you say, but how you say it . . . and who would know that better than me!

But I love you, kid . . . even though those cigars of yours are killing me!

Rich Little

Dear George—

No, I won't testify for you. And I wish you'd stop telling everyone we're such good friends.

You Know Who

He not only didn't sign his name, but he didn't want anyone to see his face.

• • •

Dear George—

I just heard about your lawsuit, and I'm really proud to know you. Here you are, 89 years old, and you're being sued. What an honor. Some of the biggest people in the history of the world never got sued.

Adam, who said to Eve in the Garden of Eden, "What do you mean you got nothing to wear?"—never got sued.

Moses, who said to the Children of Israel, "Stop calling me Charlton!"—never got sued.

Cain, whose wife divorced him because he wasn't Abel—never got sued.

King Solomon, who said to his thousand wives, "Who hasn't got a headache?"—never got sued.

John Wilkes Booth, who said, "Sorry, I thought he was a critic"—never got sued.

I could go on and on, but of all the biggies I know, George, you're the only one being sued. My hat's off to you. And if you lose the case, I'll be the first one to congratulate you. And you can also have my hat. Love ya.

Red Buttons

• • •

Dear George—

It was great hearing from you, and I'd love to take the stand on your behalf.

The problem is, if I do it for you, then I'd have to do it for all my other friends who are being sued. Also, I might be away on location at the time of your trial. And even were I available, I've wrenched my right arm and I'm having trouble raising it, so they wouldn't take me.

Sorry, but I'll make it up to you, even if it means doing another picture together.

Walter Matthau

• • •

Dear George—

Your esteemed barrister enlightened me on the act of vindictive litigation by an obviously pathetic and malcontent provocateur. This scandalous and truculent attack can only be construed, by any reasonably intelligent and cognizant person, as nothing more than a lame attempt to vilify you and your age-earned unimputable reputation.

I, therefore, offer my untiring assistance in establishing the indisputable quality of your unimpeachable character to the fair jurists sitting in judgment of your suit.

Personally, George, it's not the suit that bothers me, it's your tie that's a little too loud.

Howard Cosell

Author and his c~~lo~~se friends.

Author and his fri~~e~~nds.

Danny Thomas

Kenny Rogers

Milton Berle

Walter Matthau

Rich Little

HARRY LANGDON

Phyllis Diller

Steve Allen and Jayne Meadows

Red Buttons

Howard Cosell

Still waiting to hear from Laurence Olivier.

END OF CHAPTER

Dear George—
    Can weight lifting be overdone?—

NBC

—Not the way I do it.

Dear George—

You were right after all. My wife and I are back together. She loves me, she loves the blue convertible, and we're expecting our first child in May. So forget the lawsuit, and thanks for that good advice.

Farley in Fairfield

(What do you know! We have a happy ending.)

DEAR READERS

Well, that's it. Now you can go back to whatever you were doing, and I can go back to my Tuesday-night bowling.

I hope you enjoyed the book. If you did, feel free to drop me a line, but please don't start it "Dear George." And don't expect an answer. I'm answered out.

At the end of every book of mine, I've always made it a point to name all those who helped me with it. Some authors don't do this. But I'm a firm believer in spreading the blame. I'm generous that way.

Let me begin the credits by mentioning Hal Goldman, Harvey Berger, Bob O'Brien and Jay Grossman. They're not my backup singers, they are the accomplished, creative, imaginative and prolific writers who contributed so much to these pages, including this line. For my part, I have to say we were a good team, and we had lots of laughs together. The chemistry couldn't have been better—the writing, maybe, but not the chemistry.

This is now Hal's fourth book with me, so he knows exactly how I think, which amazes me, because *I* don't know how I think.

For Harvey it's the third time around. It's great working with him, too, because he knows how Hal thinks. This is the first book with me for Bob and Jay, so they don't know how anybody thinks, and they don't care.

And now I come to someone who has been invaluable to me, my secretary, Jack Langdon. Jack's been with me for 26 years, and every year he's asked me for a raise. This year I'm finally giving it to him. I hope he doesn't read the book, because I want it to be a surprise.

Nothing dresses up a book like a lot of pictures. I'm sure you have noticed all those photographs of me and the four models, Sheila Aldridge, Camille Calvet, Monica Maynor and Lori Goldstein. Believe me, it's not easy taking a picture standing next to a sexy body. But the girls held up well.

While we're on pictures, I should mention the fine photographer who took most of them, Peter Borsari. In fact, he's taken hundreds of pictures of me for my last three books, so I thought I'd take one of him. Here it is:

I forgot to tell him to say cheese.

Of course I want to thank all my close show-business friends who wrote all those nice, complimentary things about my character. They may not have seemed complimentary to you, but I know my character better than you. Believe me, ladies and gentlemen, they were complimentary.

Now to my personal manager, Irving Fein. I can't say enough nice things about Irving, so I won't. Yes, I will, I changed my mind. He's bright, he's dependable, he's conscientious, he's trustworthy, he's warm, he's giving, he's nice. In fact, it's because I think so much of him that I keep working all the time. I'm not doing it for me, it's for him. I want this nice guy to keep living well.

Then there are my literary agents, Arthur and Richard Pine. I must give credit where credit is due, and despite what you read in the introduction, they were the ones who thought of the title. Arthur came up with "Dear," and Richard came up with "George." Or was it the other way around? I wouldn't want to hurt their careers.

I'd never forgive myself if I neglected to thank Phyllis Grann. She not only has a sense of what the public wants, but she has great taste. I know that, because every time she sees me, she asks, "Where do you get your shirts?"

Finally, I better thank Cathy Carr from Dallas. She really didn't have anything to do with the book, but if I don't thank her, she may not have anything to do with the author.

Well, that takes care of just about everyone except you readers, especially those of you who bought the book. If there are enough of you, I'm sure my literary agents will come up with another good idea that Phyllis Grann will try to talk me into writing. And she just might succeed. How could I turn her down, she loves my shirts. Besides, between you and me, I'm sick of bowling.

The last and most important letter—the author's check!